NORTH KOREA'S MILITARY-DIPLOMATIC CAMPAIGNS, 1966–2008

This book examines North Korea's nuclear diplomacy over a long time period from the early 1960s, setting the dangerous brinkmanship in the wider context of North Korea's military and diplomatic campaigns to achieve its political goals. It argues that the last four decades of military adventurism demonstrates Pyongyang's consistent, calculated use of military tools to advance strategic objectives *vis-à-vis* its adversaries. It shows how recent behavior of the North Korean government is entirely consistent with its behavior over this longer period: the North Korean government's conduct (rather than being haphazard or reactive) is rational – in the Clausewitzian sense of being ready to use force as an extension of diplomacy by other means. The book goes on to demonstrate that North Korea's "calculated adventurism" has come full circle: what we are seeing now is a modified repetition of earlier events – such as the *Pueblo* incident of 1968 and the nuclear and missile diplomacy of the 1990s. Using extensive interviews in the United States and South Korea, including those with defected North Korean government officials, alongside newly declassified first-hand material from U.S., South Korean, and former Communist-bloc archives, the book argues that while North Korea's military-diplomatic campaigns have become more intensified, its policy objectives have become more conservative, aimed at regime survival, normalization of relations with the United States and Japan, as well as obtaining economic aid.

Narushige Michishita is Assistant Professor of the Security and International Studies Program at the National Graduate Institute for Policy Studies (GRIPS) in Tokyo, Japan. Previously, he served as senior research fellow at the National Institute for Defense Studies, Ministry of Defense and assistant counsellor at the Cabinet Secretariat for Security and Crisis Management of the Government of Japan.

ROUTLEDGE SECURITY IN ASIA PACIFIC
SERIES
Series Editors
Leszek Buszynski
International University of Japan and
William Tow
Australian National University

Security issues have become more prominent in the Asia Pacific region because of the presence of global players, rising great powers, and confident middle powers, which intersect in complicated ways. This series puts forward important new work on key security issues in the region. It embraces the roles of the major actors, their defense policies and postures and their security interaction over the key issues of the region. It includes coverage of the United States, China, Japan, Russia, the Koreas, as well as the middle powers of ASEAN and South Asia. It also covers issues relating to environmental and economic security as well as transnational actors and regional groupings.

BUSH AND ASIA
America's Evolving Relations with East Asia
Edited by Mark Beeson

JAPAN, AUSTRALIA AND ASIA-PACIFIC SECURITY
Edited by Brad Williams and Andrew Newman

REGIONAL COOPERATION AND ITS ENEMIES IN
NORTHEAST ASIA
The Impact of Domestic Forces
Edited by Edward Friedman and Sung Chull Kim

ENERGY SECURITY IN ASIA
Edited by Michael Wesley

AUSTRALIA AS AN ASIA PACIFIC REGIONAL
POWER
Friendships in Flux?
Edited by Brendan Taylor

NORTH KOREA'S MILITARY-DIPLOMATIC CAMPAIGNS, 1966–2008

Narushige Michishita

Routledge
Taylor & Francis Group

LONDON AND NEW YORK

First published 2010
by Routledge
2 Park Square, Milton Park, Abingdon, Oxon, OX14 4RN

Simultaneously published in the USA and Canada
by Routledge
711 Third Avenue, New York, NY 10017

Routledge is an imprint of the Taylor & Francis Group, an informa business

First issued in paperback 2011

© 2010 Narushige Michishita

Typeset in Times New Roman by Taylor & Francis Books

British Library Cataloguing in Publication Data
A catalogue record for this book is available from the British Library

Library of Congress Cataloging in Publication Data
Michishita, Narushige.
North Korea's military-diplomatic campaigns, 1966-2008 /
Narushige Michishita.
p. cm. – (Routledge Security in Asia Pacific series ; 12)
"Simultaneously published in the USA and Canada"–T.p. verso.
Includes bibliographical references and index.
1. Korea (North)–Military policy. 2. Nuclear weapons–Government policy–
Korea (North) 3. Korea (North)–Foreign relations–20th century. 4. Korea
(North)–Foreign relations–21st century. 5. Korea (North)–Politics and
government. I. Title.
UA853.K5M53 2009
327.5163–dc22
2009010625

ISBN10: 0-415-44943-X (hbk)
ISBN10: 0-415-66689-9 (pbk)
ISBN10: 0-203-87058-1 (ebk)

ISBN13: 978-0-415-44943-4 (hbk)
ISBN13: 978-0-415-66689-3 (pbk)
ISBN13: 978-0-203-87058-7 (ebk)

TO MY WIFE MIHO
AND MY PARENTS
YOSHITO AND MICHIKO

CONTENTS

MAPS

ACKNOWLEDGMENTS

This study would not have been possible without the help of my mentors, colleagues, and institutions. Nathaniel Thayer, Eliot Cohen, Charles Doran, Michael Green, John Merrill, and William Zartman directly advised me on this study. Kang In-duk, Kim Hee Sang, Kim Kook-Hun, Lee Ki-Tak, and Rhee Sang-Woo were South Korean mentors who always provided me with incredible insights.

For comments and advice, I thank Kiyohiko Azuma, Bruce Bechtol, Jr., Joseph Bermudez, Jr., Stephen Bradner, Leszek Buszynski, Robert Carlin, Cha Jaehoon, Cheong Seong-Chang, Choi Kang, Robert Collins, Toby Dalton, Robert Dujarric, James Foster, Yoichi Funabashi, Richard Halloran, Hamm Taik-young, Seigo Iwamoto, Hajime Izumi, Jun Bong-Geun, Bruce Klingner, Hideya Kurata, Lee Chung Min, Lee Jong-Seok, Lim Sungnam, Satoru Miyamoto, Moon Seong-Mook, Tetsuo Murooka, Don Oberdorfer, Shinichi Ogawa, Masao Okonogi, Paik Haksoon, Park Jin, Jonathan Pollack, Charles Pritchard, Kenneth Quinones, Ryoo Kihl-jae, Heigo Sato, Scott Snyder, Peter Sowden, David Straub, Noriyuki Suzuki, Sugio Takahashi, Stephen Tharp, Aaron Trimble, Ichiro Ue, Chikako Ueki, Joel Wit, Yang Un-Chul, Yoon Taeyoung, Tomonori Yoshizaki, and other anonymous former and incumbent DPRK, ROK and U.S. government officials.

For providing materials, I am grateful to Gunnie Boman, Michael Chinworth, Cho Ah Ra, Chung Kyung A, Richard Davis, Richard Devine, Vicki Futscher, Yukari Harada, Ryo Honta, Atsuhito Isozaki, Shigeo Kikuchi, Kim Yong Kyu, Amiko Nobori, Park Young-June, James Person, Robert Richardson, Yasuyo Sakata, Katsumi Sawada, Junichi Shimo, Tadashi Takayama, Kaoru Tomobe, Yi Han Ki, Kimitaka Yoshimura, and Robert Wampler. I thank Paola Celli, Emma Davis, Megan Graieg, Nigel Hope, Arthur Lord, Dean Ouellette, Katsuya Tsukamoto, and Kori Urayama for their help during editing and production.

The National Graduate Institute for Policy Studies, the National Institute for Defense Studies, Kyungnam University's Institute for Far Eastern Studies, the Reischauer Center for East Asian Studies at the Johns Hopkins University's School of Advanced International Studies, the Sejong Institute, and the Chinese Academy of Social Sciences provided the most favorable academic environments to me. I am grateful to Kent Calder, Jin Changsu, Masashi Nishihara, Park

Kie-Duck, Piao Jianyi, Shin Jong-Dae, Takashi Shiraishi, Seiichiro Takagi, and Zhang Yuyan for generously supporting me in conducting this study. This work was also supported by the Abe Fellowship administered by the Japan Foundation Center for Global Partnership in Tokyo and the Social Science Research Council in New York, and a fellowship provided by the Japan-Korea Cultural Foundation in Tokyo.

A NOTE ON TRANSLITERATION AND STYLE

Generally, I used the "New Romanization System," released in July 2000 by the ROK Ministry of Culture and Tourism, available at http://user.chollian.net/~lyh220/urimal/romanization.htm, in transliterating Korean words. However, in order to enable the readers to easily identify the precise spelling of the original Korean words, I made one adjustment to the system. Instead of reflecting irregular sound changes (when pronounced) on the spelling, I decided to simply use one English character for a specific Korean character. For instance, the Korean letter for "g" (ㄱ), which is pronounced either as "g" or as "k" depending on the context, is always spelled as "g." This rule applies to the case where the consonant appears as the last letter in a word. For example, the word meaning South Korea (한국) is spelled as "Hangug."

Other exceptions are as follows. For North Korean first and family names, I used Radiopress, *Chousen Minshushugi Jinminkyouwakoku Soshikibetsu Jinmeiroku* (North Korea Directory) (Tokyo: Radiopuresu, various years), which followed the official North Korean transliteration system.

For South Korean first and family names, I used the "New Romanization System." However, when a specific spelling is preferred and/or used by a particular individual (where it is known) or when it is commonly used, I followed suit. For example, Roh Tae Woo (노태우) is not spelled as "No Tae Wu" as the New Romanization System would suggest. Moreover, Kim (김), Lee (이), and Park (박) are spelled as "Kim," "Lee," and "Park." Simply following the transliteration rule, Kim must be spelled as "Gim," Lee as "I," Park as "Bag." However, these names are common enough to stand as exceptions.

For North Korean location names (e.g. cities, mountains, rivers), I followed Sin Dae Heung, ed., *Saishin Chousen Minshushugi Jinminkyouwakoku Chimei Jiten* (New Dictionary of Location Names in the Democratic People's Republic of Korea) (Tokyo: Yuuzankaku, 1994). When the spelling of the location names differ from the one widely used internationally, I have indicated the latter in parentheses. For South Korean location names, I referred to Kim Myong Taek, ed., *Gyotong-Gwangwang Hangug Doro Jido* (Korea Tour-Road Atlas: Chinese-English Edition) (Seoul: Jungang Jido Munhwasa, 2001).

For book, journal, and article titles in notes, I followed the New Romanization System. However, I used official names, when available, for book, journal, and article titles in the main text. For this reason, the title of the same journal can be spelled differently in the text and in notes in a few cases. For example, *Kyunghyang Sinmun*, a South Korean daily, is spelled as *Kyunghyang Sinmun* (official English name) in the main text, but *Gyeonghyang Sinmun* (transliteration) in notes. This method is used to make it easy for the readers to identify and locate source materials.

The Democratic People's Republic of Korea is abbreviated as the DPRK, and the Republic of Korea as the ROK without note. Korean names are written with surnames preceding given names, while American and Japanese names are given with the surname following the given name. The time and dates are indicated in local time. All the titles and positions reflect those in the period under discussion. Electronic addresses (URL) for a book or a journal article published and available on the internet are indicated where appropriate. The date of access is March 17, 2008 unless otherwise indicated.

ABBREVIATIONS

AGER   Auxiliary general environmental research
BDA   Banco Delta Asia
CFC   Combined Forces Command
CIA   Central Intelligence Agency
CINCCFC   Commander in Chief, U.S.–ROK Combined Forces Command
CINCPAC   Commander in Chief, U.S. Pacific Command
CINCUNC   Commander in Chief, United Nations Command
CPV   Chinese People's Volunteers
CVID   Complete, verifiable, and irreversible dismantlement
DEFCON   Defense Condition
DMZ   Demilitarized Zone
DPRK   Democratic People's Republic of Korea
EUSA   Eighth United States Army
GNP   Gross national product
GOT   General-Officer Talks
HEU   Highly-enriched uranium
HFO   Heavy fuel oil
IAEA   International Atomic Energy Agency
ICBM   Intercontinental ballistic missile
JCS   Joint Chiefs of Staff
JSA   Joint Security Area
JSAO   Joint sea air operation
KATUSA   Korean Augmentation to the U.S. Army
KCNA   Korean Central News Agency
KEDO   Korean Peninsula Energy Development Organization
KIA   Killed in action
KPA   Korean People's Army
KPA/CPV   Korean People's Army/Chinese People's Volunteers
LWR   Light-water reactor
MAC   Military Armistice Commission
MDL   Military Demarcation Line
MFA   Ministry of Foreign Affairs

MND	Ministry of National Defense
MPAF	Ministry of People's Armed Forces
MTCR	Missile Technology Control Regime
MW	Megawatt
NAM	Non-Aligned Movement
NDC	National Defence Commission
NIC	National Intelligence Council
NK	North Korea/North Korean
NLL	Northern Limit Line
NMD	National Missile Defense
NPLL	Northern Patrol Limit Line
NPT	Treaty on the Non-Proliferation of Nuclear Weapons
NSC	National Security Council
NWI	Northwest Islands
OPCON	Operational control
OPLAN	Operation Plan
PSI	Proliferation Security Initiative
PRC	People's Republic of China
ROE	Rules of engagement
ROK	Republic of Korea
ROKG	Republic of Korea government
SEAL	Sea, Air, Land
SPA	Supreme People's Assembly
TCOG	Trilateral Coordination and Oversight Group
TEL	Transporter-erector-launcher
TMD	Theater Missile Defense
UN	United Nations
UNC	United Nations Command
UNCLOS	United Nations Convention on the Law of the Sea
UNCMAC	United Nations Command Military Armistice Commission
UNCURK	United Nations Commission for the Unification and Rehabilitation of Korea
UNGA	United Nations General Assembly
UNSC	United Nations Security Council
USAF	United States Air Force
USFK	United States Forces Korea
USS	United States Ship
USSR	Union of Soviet Socialist Republics
WATCHCON	Watch Condition
WFP	World Food Programme
WIA	Wounded in action
WMD	Weapons of mass destruction
WPK	Workers' Party of Korea

INTRODUCTION

Is the logic behind North Korea's military actions different from ours? In other words, does North Korea use force regardless of its policy objectives? In the following chapters, I hope to demonstrate that North Korea's logic in using force is in fact not fundamentally different from ours. North Korea has used force to achieve its policy objectives, however idiosyncratic they might be, within the structural conditions it faces. Moreover, I also hope to demonstrate that there has been a learning process on the part of the North Korean leaders with regard to the manner in which they have used military force.

A few assessments deserve being highlighted. First, North Korea's policy objectives have changed significantly over time, from ambitious, aggressive, and hostile ones in the 1960s to more defensive ones in the 1990s onwards. In 1968, for example, North Korea captured the U.S. intelligence-gathering ship *Pueblo* and attempted to overthrow the South Korean government. Since the 1990s, however, regime survival and acquisition of economic assistance have become its most important objectives. To this end, North Korea has sought to normalize relations with the United States and Japan. Despite military crises, North Korea's policy objectives since the 1990s have been minimalist.

Second, North Korea's military actions have been consistent with its policy objectives. In other words, the North Korean leaders have been rational in using military force for the purpose of achieving their policy objectives. Changing patterns of North Korea's military actions, particularly in terms of their intensity and targeting, support this contention. This does not mean, however, that the North Koreans have always been successful. Some military actions were very successful in achieving their policy objectives while others were only moderately so. Yet others were unsuccessful or even counterproductive. Simply put, North Korean leaders have been highly rational and moderately successful high-risk takers with idiosyncratic policy objectives.

Third, North Korea's military actions have been shaped and constrained by structural factors such as military advantages that it has enjoyed. More specifically, North Korea's military advantages were a motivating factor and determinant for choosing the location of its military actions. They were also a determinant of success. The history of North Korean military action strongly

1

suggests that North Korea's propensity to threaten to or actually resort to the use of force has been high, particularly when a new opportunity was created by the acquisition of new military capabilities. The preferred location of North Korea's military actions changed over time according to the shifting military balance, and where the North Koreans had military advantages, chances were high that their military actions would succeed. In other words, structural factors, instead of tactical factors such as negotiating skills, played a decisive role in determining the outcome of North Korea's military actions.

Finally, North Korean leaders have learned lessons from the past, and their skill in using military force in conjunction with diplomatic actions has become more sophisticated over time. The North Koreans have demonstrated their ability to conduct highly sophisticated and elaborate military-diplomatic campaigns since the early 1990s. In fact, what they did in Panmunjom and in the Yellow Sea in the 1990s was refined repetitions of what they had done in the 1970s; what they have been doing since 2002 is a modified repetition of what they did in the 1990s.

North Korea's military-diplomatic actions have five distinctive characteristics. First, despite the tendency to focus on the offensively oriented nature of North Korean military strategy, deterrence has been a critical enabling factor for its military actions and military-diplomatic campaigns. For North Korean military-diplomatic campaigns to succeed, North Korea has to prevent strong U.S.–ROK retaliations. The United States and/or South Korea seriously considered major military retaliations or coercive actions in response to the North Korean raid on the South Korean presidential residence and the seizure of the U.S. intelligence-gathering ship *Pueblo* in 1968, the shooting-down of the U.S. reconnaissance aircraft EC-121 in 1969, the Axe Murder incident in Panmunjom in 1976, and the nuclear crisis in 1994, but, as we know, they eventually dropped the military option in all of the cases. In other words, North Korea successfully deterred the U.S. and ROK from taking effective retaliatory measures.

Second, legal factors have significantly influenced North Korea's military actions. North Korean policymakers have proved to be extremely knowledgeable about legal issues, and well versed in exploiting them to their advantage. Their ability to make use of legal issues seems to have resulted from the nature of the North Korean political system, in which a small number of specialists tend to stay in the same position for a long time, creating a strong knowledge base of legal matters and organizational memory. When the North Korean naval vessels started repeatedly crossing the Northern Limit Line (NLL) – a quasi-maritime borderline between North and South Korea in the Yellow Sea – in 1999, the North Korean side did not have a local military advantage, as the outcome of the naval clash in South Korea's favor suggested. However, the North Koreans still took actions hoping that they could exploit legal problems pertaining to the status of the NLL.

Third, an element of surprise has almost always been an important ingredient in North Korea's military actions. The seizure of the *Pueblo*, the shooting down of

2

the EC-121, the Axe Murder incident, announcements to withdraw from the Treaty on the Non-Proliferation of Nuclear Weapons (NPT) in 1993 and 2003, the launch of the ballistic missiles in 1993, 1998 and 2006, and the nuclear test in 2006 all came to observers' surprise. The frequent use of surprise seems to have implanted in our minds an impression that the North Koreans are "crazy." However, surprise has actually worked well.

Fourth, none of North Korea's major military-diplomatic actions have been primarily caused by domestic political factors. Even in cases in which domestic political objectives played a role, they have been of secondary importance, or less, as motives of North Korean military actions. In the period directly following the end of the Korean War in 1953, North Korea did not undertake many military actions as its attention was focused on a number of serious domestic power struggles.[1] North Korea's use of force actually increased when Kim Il Sung's position was consolidated in the 1960s. Furthermore, when Kim Jong Il formalized his position in the Workers' Party in the early 1980s, North Korea continued to undertake provocative actions, such as the Rangoon Incident.

Fifth, the contention that North Korea tends to undertake military actions when it faces a hostile international environment is not true. History suggests it has initiated military actions when the international environment was favorable as well as when it was not. The 1976 Axe Murder incident took place in an international environment most favorable to North Korea while its nuclear diplomacy began in 1993 and in 2002 when the international situation was extremely negative to the country. The Taepo Dong launch took place in 1998 when the international environment was quite favorable due to the adoption of the engagement and sunshine policies by the United States and South Korea, respectively. The 1999 naval clash took place about two weeks after William Perry, special advisor to the president and secretary of state, visited Pyongyang. The international environment does not necessarily determine the outcome of their action, either. The Axe Murder, for example, failed disastrously despite a favorable international environment, while the nuclear diplomacy twice turned out to be a success under the most unfavorable international environment.

Finally, regardless of their immediate results, North Korea's military-diplomatic campaigns have in some cases produced mid- to long-term unintended consequences. In the 1960s, for example, sustained assaults along the Demilitarized Zone (DMZ) provoked the United States and South Korea to fortify the area, making it impossible for North Korean agents to penetrate the DMZ as easily as before. In the 1970s, North Korean naval and air activities catalyzed South Korea's effort to fortify the offshore islands in the Yellow Sea – the Northwest Islands – and build up and modernize its naval forces deployed in the area. The local military balance in the area had become decisively favorable to the South Korean side by the time the naval vessels of North and South Korea engaged in battle in 1999. The launch of the Taepo Dong missile in 1998 encouraged the United States and Japan to accelerate their efforts on ballistic missile defense programs. These cases demonstrate the importance of paying attention to the mid- to long-term repercussions in assessing the effectiveness of North Korea's military-diplomatic campaigns. Short-term success could turn into mid- to long-term failure.

Structure and definitions

The following chapters are structured as follows. Chapter 1 will provide a historical and analytical survey of North Korea's past conventional as well as unconventional military actions. In this, four distinct periods are identified:

(a) Genesis of military-diplomatic campaigns, 1966–72
(b) Diplomatic uses of limited force, 1973–82
(c) The rise of terrorism, 1983–92
(d) Sophisticated military-diplomatic campaigns, 1993–present

Chapters 2 to 9 will constitute detailed studies of significant cases. These case studies have been selected on the basis of one or more of the following criteria:

(a) Sustained use and/or threat of force conducted for a period of over one year for a set of coherent policy objectives; or
(b) Major crisis in which the U.S.–ROK side's Defense Condition (DEFCON) was raised to level three or above

Eight cases met these criteria. Under the first criterion, assaults along the DMZ in the 1960s, the West Sea incident in the 1970s, the first round of nuclear diplomacy, missile diplomacy, the sustained campaigns to undermine the Korean Armistice in the 1990s, and the second round of nuclear diplomacy since 2002 were selected. Under the second criterion, the *Pueblo* incident of 1968 and the Axe Murder incident of 1976 were chosen. In order to conduct a controlled comparative analysis, all case study chapters will follow the outline indicated below.

(a) Historical description
(b) Critical factors
(c) Characteristics
(d) Assessment
(e) Repercussions (when they apply)

Here, critical factors refer to the factors that motivated or enabled North Korea to use force, such as military balance, the international environment, and legal issues that played critical roles in North Korea's military-diplomatic campaigns.

In discussing characteristics of North Korea's use and/or threat of force, four important aspects will be considered. First, I will look at the location and timing of North Korea's military actions. Where and when did military actions take place? Did they take place in the DMZ, in the Joint Security Area, or somewhere else? What determined the timing of the military actions? The existence of the element of surprise will also be an important factor discussed here.

Second, I will discuss forces involved and the type of force used, examining whether they were: (a) conventional forces, unconventional forces, or weapons of mass destruction and ballistic missiles; (b) the actual or potential use of force; and (c) controlling, coercive, or subversive use of force. A quick word on definitions: the actual use of force, or simply use of force, refers to the real, physical application of force against the target. The potential/indirect use of force, or threat of force, refers to the exercise of compellence by demonstrating military force and by issuing threats, explicitly or implicitly.[2] The controlling use of force aims at establishing physical control over targets. The coercive use of force is meant to exercise influence over the targets without attempting to establish physical control over them. The subversive use of force aims at undermining the military, economic, psychological, or political strength or morale of a regime and/ or at overthrowing an incumbent government.[3]

Third, I will investigate the intensity and targeting of the threat or use of force. How intensely and what kind of targets did North Korea attempt to attack? How many people were killed and wounded? Was the target enemy armed forces, citizens, or leadership? Was it Americans or South Koreans that were attacked? Finally, I will examine the level of military-diplomatic coordination, asking how closely the specific military actions and diplomatic moves were coordinated and how deliberately or purposively military force was employed to support diplomatic actions and vice versa.

Assessing the results of the use of force is one of the most challenging parts of this study due largely to the secrecy of the North Korean system and to the inherent difficulty involved in assessing the consequences of military actions. I will take the following steps in order to produce an objective assessment. First, I will identify North Korea's original policy objectives. In doing so, I will use North Korea's official and semi-official pronouncements as the most important source of information. Since North Korea's pronouncements are quite often exaggerated or, worse, designed to mislead, I will also use an assessment of North Korean intentions made by the top leaders and high-ranking American and South Korean officials to make necessary adjustments. In addition, I will employ circumstantial evidence to make further adjustments and to identify other policy objectives that the North Koreans might have had. Second, I will identify consequences of North Korea's military actions. The most clear-cut consequences would include destruction of certain physical targets or formal agreements. Even in clear-cut cases involving formal agreements, care will be taken to find out how much of the agreement was actually implemented. Finally, I will evaluate the effectiveness of North Korea's military actions based primarily on the evaluations made by American and South Korean high-ranking officials. In particular, their private evaluations are the most useful source of information since these are considered to be highly genuine. In analyzing these case studies,

I will discuss domestic origins of North Korea's military actions where possible. After I assess the results of the military actions, I will separately discuss mid- to long-term repercussions, if any.

Regarding terminology, the term "military actions" is used throughout this study to mean overt use or threat of military force, including the use of potential nuclear force, to achieve policy objectives. Covert actions such as guerrilla infiltration operations, assassination attempts, and terrorist attacks will be referred to as "unconventional" actions or activities.

North Korea's use of force in a historical continuum

North Korea defines its military actions as part of a historical continuum and, following a military-first policy, will continue to use force as the single most important policy tool in the foreseeable future. One of the biographies of Kim Jong Il, entitled *Gen. Kim Jong Il: The Lodestar* and published in Pyongyang, claimed that Kim had enabled his country to fight and win a war of nerves against the United States, and characterized the *Pueblo* incident of 1968 as "the first war of brains (*dunoejeon*)" and the 1993–94 nuclear diplomacy as "yet another war of wisdom (*jihyejeon*)."[4] In the first case, Kim Jong Il was said to have created a situation in which the U.S. Congress, Defense Department, and State Department were "flustered and thrown into confusion," and the threatened retaliation by the United States "went up in smoke before the quick moves taken by the Leader [Kim Jong Il]." The United States was eventually forced to send a letter of apology to North Korea. This was a victory in the first war of brains against the United States for "young General Kim Jong Il in his twenties." The second war of brains came at the time when the United States and South Korea were conducting Team Spirit 93 joint military exercise and the international pressure on North Korea to accept inspections on its nuclear facilities was mounting. The "General," the biography explained, "wisely ordered the launch of a '15-day war' and snubbed the arrogant United States again for the entire world to see."[5]

On June 16, 1999, *Rodong Sinmun* and *Kulloja*, the daily newspaper and the journal of the Central Committee of the Workers' Party of Korea (WPK), jointly issued an article entitled "WPK's policy of giving priority to army is invincible." The article contended:

> The WPK's policy of giving priority to the army is a powerful policy that ensures a decisive victory in political and diplomatic confrontation with imperialism.
>
> … Today the WPK's policy of giving priority to the army is a guarantee for sure victory in diplomacy with the enemies. Our self-reliant defence capabilities, a result of scores of years of arduous efforts, instill great fear into the imperialists. We will strongly counter imperialism while saying whatever we want to say in face of any threat and blackmail.[6]

Chapter 1

NORTH KOREA'S MILITARY-DIPLOMATIC CAMPAIGNS

After the Korean War ended in July 1953, a relative calm prevailed in Korea. In 1954–60, North Korea was busy with domestic power struggles and the rehabilitation of its war-torn economy. From 1961–65, however, North Korea started to follow a revolutionary agenda *vis-à-vis* South Korea and began to invest a large amount of resources to its military build-up. This build-up eventually resulted in active conventional as well as unconventional offensives since the mid-1960s.

Genesis of military-diplomatic campaigns, 1966–72

Conventional and unconventional assaults and assassination attempts

The period between 1966 and 1972 witnessed a dramatic increase in North Korean military activities such as sustained armed assaults along the Demilitarized Zone (DMZ) and conventional attacks against U.S. intelligence-gathering assets. During this period, major actions were concentrated along the DMZ and in the Sea of Japan. North Korean actions resulted in a large number of casualties. Most of the casualties were American and South Korean servicemen, but a number of South Korean civilians were also killed. Unconventional attempts to assassinate the South Korean president as well as massive guerrilla infiltrations into South Korea accompanied the more conventional military actions.

Assaults along the Demilitarized Zone

North Korea mounted numerous armed assaults directed at U.S.–ROK forces along the DMZ in the latter half of the 1960s. It started to use larger teams and more heavily armed operatives in 1966, and the emphasis shifted from intelligence collection and subversion to overt "harassment." There were also clashes in or near the Joint Security Area (JSA) in Panmunjom in this period.

In response to the increase in North Korean armed assaults, South Korea took active retaliatory measures, causing tension between the United States and South Korea because the South Korean raids were executed without the approval of the Commander in Chief, United Nations Command (UNC), a U.S. Army general who at that time exercised operational control over South Korean forces in addition to the U.S. forces in Korea. The United States faced a serious challenge in helping South Korea; while the help was certainly necessary, there was a danger that the U.S. help might encourage the South Koreans to take unilateral, punitive actions against North Korea which might result in military escalation.

Conventional attacks

During this period, North Korea mounted a number of conventional attacks at sea and in the air. The first such attack took place in April 1965, when two North Korean MiG-17 fighters attacked and damaged a U.S. Air Force RB-47H reconnaissance aircraft in the Sea of Japan. The plane survived the attack, however, and landed safely in Japan.[1]

Two years later, in January 1967, a South Korean naval patrol craft PCE-56 was attacked and sunk by North Korean coastal guns when it was protecting South Korean fishing boats in the Sea of Japan. North Korea claimed that the ship was sailing inside its territorial sea, while the UNC claimed it was not.[2]

Then on January 23, 1968, North Korean naval vessels captured the U.S. Navy intelligence-gathering ship *Pueblo* and its crew in the Sea of Japan. In order to get the crew and the ship back, the United States agreed to hold bilateral talks with North Korea in Panmunjom. The crew, but not the ship, returned to the United States in December.

On April 15, 1969, two North Korean MiG-21 fighters shot down the U.S. Navy EC-121M reconnaissance aircraft in the Sea of Japan, killing all crew members aboard.[3] Although U.S. leaders considered a military response, given the war in Vietnam and lack of Congressional support for expanded military action, they ultimately rejected an armed retaliation.[4] Finally, in June 1970, a North Korean high-speed craft seized a South Korean Navy broadcasting ship with 20 crewmen in the Yellow Sea.

Assassination attempts

Between 1966 and 1972, North Korea conducted two separate assassination attempts against the South Korean president. On January 21, 1968, a 31-man assault team from North Korea's 124th Army Unit, a special operations unit created in 1967, attempted to mount a raid on the South Korean presidential residence – the Blue House – to kill Park Chung Hee. The team was stopped on the way to the Blue House, however, and the plan failed. The second attempt was made in June 1970, when three North Korean agents infiltrated into Seoul and tried to install a remote-controlled bomb at the gate of the National Cemetery three days before Park was scheduled to make a speech there. The bomb prematurely exploded, however, and the attempt failed.

Unconventional warfare

North Korea's unconventional warfare during this period centered on infiltrations of spies and armed guerrillas into South Korea to construct revolutionary bases or to incite instability, a Korean-style "Vietnam strategy," of sorts.[5] North Korea deployed guerrilla teams either through the DMZ or from the sea with fast boats; sightings, contacts, and firefights were reported almost daily in mid-1967.[6] Between October 30 and November 2, 1968, major North Korean infiltration operations took place in Uljin and Samcheok on the South Korean east coast. On three separate occasions, eight 15-member operation teams from the 124th Army Unit landed in these areas. Over 40,000 ROK Army and ROK National Police personnel were mobilized for several months to suppress the infiltrators.[7]

Defying the United States and overthrowing the ROK government

North Korea had highly ambitious policy objectives during this period, ranging from strategically pinning down U.S.–ROK forces on the Korean Peninsula to seriously hampering U.S. reconnaissance activities. North Korea's military actions were largely quite effective in achieving their policy objectives. Although North Korea failed to seriously challenge the stability of South Korea and to assassinate President Park, it succeeded in diverting U.S.–ROK attention and resources away from Vietnam, hampering U.S. reconnaissance activities, and straining U.S.–ROK relations.

These successes, nevertheless, were attained at tremendous cost, both in the short run and in the long run. In the short run, sustaining active military operations exacted a high human toll. Over this six-year period, as many as 715 North Korean servicemen were killed in various engagements, more than double the number of South Korean military personnel killed in the same period.[8] In the long run, the massive military buildup during this period put a heavy burden on the North Korean economy. North Korea spent approximately 30 percent of its budget on defense for the five consecutive years between 1967 and 1971, significantly hampering its economic development.[9] After South Korea's per capita gross national product (GNP) surpassed that of North Korea's in 1969, the gap between the two economies has continued to widen to date.

Diplomatic uses of limited force, 1973–82

Conventional skirmishes, assaults, infiltrations, and assassination attempts

In 1973–82, North Korea's military actions underwent a clear change. Its focus shifted from operations along the DMZ and in the Sea of Japan to operations in the Yellow Sea and in the JSA. The intensity of the use of force diminished dramatically, and military actions were better coordinated with diplomatic moves. In this period, conventional skirmishes at sea and in the air and low-intensity assaults on UNC personnel occurred frequently. Unconventional attacks such as infiltrations by sea and assassination attempts continued, but at a much lower level.

Conventional skirmishes

North Korean military activities at sea increased in the 1970s, particularly in the Yellow Sea around the Northwest Islands, five offshore islands under UNC jurisdiction which are situated much closer to the North Korean coast than to the South Korean coast. In October 1973, North Korea instigated a new military crisis around the Northwest Islands, which came to be known as the West Sea incident. (Both North and South Korea call the Yellow Sea the "West Sea.") North Korean patrol boats frequently entered the areas around the Northwest Islands between 1973 and 1975 to challenge the Northern Limit Line (NLL), a quasi-maritime border established unilaterally by the UNC after the Armistice Agreement ending the Korean War was signed. In 1975 and 1976, North Korean fighters frequently flew in the area, as well.

The strongest military action in the air during this period was North Korea's attempt to shoot down a U.S. SR-71 reconnaissance aircraft. In August 1981, North Korea launched SA-2 surface-to-air missiles at the SR-71 as it was flying over the Yellow Sea. The missiles missed the target.[10]

Low-intensity assaults

Between 1973 and 1977, assaults on UNC personnel occurred frequently in the JSA and the DMZ, which peaked in 1976 and culminated in the Axe Murder incident. On August 18, 1976, two U.S. Army officers were killed in the JSA in Panmunjom by North Korean guards wielding axes. In reaction, the United States mobilized its armed forces and concentrated them in and around the Korean Peninsula in a show of force. Then the U.S. forces in Korea, together with South Korean special forces, undertook an operation to cut down a poplar tree, which was the direct cause of the clash in the JSA. This operation caused an extremely tense situation; had there been even one accidental shot, it is quite likely the situation could have quickly escalated into a free-for-all.

Infiltrations and assassination attempts

With time, the number of known infiltrations declined noticeably, with the 1969 high of 144 declining to 86 in 1970, 52 in 1971, and only 20 in 1972. This trend continued as the number further declined in the latter half of the decade. Though the assassination attempts in 1968 and in 1970 had failed, assassination remained a popular tactic for North Korea. On August 15, 1974, another attempt was made to assassinate Park Chung Hee when a North Korean-trained South

Korean citizen fired rounds at Park. He missed Park, but the First Lady was killed in the incident.[11]

New maritime order, peace agreement, and the withdrawal of U.S. forces

North Korea's policy objectives in 1973–82 continued to be revisionist in nature. However, diplomacy became a primary channel through which the North Koreans tried to achieve their objectives. In the West Sea incident and the Axe Murder incident, coordinated diplomatic actions were indispensable for translating military actions into concrete gains.

In this period, North Korea's objectives included (a) challenging U.S.–ROK positions on the status of the waters around the Northwest Islands and the status of the NLL, (b) complicating U.S.–ROK relations, and (c) driving U.S. forces out of Korea. The failed attack on the SR-71 in 1981 seemed to have been in line with the capture of the *Pueblo* and the shooting down of the EC-121 in the late 1960s in that hampering U.S. reconnaissance activities was the primary objective. An assassination attempt was made once again, most likely in order to destabilize South Korea and obstruct its economic development.

During this period, cooperative elements started to appear in the objectives of North Korea's military-diplomatic actions. One of the objectives in the West Sea incident was to promote bilateral U.S.–DPRK talks for concluding a peace agreement, which North Korea proposed to the United States for the first time in 1974, shortly after it started the naval operations in the Yellow Sea. In the Axe Murder incident, one of North Korea's objectives was to marshal international support for its position both in the Non-Aligned Movement summit meeting and in the upcoming United Nations General Assembly meeting. Moreover, North Korea seems to have attempted to encourage those in the United States advocating the withdrawal of U.S. forces from Korea by attacking American soldiers deployed there.

North Korea's military-diplomatic campaigns in this period worked to produce some positive yet largely marginal results. In the West Sea incident, North Korea succeeded in publicly demonstrating the existence of the legal dispute involving the Yellow Sea and in underlining the arbitrary nature of the Armistice arrangements in Korea. It also succeeded in highlighting the disagreements between the United States and South Korea with regard to the status of the NLL. However, it failed to actually enforce the territorial claims it made, and to seriously undermine U.S.–ROK relations.

North Korea used the Axe Murder incident to reinforce its diplomatic offensive by claiming that the U.S. presence in South Korea was a root cause of the confrontation on the Korean Peninsula. However, the brutal killing of the U.S. servicemen backfired. The reaction of the international community to the North Korean action was extremely negative. North Korea's diplomatic offensive against the U.S. military presence in South Korea lost its momentum thereafter. In addition, the incident wrecked North Korea's position in the inter-Korean diplomatic competition at the United Nations General Assembly.

North Korea's military actions in this period were less costly in terms of casualties and physical damage than those in the previous period. The naval and air activities in the Yellow Sea involved only a few actual military clashes, and damage to the North Korean side was small. While two U.S. officers were killed, no North Korean was killed in the Axe Murder incident. Finally, the assassination attempt did not involve major forces or significant material investment.

More broadly, however, North Korea's military actions during this period did involve large costs. For instance, operations in the Northwest Islands area were made possible by continued heavy spending on defense. Although North Korea's defense expenditure during this decade was relatively smaller than in the 1960s, it remained remarkably high in absolute terms.[12] Moreover, North Korea's actions at sea provoked South Korean responses: Seoul adopted the "*sasu*" strategy entailing unconditional defense of the NLL, the offshore islands in the Yellow Sea were fortified, and South Korea's naval and air forces were strengthened.

The rise of terrorism, 1983–92

Assassination attempt and terrorist attacks

The 1983–92 period saw a relative calm in terms of North Korea's use of military force with only sporadic action in the DMZ or in the Northwest Islands area. Instead, North Korean efforts to disrupt South Korea continued with a new emphasis on terrorism. In 1983, relatively small-sized infiltration operations against South Korea increased. In July, an infiltration attempt was made near a South Korean nuclear power plant in Wolseong. In September, the office of the U.S. Information Service in Daegu was attacked, and four South Korean civilians were killed.[13] In the same year, an attempt was made to assassinate South Korean President Chun Doo Hwan in Rangoon, Burma (now Myanmar). On October 9, 1983, North Korean agents detonated a bomb in the Aung San Martyrs' Mausoleum, killing 21 people including four South Korean cabinet members. President Chun, however, survived uninjured.[14]

As the 1988 Seoul Olympic Games drew near, North Korean terrorist attempts to disrupt them became frequent and intense. The first major attempt was made in September 1986, six days before the Asian Games opened in South Korea, when a bomb exploded in the Gimpo International Airport, killing five and wounding more than 30 people. Then on November 29, 1987, Korean Air Lines Flight 858 bound for Bangkok from Abu Dhabi was bombed by two North Korean agents, exploding in midair over the Andaman Sea. All 115 people on board were killed.[15] After the incident, one of the two agents killed himself while the other female agent, Kim Hyon Hui, was captured.

Desperate attempts to reverse the tide

North Korea's policy objectives during this period were revisionist in the first half but relatively status quo-oriented in the latter half. In 1983, North Korea clearly tried to destabilize South Korea with the assassination attempt on President Chun, whose domestic political position was not very strong. By contrast, North Korea's terrorist attacks in 1986 and 1987 were limited in purpose and arguably defensive in nature. What the North Koreans tried to do was to prevent the Asian Games and the Seoul Olympic Games from succeeding. The North Koreans knew that the success of these important international sports events would enormously enhance South Korea's position in the inter-Korean competition for legitimacy both domestically and internationally. North Korea's actions were defensive in the sense that it was making a final effort to prevent the Republic of Korea from becoming a stable, rich, and internationally acclaimed state.[16]

North Korean actions during this period were unsuccessful. North Korea's conventional actions were too unfocused and too limited to produce meaningful results. The terrorist attacks, no matter how dramatic a psychological shock they might have had, largely backfired. Despite the North Korean attacks, the Asian Games and the Olympic Games were not significantly disturbed. Rather, the disclosure that two North Korean operatives bombed the Korean Air liner fueled international condemnation of North Korea as a terrorist state. In January 1988, the United States designated North Korea as a terrorist-sponsoring nation. Although North Korea's military and terrorist operations during this period were relatively inexpensive without the employment of significant military forces, the price that North Korea paid diplomatically was prohibitively high. The net effect of North Korean military and terrorist actions was clearly negative.

Sophisticated military-diplomatic campaigns, 1993–present

Nuclear and missile diplomacy and undermining the Armistice

After more than a decade, North Korea's overt military-diplomatic campaigns returned to centre stage in the next period, this time with weapons that have regional and potentially global strategic implications. In addition, North Korea initiated sustained military actions in the JSA, the DMZ, and the Yellow Sea to undermine the Korean Armistice. During this period, no known attempt was made to assassinate the South Korean president. North Korea's military assistance and material support for international terrorist and revolutionary groups also declined.

Nuclear diplomacy, round one

North Korea initiated its first foray into nuclear diplomacy in 1993. On March 12, North Korea declared it would withdraw from the Treaty on the

Non-Proliferation of Nuclear Weapons (NPT). This threat successfully brought the Americans into bilateral negotiations in June. The talks failed to produce a swift and definitive solution to the nuclear issue. Moreover, the sidelined South Koreans became frustrated and started to show a negative attitude toward U.S.– DPRK interactions. Under such circumstances, North Korea began discharging spent fuel rods from its five-megawatt (MW) nuclear reactor in May 1994, turning rising tension into crisis. In June 1994, the United States seriously contemplated imposing economic sanctions on North Korea. North Korea declared that it would regard sanctions as a "declaration of war."[17] The end of the crisis came suddenly and unexpectedly. During his unofficial visit to Pyongyang in mid-June, former U.S. President Jimmy Carter was able to reach agreement with Kim Il Sung on ways to deflate the crisis.

Missile diplomacy

North Korea's missile-related activities became an official agenda item in U.S.– DPRK bilateral talks. As a result, the first round of missile talks was held in 1996. North Korea's efforts to develop medium- and long-range ballistic missiles had long been known. In May 1993, North Korea test-launched a medium-range No Dong missile in the direction of Tokyo. A big surprise came when North Korea launched a three-stage rocket based on the Taepo Dong 1 in August 1998, with some unexpected technological breakthroughs. It was doubly shocking because the rocket flew over the Japanese main island in the direction of Hawaii.

Assaults on the Korean Armistice

At the same time, North Korea attempted to undermine the Armistice by initiating sustained military-diplomatic campaigns in 1993, causing trouble in the JSA, DMZ, and Yellow Sea. The North Koreans conducted armed demonstrations several times in the JSA between 1994 and 1996 and provoked an exchange of fire in the DMZ in 1997. They also conducted naval actions to challenge the NLL in the Yellow Sea in June 1999. The resulting naval skirmishes developed into a major exchange of gunfire between the two Koreas. In June 2001, three North Korean cargo ships sailed through the Jeju Strait, and one of them later crossed the NLL in the Yellow Sea and entered the port of Haeju. In June 2002, two North Korean patrol boats separately crossed the NLL in the Yellow Sea, and one of them suddenly opened fire against one of the South Korean patrol boats. The ensuing exchange of fire lasted for about 30 minutes, and both side suffered casualties and damage.

Covert operations

Some of North Korea's ongoing covert operations were unveiled in 1995, 1996, and 1998. In October 1995, a North Korean infiltration team was discovered while it was attempting to cross the Imjin River south of the DMZ. In the same month, two North Korean operatives infiltrated into South Korea in order to conduct political operations before being captured by South Korean security forces. In September 1996, a *Sang-o*-class North Korean special-purpose submarine was found on the South Korean east coast in a failed infiltration/exfiltration operation. In June 1998, a North Korean *Yugo*-class midget submarine was found off the South Korean east coast with nine corpses inside. Also, a North Korean semi-submersible that had infiltrated the southern coast was sunk in December 1998.[18]

Nuclear diplomacy, round two

In December 2002, North Korea set in motion a second round of nuclear diplomacy by announcing that it would restart the construction and operation of its nuclear facilities. Faced with financial sanctions imposed by the United States and America's refusal to seriously engage with Pyongyang, North Korea launched ballistic missiles in July 2006 and conducted a nuclear test in October.

Coercing to survive

North Korea's policy objectives in this period were predominantly intended to preserve the status quo. Through its active military-diplomatic campaigns in this period, North Korea sought to create a mechanism that would ensure its regime's survival. Normalization or at least improvement of its relations with the United States was the single most important means of achieving that goal. Economic gain also emerged as another of the most important policy objectives in this period. This was a significant development given that North Korea had never before demanded direct economic rewards in its military-diplomatic campaigns.

North Korea's military-diplomatic campaigns in this period were quite successful. The most tangible success was won with the signing of the 1994 Agreed Framework in which the United States promised to provide light-water reactors to North Korea and offered to improve U.S.–DPRK relations in response to North Korea's promise to freeze its nuclear development and to accept full nuclear inspections in the future.

Together with the discovery of a suspected underground nuclear facility in Kumchangri, North Korea's active missile diplomacy initiated in 1998 prompted the United States to undertake a major review of its policy toward the country. As a result, the United States and the DPRK issued the "Joint U.S.–DPRK Statement on International Terrorism" and the "U.S.–DPRK Joint Communiqué" in 2000.

In the second round of nuclear diplomacy, North Korea successfully used nuclear coercion to force the United States to reengage with it. After the nuclear test in 2006, the United States shifted its policy toward North Korea, eventually ceasing to apply the Trading with the Enemy Act in June 2008 and removing North Korea from its State Sponsor of Terrorism list four months later.

In parallel with nuclear and missile diplomacy, North Korea proposed the conclusion of a U.S.–DPRK peace agreement in October 1993, and a "tentative agreement" in February 1996 as a first step toward the conclusion of a peace agreement with the United States. These proposals were made while North Korea simultaneously undertook a series of military actions and armed demonstrations. North Korea's logic was that since the danger of war was looming large on the Korean Peninsula and military tensions rose because the current Armistice mechanism was ineffective, the United States and the DPRK must conclude a peace agreement or at least establish a better peace mechanism in order to avoid another war. With its series of military actions, North Korea tried to create the reality to fit its argument. Nevertheless, North Korea has so far failed to conclude a tentative agreement, let alone a peace agreement, with the United States.

North Korea's military-diplomatic campaigns were quite costly in this period. North Korea devoted a large amount of its resources to nuclear and missile development and in the second nuclear crisis endured tremendous socioeconomic pressure from the United States. North Korea also suffered a number of casualties and loss of naval vessels in the naval battles in 1999 and 2002. North Korea's covert operations also proved to be a costly venture. Within a matter of two years, North Korea lost two special-purpose submarines, a *Sang-o*-class submarine in 1996 and a *Yugo*-class submarine in 1998. These incidents were an indication of the growing difficulties the North Koreans faced in successfully executing covert operations.

Finally, North Korean military actions during this period also produced negative results. Partly as a result of North Korea's nuclear and missile diplomacy, the United States and Japan accelerated their joint efforts on ballistic missile defense and Japan started to deploy ballistic missile defense systems in 2007. Also, the naval battle of June 1999 undermined North Korea's ability to exercise conventional military-diplomatic campaigns by demonstrating that its conventional military assets were outdated and were no match for their South Korean counterparts. The only way for the North Koreans to match South Korea now was by means of surprise, as it did in 2002.

Chapter 2

ASSAULTS ALONG THE DEMILITARIZED ZONE, 1966–68

North Korea mounted numerous armed attacks directed against U.S.–ROK forces along the Demilitarized Zone (DMZ) in the latter half of the 1960s. With its sustained military operations along the DMZ, North Korea succeeded in diverting U.S.–ROK attention away from Vietnam, straining the U.S.–ROK relationship, and bolstering Kim Il Sung's position both domestically and internationally.

Attacks and counterattacks

Armed attacks against U.S.–ROK forces

After North Korean leader Kim Il Sung announced in October 1966 that the U.S. forces should be "dispersed to the maximum everywhere and on every front of the world," guerrilla-type assaults against U.S. and South Korean forces surged.[1] North Korea started to use larger teams and more heavily armed operatives.[2] Between October 15 and 19, 1966, 11 South Korean servicemen were killed in ambush. On October 21, a South Korean truck was attacked in the western DMZ, killing six South Korean soldiers. During the early morning hours of November 2, the last day of the U.S. President Lyndon Johnson's visit to South Korea, six U.S. and three South Korean soldiers were killed in two separate clashes with North Korean troops south of the DMZ. On one occasion, a Korean People's Army (KPA) squad attacked an eight-man U.S. patrol with hand grenades and submachine guns, about one kilometer south of the DMZ, killing six Americans and one South Korean soldier serving in the U.S. unit as Korean Augmentation to the U.S. Army (KATUSA). In another simultaneous attack, a KPA squad attacked a South Korean patrol, killing two soldiers.[3] The November 2 attack on the U.S. patrol became a front-page story in the U.S. media, although the story itself did not attract sustained public attention.[4] Between January and November 1966, six U.S. and 30 South Korean soldiers been killed in 40 such incidents.[5]

The emphasis of North Korean assaults along the DMZ since mid-October shifted from intelligence collection and subversion to "harassment."[6] Before that, North Korean infiltration agents usually wore civilian clothes and rarely engaged in firefights except when challenged by the South Korean military or security services. In mid-October, North Korean infiltration teams started to seek out and attack South Korean forces. An intelligence memorandum produced by the U.S. Central Intelligence Agency (CIA), dated November 8, argued that (a) although there had been a marked increase in North Korean harassment attacks along the DMZ since mid-October, these actions probably did not reflect a decision to engage in wholesale violations of the Armistice Agreement, (b) there was no evidence that the North Koreans intended to open a "second front" in the Vietnam War, and (c) the North Koreans might have heightened tensions along the DMZ to warn the United States and South Korea against further deployment of ROK forces to Vietnam and to demonstrate North Korean support of Hanoi to other Communist states.[7]

North Korea's official position was that the United States was intensifying military provocations against North Korea and was creating tension on the Korean Peninsula. On November 5, the North Korean Ministry of Foreign Affairs (MFA) stated that "[o]n the occasion of Johnson's visit to South Korea, the frantic armed provocations by the U.S. imperialist aggressor army and their puppet troops in South Korea" reached the "stage of foolhardiness," and demanded that the United States "stop hostile provocations against the D.P.R.K. and quit South Korea at once, taking all their murderous weapons."[8] In June 1967, an MFA official said: "following U.S. President Johnson's visit to South Korea in October last year various provocations have been staged in a more premeditated way" on the Military Demarcation Line (MDL), warning that a "grave danger of war breaking out again in Korea at any moment" had been created due to the "U.S. imperialists' schemes for another war."[9]

North Korean attacks along the DMZ continued in 1967. In February, a U.S. soldier was killed when North Koreans fired upon his nine-man patrol south of the DMZ. In April, 40–60 North Korean soldiers crossed the eastern MDL. In the following six-hour engagement, the U.S.-led United Nations Command (UNC) side used artillery for the first time since the Armistice. It was in the midst of these events that the MFA issued a statement contending that the "ceaseless military provocations of the U.S. imperialist aggressors have increased tension in Korea to a higher pitch and led the situation to an unbearable, grave stage."[10] On May 22, North Korean intruders exploded satchel charges in the barracks of the U.S. Second Infantry Division in the first incident of the kind since 1953. Two U.S. soldiers were killed, 16 were seriously injured, and two U.S. army barracks south of the DMZ were completely demolished.[11] On July 16, the KPA killed three U.S. soldiers south of the southern boundary of the DMZ.

Faced with the new developments, Gen. Charles Bonesteel III, Commander in Chief of the United Nations Command (CINCUNC), reported in July that:

> Actions along DMZ are also continuing with increasing viciousness with more planned, small-scale attacks being made. Firefights are occurring almost every night. A few days ago three more U.S. soldiers

18

were killed. This year's score along DMZ to date: firefights 69; NKs [North Koreans] 64 KIA [killed in action], 2 captured; ROK/US 35 KIA, (including 6 U.S. KIA), 87 WIA [wounded in action]. Irritating factor is that in last few weeks NK along DMZ are improving their kill ratio.[12]

North Korean attacks on UNC vehicles also increased. On August 10, a truck was attacked south of the southern boundary of the DMZ, killing three South Korean soldiers. On August 22, the KPA attacked a U.S. vehicle carrying straw, killing one soldier and injuring another. Then on August 29, three U.S. soldiers were killed and five were wounded when two U.S. vehicles were destroyed by mines planted by North Koreans.

During this period, there were also clashes in and near the Joint Security Area (JSA) in Panmunjom where the Military Armistice Commission (MAC) meetings were held. On August 28, 1967, North Koreans attacked a U.S. Army Engineer Company working 200 yards northeast of the JSA advance camp, killing two U.S. soldiers and two KATUSAs and injuring 26 others. On September 8, a brief free-for-all, involving some 40 personnel from both sides, began when a KPA guard hit a UNC officer as he tried to take a picture. On November 29, three KPA guards attacked a UNC guard near the MAC conference building. A fist fight ensued but was stopped by Security Officers from both sides. There were also two sabotage attacks on trains near the DMZ in September.[13] Of 114 North Korean infiltrations in 1967, 69 cases involved armed attacks.[14]

In December, Kim Il Sung stated that the present situation required a "more enterprising, more revolutionary" approach to "accomplish the south Korean revolution. ... "[15] This statement was followed a month later, in January 1968, with an attempted guerrilla raid on the Blue House, the South Korean presidential residence, aimed at assassinating South Korean President Park Chung Hee. The same month, a U.S. intelligence-collection vessel – the USS *Pueblo* – was captured off the North Korean east coast. North Korean attacks in the DMZ continued and even intensified after these incidents.

On January 22, KPA infiltrators attacked a U.S. guard post and wounded three U.S. soldiers. Two days later, two U.S. soldiers were killed by North Korean agents while in a blocking position to trap remnants of a group of North Korean infiltrators who had attempted to assassinate President Park. On January 25, KPA soldiers mounted raids in the DMZ in an area defended by the U.S. Second Division, killing one U.S. and two South Korean servicemen. On the next day, a U.S. soldier was killed by North Korean agents south of the DMZ.

After a temporary pause in February and March, North Korean attacks resumed in April. Interestingly, after the Senior Members meetings with regard to the *Pueblo* began in February in the MAC in the JSA, incidents in and near the JSA increased, and U.S servicemen became the preferred targets of North Korean assaults. On April 12, 15 KPA guards armed with clubs hit UNC Joint

19

Duty Office personnel who were inspecting the perimeter on the northern edge of the MDL in the JSA. Two days later, North Korean intruders ambushed a UNC JSA security guard truck en route to the JSA, killing two U.S. soldiers and two KATUSAs. On May 2, one KPA security guard knocked down an unarmed UNC guard near a MAC conference room. On August 26, KPA guards dragged a UNC Security Officer off a UNC jeep and attacked him near KPA Guard Post No. 5 in the JSA. On September 2, some 15–20 North Korean workers assaulted U.S. officers in the JSA after they attempted to return a dropped hat to a North Korean guard. Then on December 1, one UNC officer and one enlisted member were attacked and beaten by at least 15 KPA security guards in the JSA.

There were also attacks along the DMZ. On July 20, two U.S. servicemen were killed in two separate incidents near the DMZ. On August 18, the KPA mounted a surprise raid on the U.S. Seventh Division area, killing two U.S. soldiers. On September 27, two U.S. soldiers were killed when North Korean intruders ambushed their jeep south of the MDL. On October 18, a U.S. vehicle was attacked and four were killed.

While attacks in the JSA drastically diminished after the crew of the USS *Pueblo* was released on December 23, attacks outside the JSA continued. On April 7, 1969, North Korean soldiers fired some 300 rounds in 40 minutes into UNC positions in the central sector of the DMZ. On September 22, North Korean howitzers and recoilless guns opened fire on a ROK Army guard post in the central sector of the DMZ. On October 18, a U.S. vehicle was attacked in daylight in the western DMZ, and four U.S. soldiers were killed.

South Korean counterattacks

Given North Korea's statements, the attack on November 2, 1966, against a U.S. patrol unit seems to have been related to Johnson's visit to South Korea. However, it might not have been the only reason for the particular timing. A less known factor was that some 30 South Korean troops had mounted a raid on October 26, a week before the November 2 attack, against North Korea. The South Korean attack team penetrated through the DMZ into North Korean territory to mount the raid, claiming some 30 casualties on the North Korean side. The United States assessed that by attacking American troops on November 2, the North Koreans might have sought to encourage the United States to take measures to prevent any repetition of the South Korean raid across the DMZ.[16]

The South Korean raid caused some tension between the United States and South Korea primarily because it was executed without approval by General Bonesteel, who at that time exercised operational control over South Korean forces. The raid was thus a violation of the command relationship. After the incident, the CINCUNC and the U.S. ambassador to South Korea warned South Korean leaders against any repetition of such incidents.[17]

Violations of the command relationship continued after the December 2 incident, nevertheless. South Korean Defense Minister Kim Sung Eun organized elite anti-infiltration units with 2,400 men under his command and by February 1968 had conducted on average two raids a month against the North. In particular, 11 such raids were mounted between October 26 and December in 1967. Among them was a raid mounted against a KPA division headquarters in November 1967. The headquarters was blown up and the 12-man South Korean strike team returned without any casualties. Most South Korean cabinet members did not know about these activities since the South Korean infiltration units were under the personal control of the Defense Minister and their activities were closely held secrets even within the South Korean government. South Korea had about 200 anti-infiltration troops in each division near the DMZ and was training an additional group. Also, there was one airborne battalion that could be parachuted in for guerrilla activity.[18]

Cyrus Vance, who visited Seoul in February 1968 as a U.S. special presidential envoy, wrote on the possible unilateral military retaliations made by South Korea against North Korea:

> If counter-actions by the Republic of Korea resulted in the outbreak of war with North Korea, the lives of some 12,000 American civilians (most of whom are located in the vicinity of Seoul) would be immediately endangered. Similarly, since American aircraft are parked wing to wing on the six ROK airfields and American military forces are deployed along a key portion of the DMZ – to the West and North of Seoul and across two of the most likely attack routes into South Korea – the prospects of American troops becoming immediately involved in combat with North Korean forces are extremely high.
>
> The outbreak of war in Korea could thus be ignited either by a serious North Korean incursion into the South or by a South Korean foray into the North.[19]

The United States emphasized the "provocative nature" of the South Korean cross-MDL attacks directed by Defense Minister Kim, and suggested that some of the most serious North Korean incursions into the South in the past might actually have been launched in retaliation for the South Korean raids.[20] The U.S. side also pointed out that there was no evidence that the South Korean raids had had dampening effects on North Korean actions, and refused to commit itself to an "agreed retaliation policy" suggested by the South Koreans that involved "instant, punitive, retaliatory action" against future North Korean violations of the Armistice Agreement.[21] Moreover, Vance warned President Park that were the South Koreans even to consider removing troops from South Vietnam, the United States would pull its forces out of Korea.[22] Defense Minister Kim was replaced by Choi Young Hee on February 28, 1968, shortly after the Vance visit.

The U.S. officials were also concerned that South Korean decision-makers might lose their temper and take irrational actions. They were particularly worried about President Park's mental condition. This element compounded their concern about the possible unilateral retaliatory actions by the South Koreans. Vance wrote:

> ... the raid on the Blue House had unfortunate psychologic effects on him. He felt that both he and his country had lost face and his fears for his own safety and that of his family were markedly increased. Compounding this problem has been his heavy drinking. This is not a new development but it may be having cumulative effects. Highly emotional, volatile, frustrated and introspective, Park wanted to obtain from me a pledge for the United States to join his Government in instant, punitive, and retaliatory actions against North Korea in the event of another Blue House raid or comparable attack on some other important South Korean economic, governmental, or military facility. He wanted my assurance of an "automatic" U.S. response in the event of another serious raid against the ROK. I refused to give any such assurances. Park's views were mirrored by almost every member of his Cabinet, who, while now civilians, are mostly retired colonels and generals.[23]

Although the Vance visit improved U.S.–ROK relations in the short run, Vance was not optimistic about the long-term prospects. Specifically, Vance was concerned that (a) North Korea might try to get South Korea to take some unilateral action to further divide the United States and South Korea, (b) there was an unstable political situation with Park's mood and attitude, (c) a serious problem could be raised with the possibility of South Korea's unilateral action, and (d) Park might not "last."[24] The United States faced a dilemma in helping South Korea. While the help was certainly needed, there was a danger that the U.S. help might encourage the South Koreans to take unilateral, punitive actions, which could result in escalation.[25]

Critical factors

The war in Vietnam

In the late 1960s, the United States was deeply involved in the war in Vietnam and a large number of South Korean troops were also committed. The U.S.–ROK involvement in the Vietnam War seemed to have convinced the North Koreans that even if they posed serious military challenges to the two countries, the U.S.–ROK side would not be able to react boldly. In April 1967, Kim Il Sung suggested that the situation in the DMZ would not develop into war because "the U.S. imperialists are heavily involved in Vietnam and the fighting is going against them there."[26] Interrogations of captured North Korean agents pointed to the same conclusion; North Koreans evaluated the United States as "so overextended" in support of South Vietnam that it would be unable to adequately reinforce Korea in case of war.[27] Pointing out that North Korea was determined to create conditions for a "peoples' war" in South Korea, a U.S. intelligence estimate in May 1968 assessed that North Korean leadership rated the risks of this enterprise as "not very high" due to the U.S. involvement in Vietnam and the resultant discord in the United States limiting the military capabilities and the will to support any serious South Korean retaliations against the North.[28]

North Korea's military buildup

North Korea's improved special operations capabilities, together with the more or less balanced overall military power between the North and the South, contributed to its active military campaign in the late 1960s. North Korea initiated a major military buildup in 1962. With its "Party military lines" to arm the population and fortify the entire nation, North Korea had by the late 1960s equipped itself with sufficient deterrent capabilities against possible U.S.–ROK retaliations and with defense infrastructure to guarantee its survival even if the U.S.–ROK side actually mounted military retaliations against it. By the late 1960s, a short, decisive war was difficult for either side to accomplish. Samuel Berger, Director of the Korean Task Force, elaborated in February 1968 why escalation would be futile:

> The temptation to strike back in reprisal is understandable, but it will produce no decisive outcome. The danger in retaliatory or punitive air attacks against North Korea is that they could invite air attacks against the South. If Pyongyang or other NK [North Korean] site is hit, what is to prevent an attack against Seoul or some other site? Action and counter-action could lead to resumed fighting along the DMZ, but both sides are too strong to move successfully against each other in this area. The end result would be to call off the reprisal policy, after physical damage had been done to both sides and a period of fighting in the DMZ with no decisive result (it would not end infiltration), or move to full scale war. None of these outcomes is in the South Korean or our interest.[29]

In short, strong retaliations by the U.S.–ROK side were not likely. Given such a military environment, North Korea could take limited military and unconventional actions against the U.S.–ROK side with impunity.

The North Koreans understood this. For instance, the MFA declared on April 14, 1967:

> Our heroic People's Army has now grown into an invincible, modernized combat detachment of cadres and is standing like an iron wall at the defence post of the country.

The entire people are under arms in the northern part of the country and the whole country has been converted into a fortress.[30]

In addition, improved special operations capabilities gave North Koreans an offensive edge over South Korea in the areas of unconventional operations. In April 1967, North Korea established an elite special operations unit, the 124th Army Unit. By July, North Korea had trained and made available for dispatch some 1,200 or more specially selected agent-guerrilla personnel, capable of conducting subversion, espionage, agitation, and supporting or carrying out militant guerrilla action. Moreover, the North Koreans had been training for two years some 500 subversives in each of the nine provinces, or a total of 5,000 or more, for guerrilla activity in a target province in South Korea. Together with a 4,070-man reconnaissance brigade, special-forces-type personnel added up to about 10,000.[31]

Coping with hit-and-run-type assaults was an inherently daunting task. General Bonesteel wrote:

> Our ability to effectively cope with the NK [North Korean] aggressive killer-patrol actions in or near the DMZ is not as good as I'd like it to be. There are three major reasons: (a) the NK flagrant violations of the DMZ while we abide by it and require the ROK's [South Koreans] to do likewise; (b) the basic military difficulty of reacting effectively against guerrilla hit and run tactics at NH's [*sic*, North Korea's] initiative, usually at night, in a 150 mile band of generally rugged terrain covered now with fairly dense vegetation and natural cover and from which the DMZ offers an immediate sanctuary (this is what is very seriously intensifying ROK frustration, anger and desire to make retaliatory raids); and (c) inexperienced soldiers and junior leaders.[32]

North Korea's military advantage was further reinforced by the lack of adequate defense on the U.S.–ROK side. Both inland and on the coast defense systems against North Korean infiltrations were primitive and weak. The DMZ area was a gigantic, rugged, unexploited natural reserve. Most of the area was covered with plants and, therefore, visibility and accessibility were severely limited.

North Korea's treaty relationships with the Soviet Union and China

In addition to the shift in the overall military balance, the treaties that North Korea had concluded with the Soviet Union and the People's Republic of China (PRC) worked as a reassurance to North Korea and a deterrence against the United States and South Korea. As ROK forces were under the operational control of an American general, North Korea's ability to deter a strong reaction from the United States was of utmost importance.

North Korea signed treaties of Friendship, Cooperation, and Mutual Assistance separately with the Soviet Union and the PRC in 1961. What was significant militarily was the treaties' emphasis on mutual defense. Article 1 of the Soviet–DPRK treaty and Article 2 of the PRC–DPRK treaty stipulated that in the event of one of the parties being the object of an armed attack by any state or coalition of states and being thus in a state of war the other party would immediately render military and other assistance with all the means at its disposal.[33] In November 1967, North Korean Foreign Minister Pak Song Chol told his Soviet counterpart that in addition to its strong army, the DPRK had strong allies – the Soviet Union and China. In such circumstances, the Americans would "hardly attempt to resume the war."[34] A U.S. intelligence memorandum produced in February 1968 stated that the North Koreans might be counting heavily on U.S. preoccupation with Vietnam, and on the deterrent value of their own mutual defense treaties with China and the Soviet Union.[35]

Different approaches

The United States and South Korea disagreed over how to react to North Korean actions. On the one hand, being pinned down in Vietnam militarily and faced with strong domestic opposition, the United States was not in a position to take a strong response against North Korea. On the other hand, with the life of their own president threatened, the South Koreans were inclined to take strong countermeasures. As a result, South Korea took military actions against North Korea without approval by General Bonesteel. Against this backdrop of rising tension, President Park Chung Hee announced in February 1968 that South Korea would seek "Self-Reliant National Defense (*Jaju Gugbang*)" to reduce its reliance on U.S. forces.[36]

The United States and South Korea differed on their approaches to the Korean unification issue. While South Korean leaders were inclined to push for unification should an opportunity arise, American leaders tried to avoid creating a situation in which Koreans might start pushing for unification. U.S. Ambassador to South Korea William Porter wrote in May 1968 that it was not very difficult to specify evidence to support existence of "Korean ardor for reunification," and that it was the natural impulse of a homogeneous people living in one half of a divided nation, and this impulse was only strengthened by the fact that many South Korean leaders were born in the North. On the basis of such an assessment, the United States was paying serious attention to the mood among South Korean personalities at the decision-making level, and to the possible implications of improved military preparedness of the ROK armed forces.[37] The U.S. leadership was concerned about the South Korean military buildup plan formulated in April 1968 because given the increased military capability the ROK leadership might take military moves which ranged from larger retaliatory actions to a preemptive strike against the North to effect reunification. Porter concluded that full support of the South Korean plan was, therefore, not justified in terms of present U.S. objectives in Korea because it could lead to a military force capable of "independently taking courses of action inimical to the U.S. national interest."[38]

The danger of the "March North" was subsequently discounted on the ground that there were only a few "fanatics" in the South Korean leadership and South Korea depended on U.S. logistical support in making such a move. The U.S. government recognized that it was worth worrying about such a scenario, however, and decided that it had better keep ROK forces defensively oriented and continue to make clear that the U.S. defense guarantee would not apply to hostilities arising from a South Korean attack in order to prevent such a scenario from coming into reality.[39]

Characteristics

Location and timing

Most of the North Korean attacks on the U.S.–ROK forces took place in or near the DMZ as well as in the JSA. The North Korean armed campaign along the DMZ lasted for about three years. Armed attacks occurred 15 times in 1966, 69 times in 1967, 175 times in 1968, and 21 times in 1969.[40] With regard to the timing, there were several cases where North Korea took military actions when important diplomatic events were taking place. For example, a South Korean truck was attacked in the western DMZ in October 1966 while President Park Chung Hee attended a summit meeting in the Philippines for countries participating in the Vietnam War. The November 2, 1966, attacks occurred on the last day of the Johnson visit to South Korea. Furthermore, attacks in and near the JSA increased after the MAC Senior Members meetings on the *Pueblo* issue were initiated in February 1968 and diminished after the *Pueblo* affair was wrapped up in December of the same year.

Forces involved and the type of use of force

In most cases, a small number of specially trained forces were used to undertake assaults on U.S.–ROK forces along the DMZ. Joseph Bermudez, Jr. identified incidents on May 22 and August 27 in 1967 and on April 14 in 1968 as executed by the foot reconnaissance stations within the Reconnaissance Bureau under the KPA General Staff. The foot reconnaissance stations "normally utilized teams of three to five lightly armed and equipped troops who operated within the army groups' area of responsibility."[41]

North Korea's use of force was actual and caused a number of human casualties and material damage to the U.S.–ROK side. However, North Korea did not go so far as to actually seize and hold South Korean territories. There was no indication that North Korea was willing to escalate the situation into war. In this sense, the use of force here was primarily coercive and not about controlling the target.

26

North Korea's use of force along the DMZ during this period was thus designed to influence the perception and behavior of the target countries.

Intensity and targeting

In terms of casualties, U.S. forces suffered six deaths in 1966, 16 in 1967, 18 in 1968, and 35 in 1969. The ROK forces suffered 29 deaths in 1966, 115 in 1967, 145 in 1968, and 10 in 1969. The largest number of deaths recorded on one day was nine (six U.S. and three South Korean), caused by two separate attacks on November 2, 1966. On the other hand, the attrition rate was much higher for North Korean forces than U.S.–ROK forces, as the KPA suffered 43 deaths in 1966, 228 in 1967, 321 in 1968, and 55 in 1969.[42] The incidents inside the JSA, however, were relatively low-key. No death was recorded and most of the incidents only involved the use of fists and clubs.

No particular pattern can be identified in the targets of North Korean actions. Most of the time, both U.S. and South Korean forces were targets of North Korean assaults, although North Korea focused heavily on U.S. forces in its military actions while negotiations on the *Pueblo* issue were ongoing. After the *Pueblo* crew was released, U.S. and ROK forces were again targeted fairly equally. One caveat here is that since the U.S. Forces Korea had South Koreans working with them as KATUSA, an attack on a U.S. unit often meant an attack on both Americans and South Koreans. This partly explains why U.S. and South Korean soldiers were killed together in many cases.

Military-diplomatic coordination

There was little coordination between North Korea's military actions and its diplomatic moves. Military actions were sometimes executed with concurrent diplomatic action, most frequently statements issued by the MFA, but such coordination did not translate into concrete outcomes due largely to the lack of direct diplomatic channels between the United States and the DPRK. The military-diplomatic coordination in this period was thus mostly primitive.

It is also important to note that not all clashes were necessarily deliberate, as unintended clashes also occurred. A fist fight in Panmunjom on November 29, 1967, which was eventually stopped by the Security Officers from both sides, stands as a case in point. This incident demonstrated that men on the ground could not be perfectly controlled all the time.

Assessment

Diverting U.S.–ROK attention and resources away from Vietnam

In his report at the Workers' Party Conference in October 1966, Kim Il Sung said, "In the present situation, the U.S. imperialists should be set back and their

27

forces should be dispersed to the maximum everywhere and on every front of the world."[43] As the war in Vietnam intensified, the best way for North Korea to strengthen international revolutionary forces was to help the North Vietnamese "struggle" against the United States.

There were two primary means for helping the North Vietnamese effort. One was to provide military or other assistance, which North Korea did by sending pilots and aircraft to North Vietnam.[44] (In mid-1966, North Korea also offered the dispatch of a KPA division to North Vietnam. However, the North Vietnamese seemed to have declined the offer for they did not need additional troops. Instead, they accepted North Korean fighter pilots.[45]) The other was to distract U.S. and South Korean attention away from the war in Vietnam. Given the fact that the United States and South Korea had committed sizable forces to the war in Vietnam, it was strategically wise to raise tension in Korea where the Americans, let alone the South Koreans, had high political and military stakes. In November 1966, shortly after North Korea intensified assaults against U.S.–ROK forces, the MFA issued a statement saying that the "fresh moves of the U.S. imperialists and the Pak [Park Chung Hee] clique for the dispatch of troops are an unpardonable criminal act against the Korean and Vietnamese peoples," and that the South Korean "puppet regime must stop immediately the criminal act of driving South Korean youths to the aggressive war in South Vietnam."[46] In January 1967, the North Korean Ambassador to the Soviet Union suggested that keeping tensions high along the demarcation line was "a kind of help for the Vietnamese people," because it was distracting a part of the U.S. forces from Vietnam.[47]

The North Korean actions affected U.S.–ROK behavior as early as November 1966. In that month, Winthrop Brown, U.S. Ambassador to South Korea, informed Washington that political problems surrounding the dispatch of more South Korean troops to Vietnam had been compounded by the increase in the number of incidents along the DMZ.[48] In September 1967, President Park explained to U.S. Ambassador Porter that public concerns about South Korea's own security and defense capabilities were affecting his ability to dispatch additional ROK troops to Vietnam, particularly when the North Korean actions along the DMZ and infiltrations were escalating.[49] The U.S. embassy in Seoul wrote in September 1967 that:

Our task [to help Park overcome domestic political obstacles] is not becoming easier because boldness of NK [North Korean] sabotage of DMZ and pressure on DMZ itself is creating (as it is undoubtedly designed to do) in public mind much uneasiness about ROK ability to defend itself. Moreover, when railroad sabotage is carried out miles south of DMZ and relatively close to nation's capital, it involves face and builds up ROKG [ROK government] desire for riposte. In [such] circumstances, question naturally arises whether new military manpower should be used at home rather than in defense of country two thousand miles away.[50]

28

With the anticipated increase of North Korean activities, influential voices within South Korea had started to argue by November 1967 that South Korean troops could not be spared and any such dispatch would spur the North to increase pressure against the South.[51]

North Korean military actions were successful in preventing the dispatch of additional South Korean forces to Vietnam although they failed to force the withdrawal of South Korean forces already present in Vietnam. In April 1968, President Park told President Johnson that it would be "impossible" to send more active forces to Vietnam at present because of the situation in South Korea. This was a marked departure from comments made earlier in December 1967, when President Park indicated his willingness to send 5,000 civilians and 6,000 additional troops to Vietnam to augment forces in Vietnam.[52] The North Korean operations successfully reversed Park's earlier position.

Straining U.S.–ROK relations

In January 1969, the CIA assessed North Korean tactics against South Korea in the previous year and reported that the North Koreans almost certainly believed that large-scale armed incursions would cause frictions between Seoul and Washington over measures to counteract them.[53] Although it is not clear whether North Korea had deliberately set straining U.S.–ROK relations as a major policy objective in planning their active military actions against U.S.– ROK forces, it was one of the most successful aspects of the North Korean military campaign.

In October 1967, the U.S. Vice President Hubert Humphrey told the South Korean Prime Minister that although the United States was aware of the great problem presented by the North Korean infiltrations, South Korea must not respond unilaterally. Humphrey emphasized the importance of concerted actions, and cautioned that unilateral action could only lead to "misunderstanding." The Prime Minister made no response to the Vice President's remarks on this subject.[54] In November 1967, Secretary of State Dean Rusk suggested to South Korean Foreign Minister Choi Kyu Hah that South Korea respond to North Korean actions "with considerable restraint." Rusk cautioned the Foreign Minister of the possible consequences of a significant North–South conflict, and stated that if any such clash occurred South Korea should appear to be the victim of aggression. Rusk contended that since South Korea needed the support and sympathy of many foreign governments, it should "keep its record clean."[55]

The heightened level of the North Korean provocations exacerbated the disagreements between the United States and South Korea, however. An internal U.S. government memorandum in February 1968 assessed that the North Korean actions had hardened Seoul's attitude and increased the likelihood of a major ROK reaction to North Korean harassments, and that the North Koreans probably believed that the United States would impose restraints on the ROK. The memorandum concluded that the North Koreans now probably saw "great and continuing opportunities" to exacerbate relations between Seoul and Washington.[56]

Impact on negotiations over the USS Pueblo

North Korea seems to have used armed clashes in and near the JSA as leverage to influence negotiations over the detained U.S. reconnaissance vessel *Pueblo*. North Korean assaults occurred frequently in April and early May, just before it presented a draft document of a U.S. apology on May 8. The North Koreans might have thought it useful to put military pressure on the United States before it made a concrete proposal. However, declassified U.S. documents do not suggest that the North Korean military actions actually affected the U.S.–DPRK negotiations over the *Pueblo*.

Eliminating the United Nations Command

The U.S. embassy in Seoul suspected that North Korea might exploit the South Korean retaliatory actions against the country for diplomatic purposes, particularly in places of high international visibility such as the United Nations General Assembly. In November 1966, U.S. Ambassador Brown assessed that the North Korean military actions might have been related to its effort to undermine the status of the UNC in South Korea. North Korea and its supporters in the United Nations were mounting an organized and vigorous diplomatic assault on the U.S.–ROK position in the Korean unification debate. The U.S. embassy suspected that North Korea and its friends might be using a new tactic to seek to eliminate the UNC and the United Nations Commission for the Unification and Rehabilitation of Korea, or at least obtain more sympathizers. One possible way to do so was to accuse the U.S.–ROK side of violating the Armistice Agreement. In fact, the MFA and the media alleged that the United States and South Korea were stepping up armed attacks and military provocations in violation of the Armistice Agreement.[57] Such claims were contrary to the truth since the North Koreans were the ones who were violating the Armistice Agreement much more frequently than the U.S.–ROK side. However, the U.S.–ROK position could have been damaged if the occasional South Korean punitive raids against North Korea across the MDL were revealed. The United States was concerned that the North Koreans might have obtained photographic and physical evidence to support their allegations.[58]

This concern, however, did not materialize. North Korea did not mount diplomatic propaganda campaigns by making use of the South Korean retaliatory actions. In the meanwhile, the U.S. embassy, the Department of State, and the U.S. Mission to the United Nations decided in August 1966 to take a preventive measure by preparing a "White Paper" documenting North Korean violations of the DMZ for presentation to the United Nations General Assembly. The report was submitted to the United Nations on November 2.[59]

Strengthening Kim Il Sung's position

Military actions in the DMZ might have worked as a political tool for Kim Il Sung to enhance his prestige as a revolutionary and counter his political opposition both at home and abroad.[60] When North Korea initiated the active military actions in 1966, important domestic political developments were taking place in North Korea. In October 1966, the pro-Kim Il Sung partisans strengthened their position within the Party, and in May 1967 the monolithic ideological system was adopted, paving the way for the supremacy of Kim's position within the Workers' Party. In this process, however, Kim faced a political challenge from Pak Kum Chol, who was critical of Kim's single-minded focus on military buildup implemented at the expense of economic development. Kim used the tension created by the DMZ incidents to justify his military-first policy, and purged Pak and his followers at the May 1967 fifteenth plenum of the Fourth Party Central Committee.[61]

Kim also used the military actions in the DMZ to bolster his international prestige. After North Korea embarked on the military offensive, Kim started to boast that North Korea was taking the leading role in international revolutionary struggle against the United States in support of North Vietnam. In doing so, Kim distinguished himself from Chinese and Soviet leaders, whom he characterized as not doing enough to advance the Communist cause. Given the anti-Kim Red Guard criticism coming from China, it was particularly important for Kim to appear like a true revolutionary in the international Communist movement.[62] Kim succeeded in winning the highest praise from Fidel Castro, the Cuban leader, who characterized him as "one of the most distinguished, brilliant, and heroic socialist leaders in the world today. ... "[63]

Repercussions

The military actions against the U.S.–ROK forces produced unintended consequences as well. The most apparent and immediate repercussion was the strengthening of the defense in the DMZ. In this regard, particularly important was the North Korean attack on U.S. forces on November 2, 1966. As Daniel Bolger wrote, patrols in the DMZ had by then actually become "rather pro forma affairs." However, the November 2 attack changed the situation, and the Americans started to pay serious attention to the North Korean infiltrations.[64] As a result, General Bonesteel loosened the rules of engagement in early 1967 and gave the commanders of the I Corps (Group) and the ROK First Army the authority to use artillery and mortar against enemy elements in or south of the DMZ and against KPA units shooting from hostile territory.[65] Furthermore, in July 1968, the UNC changed its rules of engagement and allowed ROK units in the DMZ to counter North Korean intrusions and ambushes at their own discretion. This change was an important departure from the previous arrangement with which military actions taken by ROK units in border clashes were subject to prior approval by the CINCUNC.[66] Following the new rule, South Korean units used significant artillery and mortar fires along the DMZ three times by 1969.[67]

In addition, toward the end of 1967, General Bonesteel and President Park produced two documents on combined counter-guerrilla operations – the UNC Counterinfiltration-Guerrilla Concept Requirement Plan and ROK Presidential Instruction No. 18. According to these decisions, the ROK Army introduced infrared night-vision equipment, searchlights, and infrared gun-sights while it strengthened the protection of guard posts and command posts.[68] In addition, the ROK Army replaced wooden fences with iron fences in the DMZ by mid-1968.[69] At the same time, the UNC developed a four-layer defense – patrols and guard posts in the DMZ, a barrier defense system just south of the southern edge of the DMZ, and mobile quick-reaction forces behind them – against North Korean infiltrations throughout 1967. By July 1968, the chain-link fence and the new barrier system were installed along the entire southern boundary of the DMZ.[70] As a result, the capabilities of the U.S.–ROK forces in dealing with North Korean provocations had improved dramatically by the end of the 1960s.[71]

Chapter 3

THE *PUEBLO* INCIDENT, 1968

On January 23, 1968, two days after North Korean armed agents mounted an assault on the South Korean presidential residence, North Korean naval vessels captured the U.S. Navy intelligence-gathering ship *Pueblo* and its crew in the Sea of Japan. In order to get the crew and the ship back, the United States agreed to hold direct talks with the DPRK in Panmunjom.

The crew, but not the ship, was returned to the United States in December 1968 after the conclusion of the talks, which lasted 11 months. The *Pueblo* incident was a total victory for North Korea. By capturing the ship, North Korea succeeded in hampering U.S. intelligence activities, diverting U.S.–ROK attention away from Vietnam, and straining U.S.–ROK relations.

The seizure of the *Pueblo* and the "U.S.–DPRK" negotiations

Detention of the USS Pueblo[1]

Just before noon on January 23, 1968, the USS *Pueblo* was sailing approximately 16 nautical miles off the North Korean east coast. Suddenly, a North Korean SO-1 patrol craft, with its crew in battle position, appeared and approached the *Pueblo*. At 1210 hours, the SO-1 communicated with a base on the shore that it judged the *Pueblo* to be an unarmed American reconnaissance ship. At 1227 hours, the SO-1 signaled, "Heave to or I will open fire." The *Pueblo* answered, "I am in international waters," and "intend to remain in present location until tomorrow."

At this point, three P-4 torpedo boats approached from the west, again with their crew in battle position, and joined the SO-1 in surrounding the *Pueblo*. The SO-1 sent in international code, "Follow in my wake; I have pilot aboard." As another P-4 sailed toward the *Pueblo*, two MiG-21s flew over the area. When one of the P-4s with eight to 10 fully armed troops on board started to move toward the *Pueblo*, Lloyd Bucher, the commander of the *Pueblo*, decided to leave the area. Then, another SO-1 appeared and joined in chasing the *Pueblo*. At 1306 hours, the SO-1 sent a message ashore: "According to the present instructions, we will close down the radio, tie up the personnel, tow it and enter port at Wonsan. At present, we are on our way to boarding. We are coming in."[2] The first SO-1 started to approach the *Pueblo*. At 1327 hours the SO-1 finally opened fire on the *Pueblo*, quickly followed by fire from the P-4s. The *Pueblo* was escaping at almost full speed. While the SO-1 had a maximum speed of 28.5 knots and the P-4 55 knots,[3] the *Pueblo*'s maximum speed was just 13.1 knots. Bucher immediately ordered destruction of all classified materials. As the North Korean boats attacked the *Pueblo*, a MiG fighter launched rockets in the sea.

After taking continued fire, Bucher decided to surrender. At 1345 hours, the *Pueblo* gave in and followed the SO-1 to the port of Wonsan. As confirmed by radio intercepts of the communication of the North Korean side, the *Pueblo* was between 15.5 and 17.5 nautical miles from shore when it was detained.[4] The entire North Korean nation went on alert after the *Pueblo* capture. North Korean nationals living in the east coast were evacuated and anti-aircraft guns were mobilized and concentrated there.[5]

The *Pueblo* had departed Sasebo, Japan on January 11 and moved into the Sea of Japan to perform surveillance of North Korean ports in Kimchaek (formerly called Songjin), Chongjin, Mayangdo, and Wonsan, as well as Soviet naval vessels operating in the Tsushima Straits. The missions of the *Pueblo* were to:

- Determine the nature and extent of naval activity [in the] vicinity of North Korean ports of Chongjin, Songjin [Kimchaek], Mayang Do [Mayangdo] and Wonsan;
- Sample electronic environment of East Coast North Korea, with emphasis on intercept/fixing of coastal radars;
- Intercept and conduct surveillance of Soviet naval units;
- Determine Korcom [Korean Communist] and Soviet reaction respectively to an overt intelligence collector operating near Korcom periphery and actively conducting surveillance of USSR [Union of Soviet Socialist Republics] naval units;
- Evaluate USS *Pueblo*'s (AGER-2) capabilities as a naval intelligence collection and tactical surveillance ship; and
- Report any deployment of Korcom/Soviet units which may be indicative of pending hostilities or offensive actions against U.S. forces.[6]

Since it was known that Soviet submarines operated from Wonsan during the winter time, it would have been a great achievement if any information on their submarine operations was obtained.

In hindsight, the *Pueblo* had actually been under close North Korean surveillance. When the *Pueblo* was operating in the area, one of the *Pueblo* crewmen realized that North Korea had its fire control radar locked on the ship for days. On January 21, the *Pueblo* noticed a SO-1 approach and then pass 300 yards in front of it before heading to Wonsan. Finally, on January 22, two North Korean fishing trawlers came close to the *Pueblo*. One of the trawlers approached the

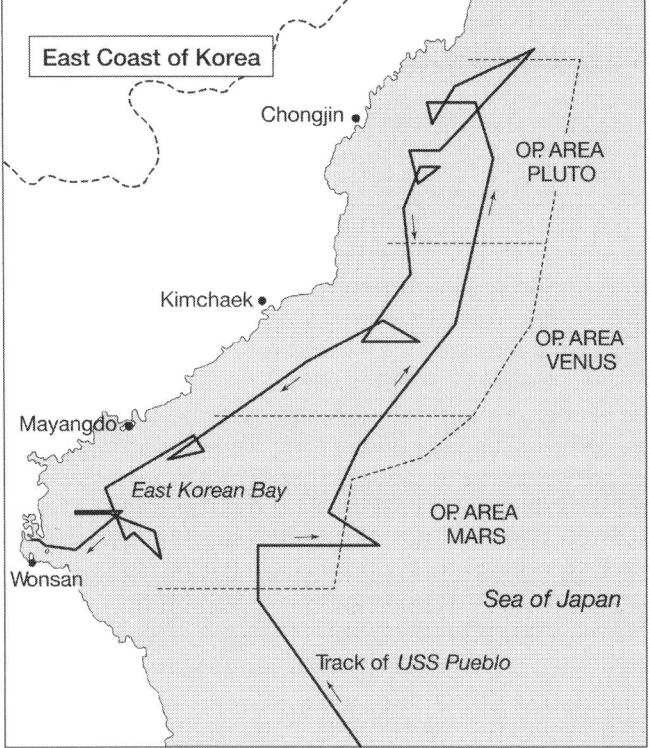

Map 3.1   *Pueblo* navigation chart
Source: Back inside cover of Lloyd M. Bucher, with Mark Rascovich, *Bucher: My Story* (Garden City, NY: Doubleday & Company, 1970), reprinted with permission of the copyright holder.

Pueblo, passed in front of it only 100 yards away, and then circled it before going back to the north. After a while, the two trawlers together approached the *Pueblo* again. This time, they came as close as 30 yards and again circled it before leaving the area.

Initial moves

North Korea was quick in putting its demands on the table. At the 261st Military Armistice Commission (MAC) meeting on January 24, Maj. Gen. Pak Chung Kuk, Senior Member of the Korean People's Army/Chinese People's Volunteers (KPA/CPV) delegation to the MAC, first denounced the United States for "infiltrating an armed spy ship" into "the coastal waters of our side up to the point 39°17.4′N and 127°46.9′E off the Wonsan Port."[7] Pak then demanded that the United Nations Command (UNC) (a) admit the "aggressive act" committed by the "armed spy ship," (b) apologize for the act, (c) severely punish those who were responsible for it, and (d) give assurance that such provocation would not be repeated.[8] On the other side of the table, the U.S.-led UNC demanded immediate release of the *Pueblo* and its crew, expression of apology for the illegal detention, and compensation for the damages incurred on the United States by the incident. North Korea also took measures to strengthen its bargaining power. On January 25, Radio Pyongyang reported that Bucher had written a letter of confession acknowledging that the *Pueblo* had spied on military installations along the east coast and intruded into the coastal waters of North Korea. Bucher's confession was followed by confessions by other crew of the *Pueblo*.

At the same time, North Korea put extra military pressure on the UNC side. On January 25, soldiers of the Korean People's Army (KPA) mounted raids in the Demilitarized Zone (DMZ) in an area defended by the U.S. Second Division and killed one U.S. and two South Korean servicemen.[9] North Korean MiG fighters came as close as five miles to the north of the Military Demarcation Line, breaking away from the ordinary procedure of remaining at least 30 miles away from the line. North Korea went into full mobilization, and its population, administrative institutions, industries, and factories in Pyongyang began to evacuate.[10] Later on the same day, the KPA/CPV Senior Member to the MAC sent a letter to the UNC stating that it was possible to solve this problem if the United States acknowledged that the people of the ship were prisoners of war and showed its willingness to negotiate under such terms.[11] Then on February 8, Kim Il Sung made nuanced comments, suggesting that although North Korea would stand firm, it did not want war. Kim said:

> If the U.S. imperialists persist in their attempt to solve this matter by mobilizing their armed forces to threaten and blackmail us, they will get nothing out of it. If they do get anything it will be only corpses and death.
>
> We do not want war, but we are not afraid of it. Our people and People's Army will retaliate for the "retaliation" of the U.S. imperialists, return all-out war for all-out war.[12]

The Director of Central Intelligence Richard Helms assessed that Kim's position was not to reopen the war, but to make the situation as tough as possible for the United States.[13]

The United States took both military and diplomatic steps to cope with the situation. Just after the *Pueblo* was detained, the USS *Enterprise* carrier task force heading for Vietnam from Japan was ordered to move north, and other naval assets were ordered to deploy near the port of Wonsan. By January 24, a task group composed of the *Enterprise* and five destroyers was deployed southeast of the Korean Peninsula, and on January 31, the second task group with the aircraft carrier *Ranger* and three destroyers arrived in the area. On February 2, the third task groups with the carrier *Yorktown* and six destroyers joined the already deployed forces. Finally, the carriers *Kearsage* and *Coral Sea*, the frigate *Truxton*, the *Pueblo*'s sister ship *Banner*, and four additional destroyers arrived.

These forces constituted Task Force 77.[14] The U.S. Fifth Air Force set up advance headquarters at Osan Air Base in South Korea. Two fighter-bomber squadrons were sent to South Korea and Strategic Air Command bombers were sent to the west Pacific from the United States.[15] President Johnson decided to activate more than 14,000 Air Force and Navy air reservists on January 25, the first call-up of U.S. reserves since the 1962 Cuban missile crisis. The call-up was expected to put pressure on North Korea as well as prevent the North Koreans from thinking about taking offensive actions against South Korea.[16] The United States also flew an A-12 reconnaissance aircraft on a three-pass "Black Shield" mission over North Korea on January 26. The aircraft found the *Pueblo* in a small bay north of Wonsan, but detected no signs of military reaction in the North Korean forces.[17] Because of the North Korean attempt to raid the South Korean presidential residence on January 21, the Defense Condition (DEFCON) had already been raised to level three on January 22.[18]

The effectiveness of this show of force, however, was questioned by some top U.S. decision-makers. For example, while Secretary of Defense Robert McNamara thought that the diplomatic initiative would be reinforced by a call up, Llewellyn Thomson, U.S. Ambassador to the Soviet Union, commented that the presence of U.S. naval force off Wonsan would make it virtually impossible for the North Koreans to return the *Pueblo* and its crew, and that the show of force would prevent the Soviets from acting as an intermediary or quietly exerting influence on the North Koreans to ease the crisis.[19]

Despite all the contemplated military options, the prevailing U.S. policy direction was to seek peaceful solution. After all, the capture of a spy ship was "not worth us going to war," as presidential adviser Clark Clifford put it.[20] On January 26, President Johnson announced that the United States would continue to use every means available to find a prompt and peaceful solution to the problem.

By January 29, the U.S. leadership had reached consensus as to what U.S. objectives should be in the crisis. The objectives were to: (a) get back the crew of the *Pueblo* and, possibly, the ship; (b) keep the confidence of the South Koreans and their willingness to provide an increment of force in South Vietnam; and (c) avoid a second front in Asia.[21]

In response to the January 27 message, a UNC Senior Member requested an immediate closed meeting between the Senior Members of each side. The two sides agreed that the meetings would be held in the conference room of the Neutral Nations Supervisory Commission in the Joint Security Area. With this agreement, North Korea successfully brought the Americans to the negotiating table. The first meeting was held on February 2.[22]

U.S.–ROK relations

The capture of the *Pueblo* took place only two days after the January 21 raid on the Blue House. Although that attempt failed, South Koreans were shocked that the infiltrators managed to come close to the presidential residence. As a result,

South Korean leaders became emotional and were looking for ways to retaliate against the North Koreans. Worried about a possible escalation of the situation, the United States dissuaded South Korea from taking strong actions in retaliation. The South Korean government did not like the American attitude that not only North Koreans but also South Koreans could not be trusted to stay calm in a crisis.[23]

The South Koreans were also frustrated by the contrast between the restraint that the United States exercised after the North Korean raid on the Blue House and the strong reaction that it showed after the capture of the *Pueblo*. This gave the impression that the United States did not care about the life of the South Korean president as much as 82 American sailors detained with the *Pueblo*.[24] South Koreans' feeling was further hurt by the fact that the North Korean raiders who attacked the Blue House had infiltrated into South Korea through a DMZ area defended by the U.S. Army.[25] South Korean forces tended to do better in patrolling, and some U.S. soldiers handled the mission poorly due partly to primitive conditions in the bunker complexes and weak junior leadership.[26] As a result, the South Koreans had strong doubts about the ability and seriousness of the U.S. forces in defending South Korea. To ease tensions, Washington recommended on January 23 that the UNC Senior Member make "strong, dignified and hard statements" on the North Korean raid on the Blue House as well as on the seizure of the *Pueblo* so as not to give South Koreans the feeling that the United States attached more importance to the latter.[27]

As the United States and North Korea moved toward bilateral negotiations to solve the *Pueblo* issue, the relationship between the United States and South Korea became further strained. The United States failed to immediately inform the South Korean government of the receipt of the January 27 letter from the KPA/CPV Senior Member. Left out, the South Korean government was worried that the United States might be trying to establish direct contact with North Korea at locations other than the Joint Security Area, and that the United States might forgo force augmentations and leave the situation in status quo ante without solving President Park's political or security problems once the United States obtained the release of the *Pueblo* and its crew. In order to pressure the United States not to take that path, the South Korean side even hinted at the possible withdrawal of its forces from operational control of the Commander-in-Chief of the United Nations Command (CINCUNC) and the withdrawal of South Korean forces from Vietnam.[28]

Once the secret talks began between the United States and North Korea, the South Koreans showed more negative reactions. Public opinion in South Korea and the views expressed in the National Assembly were also negative. The South Koreans were particularly frustrated by the fact that issues related to South Korea such as infiltrations in the DMZ and attacks on its citizens were not being discussed in any forum.[29] The United States appeared to be interested only in saving its own nationals. In a meeting with U.S. Ambassador William Porter and Gen. Charles Bonesteel, III, CINCUNC, on February 6, South Korean Prime Minister

Chong Il Kwon complained that although there had been innumerable violations by North Korea, and South Korea was abiding by international agreements, the South Koreans had no means of retaliation because the UNC tied the ROK government's hands. Chong then demanded that if more closed meetings with North Koreans were necessary, South Korean representatives must be included, or at least the U.S. must consult with South Korean representatives before acting. Finally, the prime minister said that if there was another incident, South Korea would have to act, suggesting limited retaliations. Although the U.S. side did not take the threat of retaliation too seriously, it thought that the South Koreans felt deep down that "this may be moment to reunify the country and that if opportunity is lost, it may not come again."[30]

To calm the situation in South Korea, the United States sent Cyrus Vance to Seoul in mid-February as a special presidential envoy. One of the main objectives of his mission was to reassure the South Koreans that the United States would not abandon South Korea when the *Pueblo* and its crew were returned, and to urge President Park to remain calm and patient and not to permit any of his men to engage in rash acts that would create a wholly new set of problems and strains for the U.S.–ROK alliance.[31]

During his visit to Seoul, Vance agreed that the United States would take necessary measures to deal with the North Korean threat, regularize U.S.–ROK defense ministerial meetings, and that the U.S. president would ask Congress to provide $100 million to South Korea in military assistance. In return, the South Korean leaders promised that (a) they would take actions to dampen public agitation for retaliatory actions, (b) they would stand by during the closed door sessions between the United States and North Korea unless it was to go on for a long period of time, (c) South Korea would make no reprisals for the Blue House raid or the *Pueblo* capture, and (d) there would be no significant reprisals in the future without consulting the United States. The United States promised to inform the South Korean government of the proceedings of the closed MAC meetings.[32]

Special MAC Senior Members meetings

By the time the special MAC meetings began, North Korea had created a situation where time was on its side. A U.S. National Security Council (NSC) staffer wrote on February 2 that this was the case since (a) the status quo was a victory for the North Koreans, (b) prolonged meetings without result would exacerbate U.S.–ROK relations, (c) the detained ship and the crew would be further exploited, (d) the North Koreans would get enormous prestige from keeping the United States "on the hook," (e) the North Koreans seemed to believe that the U.S. reaction would be mild, and (f) the North Koreans would enhance their prestige by remaining equal to the United States in bilateral talks.[33] It was against such a backdrop that special MAC Senior Members meetings began on February 2.

Before the negotiations got into substantive issues, the status of the meetings became a point of contention between the UNC and the KPA. In the process of negotiation, the United States unintentionally verged on giving North Korea a higher diplomatic status by upgrading the status of the meetings, and the North Korean side attempted to turn the special MAC meetings into direct U.S.–DPRK bilateral talks.

Usually, the MAC meetings were held between the UNC on one side and the KPA/CPV on the other. The special MAC Senior Members meeting organized for negotiations on the *Pueblo*, however, was a closed forum with representations only from the United States and North Korea. The UNC Senior Member in the meetings was getting his directions from the State Department via the U.S. embassy in Seoul instead of the CINCUNC. This was largely because the *Pueblo* was not under the command of the CINCUNC but under the command of the Commander in Chief, U.S. Pacific Command and, therefore, the matter was dealt with as an issue outside of the Korean Peninsula. The United States decided to use the MAC meeting as a forum to discuss the *Pueblo* issue largely because it did not have diplomatic relations with North Korea and, therefore, lacked other useful channels to talk with the North Koreans. As a result, the special MAC meetings, though not intending to, became virtual diplomatic talks between the government of the United States and the government of the DPRK.

The North Koreans did not deliberately attempt to make this happen, but they quickly realized the potential implications of such a development and tried to make use of it. In the second MAC Senior Members meeting on February 4, the KPA/CPV Senior Member asked whether he could understand that the case was to be dealt with as a matter between the DPRK and the United States, and not between the KPA and the UNC. He also added that if this understanding was correct and the U.S. side appointed a representative of the United States, his side would also appoint a representative of the DPRK.

The U.S. government recognized the potential problem that such a definition might create. Samuel Berger, Director of the Korean Task Force, wrote that the North Koreans appeared to have picked up the UNC point in order to make a bid to raise the level of discussion on the *Pueblo* to "government-to-government," and pointed out two problems that might arise. First, by holding the bilateral talks, the United States might end up giving North Korea a certain level of diplomatic recognition and status. Second, the United States might be raising the profile of the special MAC meetings and treating the *Pueblo* issue at a level higher than the MAC where the issues that the South Koreans were most concerned about, such as the Blue House raid, were discussed.[34] The South Koreans would loath to see such a development.

For these reasons, the UNC Senior Member was instructed to walk a thin line. The UNC Senior Member explained in the third meeting on February 5 that he was the Senior Member of the MAC and represented the U.S. government "with full authority to discuss the release of the U.S.S. *Pueblo* and its crew." He did not say that he was a representative of the U.S. government, though, and hence the official U.S. position was that the meeting was not between the U.S. and DPRK governments. In response, the KPA/CPV Senior Member unilaterally noted UNC Senior Member's "acknowledgement" that the *Pueblo* case was a matter to be handled by the governments of the DPRK and the United States.[35]

The North Korean side tried to exploit this issue further in the fourth meeting on February 7. In that meeting, the North Korean side requested the addition of a deputy and the exchange of minutes and more formalized procedures such as press releases. Such a move was interpreted as an effort to (a) enhance North Korea's prestige by characterizing itself as an equal interlocutor of the United States, (b) prolong the negotiations, (c) further strain U.S.–ROK relations, and (d) keep U.S. forces pinned down in Korea.[36] In the meantime, U.S. Ambassador Porter's suggestion to move the talks outside Korea was turned down by the State Department for the change from military to diplomatic channels would go farther toward giving appearance of recognition of North Korea than present procedures.[37] This problem faded away in the fifth meeting on February 10 in which the KPA/CPV Senior Member neither went back to the question of the precise status of the UNC Senior Member, nor referred to the point that the governments of the DPRK and the United States were being represented.[38]

In the sixth meeting on February 14, the North Korean side finally put forth their terms for the release of the *Pueblo* crew, which did not include the release of the ship. The KPA/CPV side stated:

> … we will give considerations to (will be able to consider) the issue of returning the crew members only when your side apologizes for the fact that the U.S. Government dispatched the armed spy ship *Pueblo* to the territorial waters of the Democratic People's Republic of Korea, conducted espionage activities and perpetrated hostile acts, assuring (and assure) that it will not commit such criminal acts again.[39]

In the seventh meeting on February 16, the KPA/CPV side made it clear that return of the ship itself could not be the subject of discussion on the grounds that it was equipment used in espionage. While taking diplomatic steps, North Korea strongly warned against possible U.S. military actions. For example, on February 17, North Korean Vice Premier Pak Song Chol issued a statement in which he said:

> If the U.S. imperialists and the Pak Jung Hi [Park Chung Hee] clique should dare attempt any "retaliatory act," it will in itself mean the start of war.
>
> U.S. imperialism and its stooges should look straight at the reality and act with discretion.
>
> Whether a new war breaks out in Korea or not entirely depends on the attitude of the U.S. imperialists and their stooges.
>
> The more the U.S. imperialists resort to threat and blackmail and war racket, the more it will complicate the present situation, and if there is anything for them to get from this, it will be only corpses and death.[40]

In this period, the United States had three realistic means of pushing the negotiation ahead. First, the strengthening of the overall strategic posture would enable the United States to speak and be listened to. Based on this assumption, the U.S. force level in and around the Korean Peninsula was substantially increased. It was also recognized, nevertheless, that even these measures would not make the overall situation advantageous to the United States.

Second, the redeployment of the carrier force away from Korea would give a reason for the North Koreans to take positive steps in resolving the issue. This option was made available by the deployment of the carrier battle group in the Sea of Japan in the first place. By February 7, the *Enterprise* task group had been ordered and was moving southward through the Tsushima Straits to an area 12 hours' sailing time from the former position. It was expected that the Soviet Union would report this movement to North Korea. The timing of this movement was calculated to give the impression to North Korea that the United States was prepared to ease pressures while talks were still in progress.[41] By February 20, the *Enterprise* was in Subic Bay in the Philippines.

Finally, the United States regarded the military assistance to South Korea as an important bargaining chip in its negotiations with North Korea since it would not only ease the concerns of the South Koreans but also make the North Koreans think that their advantage would be undercut as time went by. A member of the NSC recommended on March 4 a building up of South Korean capabilities "rapidly, substantially, and very overtly." In fact, when Vance visited Seoul, he offered an additional $100 million in military assistance to South Korea.[42]

The *Pueblo* issue loomed large in U.S. domestic politics during the 1968 presidential election campaign. The fact that Johnson was receiving letters from the *Pueblo* crew had a large impact on public opinion.[43] Undersecretary of State Nicholas Katzenbach, noting that the biggest ovation Richard Nixon received during one of his addresses was for his reference to do something about the *Pueblo*, predicted that the *Pueblo* would undoubtedly be an issue in the presidential campaign.[44]

In the 11th meeting on March 9, the KPA/CPV Senior Member again implied that the *Pueblo* crew might be punished. The North Korean delegation also complained that the United States was requesting the return of the crew in exchange for nothing.[45] In the 16th meeting on May 8, North Korea presented a draft document of a U.S. apology to North Korea.[46] The U.S. side considered a so-called "overwrite" plan, in which the UNC Senior Member would write across the face of a document presented by the North Koreans an acknowledgment of the receipt of the crew and sign it.[47] By agreeing to do this, the North Koreans could claim that the Americans had signed the document and the Americans could say that they had signed only on what the U.S. Senior Member had written.[48] In the 22nd meeting on September 30, however, the North Korean side submitted to the UNC Senior Member an exact statement to be signed. This new document undercut the effectiveness of the "overwrite" idea as it included the sentence, "Simultaneously with the signing of this document, the undersigned acknowledges receipt of 82 former crew members of the *Pueblo* and one corpse," thus making the overwrite repetitive.[49]

Finally, on December 23, the UNC Senior Member issued a brief statement – "I will sign the document to free the crew and only to free the crew" – and then proceeded to sign the documents as prearranged.[50] At 1130 hours, the 82 members of the *Pueblo* crew, with the remains of a killed sailor, walked across the Bridge of No Return into the southern section of the DMZ. After moving to a nearby U.S. Army camp, the *Pueblo* crew held a press conference, in which the commander of the *Pueblo* stated that at no time had the *Pueblo* entered North Korean territorial waters and described the beatings and abuse of the crew by the North Koreans while in captivity. The crew arrived in the United States on December 24, reunited with their families for the Christmas holidays.[51]

Toward the end of Johnson's presidency, measures to induce the North Koreans to return the *Pueblo* were discussed. All the options were declined, however, and the ship did not return.[52] By 1999 the *Pueblo* had been brought from Wonsan to Pyongyang, and is currently displayed in the Taedong River as "an epitome of disgraceful defeat the U.S. suffered in its aggression against the north and a symbol of severe punishment meted out to the U.S."[53]

Critical factors

Overall and local military balance

The more or less equal military balance between the North and the South in this period seems to have made the North Korean leaders confident of their ability to deter U.S.–ROK forces from taking meaningful retaliatory actions against their military provocations. In 1968, North Korean air power was substantially superior to that of South Korea, while South Korea enjoyed superiority in ground forces.[54] In naval power, while South Korea had an advantage in terms of tonnage, North Korea possessed a larger number of high-speed torpedo boats and other patrol boats useful in limited and surprise attacks near its coasts. Soviet help was indispensable to North Korea in arming itself. It was reported in February 1968:

> The North Korean air force is estimated to include 21 MiG-21, 350 MiG-17, and 80 MiG-15 fighters plus 80 Il-28 bombers. Moreover, since 1965, North Korea's air defense missile complexes have grown with Soviet help from two to ten, of which at least five are now operational. North Korea is said to have 500 air-defense missiles. ...
>
> The North Korean army of 350,000 to 400,000 is equipped almost exclusively with Soviet equipment including medium tanks, and the North Korean Navy is said to have two Soviet W-class [*Whiskey*-class] submarines, four *Komar*-type guided-missile ships, forty motor torpedo

boats and two coastal defense complexes with Soviet radar and shore-to-ship missiles.[55]

The U.S. Special National Intelligence Estimate prepared in May 1968 assessed that the number of SA-2 surface-to-air missile sites had increased from two to 20 over the previous three years.[56] The area around Wonsan was heavily armed. There was a large air base, 14 air-defense sites each consisting of six guns, and two surface-to-air missile sites around the city.[57] North Korea had approximately 400 jet fighters, compared to 200 in South Korea. More specifically, there were 67 MiG-15/17s and five MiG-21s in the area around Wonsan while the United States had only 24 fighters in Japan.[58] On January 9, 1968, two MiG-21s flew close to the DMZ in a counter-patrol and inspection flight. By then, basic MiG-21 pilot training, which started in June 1966 with Soviet help, had been completed.[59]

At the time of the *Pueblo* capture, the U.S. aircraft carrier *Enterprise* and the frigate *Truxton* were 510 miles away from Wonsan. Although there were four F-4Bs on five-minute alert, they were only equipped with air-to-air missiles and were incapable of attacking targets on the sea. There were two A-4 and F-4 U.S. Marine squadrons deployed in Japan that could have arrived in the area near Wonsan within two hours, but they were not informed of the *Pueblo* incident until the morning after the incident. In addition, at the time the *Pueblo* was under attack, there were no U.S. fighters on a strip alert that could provide a quick response to the situation. Furthermore, the first boarding attempt on the *Pueblo* was made at 1315 hours; on that day, twilight came at 1709 hours and darkness at 1738 hours. There were only three and a half hours of light for the U.S. Air Force to effectively react after the *Pueblo* was captured. The Commander of the U.S. Fifth Air Force issued an order to send aircraft but later reversed the order because of the approach of darkness and the superiority of enemy forces in the area.[60]

In addition to the Vietnam War that constrained the U.S. actions as discussed in the previous chapter, North Korea's ability to prevent successful military countermeasures on the part of the United States played a critical role in the crisis. After assessing different military options, Secretary Rusk concluded that the use of military force would "make us feel better about it, but does not get our ship and our men back."[61]

North Korea's cooperation with the Soviet Union and China

North Korea's improved relationship with the Soviet Union worked to facilitate its decision to capture the *Pueblo*. The Soviet Union had provided a large volume of military assets to North Korea before the incident and supported its position after it happened. In the late 1960s, after the downfall of Nikita Khrushchev and the onset of the Great Cultural Revolution in China, the Soviet–North Korea relationship improved greatly.[62] The Soviet Union decided to provide a large amount of military and financial aid to North Korea in 1965. In May 1965, Kim Il Sung expressed his "great satisfaction" for the promised Soviet assistance of weapons and military equipment in the amount of 150 million rubles, which made the significant military buildup possible.[63] In addition, North Korea's alliance treaty relationships with the Soviet Union and China also influenced the North's decision to capture the *Pueblo* since they provided deterrents against U.S. retaliation.

When President Johnson sent a letter dated February 5, 1968 to Soviet Foreign Minister Alexei Kosygin, calling on the Soviets to work with the Americans for peace in Korea, he replied that when Soviet ships intruded into U.S. territorial waters, the Soviets used diplomatic channels, apologized, paid fines, and then settled the matter. He suggested that the United States work through diplomatic channels and not resort to a show of force.[64] The United States even received a message from the Soviet Union suggesting that the United States pretend that the *Pueblo* had actually violated the territorial waters of North Korea.[65]

Behind the scenes, however, the Soviet attitude was more mixed. The Soviets did not have prior knowledge of the intended capture of the *Pueblo* and, when it happened, they sought to prevent both North Korea and the United States from escalating. The most important Soviet objective in the crisis was to avoid getting dragged into a war with the United States.[66] In April 1968, Leonid Brezhnev, General Secretary of the Communist Party of the Soviet Union, expressed his concerns about the Korean intention to "bind the Soviet Union somehow, using the existence of the treaty between the USSR and the DPRK [as a pretext to] involve us in supporting such plans of the Koreans friends about which we knew nothing." He also said that the Soviet leaders were "against taking the matter towards unleashing a war. ..."[67] The North Koreans were similarly duplicitous. During the crisis, they even attempted to obtain additional economic aid from the Soviets in return for inside information on developments.[68]

U.S. domestic politics

Regardless of what the North Korean decision makers thought, American leaders actually believed that North Korea had taken American domestic politics into account when it made the decision to capture the *Pueblo*. Several factors were of particular importance. First, the presidential election was scheduled in November 1968. As the United States was already deeply involved in the Vietnam War, it was politically difficult for the U.S. president to mobilize additional forces for another major contingency in Asia. As presidential advisor Berger wrote, the North Koreans knew about "our foreign exchange problems, budgetary deficit, and the President's domestic difficulties," assessing that North Korea might have thought that maintaining a certain amount of tension in Korea would put "added strains on our resources and add to the President's troubles at home."[69] When McNamara suggested on January 25 that the President ask for legislation extending the tours of duty of those serving, Johnson responded negatively, commenting that such legislation would put the American boys on North Korean side. "We must keep them on our side," he put it.[70]

Second, the lessons of history seem to have worked against the United States. When the *Pueblo* was seized, the Senate Foreign Relations Committee was considering whether or not to hold formal hearings on the 1964 Gulf of Tonkin incident. At the time, misinterpretation of the incident was suspected to have led the U.S. Congress and the American public into supporting the substantial military commitment to the war in Vietnam. This precedent led the respected Senator William Fulbright to remark soon after the *Pueblo* was captured that the United States should be very careful in this instance not to jump to conclusions until "we know all the facts."[71]

Finally, the general public in the United States did not support military options, as Johnson rightly predicted. In a public opinion poll, only 3 percent of the respondents supported retaliation even at the risk of war while 47 percent supported a diplomatic solution.

Characteristics

Location and timing

The military operation to detain the *Pueblo* took place in a geographically limited theater, about 16 nautical miles off the east coast of North Korea near the major port city of Wonsan. The Sea of Japan has traditionally been an area with active naval activities. This was particularly true for the Soviet Union and North Korea, who used Vladivostok, Wonsan, and Chongjin as major port cities.

Although it is unclear when the plan to capture a *Pueblo*-type vessel was first conceived by the North Koreans, the first such ship – the USS *Banner* – began operating in the area in February 1967, about a year prior to the *Pueblo* incident. The North Koreans achieved perfect surprise in the *Pueblo* seizure. Presidential adviser McGeorge Bundy confessed about a week after the *Pueblo* incident that "no one ever thought a small power such as North Korea would take offensive action against a major power in a situation such as this."[72] Although the North Korean broadcast on January 6 criticizing the United States for "incessantly committing provocative acts lately on the sea off of the eastern coast" and for dispatching "many armed boats" into the North Korean coastal waters was an ominous warning of the coming detention of the U.S vessel, such a statement was not exceptional amidst the customarily harsh North Korean rhetoric.[73] It was only in hindsight that such a comment could be considered a warning. It was judged that the Blue House raid and the *Pueblo* incident had not been planned in a coordinated manner because the raid on the Blue House must have needed considerable advance planning and training. In addition, the *Pueblo* embarked on its mission on January 10, only 11 days prior to the raid on the Blue House.[74] Military operations to capture the *Pueblo* lasted for about two and a half hours. After the capture of the *Pueblo*, it took about 10 days before the special MAC meetings started. The bilateral negotiations lasted for almost 11 months.

46

The timing of the release of the *Pueblo* crew was noteworthy: just after Richard Nixon, who was supposedly a tough negotiator, was elected U.S. president. It is quite possible that the election of Nixon affected the North Korean negotiation behavior.

An operation in reaction to hostile reconnaissance activities or to attack a naval vessel was not new to the North Koreans. North Korea had already attacked U.S. reconnaissance aircraft in January 1954, February 1955, June 1956, June 1959, and April 1965. Incidents at sea were also not without precedent. For example, in January 1967, an ROK Navy patrol craft PCE-56 was sunk by North Korean coastal artillery, with 39 crewmen killed and 15 wounded. In October 1967, a South Korean and a U.S. patrol boat were attacked at the mouth of the Imjin River. Furthermore, there had been a number of cases where the North Koreans captured South Korean fishing boats. In other words, the North Korean navy and air force had some experience in this kind of operation before the capture of the *Pueblo*.

Forces involved and the type of use of force

Only a limited number of naval and air assets were involved in the capture of the 895-ton *Pueblo*. North Korea employed two 215-ton SO-1 patrol craft, four 25-ton P-4 fast attack torpedo craft, and two MiG-21 fighters in the operation.[75]

The seizure of the *Pueblo* involved the actual application of military force to take control of the ship, its crew, and intelligence-gathering equipment and related documents. The physical possession of the American citizens provided significant bargaining power to the North Koreans *vis-à-vis* the United States. The steps the North Koreans took to highlight this point, such as showing the pictures of the *Pueblo* crew to the outside world through various channels and sending letters written by the crew to the U.S. president, were quite effective.[76] By repeatedly referring to crew welfare and possible punishment, the North Korean negotiators tried to make the best use of the U.S. concern for crew safety.[77]

Intensity and targeting

The North Koreans used 57-millimeter guns and machine guns in attacking the *Pueblo*. As a result of the gunfire, one crew member was killed. The physical target in this case was a reconnaissance vessel, its crew, and all the equipment and documents related to U.S. intelligence-gathering activities aboard the *Pueblo*. The political target was clearly Washington, and not Seoul. The fact that an American vessel was targeted was highlighted by the simultaneous attack on the Blue House, in which the target was distinctly South Korean. This clear target discrimination worked effectively in separating the United States and South Korea in the period following the *Pueblo* incident, a significant strength in the North Korean negotiating strategy.

Military-diplomatic coordination

In the *Pueblo* incident, North Korea's military actions and diplomatic moves were well coordinated. It was only one day after the seizure that North Korea put its four demands on the table. North Korea immediately followed this by trying to strengthen its negotiating position, broadcasting a report that the commander of the *Pueblo* had written a "confession" acknowledging that the *Pueblo* had spied on North Korea.

As North Korea went into full mobilization, it issued statements demonstrating its will to resist U.S. military pressure. At the same time, however, it quickly conveyed its willingness to negotiate with the United States. The first bilateral meeting was held on February 2, only 10 days after the capture of the *Pueblo*. After the negotiations began, North Korea continued to generate tension, meaningful but not excessive, by provoking military clashes near the negotiation site in the Joint Security Area.

Assessment

Hampering U.S. intelligence-gathering activities

The most direct and immediate objective of the *Pueblo* seizure was to hamper U.S. intelligence-gathering activities. The *Pueblo* seizure produced several positive results for the North Koreans. First, the *Pueblo* seizure put an additional burden on U.S. reconnaissance activities. After the *Pueblo* was captured, U.S. reconnaissance had to observe self-imposed restrictions on flight areas for a long period; fighter escort was provided when the reconnaissance aircraft was over water; and strip alert was ordered when it was over land.[78] In April 1969, the U.S. Congress institutionalized this heightened security precaution by passing a resolution stating that "no manned ship or plane of the Armed Forces of the United States should be sent into danger areas on an intelligence-gathering mission without adequate protection against attack or capture by foreign armed forces."[79] Also, as a result of the *Pueblo* affair, all intelligence operations using *Pueblo*-type ships were terminated, and the vessels were decommissioned by late 1969.[80]

Second, the loss of the intelligence-gathering equipment and related information to the North Koreans, and to the Soviets and Chinese indirectly, was a serious blow to U.S. intelligence efforts. After the *Pueblo* was captured, the Soviet Union sent a team of electronics and decoding experts to North Korea to assist with the interrogation of the *Pueblo* crew, and China sent an interrogation team to question *Pueblo* crew members who had previously gathered intelligence off the Chinese coast.[81] The Director of the U.S. National Security Agency evaluated the loss of the *Pueblo* as "a major intelligence coup without parallel in modern history" with regard to its effect on communications security, stating that the overall loss and impact on U.S. ability to conduct signals intelligence was considered "very severe."[82] An assessment made on the impact of the loss of approximately 7,000–8,000 documents aboard the *Pueblo* concluded that it had given North Korea as well as other Communist countries significant insight into U.S. intelligence-collection capabilities and constituted a major compromise of intelligence-gathering sources and methods in Southeast Asia. Another review by the National Security Agency concluded that the compromise to the Cryptologic Community was "without precedence in U.S. cryptologic history."[83]

Although cryptographic communications were thought to have been secure due to the inability of the North Koreans or others to decrypt messages without cryptographic keys, it was revealed in mid-1985 that a spy ring within the U.S. Navy, led by John Walker, a communications specialist, had been passing the keys to coded communications to the Soviet Union for more than 17 years.[84] On this point, retired Maj. Gen. Oleg Kalugin, former deputy chief of the KGB station at the Soviet embassy in Washington, D.C., said:

> [We] read all cryptographic traffic between the United States Naval Headquarters and the Navy across the world. ... So by keeping control of the movement of U.S. nuclear submarines, by controlling the coded traffic between the Navy and the units in the open seas, we could really protect our country's security. ... I think this was the greatest achievement of Soviet intelligence at the time of the Cold War.[85]

Diverting U.S. and South Korean resources away from the Vietnam War

By the time of the *Pueblo* incident, the North Koreans had actively been helping the North Vietnamese war effort by sending 30 pilots and providing 10 MiG-21s and by conducting sustained assaults on the U.S.–ROK forces in South Korea.[86] The seizure of the *Pueblo*, as well as the Blue House raid, was yet another way of helping North Vietnam by diverting U.S. and South Korean attention.

North Korea was quite successful in this regard. The effects of the *Pueblo* seizure were clear and immediate. Soon after the *Pueblo* capture, the United States diverted the aircraft carrier *Enterprise* from South Vietnam to the Sea of Japan, as well as 10,000 tons of bombs en route to South Vietnam to South Korea.[87] On January 24, Defense Secretary McNamara remarked that if the North Korean effort was aimed at tying U.S. hands in other theaters, they had "succeeded" since the United States could not move in South Vietnam until the *Pueblo* incident was resolved.[88] The seizure of the *Pueblo* was also effective in influencing U.S. policy in Vietnam more broadly. A CIA report in January 1968 assessed that all the Communist parties would wish to handle the *Pueblo* affair in such a manner as to "increase pressures on the U.S. Government, at home and abroad; the effect, they would hope, would be to make it more difficult for the US to sustain its present course in Vietnam."[89]

Straining U.S.–ROK relations

One of the most important consequences of the *Pueblo* incident was the strain it caused in U.S.–ROK relations. Although it appears that North Korea did not necessarily intend to do so by seizing the *Pueblo*, it was a significant consequence. Once such effects were recognized, North Korea attempted to make use of and exacerbate the friction between the United States and South Korea. For example, North Korea tried to put the special MAC meetings, or virtual bilateral U.S.– DPRK talks, above the MAC meetings at which South Korea was represented. In the 13th MAC meeting, the North Korean Senior Member asserted that the meetings were taking place between representatives of the DPRK and U.S. governments, and complained that the U.S. side had continued the "discourteous act" of calling the DPRK "North Korea." He went on to warn that unless the United States decided to deal with the government of the DPRK, the question of the *Pueblo* crew would never be solved.[90] Such a demand seems to have been designed to elevate U.S.–DPRK relations, demean South Korea, and drive a wedge between the United States and South Korea.

Defending Kim Il Sung's position

The North Korean leadership might have also used the *Pueblo* incident to justify its "dual-track development policy." Adopted in 1962, this policy called for the simultaneous development of economic and military strength. By the time of the *Pueblo* incident, the negative consequences of that policy had become apparent. It was already revealed in 1966 that North Korea could not achieve the goals set in the seven-year plan by the target date of 1967 and was forced to extend the deadline by three years.[91]

In a speech on March 21, 1968, Kim Il Sung said that the North Koreans did not have to fear the "U.S. imperialists" because North Korea was "incomparably stronger" than in the days of the Korean War and had adequate means for defeating them. He also pointed out that North Korea had "an impregnable defence coping with any imperialist aggression" as a result of the work of "arming all the people and fortifying the whole country."[92]

Kim Il Sung also used the *Pueblo* incident, after the event, in purging his political rivals in the military. In criticizing some of North Korea's top military leaders including Defence Minister Kim Chang Bong, Kim Il Sung said in January 1969:

> Had it not been for revisionist influence, they [the North Korean military leaders under criticism] would not have objected to shooting down American aircraft. Also, how was it different from Khrushchev's order [to back off during the Cuban Missile Crisis] when they suggested capturing the Americans [USS *Pueblo*] instead of shooting at them when they came close to the coast? Why on earth are we preparing for war?[93]

From these remarks, it can be inferred that while Kim Il Sung wanted to sink the *Pueblo*, the North Korean military leaders suggested capturing the ship. The capture, and not the destruction, provided the North Koreans with precious assets – U.S. intelligence equipment and documents as well as live American hostages. Despite the positive outcome of the decision to capture the *Pueblo*, Kim Il Sung was willing to use it to purge his rivals. In this context, it is telling that North Korea shot down a U.S. Navy EC-121 reconnaissance aircraft on April 15, 1969, Kim Il Sung's birthday. On the next day, Kim sent a message to congratulate the officers and men of the KPA Unit 447 which was responsible for the operation.[94] These facts strongly suggest that the action was deliberately executed at Kim's order to distinguish himself from the purged military leaders and strengthen his position in the military establishment.

Chapter 4

THE WEST SEA INCIDENT, 1973–76

In October 1973, North Korea initiated a long and systematic military and diplomatic campaign in the area surrounding five offshore islands in the Yellow Sea.[1] These five islands – Baengnyeongdo, Daecheongdo, Socheongdo, Yeonpyeongdo, and Udo – are much closer to the North Korean west coast than the South Korean west coast but remain under the military control of the Commander in Chief, United Nations Command (CINCUNC), as stipulated by the Armistice Agreement signed in July 1953. This group of islands lying around the Ongjin Peninsula came to be called the Northwest Islands (NWI).[2]

The North Koreans undertook a series of military actions in the NWI area between 1973 and 1976 to back their claim that the waters around the NWI were under their jurisdiction and that the Northern Limit Line (NLL), a quasi-maritime borderline between North and South Korea established by CINCUNC, was not valid. They succeeded in making their legal claims widely known and also in complicating U.S.–ROK relations. At the same time, however, the North Korean actions also ended up encouraging the fortification of the NWI and a South Korean naval buildup.

Coordinated military-diplomatic offensive

Claiming the 12-nautical-mile "coastal waters"

On October 23, 1973, a North Korean gunboat and torpedo boat crossed the NLL to the south. While the North Korean vessels crossed the NLL, they did not violate the 3-nautical-mile "contiguous" waters around the NWI claimed by the U.S.-led United Nations Command (UNC). In short order, the North began to escalate, and not only cross the NLL but also intrude into the contiguous waters of the NWI. Between November 19 and December 1, North Korean patrol boats entered the waters around Baengnyeongdo, Daecheongdo, Socheongdo, and Yeonpyeongdo six times.[3] Between October and December 1973, North Korean vessels crossed the NLL 43 times, including nine guided-missile boats crossing the line six times.[4]

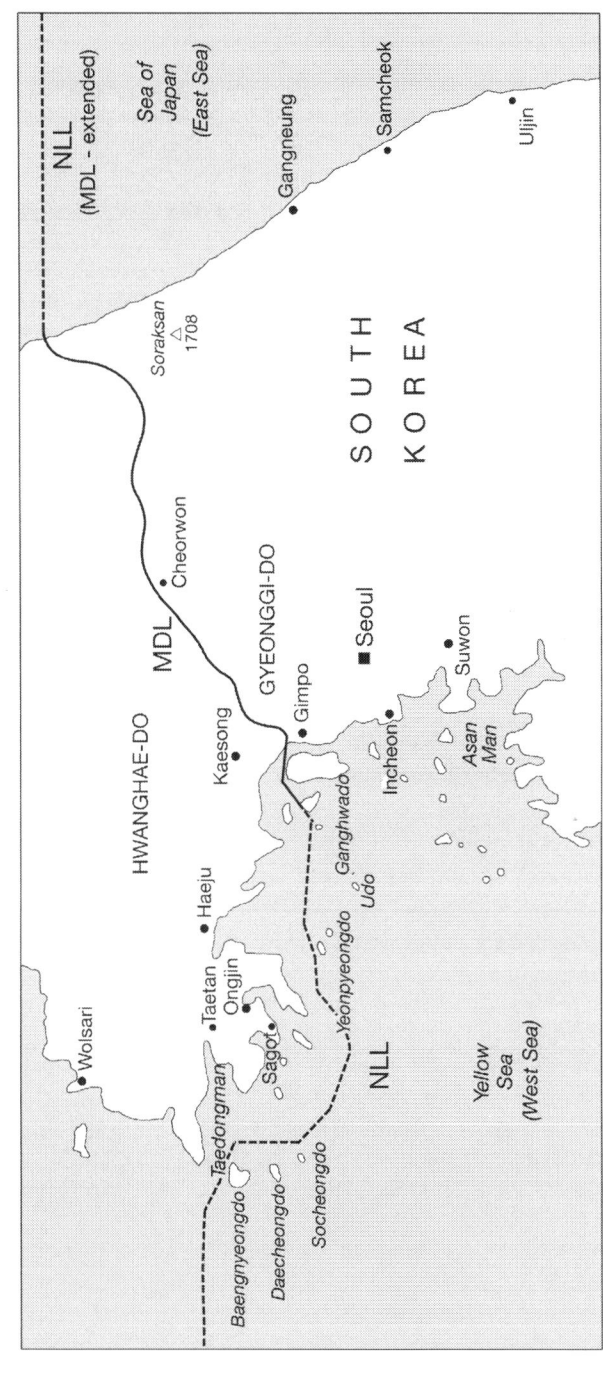

Map 4.1 The Northern Limit Line and the Northwest Islands
Designed by Routledge based on information provided by the author.

The first territorial dispute under the Korean Armistice surfaced at the 346th Military Armistice Commission (MAC) meeting on December 1.[5] In the meeting, the North Korea-led Korean People's Army/Chinese People's Volunteers (KPA/CPV) delegates claimed jurisdiction over the area 12 nautical miles from the North Korean west coast, and alleged violations of the Armistice Agreement by South Korean naval vessels. This formal complaint came from the long-held North Korean position that South Korean naval vessels had repeatedly intruded into their 12-nautical-mile zone of jurisdiction since the early 1960s.[6] The NWI, according to North Korea, were in its "coastal waters," so the sea contiguous to the NWI belonged to North Korea.

The KPA/CPV representatives also suggested that the NLL was not valid. It stated:

> ... you U.S. imperialist aggressors organized the south Korean naval craft into our coastal waters ... to enforce a sea blockade and what is worse, commit without hesitation such outrageous act as to hinder the free navigation of many foreign merchant ships entering the ports in the West Sea [Yellow Sea] of our country.[7]

This statement implicitly referred to U.S.–ROK enforcement of the NLL causing North Korea's maritime traffic, particularly vessels departing from the port town of Haeju, to make a detour around the NLL instead of sailing across the line to the high seas. The KPA/CPV side warned that because of "reckless commotions" on the UNC part, an armed conflict between both sides might occur and "a grave irretrievable situation" might be created.

The KPA/CPV representatives then argued that the waters north of the maritime boundary line of Hwanghae-do province and Gyeonggi-do province, which extended southwest from the western end of the inland boundary between the two provinces, belonged to the coastal waters of North Korea. It was clear that the North Koreans were attempting to interpret Paragraph 13b of the Armistice Agreement to mean that the waters to the north and west of the provincial boundary line were under the military control of the Supreme Commander of the Korean People's Army (KPA).

The North Korean side finally insisted that the UNC submit a request and get KPA's approval in advance if it wanted to sail in North Korea's coastal waters en route to the NWI, warning that "proper steps" would be taken resulting in "severe punishment" if the UNC side did not adhere to this new demand. A memorandum that the CINCUNC sent to Washington characterized this MAC meeting as "the most belligerent [sic] since the *Pueblo* period."[8]

Probing UNC and South Korean reactions

North Korea then embarked upon an interesting series of actions most likely designed to probe UNC and South Korean reactions. The ROK Ministry of

National Defense (MND) announced on December 7 that a North Korean patrol boat had "violated" South Korean waters by coming close to Baengnyeongdo.[9] On December 10, a North Korean patrol boat came as close as 3.6 nautical miles to the southwest of Socheongdo, and stayed there for about two hours. The ROK Navy claimed that the North Korean patrol boat had violated South Korean waters.[10]

Then on December 11, three North Korean torpedo boats in combat formation launched an extremely provocative high speed run near UNC naval vessels escorting a landing ship on a routine supply run to Baengnyeongdo.[11] On December 18, two North Korean patrol boats entered the contiguous waters of Socheongdo to a point near the path routinely traveled by a civilian ferry between the South Korean port of Incheon and Baengnyeongdo. Later on the same day, two North Korean patrol gunboats again violated the contiguous waters of Socheongdo.[12]

Interestingly, while the UNC charged the North Korean side at the December 24 MAC with violating the Armistice Agreement on December 11 and 18, it did not mention the North Korean actions on December 7 or 10, which the South Koreans claimed had constituted violations of their waters.[13] The North Koreans probably learned from these events that the UNC and the ROK government interpreted the legal status of the waters in the area differently.

In the 347th MAC meeting, the UNC side clarified its position. It warned that (a) any intrusion by naval vessels into waters contiguous to the NWI would be a violation of Paragraph 15 of the Armistice Agreement (Note that the crossing of the NLL was not deemed as a violation), (b) any attempt to interfere with or interrupt the passage of UNC vessels traveling directly to and from the NWI would constitute an attempt to modify the terms of Paragraphs 13b and 15, (c) the UNC would take all necessary means to stop North Korean intrusions into contiguous waters of the NWI and to insure the unimpeded progress of the ships to and from the NWI, and (d) the UNC would not request North Korean permission to sail to the NWI. The UNC pointed out that North Korea had actually recognized and respected the NLL delineation over the past twenty years. The UNC also rejected the KPA/CPV contention that the provincial boundary line referenced in Paragraph 13b ceded the KPA/CPV side the contiguous waters surrounding the NWI. Finally, the UNC insisted that North Korea's provocative actions cease, as they were dangerous, served to heighten tensions and, therefore, were "clear violations of the spirit of the Armistice Agreement."

On February 15, 1974, North Korean naval vessels attacked two South Korean fishing trawlers – *Suwon-ho* No. 33 and *Suwon-ho* No. 32 – that were fishing in waters north of the NLL, some 30 nautical miles northwest of Baengnyeongdo in the first such attack since the North-South Joint Communiqué was issued in July 1972. One of them was sunk and the other was seized.[14] The incident was assessed to have been a result of aggressive patrolling action by North Korean boats.[15] Six months later, on June 28, 1974, three North Korean gunboats attacked and sank South Korean Maritime Police patrol boat No. 863

after a two-hour firefight in the Sea of Japan, north of the seaward extension of the Military Demarcation Line (MDL), killing 26 crew members and detaining two. When the boat encountered the North Korean gunboats, it was estimated to have been located near the 12-nautical-mile limit and about six nautical miles north of the extension of the MDL. However, it was not clear whether it was inside or outside of the 12-nautical-mile limit.[16]

Escalation

After a period of relative calm, tensions rose once again in February 1975.[17] At 1505 hours on February 26, two unidentified boats were detected in the international waters 20 nautical miles south of the NLL and 23 nautical miles west of Socheongdo, an area where fishing boats did not normally operate. At 1635 hours, two South Korean patrol boats dispatched to the area found them. They then approached the unidentified vessels to ascertain their identity. However, they did not respond to the demand. At 1909 hours, a South Korean destroyer arrived on the scene. After a while, the unidentified boats headed for a fleet of eight other boats which appeared like fishing boats, and maneuverings on both side continued. Then at 2026 hours, in an attempt to prevent the North Korean vessels from operating south of the NLL, the South Korean destroyer hit one of them. The 200-ton ironclad fishing boat sank as a result.[18]

In reaction to the incident, North Korea sent 11 vessels including torpedo boats, gunboats, and guided-missile boats to the south, and flew a total of 85 sorties of MiG fighters in the areas near Baengnyeongdo. The entire North Korean fleet and SA-2 surface-to-air missiles deployed in the Ongjin Peninsula were put on alert. The heightened tension continued until the next morning.[19] Some of the North Korean fighters intruded into the airspace above Baengnyeongdo, Daecheongdo, and Socheongdo islands on 11 separate occasions between 2341 hours on February 26 and 0917 hours on February 27. In reaction to the situation, South Korean fighters as well as U.S. Air Force (USAF) F-4 fighters took off. The North Korean jets and the South Korean fighters came within 17 nautical miles of each other, creating a precarious situation.[20] After these hostilities, the North Korean Ministry of Foreign Affairs denounced the USAF involvement in the incident, claiming that it indicated that the United States was "the ringleader" who was "exacerbating tension in Korea and indulging in the war provocative moves."[21] The U.S. Department of Defense contended that the USAF F-4s remained above the Osan Air Base and did not participate in the pursuit of North Korean fighters in the Yellow Sea.[22]

The events on February 26–27 were discussed in the 360th MAC meeting held on March 3. The KPA/CPV side claimed that the South Korean naval vessels had rammed and sunk a North Korean fishing boat in international waters. The UNC argued that the North Korean armed vessels were in an area of the Yellow Sea which was normally patrolled by the UNC side and that their unexplained presence in the area presented a possible threat to the security of South

Korea and its fishing vessels in adjacent areas. In other words, the UNC tacitly acknowledged that the North Korean vessels were in international waters and that the presence of these vessels in the area was not a violation of the Armistice Agreement in itself.[23]

South Korea had a different interpretation. The MND announced that the North Korean boats had "violated" South Korea's "maritime operating area (*jagjeon haeyeog*)" south of the Northern Patrol Limit Line (NPLL) which defines an area, based on the NLL, in which patrol activities are conducted.[24] In other words, South Korea regarded the crossing of the NLL and the intrusion into its maritime operating area as illegal. The South Korean position did not have a solid legal basis, however. For this reason, just before the 360th MAC meeting, the United States informed South Korea that the UNC would not try to justify the sinking of the North Korean vessel based on South Korea's claim on the maritime operating area.[25] In the MAC meeting, the UNC used the phrase "in accordance with internationally accepted maritime practices" throughout in referring to South Korea's naval challenges.[26]

The United States did not view armed enforcement of ROK fishing claims, especially in areas it regard as international waters beyond the armistice zone, within the scope of its obligations, either.[27] In fact, after the February 1975 incident, the UNC requested that the MND not disclose the fact that U.S. air assets had been involved in the operations. The MND agreed, although they later disclosed the USAF F-4 participation, after which the CINCUNC conveyed the "strongest personal protest" to the MND. The U.S. side suspected that South Korea had played up the USAF involvement for the purpose of demonstrating to the North Koreans the "credibility and consistency of U.S. commitment" to South Korea.[28]

Provocations in the air

North Korean air activities continued in the area. On March 24, 1975, 30 North Korean fighters conducted active air maneuvers in the NWI area between 0800 and 1300 hours. They took 15 different routes in the airspace, and flew across the NLL sometimes as deep as 50 nautical miles. There were two intrusions of the airspace above Baengnyeongdo and Socheongdo islands. In reaction, South Korean aircraft scrambled to challenge the North Korean fighters.[29] The North Koreans seem to have done in the air what they had been doing at sea. They crossed the NLL frequently, and occasionally violated the airspace above the NWI. Again, North Korea was taking steps to consolidate its legal claims and to highlight the difference between the UNC and the ROK government over the interpretation of the legal status of the NLL.

The MND requested the UNC to make a strong protest against the North Korean action at the MAC. In the 362nd MAC meeting on May 27, the UNC side claimed that the two North Korean overflights above Baengnyeongdo and Socheongdo were serious violations of the Armistice Agreement. When the UNC mentioned the other maneuvers, however, it characterized them simply as "highly provocative" activities that took place far south of North Korea's normal operating area and adjacent to the South Korean territory. The UNC did not claim that these air maneuvers constituted violations of the Armistice Agreement.[30]

More importantly, U.S. air assets were not used in the March 24 incident, as they were in the February 26 case.[31] In July 1975, it was reported that the U.S. Department of Defense had instructed the CINCUNC to formulate a U.S.–ROK combined operation plan to defend the NWI. However, it also instructed the CINCUNC not to include U.S. military assets in such a plan.[32] Taken as a whole, the United States tried as much as possible to avoid becoming entrapped by South Korean positions where the issues were not directly related to the enforcement of the Armistice Agreement or obligations under the U.S.–ROK Mutual Defense Treaty.[33]

The North Korean operations in the NWI area continued sporadically after the incident in March. A North Korean patrol craft violated the waters contiguous to Baengnyeongdo on May 14.[34] On June 9, two MiG-21 fighters flew over Baengnyeongdo.[35] The North Korean fighters returned when ROK Air Force aircraft scrambled.[36] On July 12, three North Korean fishing vessels and one patrol craft intruded into the waters contiguous to Baengnyeongdo.[37] Then on January 23, 1976, two North Korean MiG fighters flew over Baengnyeongdo.[38] A South Korean source also recorded that eight North Korean vessels crossed the NLL 18 times between March 7 and March 27.[39]

North Korea's proposal for a peace agreement with the United States

While taking sustained military actions, North Korea made a new proposal on March 25, 1974, calling for the conclusion of a bilateral peace agreement with the United States.[40] In the report presented at the Third Session of the Fifth Supreme People's Assembly, Ho Dam, North Korean Vice-Premier and Minister of Foreign Affairs, stated:

> ... today's reality of our country makes it necessary to settle the question of signing a peace agreement directly with the United States in order to create prerequisites for the removal of the tension in Korea and promotion of her independent and peaceful reunification.
> ... it is right and proper to settle the question between the parties concerned which hold real power to guarantee it with certainty. The Democratic People's Republic of Korea and the United States of America are the two signatories to the Korean Armistice Agreement and the actual parties concerned.
> The Korean Armistice Agreement was signed at first between the Korean People's Army and the Chinese People's Volunteers on the one hand and the "United Nations forces" on the other, but the Chinese

People's Volunteers withdrew from Korea already long ago and the so-called "United Nations forces" present in south Korea are, in fact, none other than the U.S. Army.

... the question of signing a peace agreement must be solved directly with the United States, the party concerned which has its troops stationed in south Korea, holds the whole supreme command of the armed forces and signed the armistice agreement.

In proposing a peace agreement with the United States, we seek, in the long run, to put an early end to foreign interference in our internal affairs, the root cause of the permanent tension in out country, and open a favourable phase for settlement of the internal affairs of the nation by the efforts of Koreans themselves, on all accounts. ... [41]

Ho Dam justified his proposal by pointing out that South Korean authorities had "turned down all the reasonable proposals of ours" and were "continuously stepping up war preparations and ceaselessly perpetrating armed provocations," adding that the U.S. government was "chiefly to blame for the strained situation and the danger of war created in Korea today." On this basis, Ho Dam insisted that the peace agreement include the following four points:

(a) Both sides shall pledge to each other not to invade the other side and shall remove all the danger of direct armed conflict. The United States shall be obliged not to "instigate the south Korean authorities to war provocation manoeuvres"
(b) The two sides shall discontinue arms reinforcement and arms race
(c) The berets of the "United Nations forces" shall be taken off the foreign troops stationed in South Korea and they will be withdrawn at the earliest possible date along with all their weapons
(d) Korea shall not be made a military base or operational base of any foreign country after the withdrawal of all foreign troops from South Korea.[42]

On this basis, Ho Dam proposed discussions to negotiate a peace agreement with delegates "of a rank higher than those of the MAC" participating from both sides. This proposal was designed to place direct U.S.–DPRK talks above the MAC meeting where the South Koreans were also represented. The Supreme People's Assembly sent a letter to the U.S. Congress on March 25.[43]

This proposal was a significant departure from North Korea's previous position that a peace agreement must be concluded between the North and the South. Also significant was its new claim that the foreign troops stationed in South Korea should be withdrawn "at the earliest possible date." In a reversal of its previous position, the withdrawal of U.S. forces from Korea was to be realized after, and not before, the conclusion of the peace agreement. The new proposal was apparently influenced by the conclusion of the Paris peace treaty under which U.S. forces withdrew from Vietnam.[44] North Korea seemed to have thought that the same kind of peace agreement could result in the withdrawal of U.S. forces from South Korea in the long run.

Critical factors

Significance of the Northwest Islands

Located much closer to the North Korean west coast than to the South Korean west coast but under UNC jurisdiction, the NWI have enormous strategic significance both to the U.S.–ROK side and to North Korea.[45] The NWI are located approximately 45 to 110 nautical miles west of Seoul in the Yellow Sea, surrounding the Ongjin Peninsula in North Korea. Baengnyeongdo is located approximately seven nautical miles away from the North Korean west coast and approximately 93 nautical miles from the South Korean port of Incheon. Yeonpyeongdo is located approximately six nautical miles from the Ongjin Peninsula and approximately 44 nautical miles from Incheon.[46]

UNC jurisdiction over the NWI was important for several reasons. First, the NWI are located in positions that can block entrance to the Taedongman and Haejuman bays in North Korea. Second, the NWI are critical military assets for the defense of the western front and the capital area of South Korea, and thus are useful for (a) stopping North Korean seabound infiltration, (b) stopping North Korean advance into the mouth of the Hangang river, Ganghwado island, and the Gimpo Peninsula in the western front, (c) blocking the southward advance of North Korean naval forces, (d) disrupting the sea lines of communication between China and North Korea, and (e) maintaining sea control in the Yellow Sea. Third, the NWI served as an important base for intelligence collection. A radar site in Baengnyeongdo could detect movements of Chinese aircraft as far away as Shenyang. Finally, the NWI could be used as a base from which landing operations on the Ongjin Peninsula could be conducted.[47] In a way, the NWI are a dagger at North Korea's belly.

Differing interpretations of the "contiguous" waters

Differing interpretations between the UNC and North Korea over the definition of "contiguous" waters was yet another important backdrop to the North Korean actions. The disagreement between the UNC and North Korea over maritime jurisdiction dated back to the armistice negotiations, when the UNC insisted on three-nautical-mile territorial sea while the KPA/CPV side upheld the 12-nautical-mile territorial sea. Having failed to agree on the width of the territorial sea, they decided to use an ambiguous expression in Paragraph 15 of the Armistice Agreement. It read:

> This Armistice Agreement shall apply to all opposing naval forces, which naval forces shall respect the waters *contiguous* to the

Demilitarized Zone and to the land area of Korea under the military control of the opposing side, and shall not engage in blockade of any kind of Korea. [*Italic* added]

As a result of this ambiguity over the maritime jurisdiction, when naval hostilities broke out in the early 1970s, the UNC regarded the three-nautical-mile zone surrounding the NWI as contiguous waters under its jurisdiction, while North Korea regarded the 12-nautical-mile zone from its coasts as contiguous waters under its jurisdiction.[48] Moreover, the North Korean side suggested that islands such as the NWI did not have contiguous waters and, therefore, the waters surrounding the NWI were under the military control of the Supreme Commander of the KPA.[49]

The North Korean attempt to refute the UNC argument gained new momentum as the 12-nautical-mile territorial waters became a new international legal norm in the early 1970s. In the 1970s, the number of the nations which claimed 12-nautical-mile territorial sea exceeded the number of the nations claiming the territorial waters of less than 12 nautical miles.[50] If the 12-nautical-mile line from the North Korean west coast is superimposed on a map, Baengnyeongdo and Yeonpyeongdo would fall inside the line, while Daecheongdo and Socheongdo would be on it.[51] In the Third United Nations Conference on the Law of the Sea initiated in New York in December 1973, the 12-nautical-mile limit came to be widely accepted as an international norm.[52] This came about partly from pressure by developing countries with which North Korea had affinity, serving as encouragement for Pyongyang.[53] It was against this backdrop that North Korea declared in December 1973, that it would exercise territorial rights over the waters surrounding the NWI. According to a U.S. embassy wire cable in December 1973, North Korean vessels had operated by then up to but not beyond 12-nautical-mile reach of their own shores.[54]

This was a challenge to the UNC, headed by an American general, since the United States was one of the countries which still upheld the three-nautical-mile territorial sea and was therefore on the defensive within the international legal community. In fact, the United States privately acceded to the North Korean position. On December 22, 1973, a telegram from the State Department to the U.S. embassy in Seoul even argued:

There is, of course, no definition of "contiguous waters" in Article 15 [*sic*, Paragraph 15] of the Armistice Agreement. In this regard, based on the records and information available to us here, it would appear that we have in fact respected a "contiguous waters" limit of twelve miles off North Korean coast as claimed by North Korea (except where access to islands or conflicting ROK territorial sea claim involved). In accordance with the JSAO (joint sea air operation) ROK likewise patrols out to at least twelve miles from its coast for Armistice Agreement purposes. Under these circumstances, it would appear difficult to claim other than twelve miles "contiguous waters" limit for islands under Article 15. (This, of course, would be limit solely for purposes of definition of "contiguous" in Article 15 of Armistice Agreement and hence for definition of rights and duties of parties under Armistice Agreement, and would have no rpt [repeat] no implication in terms of territorial sea question or claims.)

The U.S. does not recognize territorial sea claims beyond three miles and protests such claims. Consequently we should not recognize the North Korean claimed twelve mile territorial sea limit. We should, however, continue to respect DPRK claimed twelve mile "contiguous waters" limit in areas where it does not relate to access to islands and where ROK territorial waters do not overlap in accordance with current rules and authorities issued to U.S. forces.

... On this assumption we believe Patrol Limit Line should reflect median line as described above rather than NLL.[55]

As a result, the UNC took the neither-confirm-nor-deny position. On the one hand, the UNC did not publicly and explicitly set the three-nautical-mile definition of contiguous waters in order for South Korea to preserve its options. On the other hand, the UNC rejected the suggestion to redefine the contiguous waters limit to 12 nautical miles on the basis that such an action would appear to be precedent setting in legal terms, it would incite strong North Korean reaction, and would inevitably enmesh the United States in territorial waters dispute.[56] In the meantime, the South Korean Foreign Ministry thought that upholding the three-nautical-mile territorial sea would not be supported internationally and seriously examined the adoption of the 12-nautical-mile territorial sea as an option in response to the North Korean naval actions.[57] However, South Korea did not adopt the new norm until much later, in December 1977.[58]

Finally, the term "contiguous" in the Armistice Agreement was not used in the way it is usually used in international law. For example, the United Nations Convention on the Law of the Sea (UNCLOS) provided that in "a zone contiguous to its territorial sea," or "the contiguous zone," the coastal State may exercise the control necessary to: (a) prevent infringement of its customs, fiscal, immigration, or sanitary laws and regulations within its territory or territorial sea; and (b) punish infringement of the above laws and regulations committed within its territory or territorial sea. It also said that "the contiguous zone" may not extend beyond 24 nautical miles from the baselines from which the breadth of the territorial sea is measured.[59] This contiguous zone in the UNCLOS is thus a totally different concept from the "contiguous" waters in the Armistice Agreement. Furthermore, the Korean text of the Armistice Agreement uses the word comparable to "adjacent" (*rinjeob*) instead of "contiguous" (*jeopsog*) in Paragraph 15.[60] These complexities provided North Korea with legal opportunities that it could exploit in the military-diplomatic campaign in the areas surrounding the NWI.

Status of the Northern Limit Line

Although the Armistice Agreement clearly defined the demarcation line on the ground, it failed to do so at sea. As a result, it created a situation where it was not clear how the waters in the NWI area might be controlled. The failure to draw maritime demarcation lines resulted largely from the fact that the UNC wanted to end the Korean War as soon as possible. Since the UNC maintained military superiority over North Korea both in the Yellow Sea and in the Sea of Japan during the Korean War, the UNC did not see a practical need for such lines at the time of signing the Armistice Agreement.[61] The decision not to draw maritime demarcation lines was also in the interest of North Korea since Pyongyang realized that it was in a militarily disadvantageous position and therefore if such lines had been negotiated it would have had to make significant concessions.[62] Consequently, both sides signed the Armistice Agreement without agreeing on demarcation lines at sea.

It was in this context that the UNC unilaterally established the NLL in August 1953.[63] As its name indicates, the NLL was originally established to regulate the movement of UNC/South Korean – not North Korean – vessels and aircraft, preventing them from traveling too close to North Korea.[64] Its most important objective was to prevent South Korean fishing boats from getting seized by North Korean patrol boats and to prevent accidental clashes between the UNC and KPA sides.[65]

Several problems emerged when South Korea started to use the NLL to regulate North Korean maritime activity in the Yellow Sea as it increased. First, this line was not based on any statute and therefore it remained arbitrary in nature. The NLL was a "control line" and not a "demarcation line" or, let alone, a "borderline."[66] Second, the UNC did not officially inform the North Korean side of the establishment of the NLL, which was only natural given its original purpose.[67] Third, according to the assessment by the Central Intelligence Agency, the NLL in the Yellow Sea lay completely within North Korea's claimed territorial sea and intruded into inland waters in at least three places.[68] Finally, the NLL was not even strictly observed by the South Koreans. The most lucrative fishing grounds were in shallow waters around Yeonpyeongdo and Udo, termed the "Golden Fishing Site." South Korean fishing boats regularly ignored the NLL or the Fishery Control Line established south of the NLL to create a buffer zone, to tap into the "Golden Fishing Site."[69]

Furthermore, there were important differences between the UNC and South Korea with regard to the interpretation of the status of the NLL. The most important question was whether to regard the crossing of the NLL as a violation of the Armistice Agreement. In short, the UNC did not regard the NLL crossings as a violation of the Armistice Agreement, while South Korea did. The U.S.-controlled UNC never protested when North Korea crossed the NLL.[70] In fact, the United States specifically conveyed this position to South

Korea in December 1973, stating that it did not regard the crossing of the NLL as an Armistice violation.[71] Moreover, the State Department privately discussed that:

> We have reservations about [South Korean] MOFA's [Ministry of Foreign Affairs] attempt to give NLL validity as a "respected" element of "armistice regime" which has developed over past 20 years. We are aware of no evidence that NLL has ever been officially presented to North Koreas [*sic*]. We would be in an extremely vulnerable position of charging them with penetrations beyond a line they have never accepted or acknowledged. ROKG is wrong in assuming we will join in attempt to impose NLL on NK.[72]

This was a notable disagreement with the South Koreans, who announced on February 15, 1974, that North Korean patrol boats had violated the "Northern Patrol Line [the NLL]" more than 219 times since October 23, 1973, in violation of the Armistice Agreement.[73]

Local military balance

In October 1973, North Korea enjoyed local military superiority in the NWI area. North Korea had a naval port in Sagot, only about 31 nautical miles away from Baengnyeongdo and about 18 nautical miles away from Yeonpyeongdo. The North Korean air base in Taetan was only about 26 nautical miles away from Baengnyeongdo and about 34 nautical miles from Yeonpyeongdo. The forward naval port in South Korea at Incheon, in contrast, was about 93 nautical miles away from Baengnyeongdo and 45 nautical miles from Yeonpyeongdo. The nearest major air base in South Korea was Suwon, about 115 nautical miles from Baengnyeongdo and 67 nautical miles from Yeonpyeongdo. For this reason, North Korean high-speed boats could reach Baengnyeongdo within 12 minutes and North Korean aircraft could do the same within three minutes, much faster than their South Korean counterparts.[74]

In 1968–70, North Korea began to physically enforce the 12-nautical-mile zone as its naval buildup bore fruit. Improvements in North Korean naval forces resulted in the seizure of the USS *Pueblo* in 1968 and a South Korean navy broadcast ship I-2 in June 1970.[75] By 1973, North Korea had dramatically improved its capabilities both at sea and in the air. North Korea had by then fielded a total of 598 combat aircraft including 130 MiG-21s and 60 An-2s.[76] Twelve *Osa I*-class fast attack craft and 10 *Komar*-class fast attack craft with *Styx* guided-missiles were transferred from the Soviet Union in 1968.[77] North Korea also activated the West Sea Fleet Headquarters in Wolsari in late 1973.[78] The establishment of the West Sea Fleet Headquarters was a clear indication that the North Korean naval force was being strengthened in the west coast. Finally, the Korean People's Navy reportedly conducted its first major amphibious combat exercise on the west coast in the fall of 1973.[79]

Here, of particular importance was a deployment of MiG-21s and *Osa I-* and *Komar*-class guided-missile boats, which played a central role in the military-diplomatic campaigns in the NWI area. Although the size of the missile boats limited their operations to coastal waters and calm seas, they were effective in the NWI area.[80] North Korea continued to strengthen its forces in the area even after 1973. By 1975, North Korea had deployed 130-millimeter coastal guns with a range of 27 kilometers and reinforced its bases in Ongjin, Haeju, and Taetan.[81]

On the South Korean side, the main combat ships in the ROK Navy were two *Gearing*-class destroyers with 127-millimeter guns. They were slow in speed and did not have missiles in late 1973.[82] These destroyers were seriously threatened by possible standoff attack by North Korean missile boats.[83] South Korea built two fast missile boats with *Exocet* surface-to-surface missiles between 1971 and 1972; however, it was only after the mid-1970s that a militarily significant number of patrol boats equipped with *Standard* and *Harpoon* surface-to-surface missiles were procured.[84] Moreover, the NWI were not fortified back then. It was a surprise and a major revelation to the South Koreans that the local military balance was in favor of their adversary and that there was a military vacuum in such an important strategic area. The U.S. assessment in the period was that the NWI, particularly the northernmost three, could not be successfully defended against a determined attack by the North.[85] A South Korean National Assembly member accused the MND on December 10, 1973, saying that it was incomprehensible why the strategically important NWI were left undefended without any meaningful defense facilities such as coastal guns.[86]

As the military balance shifted over time, the tentative nature of the NLL became problematic. The improvement in the North Korean naval and air forces challenged the assumption that the UNC retained superiority at sea, on which the lack of maritime demarcation lines and the enforcement of the NLL depended.[87]

Finally, there were no significant U.S. forces deployed at sea around the Korean Peninsula and therefore it was not likely that a confrontation at sea would involve U.S. forces. In other words, the automaticity of the U.S. military involvement in contingencies was much lower at sea than on the ground, where the U.S. Second Infantry Division functioned as a "tripwire." The confrontation at sea, therefore, would likely be a limited North–South confrontation.[88] This situation gave the North Koreans room for driving a wedge between the United States and South Korea. By taking provocative actions that would only provoke South Korea, the North Koreans could harass the South Koreans without offending the Americans.

Characteristics

Location and timing

As a result of the fortification of the DMZ and improvement in North Korean naval capabilities in the late 1960s and the early 1970s, the concentration of North Korean military activities moved from land to sea.[89] The increased naval and air activities in the areas surrounding the NWI were something new and came as a surprise in the beginning, although they eventually proved to be a sustained effort that lasted for more than two years. Major actions took place in November–December 1973, February 1974, and February and March 1975. It was significant that the beginning of North Korea's military-diplomatic campaigns concurred with the beginning the Third United Nations Conference on the Law of the Sea in December 1973.

Forces involved and the type of use of force

Usually, the size of forces involved in actions in the NWI area was not large. Typically, conventional naval and air assets such as patrol boats, torpedo boats, and fast missile boats as well as MiG-21 fighters executed the crossings of the NLL and/or the intrusions into the contiguous sea and air space of the NWI. A large number of these assets were employed at the same time in February and March 1975.

The overwhelming majority of North Korean actions in the Yellow Sea were the indirect and coercive use of force aimed at supporting its diplomatic moves. It was intended neither to destroy any targets nor to occupy territories. During the target period, there was no exchange of fire between conventional military assets on both sides. The February 1974 incident was an exception in which the South Korean fishing boats operating in waters north of the NLL were attacked. In February 1975, it was a South Korean destroyer that sank a North Korean fishing boat.

Intensity and targeting

In 1973–76, no known deaths on the U.S.–ROK side resulted from North Korea's military-diplomatic campaigns in the NWI area except for the deaths of crew members of the *Suwon-ho* which was sunk in February 1974. On the contrary, North Korean fishermen were killed when a South Korean destroyer sank a North Korean fishing boat in February 1975. Although the overt use of conventional naval and air forces increased in the first half of the 1970s, casualties created by such activities remained minimal. In this sense, it is paradoxical that as more modern weapons came to a central stage in North Korea's use of force in the 1970s, fewer casualties and material damages resulted.

66

In the NWI-related actions, the major targets of North Korean military maneuvers were abstract "lines," namely the NLL and the three-nautical-mile lines around the NWI. This fact implies that North Korea's military maneuvers in this period were predominantly diplomatic and legal rather than military in nature.

Military-diplomatic coordination

North Korea's military actions and diplomatic moves were extremely well coordinated. For example, naval intrusions in the contiguous waters of the NWI were followed by the claim made in the MAC meeting in December 1973 that the waters around the NWI were under the jurisdiction of the Supreme Commander of the KPA. Also, it was only five months after the North Korean activities in the NWI area surged that North Korea sent a letter to the U.S. Congress calling for the conclusion of a bilateral peace agreement with North Korea to "create prerequisites for the removal of the tension in Korea."

In addition, the North Koreans demonstrated their ability to skillfully exploit legal loopholes and developments in international law by employing military force in a limited manner. They exploited the failure of the Armistice Agreement to establish demarcation lines at sea; made use of the trend of an increasing number of countries accepting the 12-nautical-mile territorial sea; and conducted elaborate naval and air campaigns to consolidate their claims, undermine the UNC position, and highlight the differences that existed between the UNC and the ROK government.

Assessment

Formalizing territorial claims and undermining the Northern Limit Line

North Korea's most direct objectives in its military-diplomatic campaigns in the NWI area were to formalize and publicize its territorial claims and to undermine the validity of the NLL. The North Korean military and diplomatic actions produced several results. First, the military tension in the NWI area was widely publicized and North Korea's territorial claims became widely known.[90] In legal terms, publicizing and enforcing one's territorial claims is always important. By repeatedly publicizing its territorial claims and operating in the target areas, North Korea succeeded in formalizing and buttressing its territorial claims. North Korea succeeded in turning the Yellow Sea into areas in dispute.

Second, North Korea undermined the NLL by making its own territorial claims. Although North Korea failed to force the UNC and South Korea to abandon the NLL, it succeeded in posing a serious challenge to the validity of the line at least.

Third, introduction of the *Osa-* and *Komar*-class missile boats forced South Korea to adopt defensive tactics and South Korean vessels stopped operating in the triangle area between 37°30'N, 125°00'E, and 125°30'E with apex at 37° 25'N, 125°15'E, in which it had previously operated.[91]

In the end, North Korea failed to nullify the NLL. North Korean forces enjoyed local superiority in the area in the early 1970s, but South Korea never gave up the defense of the NLL. Also, North Korea failed to enforce its demand that UNC traffic to and from the NWI seek advance approval from the KPA/CPV.

Advancing economic gains

There seemed to have been practical economic reasons involved in North Korea's territorial claims. First, the North Koreans wanted to prevent South Korean fishing boats from fishing in the vicinity of its coasts and to increase its own gains from fishing in larger areas. On this point, North Korea's military actions were successful. Due to the increased risk of being detained or fired upon, South Korean fishing boats gradually became cautious in approaching the areas near the North Korean coast. In January 1974, the U.S. government argued that in order to avoid confrontation, South Korean fishermen should be urged to remain south of their "winter fishing line" instead of moving northward to the summer limits as they traditionally did on April 30 every year in area south of Yeonpyeongdo. It also estimated that South Korea's police and naval forces were already stretched to their limit and could not provide effective security for South Korean fishermen in the area.[92] Subsequently in April 1974, a couple of months after the sinking of the *Suwon-ho* incident, South Korea actually moved the Fishery Control Line to the south to distance its fishing fleet and North Korea.[93] As the North Korean military-diplomatic actions on the NLL progressed, fewer South Korean fishing boats fished across the NLL in the Yellow Sea and the MDL-extended in the Sea of Japan.[94]

Second, North Korea wanted to use a shortcut for its maritime traffic. Such an intention was explicitly revealed on December 1, 1973 when the North Korean side charged that the United States was letting the South Korean naval craft "enforce a sea blockade." In fact, while foreign commercial ships could cross the NLL between Socheongdo and Yeonpyeongdo islands to enter or to sail out from the port of Haeju, North Korean vessels were not allowed to do so.[95] Since the NLL was in a position surrounding the Ongjin Peninsula, North Korean ships had to make a long detour sailing first to the west and then to the north around the peninsula to sail out from Haeju to high seas without crossing the NLL. For the North Koreans, it was a time- and money-consuming detour imposed by the NLL and, therefore, it was natural that they wanted to eliminate the line. In this instance, the result was not favorable for North Korea. Even after the active military-diplomatic campaigns, North Korea's maritime traffic to and from the ports in the vicinity of the NWI continued to make a detour in order to avoid crossing the NLL.

U.S.–DPRK peace agreement and the withdrawal of U.S. forces from Korea

Another clearly pronounced North Korean objective was to conclude a peace agreement or at least open a direct communication channel with the United States. On December 19, 1973, the Swedish Senior Officer of the Neutral Nations Supervisory Commission stationed in Panmunjom confided that with the naval actions in the Yellow Sea:

> ... the North Korean side is executing the strategy to bring about the withdrawal of the UN [United Nations] or U.S. forces by undermining the Armistice Agreement regime built upon the UN forces and by demonstrating the necessity of concluding a new armistice or peace agreement with South Korea.[96]

It turned out that he was half right. In March 1974, North Korea actually proposed the conclusion of a peace agreement with the United States, and not with South Korea. Given the withdrawal of the U.S. Seventh Infantry Division from South Korea in 1971 and the withdrawal of the U.S. forces from Vietnam in 1973, the North Koreans now sought to induce the dissolution of the UNC and the withdrawal of the remaining U.S. forces from South Korea by directly talking to the Americans. Also, by challenging the status quo under the Armistice Agreement, North Korea might have attempted to induce and/or prepare for the dissolution of the UNC, which was being debated at the United Nations as well as within the U.S. government.[97]

The North Koreans attempted to encourage the Americans to talk to them by first creating tension and then arguing that dialogue was needed to reduce the tension. The March 25 letter to the U.S. Congress argued that although tension had been eased temporarily, it was aggravated again and "military confrontation and war danger have daily been increasing. ..." On this basis, the letter demanded that "proper measures for the solution of the situation be adopted." North Korea attempted to justify conclusion of a bilateral peace agreement with the United States by emphasizing the fact that the CINCUNC, an American general officer, had "the prerogative of the supreme command of the army in south Korea."[98] The military tension in the NWI area was useful in illustrating this point. By creating tension in the NWI area, North Korea could show that even in the areas where South Korean forces played a dominant role, they were strictly controlled by the CINCUNC, an American general officer.

In addition to its approach to the Congress, North Korea secretly conveyed to the U.S. government its intention to negotiate normalization by proposing a meeting to Secretary of State Henry Kissinger in August 1974 through the Romanian emissary. Kissinger ruled out the possibility of withdrawing U.S. forces from South Korea in the foreseeable future, but he expressed willingness to have contacts with the North Korean side on the condition that Kim Il Sung gave the United States assurances on positive developments in the situation.[99]

In this context, it is noteworthy that Kissinger had already suggested to the Chinese government in July 1971 that if the relationships between the United States and China developed, it would be "quite conceivable" that most, if not all, American troops would be withdrawn from Korea before the end of Nixon's next term.[100] This conversation might well have been conveyed to the North Korean government. In addition, the U.S. government had decided in April 1973 that to move on a step-by-step basis toward improvement of bilateral relations with North Korea was one of its policy options.[101] Furthermore, in March 1974, it decided to seek United Nations Security Council endorsement of the agreed package of substitute security arrangements on the Korean Peninsula.[102] In October, Kissinger suggested to his Chinese counterpart that he wanted to eliminate the UNC without abrogating the Armistice.[103]

North Korea's military-diplomatic campaigns in the Yellow Sea did not produce concrete results in this respect, however. The U.S. Congress did not respond to the North Korean proposal, and no bilateral government-to-government talks were held to discuss the conclusion of a peace agreement. The U.S. position was that South Korea must be included in any peace agreement negotiations. The UNC was not dissolved. Finally, the U.S. decision in March 1974 suggested that there should be no substantial changes in the level or missions of U.S. forces in South Korea during the period of transition to new security arrangements.[104]

Driving a wedge between the United States and South Korea

North Korea attempted to separate the U.S. and the ROK governments by magnifying the disagreements between the two. As already mentioned, the UNC as headed by an American general and South Korea disagreed as to the legal status of the NLL. Also, the United States was concerned that South Korea's strong reaction to North Korea might escalate the situation in which the United States might get embroiled, while South Korea thought that the U.S. response to North Korean military actions was not strong enough, and cast doubts on the U.S. commitment to the defense of the country.

In a U.S.–ROK meeting on December 1, 1973, for example, the South Korean defense minister suggested "shouldering tactics" and patrols close to the NLL to defy North Korean naval activities. The U.S. side rejected the suggestion, however, claiming it would be too "provocative."[105] The U.S. side thought:

> It is clear that ROKG [ROK government] will continue to take North Korean incursions seriously and wish to involve, in first instance, the UNC and secondly ROK navy units under our [UNC] operational control. ... However ... we must continue to resist involving the command or units under its control in anything but its mission.[106]

Moreover, the United States assessed that South Korea was consciously attempting to involve it in the situation and keep it "in the center of the picture" by defining the problem as an "armistice matter," and that South Korea's reluctance to use the direct North–South communications mechanism might in part be to give the United States "no way to shift any of this responsibility."[107] On the South Korean side, their frustration was reinforced by U.S. decisions in 1975 not to commit U.S. air assets to the NLL-related operations in the Yellow Sea.

In the final analysis, however, there was a clear limit to what North Korea could achieve in this respect. The U.S. objective in the dispute was not only to "prevent the outbreak of hostilities" but also to "assure the retention of those islands under the continued control of the ROK."[108] The North Korean naval activities certainly strained the U.S.–ROK relationship, but did not undermine it in a fundamental way.

Repercussions

Adoption of the "sasu" strategy

In reaction to the North Korean actions in the Yellow Sea, South Korea came up with a concept of "*sasu*" (literally "defense to the death," or unconditional defense) in 1974. It was a major change in South Korea's approach to the NLL. South Korea made a unilateral policy decision to defend the NLL for all practical purposes, regardless of the legal standing of the NLL or the North Korean position. After the decision was made, defense of the NLL was no longer an issue of law enforcement but an issue of policy implementation.[109]

Fortification of the Northeast Islands

In response to the North Korean challenge, South Korea decided to fortify the NWI. Military facilities were built in the NWI, artillery was deployed, and M-16 rifles were given to the marine units in Baengnyeongdo even before they were distributed to the ROK Army. As a result, the NWI were turned into South Korea's forward-deployed military bastions.[110]

In the latter half of the 1970s, defense of the NWI was further strengthened.[111] In January 1977 the Sixth Marine Brigade was established and tasked with its defense.[112] Command of the defense of Baengnyeongdo changed from a lieutenant-colonel to a brigadier-general. The operational plan was revised so that the NWI would be defended even in an all-out war.[113] Finally, deployment of air-defense assets on Baengnyeongdo during this period was an important reason for the decrease in North Korean violations of the airspace over the NWI.[114] The ROK Marine Corps in Baengnyeongdo served not only to defend the NWI but also to restrain the North Korean forces near the area from being diverted for use in other areas.[115]

South Korea's military buildup

Finally, South Korea strengthened its military capabilities to defend the NLL. The ROK Navy introduced indigenous frigates, patrol craft, *Baeggu*-class and *Gireogi*-class missile craft, and *Chamsuri*-class high-speed craft. In addition to the two fast missile boats with *Exocet* missiles built between 1971 and 1972, patrol boats equipped with *Standard* and *Harpoon* ship-to-ship missiles were procured after the mid-1970s. The construction of these boats played an important role in reducing North Korean provocations at sea.[116] Ship-to-ship missiles were test-fired from indigenous South Korean vessels in August and November 1975.[117] As a result, North Korea's military-diplomatic campaigns in the NWI area petered out in the mid-1970s.

Chapter 5

THE AXE MURDER INCIDENT, 1976

In August 1976, two U.S. Army officers were killed in the Joint Security Area (JSA) in Panmunjom by North Korean guards wielding axes, in what was called the Axe Murder incident.[1] In reaction, the United States mobilized its armed forces and concentrated them in and around the Korean Peninsula in a show of force. The U.S. forces in Korea, together with South Korean special forces, also undertook an operation to cut the poplar tree in the JSA which was the direct cause of the clash. An extremely tense situation was created during the operation, which could have escalated into a free-for-all exchange of fire had there been even one accidental shot in the area.

North Korea tried to use this incident to reinforce its diplomatic offensive by claiming that the U.S. presence in South Korea was the root cause of the confrontation on the Korean Peninsula. However, the brutal killing of the U.S. servicemen backfired on North Korea. The reaction of the international community to the North Korean action was extremely negative. North Korea's diplomatic offensive against the U.S. military presence in South Korea lost its momentum thereafter.

The Axe Murder and Operation Paul Bunyan

Tree-trimming operations and the Axe Murder

In 1976, the United Nations Command (UNC) had five guard posts while the Korean People's Army and the Chinese People's Volunteers (KPA/CPV) maintained seven guard posts in the JSA. The poplar tree, thickly leafed during the summer, obstructed the view between UNC guard post No. 3 at the southwestern end of the JSA and guard post No. 5 in the central sector. The UNC guards deployed at guard post No. 3 were thus subjected to harassment by the North Korean guards who had easy, undetected, access to the spot via the "Bridge of No Return." The bridge was one of the important pathways to the JSA from North Korean territory, and had two roadblocks that the KPA/CPV side had illegally installed. UNC guard post No. 3 was vulnerably located between Korean People's Army (KPA) guard post No. 8 to the southeast and KPA guard post No. 4 located to the west of the Bridge of No Return outside the JSA. The decision to prune the tree was made in order to prevent the North Korean guards from harassing the UNC.

At about 1030 hours on August 18, five Korean Service Corps workers started trimming the boughs of the tall poplar tree. Protecting the Korean Service Corps workers were 10 UNC guards, composed of two American and one Korean officers with four American and three Korean enlisted men armed with pistols. Shortly after the UNC party started the work, two KPA officers and some nine enlisted men appeared in a truck and asked about the work. When told that the tree was to be trimmed and not to be cut down, one KPA officer indicated that was "good." The work lasted for 15–20 minutes, during which time some KPA personnel tried to direct the UNC team on how to trim the tree. But then, at approximately 1050 hours, one KPA officer told an American officer to halt the

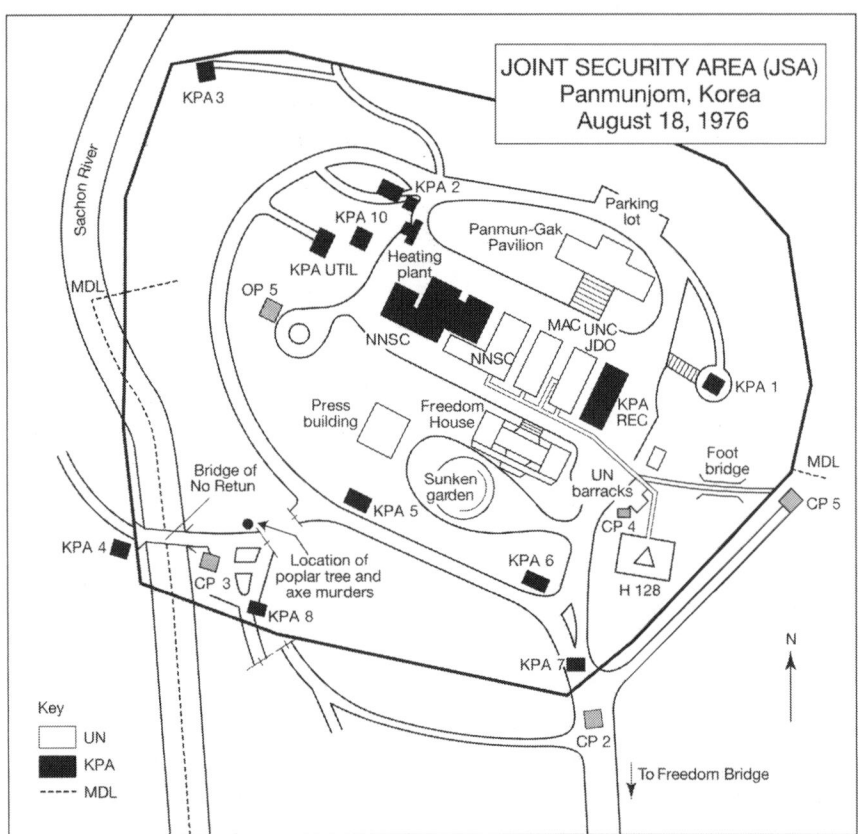

Map 5.1 The Axe Murder and the Joint Security Area
Source: Veterans of Foreign Wars Post 7591 and Eric Sprengle, Lieutenant Colonel, United States Army Reserve-Retired, Past Post Commander and Webmaster, Veteran of Foreign Wars Post 7591, http://www.vfwpost7591.org/opn-PB.html reprinted with permission of the copyright holders.

work. After a short discussion, the KPA officer threatened him. However, the American officer instructed the workers to carry on the work. At this point, the KPA officer sent a guard across the Bridge of No Return. After several minutes, there were approximately 30 KPA guards in the area. One KPA officer took off his watch, and another rolled up his sleeves.

Then, one KPA officer shouted, "Kill," and struck Captain Arthur Bonifas, knocking him down to the ground. Five KPA guards started beating him while the rest attacked the other UNC guards, beating them with clubs that they had brought and axe handles the Korean Service Corps workers had left. The clash lasted for several minutes. As a result, two U.S. officers, Captain Bonifas and First Lieutenant Mark Barrett, were killed by axes and four American and four Korean enlisted men were wounded. The heads of the two U.S. officers were clubbed beyond the point of recognition. In addition, the North Koreans destroyed three trucks and a guard post on the UNC side.

Military moves

Immediately after the incident, a National Security Council Washington Special Advisory Group was convened in Washington, D.C. to discuss options. In the meeting, it was first determined that North Korea did not intend a major attack since such an attack would not be effective without the element of surprise. With this in mind, the U.S. government decided to take military and diplomatic actions including preparing for the deployment of an F-111 bomber squadron and the aircraft carrier *Midway* from Japan to waters near Korea, and notifying the United Nations delegates and the United Nations Security Council about the North Korean assault.

On August 19, the U.S.–ROK alert status was raised to Defense Condition (DEFCON) 3. The reconnaissance status was also raised to Watch Condition (WATCHCON) 3. On the same day, KPA Supreme Commander Kim Il Sung ordered all units of the KPA and the entire membership of the Worker-Peasant Red Guards and the Young Red Guards militias to take their posts in combat readiness.[2] It was the first time that North Korea publicly announced such an alert.[3] Against this backdrop, the UNC devised a plan to enter the JSA with a show of military force and cut down the poplar tree. In addition, a contingency plan was formulated to cope with possible escalation of the situation during the tree-cutting operation. The contingency plan included an option for U.S.–ROK forces to attack and occupy Kaesong, a North Korean city located just north of the DMZ, in case the North Koreans resisted the tree-cutting operation.[4] The United States and South Korea cooperated closely in planning of the operation. Although the U.S. Joint Chiefs of Staff (JCS) and U.S. Forces Korea domi-nated the planning of the action, South Korean Lt. Gen. Lew Byong-Hion, Director of the ROK JCS, was in Gen. Richard Stilwell's office almost con-stantly during the planning phase of the operation, and the ROK JCS Chairman and the Ministry of National Defense maintained relatively close cooperation with the UNC in order to plan the first joint U.S.–ROK military action during a crisis since 1953.[5]

In addition, Secretary of State Henry Kissinger asked the U.S. JCS to examine the desirability of directing artillery fire against the KPA Military Armistice Commission (MAC) security force barracks concurrently with the tree-cutting operation. However, the JCS recommended against this option based on the superiority of the KPA artillery force, and explored other options such as the use of precision-guided air munitions, surface-to-surface missiles, and unconventional warfare Sea, Air, Land (SEAL) Teams to destroy North Korean installations of military or infrastructure significance, as well as the possibility of destroying the Bridge of No Return.[6]

On August 19, the JCS ordered the dispatch of (a) 20 F-111s from the continental United States to South Korea, (b) a naval Task Group, including the aircraft carrier *Midway*, one destroyer and four frigates, from Yokosuka to Korean waters, (c) B-52 bombers from Guam to South Korea, and (d) 1,800 troops of the U.S. Third Marine Division from Okinawa to South Korea. On August 20, U.S. President Gerald Ford approved the tree-cutting operation plan, now codenamed "Operation Paul Bunyan." Approval was given both to the plan to cut down the poplar tree and the plan to remove the road barriers put up by the KPA.

Meanwhile, North Korea was reacting nervously to the U.S. military maneuvers. In Pyongyang, air raid drills were conducted between 2000 hours on August 20 and 0200 hours on August 21. It was reported that people kept moving in and out of shelters.[7] Television and radio reports in Pyongyang were "militant" and "aggressive."[8] According to a defected former North Korean official, North Korea started to prepare for the possibility of war after the Axe Murder incident happened. Pak Pyong Yop remembered:

Once the Panmunjom Incident [the Axe Murder incident] occurred, an order for general mobilization was announced in North Korea. College students were drafted to the armed forces and reserves (Worker-Peasant Red Guards, the Paramilitary Training Units, and so forth) were called up. Retired officers up to age 50 put on uniforms again. Production facilities were getting ready to be moved to rear areas in case war broke out. ...

Between late August and mid November, approximately 200,000 people were evacuated from Pyongyang to other areas. About 8,000 households in the southern areas of the Hwanghae-do and Kangwon-do provinces were relocated when they were judged to have family members in poor health or with ideological problems. ...

North Korea was on a complete war-ready condition for three months. From August through September, men had their military uniforms ready for use when they went to bed. Workers took combat positions for three months leaving their work behind. Colleges were almost shut down with only the physically weak remaining. People were evacuated to mountainous areas to avoid possible heavy bombing. Food was not a serious issue since the distribution system remained intact. ... [9]

Diplomatic moves

From the diplomatic perspective, the Axe Murder incident was a culmination of the propaganda campaign that North Korea had initiated in the spring of 1976. In the early spring, North Korea started to accuse the United States of introducing new weapons into South Korea, conducting provocative military exercises, and keeping South Korean forces on a war path. North Korea claimed that a "grave situation" had been created and that war might break out at any time.[10] Moreover, on August 5, about two weeks before the Axe Murder incident, the Government of the DPRK issued a memorandum regarding U.S. actions in South Korea. The memorandum stated:

> ... the U.S. imperialists have completed the preparations for a new war which they had been carrying on in Korea for a long time and are going over to a stage of starting a war itself. ...
>
> If these reckless war provocation manoeuvres of the United States against the Democratic People's Republic of Korea are left unchecked, they will inevitably lead to a new war in Korea.
>
> The Government of the Democratic People's Republic of Korea firmly believes that the governments of various countries and peaceloving peoples of the world will bitterly condemn the manoeuvres of the United States to provoke a new war and positively support the struggle of the Korean people for the independent and peaceful reunification of the country.
>
> The Korean people, with the positive support and encouragement of the world peaceloving people, will force the U.S. imperialist aggression troops to withdraw from south Korea and certainly achieve the independent and peaceful reunification of the country without the interference of outside forces.[11]

Historically, North Korea had a tendency to intensify its propaganda campaign before the United Nations General Assembly (UNGA) meeting every year. However, what was new in 1976 was that North Korea, for the first time, began to accuse the United States of starting a war.[12]

When the Axe Murder incident occurred, North Korean high-ranking officials were attending the fifth Non-Aligned Movement (NAM) Summit Conference in Colombo, Sri Lanka, held on August 16–19. In the evening of August 18, North Korean Foreign Minister Ho Dam issued a statement to the NAM Summit Conference. He characterized the Axe Murder incident as "intentional provocative acts against our side" to "directly set fire on the fuse of war systematically worked out by the U.S. imperialists who have long prepared to launch a new war in Korea."[13] On August 19, a day after the Axe Murder incident, the KPA Supreme Command issued a report, describing what happened:

> As already reported, the U.S. imperialist aggressors who are making a desperate attempt to start a new war in Korea committed a grave provocative act against our side in the joint security area [JSA] at Panmunjom on August 18.
>
> Around 10:45 a.m., August 18, the U.S. imperialist aggressors sent 14 bandits carrying axes to fell a tree at random in the joint security area.
>
> In connection with this act of the enemy, four personnel of our side went to the spot and repeatedly told them that the tree must not be cut down arbitrarily but an agreement be reached between the two sides before felling it as it is a tree in the joint security area controlled by us.
>
> But the enemy side, far from complying with our just demand, collectively pounced, brandishing lethal weapons, upon the security personnel of our side, counting on its numerical superiority, and committed the outrageous provocative act of violence against our security personnel.
>
> This reckless provocation of the enemy compelled our security personnel to take a step in self-defence. Thus, a free-for-all fight took place between the two sides, injuring personnel of both sides.
>
> This is a stark fact. But the U.S. side is raising a war racket on a large scale, resorting to fabrications with the allegation that our side provoked it.
>
> Such grave provocative act committed by the U.S. side in the joint security area of Panmunjom is a premeditated act to start a war.[14]

Once the Axe Murder incident occurred, North Korea called for a meeting between UNC and KPA/CPV security officers to discuss the incident. The UNC rejected the North Korean proposal and demanded that a full MAC meeting be held immediately. In the 379th MAC meeting on August 19, U.S. Navy RAdm. Mark Frudden, UNC MAC Senior Member, read a formal protest regarding the August 18 incident by CINCUNC addressed to Kim Il Sung. It strongly accused the North Koreans and asked Kim's assurance that an incident such as this would not occur again.[15] To this, KPA Maj. Gen. Han Ju Kyong, the KPA/CPV MAC Senior Member, said the incident was provoked by the UNC side, and claimed that it was "part of your new war provocation machination in the adventurous stage of igniting the fuse of war following the completion of the preparations for a war to invade the northern half of the Republic."[16] North Korea's basic attitude was to avoid escalation of the situation, however. While the meeting was going on, the KPA guards stayed in the North Korean side of the JSA in contrast to their customary behavior of milling about the entire area surrounding the conference building.[17] The initial diplomatic moves were open-ended and inconclusive. Nothing happened that could bring the situation toward resolution.

U.S.–ROK relations

South Korean President Park Chung Hee was "calm, deliberate and positive throughout" when he met with Stilwell a day after the incident. He was much more stable than he had been at the time of the raid on the Blue House and the *Pueblo* incident in 1968. In the meeting, Park called for a two-track approach. One track was to issue a strong protest including a demand for an apology, reparations, and a guarantee of non-recurrence. The other track was to develop an appropriate counteraction. He also emphasized that South Korea and the United States should not play into North Korean hands, and suggested that the two countries take appropriate responses "without use of arms." Stilwell said that a show of force by itself would not impress the North, and referred to the fact that the major military deployment after the *Pueblo* incident did not prevent the shooting-down of the EC-121 the following year. Park also proposed that South Korean soldiers with *taekwondo* (Korean *karate*) skill participate in the tree-cutting operation, noting that these soldiers would do so without firearms.[18] Stilwell accepted the offer and instructed the ROK troops not to carry weapons since the Armistice Agreement allows only a limited number of guards with rifles or pistols in the JSA.

The U.S. willingness to take strong actions against North Korea reassured and encouraged Park. On August 20, Park said South Korea would take retaliatory steps promptly if North Korea perpetrated unlawful provocations, small or large, again. He also suggested that the recent provocation was a North Korean attempt to conceal its economic bankruptcy and serious internal power struggle.[19] To give his words teeth, Park secretly prepared his own suggested retaliatory action. On August 20, he secretly ordered the ROK First Special Brigade to "retaliate thoroughly against attacking enemies" if they attacked the South Korean forces in the JSA.[20] In order to execute this mission, the commander of the Special Brigade decided to secretly bring grenades, pistols, and M-16 rifles into the JSA.[21]

Operation Paul Bunyan

On August 21, Operation Paul Bunyan was executed. Going inside the JSA were 110 UNC personnel including 16 U.S. engineers with chain saws and axes, 30 security platoon members equipped with side arms and axe handles, and 64 ROK Special Forces troops. There was also one JSA security platoon, an ROK force, and another U.S. force stationed farther away from the tree. In addition, a U.S. infantry unit in the air with 20 utility helicopters and seven attack helicopters, U.S. and ROK artillery support, and U.S. fighters and B-52s operating south of the DMZ were on standby.

At 0700 hours, the UNC personnel entered the JSA. At 0705 hours, the KPA/ CPV side was notified of the ongoing operation to cut down the tree. The UNC personnel conducted the tree-cutting operation while a truck blocked the eastern end of the Bridge of No Return. While the operation was underway, illegal road barriers set up by the North Korean side were removed. It was later revealed that the North Koreans on the front line had been extremely scared during the operation.[22]

After the operation ended, North Korean media reported that the U.S. side had committed a "grave provocation" to try to catch North Korea in "their war provocation manoeuvres."[23] In an informal meeting on August 21, however, Han Ju Kyong conveyed a message from Kim Il Sung, the Supreme Commander of the KPA, in his first-ever personal message to the CINCUNC which said:

> It was a good thing that no big incident occurred at Pan Mun Jom [Panmunjom] for a long period. However it is regretful that an incident occurred in the Joint Security Area, Pan Mun Jom this time. An effort must be made so that such incidents may not recur in the future. For this purpose both sides should make efforts. We urge your side to prevent the provocation. Our side will never provoke first, but take self defensive measures only when provocation occurs. This is our consistent stand.[24]

At first, the reactions from the U.S. and ROK sides were negative. On August 22, the State Department announced that Kim Il Sung's statement was not acceptable since it did not acknowledge responsibility for the murders of the two UNC officers, and cautioned that the United States did not intend to lower its guard, nor fall for any propaganda ploys. On August 23, the South Korean government announced that the message was unsatisfactory because it neither acknowledged responsibility nor offered an acceptable solution.

However, on August 23, the State Department put out a more conciliatory message recognizing that North Korean's expression of regret over the incident had been "a positive step."[25] The South Korean media was critical of the U.S. actions as being not strong enough. South Korean officials also briefed the press along the similar lines. On this point, the U.S. government protested to the ROK government on August 25, and said that the United States had actually taken serious risks in the tree-cutting operation and that the United States had followed South Korean advice "exactly."[26]

Rearrangement of JSA operations

In the 380th MAC meeting on August 25, the KPA proposed a separation of the UNC and KPA/CPV personnel in the JSA along the MDL to avoid future clashes and conflicts. On the one hand, the UNC was cautious. The UNC thought that the objective of the North Korean proposal was to divert focus away from the murders and by doing so to suggest that defects in the JSA security arrangements and not KPA actions were the cause of the Axe Murder incident. At the same time, though, the UNC saw the potential benefits in the North Korean proposal. The UNC had actually proposed such a separation in 1953 and 1970, and in this sense, the North Korean proposal on August 25 could be regarded as a concession to the long-standing UNC position.[27]

As the discussions got underway, concerns about possible consequences of the negotiations were raised in South Korea. South Koreans were similarly concerned that North Korea might use this issue to avoid its responsibility for the killing. Further, it was worried that North Korea might try to open direct talks with the United States and sideline South Korea. Such a concern was reinforced when North Korea disconnected the hot line between the North and the South on August 30, a critical confidence- and security-building measure in place since 1972.

The U.S. position was to take South Korean views seriously. After the North Korean side made the proposal, Kissinger instructed U.S. ambassador to South Korea Richard Sneider to fully coordinate with the South Korean government in reacting positively to the North Korean proposal.[28] To reassure the South Koreans, the United States also announced that it would turn down the North Korean proposal if it was an opening wedge for U.S.–DPRK bilateral talks, reminding the South Koreans that North Korea had been trying to renegotiate the 1953 Armistice Agreement without South Korea.[29]

The United States was satisfied with the developments in the negotiations. In the 381st MAC Meeting on August 28, the United States extracted from the North Koreans "all the assurances" to the safety of U.S. personnel.[30] Finally, an agreement was reached on September 6, under which personnel of each side would remain in their own portion of the JSA as divided by the MDL. On September 7, U.S.–ROK forces returned to a normal alert status. The naval task force sailed back to Japan. In mid-September, the two squadrons of F-4s and F-111s left Korea, and weeks later, training flights by the B-52s ceased.

Critical factors

Declining U.S. commitment to South Korea and Jimmy Carter

By August 1976, the United States had been rearranging its security commitment in Asia and as a result U.S.–ROK relations were under serious stress. The diminishing U.S. security commitment was a source of tremendous concern to Park Chung Hee, who responded by adopting the undemocratic *Yusin* Constitution, formulating an independent defense plan, and even initiating a nuclear development plan. These measures offended an important part of the American leadership. Negative views about South Korea proliferated in the United States, and were aggravated by the abduction of Kim Dae Jung by the Korean Central Intelligence Agency and the Koreagate bribery affair. Political oppression and human rights in South Korea loomed large in the American diplomatic circle. Although the Nixon Administration remained relatively businesslike toward South Korea and South Korea decided to cancel its nuclear program under U.S. pressure, overall U.S.–ROK relations had become seriously strained by 1976.[31]

To make matters worse, Jimmy Carter, a Democratic presidential nominee, publicly called for a total withdrawal of U.S. forces from Korea in January 1975. Although he later changed his mind and limited the withdrawal plan to ground forces only, his idea was a blessing for North Korea and a nightmare for South Korea.[32] In July 1976, Carter became the Democratic presidential candidate. In the meantime, the U.S. Congress was intensifying its criticism of U.S. policy toward South Korea. In April 1976, 119 Congress members from both chambers sent a memorandum to the White House arguing that U.S. military assistance to South Korea was abetting the political oppression in the country.

Debate on the Korean Question at the United Nations[33]

Since the foundation of the Republic of Korea and the Democratic People's Republic of Korea in 1948, the Korean Question had been an important political issue for discussion at the United Nations. South Korea maintained a close relationship with the United Nations from the beginning. The Republic of Korea's founding was in fact based on the outcome of general elections held under the supervision of the United Nations Temporary Commission on Korea. A year later, by contrast, North Korea formally demanded that the United Nations not interfere with the unification of Korea and contended that any decisions made at the United Nations without its participation were invalid.

Despite the North Korean demand, the United Nations began to play a larger role in Korean affairs when the Korean War broke out in June 1950. In July, the United Nations Security Council adopted Resolution 84 calling on its member states to defend South Korea. Furthermore, UNGA Resolution 376 (V) was adopted in October, which provided for the establishment of the United Nations Commission for the Unification and Rehabilitation of Korea (UNCURK) to represent the United Nations in bringing about the establishment of a unified, independent and democratic government of all Korea. After the Korean Political Conference in Geneva failed to produce peace in 1954, the Korean Question was referred back to the UNGA. At this point, however, South Korea succeeded in preventing the North Korean delegation from being invited to the United Nations. As a result, discussions of the Korean Question at the United Nations became *pro forma* in the 1960s; every year, a pro-ROK resolution was adopted and a pro-DPRK resolution to invite North Korea to the United Nations was rejected. Against this backdrop, in 1971, a resolution to comprehensively postpone discussions of the Korean Question was adopted.

A major tuning point came in June 1973, however, when South Korean President Park Chung Hee decided to push for the peaceful coexistence of two

Koreas. Park, announcing a seven-point foreign policy for peace and unification, suggested that South Korea would not object to the admission of North
Korea into the United Nations together with the South. In July, North Korea
established an office at the United Nations. Moreover, in October, the South
Korean government suggested that dissolving the UNC could be discussed if
an alternative mechanism was established to observe the Armistice Agreement
requirements. In the 28th UNGA in the same year, competition between the
two Koreas heated up due to the rise of the non-aligned nations' support of
North Korea. As a result, the UNGA adopted a consensus statement calling for
the dissolution of the UNCURK, signaling a great diplomatic victory for North
Korea.[34]

In 1974, North Korea was gaining strength in the UNGA and was receiving
increased support. In the 29th UNGA, a pro-ROK resolution was adopted by 61
affirmative votes and 43 negative votes while a pro-DPRK resolution was
rejected by 48 affirmative votes and 48 negative votes. The support gap between
the two Koreas was shrinking. By the 30th UNGA in 1975, North Korea had
established a position almost equal to that of South Korea. During the three
years preceding the 30th UNGA, North Korea established diplomatic relations
with more than 40 countries. Moreover, it had become a NAM member in
August 1975. South Korea's attempt to do the same was blocked by pro-DPRK
and/or anti-ROK countries.

Against this backdrop, both a pro-ROK resolution and a pro-DPRK resolution
were again submitted. The pro-ROK resolution called for (a) negotiations among
the concerned countries on new arrangements designed to replace the Armistice
Agreement and (b) early completion of discussions on alternative arrangements
for maintaining the Armistice Agreement so that the UNC could be dissolved on
January 1, 1976. The pro-DPRK resolution called for (a) the dissolution of the
UNC and total withdrawal of foreign troops stationed in South Korea under the
United Nations flag, (b) replacement of the Armistice Agreement with a peace
agreement negotiated by the DPRK and the United States, and (c) reduction of
the armed forces of both sides to an equal level.

The result was puzzling. The two resolutions, which contradicted each other,
were adopted simultaneously. The pro-ROK resolution was adopted 59 to 51,
and the pro-DPRK resolution was adopted 54 to 43. Faced with deadlock and
the tide turning gradually favorable to North Korea, the South Korean government decided not to discuss the Korean Question at the United Nations.
North Korea, on the other hand, was committed to seeking a one-sided victory
by pushing ahead with a pro-DPRK resolution at the UNGA. In January–
August 1976, North Korea invited a total of 182 foreign delegations from 69
countries to Pyongyang while dispatching 147 missions to 82 countries in an
aggressive diplomatic campaign to marshal support for the forthcoming showdown in the 31st UNGA. Particularly important targets were countries in Africa
and Latin America that were associated with the NAM. In its campaign, North
Korea appealed that there was a danger of war breaking out at any moment in

Korea due to the war preparations by the United States against North Korea. In August, North Korea officially dismissed a proposal made by Kissinger in September 1975 calling for four-party talks featuring North and South Korea together with the United States and China.[35] Also, the North Korean delegation participated in the fifth NAM Summit Conference in Colombo to flex its muscles before going into the main contest at the UNGA. On August 16, just two days before the Axe Murder in the JSA, the pro-North Korean nations submitted a draft resolution to the UNGA.[36] In response, South Korea reversed its earlier decision, and pro-South Korean nations submitted their version of a draft resolution on August 20. Before the Axe Murder incident, however, the South Korean side did not expect the number of North Korea supporting countries at the UNGA to diminish.[37]

Local military balance

By 1976, shifts in the local military balance on the ground and at sea seemed to have made the JSA a relatively attractive place for the North Koreans to take actions. By then, improved defense in the DMZ made it difficult for North Korean infiltrators to penetrate the UNC defense lines. For example, in June 1976, a three-man North Korean infiltration team penetrated two kilometers south of the DMZ but were located and killed.[38] North Korea started to construct elaborate tunnels under the DMZ in 1971, partly in reaction to the improved UNC defense systems against North Korean infiltrations in the DMZ established in the late 1960s.[39] Similarly, due to the South Korean naval buildup, it was becoming harder for the North Koreans to conduct operations at sea.

In the JSA, KPA guard post No. 4 and No. 8 were located near the poplar tree in question. There were also additional North Korean forces outside the JSA across the Bridge of No Return, through which the KPA side had easy and quick access to the site. Moreover, KPA artillery dominated the area by at least a 4:1 ratio.[40] The KPA could therefore maintain local superiority in the area near the poplar tree at least for a short period of time. Since the KPA initiated the action and the fighting lasted only several minutes, it was able to maintain local superiority during the fight. When the U.S. reaction force arrived in the area, the fighting had already ended.[41]

In the aftermath of the Axe Murder incident, Ambassador Sneider pointed out that there were inadequate command and control procedures in the JSA.[42] Moreover, the United Nations Command/United States Forces Korea/Eighth U.S. Army policy directive regarding the use of force and firearms by UNC security forces specified that if something happened in the JSA the UNC forces should use a minimum of force necessary to extricate themselves, and action should be taken to terminate any physical incidents as soon as possible.[43] When the UNC personnel dispersed and left the site swiftly, they were following this directive. In a way, the North Koreans were helped by these UNC regulations.

Characteristics

Location and timing

The JSA held important symbolism and was therefore useful location for the North Koreans to plan an action for propaganda purposes. The most important factor seems to be the history of the JSA, popularly known as Panmunjom. Panmunjom became a focus of world attention when it was designed as the negotiation site for the armistice talks during the Korean War. After the Armistice Agreement was concluded in July 1953, the JSA was created. Until the bilateral communication channels for inter-Korean dialogue were established in the early 1970s, the MAC had been the only formal channel for communication, though indirect, between the two Koreas. For the United States and North Korea, the MAC had been the only effective communication channel until the late 1980s when informal channels were established between the foreign services of the two countries.

About 800 meters in diameter, the JSA is a roughly circular area in the middle of the western sector of the DMZ. MAC meetings have been held in the area since the armistice of the Korean War. In August 1976, the JSA was a neutral area, maintained and patrolled jointly by the UNC and the KPA/CPV. Each side was allowed to deploy at most five officers and 30 enlisted men equipped only with one rifle or one pistol per man.[44] Deployment of larger unarmed work forces was also permitted in the area. Maintenance work such as pruning trees was typically carried out by both sides without prior consultation with the other side.

Fighting incidents had taken place within the JSA even before August 1976. In fact, the North Koreans had heightened tensions in 1975 with threats, destruction of UNC property, and gang assaults on UNC guards.[45] In June 1975, a free-for-all fight took place between UNC and KPA soldiers for several minutes after Maj. William Henderson, Acting U.S. Army Support Group Commander, was verbally insulted, and then struck from behind and knocked down to the ground by a North Korean "reporter."[46] On June 26, 1976, less than two months before the Axe Murder incident, about 20 KPA guards assaulted two UNC guards with boards, shovels, and sticks after the KPA guards forced a UNC jeep to stop by blocking the road.[47] This assault happened just after Mark Frudden was appointed as a new UNC Senior Member.[48] Frudden stated two days after the incident:

> The subject of the uncontrolled conduct of your [KPA] guard force has been repeatedly brought to the attention of your side in the last year [1975]. There are numerous instances of direct provocations by your guard force which could have escalated into extremely serious incidents. These provocations have happened so often that it appears your side may be trying to provoke just such an incident. In addition, despite

our protests, your side has not seemed to take any action to control your guards.[49]

These facts show that when the Axe Murder incident took place, there had already been a general trend of intensifying North Korean provocations in the JSA. The Axe Murder incident was not a bolt from the blue.

Moreover, on August 6, 12 days before the Axe Murder, four South Korean workers together with guards were dispatched to the location to cut down the tree rather than trim its branches. At the time, North Korean guards told the work personnel to leave the tree as it was. It was after this event that the decision was made to trim the branches rather than cut down the tree. For this reason, the problem regarding the poplar tree was well known to both the UNC and KPA sides and, therefore, the North Koreans had enough time to contemplate the potential exploitation of this issue.[50] Finally, although the connection was less apparent, the Axe Murder incident happened about a month after Jimmy Carter officially became Democratic presidential candidate.

Forces involved and the type of use of force

The forces involved in the incident were a relatively small number of guard personnel. When the North Korean guards started to attack the UNC personnel, they used clubs that they had brought and axe handles used by the South Korean workers. In this sense, the Axe Murder occurred accidentally. Had the South Korean workers carried their axes away when they fled from the spot, there could not have been an "axe" murder, though there could have been a "club" murder. The original North Korean plan, therefore, seems to have been to beat up the Americans with the clubs they had brought in but not necessarily to kill them as brutally as they actually did.

The North Korean military actions were coercive. The North Koreans tried to encourage friendly nations to support its position and policies in international forums, and to convince Americans that the withdrawal of the U.S. forces from South Korea would be beneficial. Given the relatively favorable environment in the international arena and the existence of troop withdrawal advocates in the United States, what North Korea sought to do was not so much to coerce those who supported continued U.S. military presence in South Korea into giving up the idea but rather to encourage those who supported the withdrawal of U.S. forces to raise their voice. In this sense, this military action may be called a "positively coercive" or "collaborative" use of force.

Intensity and targeting

The Axe Murder was not a big incident by Korean standards. The death toll was much higher in the late 1960s and the early 1970s during other confrontations. What shocked observers was the fact that it was the first event in the JSA to result in deaths. On this point, the CINCUNC noted, "What is unique is the death of security personnel (the first caused by a conflict between the two sides in the 23 years since the Armistice Agreement was signed), the severity, and apparent premeditation with which the KPA attack was carried out."[51] Also, the two American officers were killed in a brutal manner. Their bodies were bloodied and battered. Captain Bonifas was "so badly beaten with the blunt end of an ax that his face was no longer recognizable."[52] As such, the incident came as a surprise, and attracted world attention.

The targets in this incident were primarily American officers. Others seem to have been of secondary value as targets.[53] According to a defected former North Korean official, Kim Jong Il told the KPA guards not to attack South Korean workers, only Americans.[54] In hand-to-hand fighting like this, distinguishing targets must have been relatively easy.

Military-diplomatic coordination

In this incident, military and diplomatic actions were well coordinated. North Korea had conducted systematic diplomatic public relations efforts, especially in NAM member countries, by sending messages through mutual visits and the media. The propaganda efforts intensified in early August. The Axe Murder was broadly synchronized with the NAM Summit Conference and the submission of the pro-DPRK draft resolution to the UNGA. Since the UNGA was scheduled to begin in late September, the North Korean military-diplomatic campaign seemed to have been designed to last for about two months, beginning in early August and aiming to produce results in late September.

Assessment

Before assessing the political results, one caveat must be made. While the Axe Murder seems to have been a premeditated, deliberate action, sheer chance also played a role. For example, the decision to trim the tree was made by the UNC and, therefore, the timing was not completely determined by the North Koreans. Also, the axes used in the killing were brought in by the UNC side and not by the KPA personnel. Had the UNC decided not to trim the tree in the first place, this incident might not have happened at all.

It also remains possible that the whole incident was initiated by the KPA officer on the spot, Pak Chol.[55] According to a defected former KPA officer, Pak Chol held a personal grudge against Captain Bonifas, and it was Pak who directly initiated the fight. Pak was later highly praised by the North Korean political leadership and was conferred a military order.[56] From available evidence, however, it is likely that although the details of the action were left for the commander on the ground to plan and execute, the decision to attack Americans was made by the highest political authority in North Korea.

Concerning the North Korean decision-making, the Soviets saw the August 18 incident as a "deliberate provocation by Kim Il-sung, done in pursuance of his campaign to win Third World political support," though he did not anticipate any sort of military crisis.[57] Also, testimony by Pak Pyong Yop, who defected from North Korea in the 1980s after having worked for the Workers' Party of Korea for more than 30 years and at one time in the same office as Kim Jong Il, described how the Axe Murder incident developed:

> The problem leading to the Panmunjom incident [Axe Murder incident] arose when the U.S. forces and South Korea attempted to cut off the branches of a poplar tree, which obstructed the vision of the northern area, without a prior consent from the North Korean side. The North Korean guards protested when the U.S. military police and South Korean workers started to cut off the branches. After this, the [North Korean] guards reported the situation directly to Kim Jong Il.
>
> ...
>
> When Kim Jong Il received the report, he ordered, "Show them the Korean way. Don't care about the South Korean workers and give the Yankees a lesson. And don't use guns." After some wrangling, the clash started. The [North Korean] guards grabbed the axes that the South Korean workers were carrying and killed [American officers]. Being upset that they actually killed men, the North Korean side again reported the situation to Kim Jong Il. Kim ordered the forces to withdraw.
>
> After it had developed into a major incident, it was reported to Kim Il Sung. Questioning the incident, Kim Il Sung said, "Why the hell did you do this?" Kim Jong Il ordered his men to tell [Kim Il Sung] that "it was the deliberate provocation by the U.S. military," and that "they did so in order to start war." The party secretaries could not tell [Kim Il Sung] that Kim Jong Il was responsible, and instead told him that people at the Ministry of People's Armed Forces were responsible. ...
>
> ...
>
> The United States was talking about retaliation and South Korea was talking about attacking North Korea. When the United States and South Korea took a tough position and demanded an apology, Kim Il Sung offered his regret. Kim Il Sung told his men, "We have to express our regret for men had been killed. The U.S. military apologized at the time of the *Pueblo* incident."[58]

Also, Pak Pyong Yop revealed that Kim Jong Il and the Ministry of People's Armed Forces considered going to war but concluded that it was not a good idea:

> It was considered that if the South Korean side should take strong counter-actions, it might be worth attacking it. Kim Jong Il and the

Ministry of People's Armed Forces thought about such an option. However, it was the time when the U.S. forces were withdrawn from Vietnam. China exercised significant influence over the North Korean foreign policy. Kim Il Sung knew very well that such an attempt would wind up in failure unless North Korea could get both material and moral support from China.[59]

Marshaling support in international forums

At the time of the Axe Murder incident, there were two specific diplomatic objectives that the North Korean leadership was seeking to achieve. One was to marshal support for its position in the fifth NAM Summit Conference. The other was to do the same at the upcoming 31st UNGA. On March 28, 1976, Kim Il Sung clearly indicated his intention by saying:

> Now, if the problem of Korea's reunification is to be solved, it is important to rouse the support of world public opinion and to expose the outrages committed by the American imperialists in south Korea to the inspection of the whole world. ...
>
> Only by rousing world opinion to support more fully the Korean people's cause of reunification, can we prevent war in Korea, preserve peace in Asia and achieve the peaceful reunification of Korea. We must work harder to rouse world feelings on the Korean question so that Korea becomes the focus of attention in Asian affairs and globally.[60]

The fifth NAM Summit Conference was the first conference the North Korean delegation attended after North Korea became a full member of the NAM in the previous year. The importance that the North Koreans attached to the conference was clear from the fact that North Korea sent a 120-man delegation. At the conference, North Korean delegates tried hard to convince other member nations that the presence of U.S. forces in South Korea was a source of tension on the Korean Peninsula and submitted a draft resolution on the Korean Question.

Due to the excessively unreasonable nature of the North Korean argument and the occurrence of the Axe Murder while the conference was proceeding, however, the draft resolution submitted by North Korea was significantly revised due to opposition from relatively moderate member nations. Five countries submitted an amendment bill, and some of the leaders of the NAM, including Yugoslavian leader Josip Broz Tito, expressed reservations about the North Korean position. North Korea was forced to submit an amendment draft as a result.

In the end, some of the points raised by the North Koreans – withdrawal of foreign troops from Korea, elimination of foreign military bases in Korea, and replacement of the Armistice Agreement with a peace agreement – were reflected in the final political declaration, due largely to concessions made by the host nation, Sri Lanka, which was concerned about the possible failure of the conference.[61] As many as 25 nations expressed objections to the declaration, however, and their reservations were recorded in the proceedings. North Korea's hard-line position failed to receive unanimous support. The Axe Murder incident damaged the North Korean position much more than it helped.[62]

The outcome of the 31st UNGA was even more disastrous to the North Koreans. The negative impact of the Axe Murder on the North Korean position was clearly recognized by American decision-makers. In a private conversation on September 15, National Security Advisor Brent Scowcroft and Ambassador Sneider shared the view that the August 18 incident had "come out better than expected – and apparently to our net advantage." Sneider thought it would have "a beneficial effect" in the United Nations.[63] The pro-North Korea draft resolution was withdrawn on September 20, just before the UNGA was convened, apparently because of North Korean expectations that its resolution would be rejected while the pro-South Korea resolution would be adopted. The Axe Murder incident seriously damaged North Korea's reputation in the international community.[64] In a meeting with Kissinger in September, South Korean foreign minister Park Tong-jin expressed his satisfaction that the Korea debate had been avoided at the UNGA and added that the North Koreans had withdrawn their resolution probably because they thought they would do considerably worse than last year. On this, Kissinger observed that the reservations entered at the NAM meeting and the lack of support the North Koreans received over the August 18 incident had also been factors.[65]

An observation made by U.S. Representative Dante Fascell after the Axe Murder is also worth mentioning. In a Congressional hearing, he pointed out that the restrained reaction on the part of the UNC at the time of the Axe Murder incident had been a blessing for the United States, noting:

> You would think they [the North Koreans] were trying to invite a response that would kill their men. In other words, they would be delighted to have their 30 people killed if that would prove their point. Their point is that the United States is aggressive and that there is great tension here.[66]

Arthur Hummel, Jr, Assistant Secretary of State for East Asian and Pacific Affairs, concurred. He responded to Fascell's remarks by saying, "We helped our point by not killing their [North Korean] men. I think your point is well taken. They would have been better served from their point of view if they had casualties on their side."[67]

By not retaliating, the UNC side lost militarily but won diplomatically. The KPA guards succeeded in doing what they were told to do – beating up the American officers. However, the action was taken in a way that defeated any reasonable expectation of achieving an international propaganda victory. The

North Koreans overshot the culminating point of victory. Under such circumstances, all North Korea could do was to lay low to wait for the wound to heal. After the Axe Murder incident, incidents along the DMZ diminished and the MAC enjoyed the "longest lull" since 1953, broken in November 1984 when a Russian defected through the JSA.[68]

Encouraging the withdrawal of U.S. forces from Korea

By provoking a serious incident in widely-known Panmunjom, North Korea seem to have tried to fuel anti-war sentiment in the United States and, by doing so, back Carter's position that the United States should withdraw its forces from South Korea. The attacks on U.S. servicemen were expected to demonstrate that keeping U.S. forces on the Korean Peninsula could draw the United States into another messy and brutal war in Asia.[69]

North Korea's attempt to encourage the withdrawal of U.S. forces from South Korea by use of force failed, however. Few people associated the Axe Murder incident with the issue of withdrawal of U.S. forces. They argued neither for nor against withdrawal based on the incident. To U.S. congressmen, human rights and the War Powers Resolution were far more important than the Axe Murder. Also, there is no evidence that U.S. public opinion was greatly affected by the Axe Murder incident, especially in terms of their preference for presidential candidates.[70] Carter was so determined to go ahead with withdrawal that the Axe Murder was simply irrelevant. Under such circumstances, North Korean military-diplomatic actions did not matter much.

One limited but potentially important impact of the Axe Murder incident on U.S. decision-makers was seen in comments made by Ambassador Sneider. On September 15, Sneider suggested that the United States pull out its security company in support of the JSA, saying that it would be better to do so "as an initiative than to retreat under domestic pressure."[71] Scowcroft rejected Sneider's suggestion, however, noting that the "exposed quality" of this particular company was the source of its value. He further expressed his concern about "an inclination within certain parts of the government to go ahead with small piece-meal moves which individually had little significance but cumulatively had the net effect of eroding our military presence in East Asia."[72] The U.S. security company was not withdrawn.

The North Koreans might have attempted to convince the United States to negotiate a bilateral peace agreement with them by showing that the tension on the Korean Peninsula could never be dissipated without such an arrangement. However, brutally killing American servicemen with axe handles did not help induce the United States to reverse its previous position regarding a bilateral peace agreement with North Korea. On this point, the U.S. position was clear. As Hummel reaffirmed on September 1, "We will not negotiate on future security arrangements on the Korean peninsula without the participation of the Republic of Korea."[73]

Consolidating Kim Jong Il's position

Although there is little direct evidence, it is worth pointing out that the Axe Murder incident might have been a part of Kim Jong Il's attempt to consolidate his position in the North Korean political and military establishment. Kim Jong Il started to exercise informal control over the North Korean armed forces in 1970, when he began to frequently visit KPA units without Kim Il Sung. During his visits to KPA units, Kim Jong Il not only listened to the briefings but also actually boarded tanks, torpedo boats, and aircraft with KPA soldiers. In 1975, Kim Jong Il's portrait was introduced to KPA barracks and offices. More importantly, Kim Jong Il changed the reporting system so that he would get reports from the KPA before they went to Kim Il Sung, thus preventing the KPA from presenting its reports directly to Kim Il Sung.[74]

Such attempts to consolidate power did not go unchallenged. The most important challenge came in June 1976. In a Workers' Party Political Committee meeting, Vice President Kim Tong Gyu criticized Kim Jong Il for failing to pay enough attention to party rules and order, and for replacing old but experienced party leaders with inexperienced young personnel at his will. Director of the KPA General Political Bureau Ri Yong Mu, Alternate Member of the Political Committee Ryu Jang Sik, Vice Minister of the People's Armed Forces Ji Kyong Hak, and others supported Kim Tong Gyu's position. These critics were purged, though, and the challenge to Kim Jong Il ended in failure.[75]

Pak Pyong Yop described the background of the Axe Murder incident:

> It was the time when Kim Jong Il had emerged as [Kim Il Sung's] successor and the monolithic ideological system was being established. It was the time when Kim Jong Il was getting reports on even the most trivial incident. At that time, Kim Jong Il tried to get all the information from all over the country, including the information on who came to the office late.[76]

It is, therefore, possible that Kim Jong Il attempted to consolidate his position *vis-à-vis* the Workers' Party and the KPA and to defy domestic opposition by actually exercising control over the KPA and by achieving a great military-diplomatic victory in Panmunjom.

Chapter 6

NUCLEAR DIPLOMACY, 1993–94

On March 12, 1993, North Korea declared it would withdraw from the Treaty on the Non-Proliferation of Nuclear Weapons (NPT).[1] As a result of its military-diplomatic campaign which lasted for a year and seven months, North Korea succeeded in getting the Washington to sign the "Agreed Framework between the United States of America and the Democratic People's Republic of Korea" on October 21, 1994, obtaining economic gains and paving the way for normalization of relations with the United States.[2]

Nuclear development, crises, and the Agreed Framework[3]

Declaration of withdrawal

North Korea's March 12 decision to withdraw from the NPT came as a direct response to the International Atomic Energy Agency (IAEA) demand for special inspections and the commencement of the 1993 Team Spirit U.S.–ROK combined military exercise. On February 9, the IAEA issued a demand for "special inspections" of suspected nuclear sites not previously declared by North Korea. On February 25, the IAEA Board of Governors issued a resolution requesting Hans Blix, Director General of the IAEA, to report on the North Korean compliance within a month. North Korea quickly announced its rejection of the demand. Then on March 9, Team Spirit 1993 commenced. Though smaller than previous years, the U.S.–ROK combined military exercise featured 70,000 South Korean troops, 50,000 U.S. troops, and the first-ever deployment of the B-2 stealth bomber to the Peninsula.[4]

Under such circumstances, Kim Jong Il issued Order No. 0034 of the Supreme Commander of the Korean People's Army (KPA) on March 8, one day before the beginning of the Team Spirit exercises, ordering the whole country, all people and the entire army, to switch to a "state of readiness for war" on March 9.[5] The announcement of the state of war readiness was the first since 1983.[6] Under the state of war readiness:

Senior military officials, told that an attack might be imminent, were ordered to evacuate to underground fortifications. All military leaves were canceled, the heads of all soldiers shaved, steel helmets were worn, and troops were issued rifle ammunition. In Pyongyang armored cars were drawn up in rows near security headquarters, and armed police checked military passes, while in the countryside the civilian population was mobilized to dig trenches near their homes as protection against air attack.[7]

Following the March 12 announcement, North Korea further intensified its military-diplomatic saber-rattling. Just after the decision to mobilize the nation was made, the North Korean government issued a statement: "If we failed to stop this conspiracy by the United States and its followers, it would drive the whole nation into confrontation and war that would result in making the nation a sacrifice for great powers."[8] At the same time, it was reported that North Korea decided to expel foreign diplomats or deny them access to North Korean officials, recall delegations from abroad, and suspend telephone lines between Beijing and Pyongyang.

The initial responses from the United States and South Korea were relatively mild. The South Korean government strongly urged North Korea to reconsider its decision as it put its armed forces on alert on March 13 and suspended all inter-Korean economic cooperation on March 15. President Kim Young Sam said, "[W]e never want North Korea to be isolated internationally nor do we want to inflict suffering on them."[9] On April 6, Kim, calling for a diplomatic solution of the nuclear issue, said, "We do not want the North Korean regime to be dismantled suddenly because this would threaten the security of the whole peninsula."[10] U.S. officials also urged North Korea to reverse its decision in a restrained manner. The Chinese attitude was a little more accommodating to North Korea than those of the United States and South Korea. China swiftly urged a diplomatic solution of the problem. After the IAEA referred the matter to the United Nations Security Council (UNSC) on April 1, China made it clear that it was opposed to the use of sanctions as a means of solving the issue.

About two weeks after the March 12 announcement, North Korea started to take steps to deflate the tension and expressed its willingness to have direct bilateral talks on the nuclear issue with the United States. On March 24, Kim Jong Il announced an end to the state of war readiness.[11] Then on March 29, North Korea's Ministry of Foreign Affairs (MFA) called for bilateral U.S.–DPRK talks.[12] In response to the North Korean overture, the United States agreed on April 22 to bilateral high-level talks while maintaining its basic position that the nuclear issue was an issue "between North Korea and the international community" and that the U.S. task was to support the efforts of the "appropriate international bodies" as they worked to resolve the situation.[13] Three preparatory meetings were held while the UNSC discussed a resolution on the North Korean nuclear issue.

On May 11, the UNSC approved a resolution calling upon North Korea to reconsider the March 12 announcement and to reaffirm its commitment to the NPT.[14] The MFA declared on the following day that if the UNSC moved ahead with sanctions, the DPRK would regard such an action as a "declaration of war against the DPRK."[15] On May 25, the United States and North Korea announced that a high-level bilateral meeting would be held in New York on June 2. At this point, North Korea conducted the most extensive missile flight tests to date. On May 29–30, it test-launched three Scud and one No Dong missiles into the Sea of Japan.

With the respective delegations headed by Assistant Secretary of State Robert Gallucci and First Vice Minister of Foreign Affairs Kang Sok Ju, the U.S.–DPRK bilateral talks began on June 2, just 10 days before North Korea's withdrawal from the NPT would take effect. In the talks, Kang contradicted previous remarks by Kim Il Sung and said that his country had the capability to build nuclear weapons. He also suggested, however, that North Korea would not manufacture nuclear weapons if the United States stopped threatening it, and even suggested that its carbon-graphite moderated nuclear technology could be traded for militarily less useful light-water technology.[16] As a result of the talks, on June 11 the two countries adopted the first-ever "joint statement" declaring that they had agreed in principle to assurances against the threat and use of force including nuclear weapons, impartial application of full-scope safeguards, and non-interference in each other's internal affairs. In this context, the two governments agreed to continue dialogue on an "equal and unprejudiced basis," and the North Korean government decided to suspend the effectuation of its withdrawal from the NPT.[17] After the talks, Kang characterized the talks as "historic."[18] The joint statement was of great symbolic value to the North Koreans. As a result of the nuclear diplomacy, North Korea "suddenly had become important to the United States."[19]

On June 18, Kang clarified the North Korean position and its ultimate objectives. He explained that the nuclear issue on the Korean Peninsula stemmed from the "anti-DPRK policy" of the United States and, therefore, the fundamental solution would be attained only by eliminating the "hostile relations between the DPRK and the USA."[20] Although dialogue between the North and the South, and between the IAEA and North Korea, eventually resumed, the key was now in the hands of the Americans and the North Koreans. The flip side of this new development in New York, however, was frustration in Seoul. Once this "joint statement" was issued, U.S.–ROK relations started to deteriorate. Although South Korea was seeking a negotiated settlement of the nuclear issue, it was reluctant to see any improvement in relations between the United States and North Korea, particularly when South Korea was sidelined in the process.

Determining the terms of trade

Once it was unofficially agreed that the nuclear issue would be handled by bilateral negotiations between the United States and North Korea, the question facing Washington concerned the terms of trade. The North Koreans were extremely straightforward in revealing their agenda. In July 1993, the second round of U.S.–DPRK high-level talks was held in Geneva. On the second day of the talks, the North Korean side officially declared that it was willing to replace its carbon-graphite reactors with light-water reactors (LWRs). In response, Gallucci was positive but cautious since he realized the immense difficulties involved in financing such a scheme.[21] North Korea had revealed its ambitious goals, which it would eventually achieve, at an early stage of the negotiations. As a result of the second high-level talks, the United States and North Korea issued a press statement on July 19:

> Both sides recognize the desirability of the DPRK's intention to replace its graphite moderated reactors and associated nuclear facilities with light water moderated reactors. As part of a final resolution of the nuclear issues, and on the premise that a solution related to the provision of light water moderated reactors (LWRs) is achievable, the USA is prepared to support the introduction of LWRs and to explore with the DPRK ways in which LWRs could be obtained.[22]

In August, however, the U.S. government spelled out a three-pronged plan for the third round of U.S.–DPRK talks, which basically said that the United States would not begin the new round of talks until North Korea began serious discussions with the IAEA and South Korea.[23] The plan was designed to encourage the resolution of the nuclear issue through the international nonproliferation regime and inter-Korean dialogue. North Korea naturally responded negatively. When the IAEA demanded that North Korea comply with all inspection requirements as a party to the NPT, it became apparent that North Korea had a peculiar interpretation of its status within the NPT: since it had only suspended its withdrawal from the NPT, it enjoyed a "unique status" by which it could determine which inspections to accept and which to reject. With this, the North Koreans claimed that all they could only accept inspections necessary to provide the "continuity of the safeguards," more limited in scope than the regular and ad hoc inspections that NPT signatories were required to accept.[24]

As a result, the visit by IAEA officials to North Korea in August was not a satisfactory one. IAEA officials were only allowed to replace film and batteries in monitoring devices. Additionally, IAEA–DPRK talks in September did not produce a positive outcome. On October 1, the IAEA General Conference adopted a resolution calling for North Korea's immediate acceptance of new inspections. Then on November 1, the United Nations General Assembly adopted a resolution urging North Korea to cooperate immediately with IAEA in the full implementation of the safeguards agreement.[25]

The inter-Korean talks were not bearing fruit, either. While the South Koreans tried to make the nuclear issue a top agenda item at the inter-Korean talks, the North Korean side insisted on prioritizing exchanges of special envoys to prepare for the inter-Korean summit meeting. Three meetings in October ended in failure. Then on November 3, North Korea announced the suspension of the meetings, blaming it on the South Korean defense minister's remarks on the previous day. On the same day, Vice-Marshal Kim Kwang Jin, Vice Minister of the People's Armed Forces, declared that North Korea was prepared to answer "dialogue with dialogue, war with war." Kim also said, "As the south Korean authorities proclaimed military countermove against us, it is inevitable for us to answer them with force of arms," adding, "Military retaliation precisely means war."[26] The North Korean accusation was simply an excuse to halt the inter-Korean talks, however. The South Korean defense minister had only said that the Ministry of National Defense should discuss how to respond to possible "accidental provocations" resulting from United Nations sanctions, and insisted that military sanctions against North Korea, therefore, be prevented.[27]

North Korea's intention was clear. It wanted a resumption of the U.S.–DPRK talks. On September 22, the MFA criticized the United States for setting "preconditions" and demanded the United States rescind them.[28] On October 4, the MFA denounced the adoption of the IAEA General Conference resolution on October 1, declaring, "The present situation proves once again that the nuclear issue can be resolved only through DPRK–USA talks."[29] In short, North Korea was closing all other doors in order to open the door for bilateral talks with the United States.

North Korea was trying to deal effectively with the outside world by employing both dialogue and saber-rattling. In the face of mounting tension and the increasing possibility of economic sanctions, it demonstrated the will to stand up against outside pressure. On November 6, it was reported that North Korea was reinforcing its forces near the Military Demarcation Line.[30] The MFA warned on November 29 that the DPRK had taken into account all possible consequences when it announced withdrawal from the NPT and was fully prepared to safeguard the sovereignty of the country even if "the worst event such as sanctions or war" was imposed upon it. If the United States discontinued the talks, it also threatened that the DPRK would end its suspension of withdrawal from the NPT.[31]

In the meantime, efforts were made on both sides to find a way out. In mid-October, North Korea informally made a new proposal to the United States. The MFA presented an American diplomat with a piece of paper proposing a series of trade-offs to settle the issue. According to the proposal, while North Korea would (a) remain in the NPT, (b) accept IAEA regular inspections, and (c) discuss the issue of the special inspections, the United States would (a) agree to end the Team Spirit military exercises, (b) lift economic sanctions on North Korea, and (c) agree to hold the third round of high-level U.S.–DPRK talks. On the other hand, on November 15, the U.S. government endorsed the so-called "comprehensive approach." This approach included having North Korea initially accept IAEA "ad hoc inspections" as well as the resumption of the North–South talks in exchange for cancellation of Team Spirit 1994 and the opening of the third round of U.S.–DPRK high-level talks. It also envisioned, in phase two, North Korea's acceptance of IAEA inspections in the two suspected waste sites in Nyongbyon (Yongbyon) in return for U.S. diplomatic recognition of North Korea and trade and investment concessions from the United States, South Korea, and Japan.[32] The United States formally presented this idea, now called a "thorough and broad" approach, on November 23 jointly with South Korea. It was a significant step in that the United States had decided to postpone the implementation of the special inspections to a later time rather than demanding it as a precondition for U.S.–DPRK talks.[33]

At the same time, the United States examined other hardline options – sanctions, the threat of military force or war, preemptive strikes, and the dispatch of additional forces to South Korea. These options had their own weaknesses, however. Sanctions would require a "staggering number of ships" but still might not work. War would be too costly. Preemption would not destroy already reprocessed plutonium and might provoke massive retaliation from North Korea. Use or threat of force had not worked well in Somalia and Haiti. The conclusion in the November 15 principals meeting was: "the available sticks were less than perfect. ..."[34] As a result, on December 29, the United States and North Korea agreed to take the following simultaneous and reciprocal actions: (a) beginning of IAEA inspections on seven declared facilities; (b) resumption of inter-Korean talks on the exchange of special envoys; (c) announcement to cancel the Team Spirit military exercises; and (d) announcement of the date to hold the third round of U.S.–DPRK talks.

During the talks between the IAEA and North Korea in January 1994, however, it was revealed that the United States and North Korea had not fully agreed on the definition of an "ad hoc inspection" and North Korea's status in the NPT.[35] While the United States had tacitly accepted the inspections needed to maintain the continuity of the safeguards, the IAEA continued to insist that its inspections be conducted on the basis of the safeguards agreement. North Korea claimed that it had only agreed to the inspections needed to maintain the continuity of the safeguards and refused the sampling and gamma mapping that were critical in inspecting nuclear activities.

In early 1994, the situation became tense. The White House announced plans to deploy *Patriot* surface-to-air missiles in South Korea. The South Korean defense ministry talked about conducting Team Spirit 1994 unless North Korea agreed to nuclear inspections. On January 31, the MFA criticized the IAEA for ignoring North Korea's "unique status" and the "hardliners and conservatives" in the United States for trying to introduce *Patriot* missiles to South Korea. The MFA declared that the DPRK could live without relations with the United States, and warned that American "hardliners and conservatives" as well as South Korean authorities, would be held fully responsible for the "catastrophic consequences" of their actions.[36] At the same time, in early 1994 the KPA conducted "unusual activities" which created serious concern. One scenario envisaged the North Koreans would "roll out of their winter training exercises into a surprise attack."[37]

The IAEA conceded and reached an agreement on February 15 with North Korea on the scope of inspections, which did not amount to full-scale inspections and were in fact close to what the North Koreans claimed to be the inspections needed to maintain the continuity of the safeguards. Based on these developments, the United States and North Korea issued a statement on February 25, entitled "agreed conclusions," in which they pledged to take "simultaneous steps" on March 1. Those steps included: (a) the U.S. announcement of its decision to agree to South Korea's suspension of the Team Spirit military exercise; (b) beginning of the inspections necessary to assure the continuity of safeguards, and the completion of the inspections within the period as agreed by the IAEA and the DPRK; (c) resumption of the working-level contacts in Panmunjom for the exchange of North–South special envoys; and (d) announcement to hold the third round of U.S.–DPRK high-level talks on March 21.[38] In early March all parties took steps to implement the agreed conclusions. The prospect of the resolution of the nuclear issue seemed promising at this point. Subsequent events led to a new and larger crisis, however.

Implementation of the agreed conclusions

In Panmunjom, the North Koreans appeared to be coming to the negotiating table with the South Koreans solely for the purpose of satisfying their end of the obligations in the agreed conclusions. For the North Koreans, the inter-Korean dialogue was just a show to be staged to satisfy the American demand. The South Korean side did not appreciate it. The Seoul delegation played it tough, and did not respond positively to the North Korean proposals regarding the agenda for the exchange of special envoys.[39] At the eighth contact held on March 19, the North Korean side complained about the South Korean attitude and threatened the South Korean side by saying that the DPRK would answer "dialogue with dialogue" and "war with war." The South Koreans demanded that the North Koreans agree that the nuclear issue would be discussed and resolved before the exchange of special envoys. The North Korean head delegate, Pak Yong Su, finally declared, "Seoul is not far away [from the DMZ]. If war breaks out, Seoul will become a sea of fire." Then the North Korean delegation walked away from the table.[40]

In Nyongbyon, North Korea did not fulfill its obligations. At the reprocessing plant known as the "Radiochemical Laboratory," IAEA inspectors were not allowed to perform certain required and agreed safeguards activities. On March 21, inspection results were reported to the IAEA, which then decided to report it to the UNSC.[41] The MFA announced on the same day that the DPRK had decided not to send its delegation to the third round of the U.S.–DPRK talks and they were no longer obliged to maintain the continuity of the safeguards. It also warned that the DPRK might have to withdraw from the NPT.[42]

In response, the United States decided to cancel the third round of talks and started preparing for the possible imposition of economic sanctions against North Korea. Concurrently, the South Korean government decided to approve the introduction of *Patriot* missiles to South Korea. On March 21, a deployment order was signed to move up to six *Patriot* missile batteries from Texas to South Korea. On March 22, the IAEA reported to the UNSC.[43] On March 31, the UNSC decided that if necessary further consideration would take place in order to achieve full implementation of the IAEA–DPRK safeguards agreement.[44]

1994 nuclear crisis

With tension already rising, North Korea took another bold step when it shut down the five-megawatt (MW) reactor in Nyongbyon on April 1. On April 19, it notified the IAEA that it would soon begin removing the spent fuel rods but it would allow inspectors to observe the operation. The IAEA decided not to send inspectors, however, since it was not allowed to take samples. As a result, the discharge operation started on May 9 without the presence of IAEA inspectors. The IAEA informed North Korea that the discharge of fuel without the required safeguard measures would constitute a serious violation of the safeguards agreement. North Korea ignored the warning but agreed to receive IAEA officials to discuss the issue. The beginning of the discharge marked a critical turning point. Until that time, the focus of the debate had basically been on past nuclear developments. Now the question also included North Korea's future nuclear development. U.S. Defense Secretary William Perry estimated that plutonium for five or six nuclear devices could be obtained by reprocessing the spent fuel discharged from the 5-MW reactor.

In early 1994, North Korea vigorously conducted military exercises. It bolstered both offensive and defensive force exercises and tested a secure communication network used in national emergencies.[45] It was reported in March that the size of the exercises increased by 40 percent for forward-deployed ground forces, 15 percent for the navy, and 30 percent for the air force.[46] In April, the number of exercises reportedly increased from the previous year by 80 percent for the ground forces and 50 percent for the air force. Maneuvering exercises by mechanized units, joint navy-air force exercises, reserve force mobilization exercises, and blackout and evacuation exercises in major cities increased significantly.[47] On April 30, a surprise exercise was conducted in which the majority of North Korea's combat aircraft were in the air at one time.[48]

At the same time, North Korea sought the resumption of the talks with the United States. On May 3, the MFA announced that when the nuclear issue was resolved "through the U.S.–DPRK talks," the spent fuel rods would be put under the IAEA control and they could be examined.[49] On May 12, Kang Sok Ju privately informed the U.S. side that the possibility to separate the key fuel rods was preserved. Also, a North Korean diplomat suggested that it would take two months to unload the fuel rods, and the United States and North Korea still had some time to negotiate a deal.[50] However, an IAEA inspector who arrived in North Korea on May 19 found out that the unloading of the fuel rods was proceeding more quickly than anticipated, without records being kept.[51]

Subsequently, discussions in late May failed. The IAEA concluded that if the discharge of fuel from the reactor continued, the opportunity to select, segregate, and secure fuel rods for later measurements would be lost within days.[52] The United States announced on June 3 that it had no basis for holding a third round of high level talks with North Korea and would seek further action in the UNSC. It also revealed that it had already begun consultations with its allies and with the UNSC on "appropriate next steps" in response to North Korea's actions, including sanctions.[53] In South Korea, the National Security Council meeting was held on June 8, for the first time under the Kim Young Sam Administration.

North Korea remained defiant. On May 31 and June 2, it test-fired *Silkworm* anti-ship missiles in the Sea of Japan.[54] On June 3, Kang Sok Ju warned that if the United States chose a "strongarm measure," (a) the DPRK would proceed with its nuclear development and could not but expand its "independent atomic energy industry," (b) the foundation of the DPRK's temporary suspension of its withdrawal from the NPT would collapse, and (c) economic sanctions would be regarded as a declaration of war. At the same time, Kang also assured the United States that the DPRK's proposal for the package solution was still valid.[55] In a letter to the IAEA on June 6, the General Director of North Korea's General Bureau of Atomic Energy insisted that the spent fuel rods had individual numbers and their original positions were all recorded so that the technical feasibility of measuring the spent fuel rods was preserved.[56]

Despite the North Korean overture, however, on June 10 the IAEA Board of Governors asked their Director General to bring the case to the UNSC and United Nations General Assembly.[57] North Korea responded strongly. On June 13, the MFA announced that the DPRK would (a) immediately withdraw from the IAEA, (b) no longer allow the inspections for the continuity of safeguards, and (c) strongly reaffirm its position that United Nations sanctions would be regarded immediately as a "declaration of war."[58] On June 14, North Korea conducted a burn test of an engine presumably to be used for the Taepo Dong missile.[59] North Korea was taking the situation to the brink.

Sanctions, preventive attack, and assessment of their consequences

In mid-June, the United States came up with a two-phase plan to impose sanctions on North Korea. Also in the same period, U.S. forces in and around Korea were reinforced and the consequences of war in Korea were given serious evaluation. In April, *Patriot* missiles arrived in South Korea and became operational. A battalion of *Apache* helicopters, M-2 infantry fighting vehicles, advanced counter-battery radar tracking systems, and about 1,000 additional U.S. troops were deployed in South Korea. Around that time, the United States deployed the aircraft carrier *Independence* to the vicinity of the Korean Peninsula,[60] to be followed by another carrier to the Yellow Sea later.[61]

In June, the United States drew up three military options, each with different levels of force buildup in Korea. The first option envisioned the dispatch of 2,000 non-combat military personnel needed to prepare for large-scale deployment. This option would be executed before any sanctions were imposed. The second option included 10,000 troops, squadrons of aircraft to be based near Korea, and another carrier battle group for the region. The third one involved over 50,000 troops, 400 aircraft, over 50 ships, multiple rocket launchers, and *Patriot* missiles. This option would require a reserve call-up and the deployment of an additional carrier battle group around Korea.[62] In addition, three military options were created for bombing nuclear facilities in Nyongbyon. In the first option, the United States would destroy the reprocessing facility only. In the second option, nuclear facilities such as the 5-MW reactor and the spent fuel storage pool would be taken out. The third option would be to remove key North Korean military assets, in addition to all of above, to degrade its ability to retaliate.[63]

The key U.S. decision-makers eventually agreed to execute the sanction option with two phases. The first phase would start 30 days after the United Nations sanctions resolution was adopted, with any trade that could contribute to North Korea's nuclear activities, North Korea's exports and imports of materials related to weapons of mass destruction or conventional weapons, flights to and from the country except regular commercial flights and humanitarian missions, and any economic and development assistance to the country banned. The United States would also urge other countries to restrict their diplomatic ties with North Korea. If North Korea took additional negative steps, the second phase would be implemented in which North Korea's financial assets would be frozen and its remittances banned. On June 15, Japan and South Korea approved the draft sanction resolution devised by the United States.[64] The U.S. general public supported the tough approach toward North Korea. In June 1994, 80 percent of the people supported economic sanctions, 51 percent supported a military strike against North Korean nuclear facilities if the country continued to reject inspections, and 48 percent said it was "worth risking war" to prevent North Korean nuclear production.[65]

The risks involved in the military and sanctions options proved to be prohibitively high, however. On May 18, a military meeting was held in Washington, D.C. to prepare for possible war in Korea. On the next day, Defense Secretary Perry, Gen. John Shalikashvili, Chairman of the Joint Chiefs of Staff, and Gen. Gary Luck, Commander in Chief, U.S.–ROK Combined Forces Command, briefed President William Clinton on the results of the meeting. In the May 19 briefing, Shalikashvili reported that in a Korean conflict, the United States would have to send 400,000 troops, and there would be 30,000 U.S. casualties and

450,000 South Korean casualties. In addition, a Pentagon estimate suggested that the war would cost one million civilian casualties, more than $60 billion, and the damage to the South Korean economy would amount to more than one trillion dollars.[66]

Furthermore, no one present in the May 27 principals meeting thought sanctions would induce North Korea to comply with NPT obligations. They also could not entirely ignore North Korea's warning that sanctions would be regarded as a declaration of war.[67] If the United States was to mount a military strike against facilities in Nyongbyon, North Korea would at least take some form of violent retaliation, be it "instigating some incident along the DMZ, lobbing artillery shells at Seoul, or staging commando attacks with special forces and fifth columnists somewhere deep in South Korea." Such actions would likely result in further escalation.[68] South Korean President Kim Young Sam later wrote in his autobiography that if the United States had bombed North Korea, North Korea would certainly have attacked South Korea "with the enormous firepower it had deployed along the Military Demarcation Line."[69]

The Agreed Framework

The end of the crisis came suddenly and unexpectedly. During his unofficial visit to Pyongyang, former U.S. President Jimmy Carter agreed with Kim Il Sung on June 17 that North Korea would (a) freeze its nuclear development until the third round of the U.S.–DPRK talks, and (b) allow two IAEA inspectors set to be ousted from the country soon to stay in North Korea. In exchange, Carter promised that he would recommend the U.S. government support North Korea's acquisition of light-water reactors.[70]

To this, the U.S. government expressed on June 20 its willingness to hold bilateral talks if North Korea assured that it would not place new fuel rods in the 5-MW reactor, not reprocess the withdrawn spent fuel rods while the U.S.–DPRK talks were ongoing, and allow IAEA inspections necessary to maintain the continuity of the safeguards. The North Korean side responded positively to the offer on June 22. On the same day, Clinton announced that the United States was ready to hold a new round of talks with North Korea, and assured Pyongyang that the United States would suspend its efforts to pursue a sanctions resolution in the UNSC.[71] On June 27, the MFA declared that the third round of U.S.–DPRK talks would be held on July 8 in Geneva.[72]

On June 30, the U.S. government approved a proposal for a two-stage diplomatic solution to the crisis. In the six-month first stage, North Korea would have to meet international nonproliferation obligations, freeze all reactor constructions, ship the spent fuel abroad, and stop ballistic missile exports. In the meantime, the United States would provide non-nuclear energy assistance, allow liaison offices to be opened in each other's capitals, lift some economic sanctions, and assure Pyongyang that it would not launch a nuclear attack against North Korea. Then in the second stage, North Korea should reduce conventional forces, adhere to international agreements against ballistic missiles proliferation, ban the possession of chemical weapons, and improve human rights conditions. In return, the United States would have LWRs provided to North Korea, lift additional economic sanctions, exchange ambassadors, and hold visits by senior government official.[73]

On July 8, the first day of the third round of high-level U.S.–DPRK talks, an unforeseen event happened: Kim Il Sung died of a heart attack at the age of 82. The hermit kingdom was inherited by his son, Kim Jong Il. Although the younger Kim had already taken charge of most of the national policies, now the country was completely under his command. Significant and indicative of North Korea's future trajectory, North Korean policy survived Kim Il Sung's death without any tangible inconsistencies in its policy lines. On August 12, at the end of the third round of talks, the United States and North Korea issued an "Agreed Statement," which became the basis for the final deal on October 21.[74]

In the period leading up to the final settlement, the United States and North Korea were again engaged in psychological war with the threat of force and harsh rhetoric. On September 22, it was reported that Commander of U.S. Pacific Fleet Ronald Zlatoper had commented, "We certainly hope for a diplomatic settlement in the Korean situation. However … some very strong military force can influence diplomacy," and "that's why we're putting the carrier battle group up there off the Korean peninsula. I think it sends a very strong message."[75] At the time, the carrier battle group, consisting of the aircraft carrier USS *Kitty Hawk*, three cruisers, a frigate and two logistics ships, had been sent to the Sea of Japan.[76] On September 24, the MFA declared that if the United States continued making military threats, the DPRK would have no other way than to put an end to the temporary freeze of the nuclear development and proceed to resume "normal, peaceful nuclear development."[77] On September 25, Defense Secretary Perry warned that the United States would use "coercive diplomacy" if North Korea did not respect its nuclear commitments.[78] On September 27, the Ministry of People's Armed Forces (MPAF) accused the United States of "reckless and provocative words and deeds," and declared that if the Americans "rashly unleash another war on the Korean peninsula," they would "pay dearly for it with blood."[79]

However, apart from the harsh rhetoric, North Korea demonstrated a significant level of restraint in terms of military actions. Moreover, the U.S. military threats eventually proved to be ineffective or, possibly, counterproductive. The U.S. position was that the aircraft carrier was sent to the Sea of Japan merely on routine deployment.[80] The *Kitty Hawk* was subsequently withdrawn on October 3.[81] A U.S. State Department official complained that the feeling among the negotiating team was, "How can I negotiate when they [North Koreans] say, 'Send the carrier away,' and we send it away?"[82]

The outstanding issues had been settled by October 17. On October 21, the United States and the DPRK signed the Agreed Framework.[83]

Critical factors

North Korea's actual and potential nuclear capabilities

Despite economic difficulties, North Korea had invested a large amount of resources in its nuclear program. North Korean nuclear development had political and military implications on the local, regional and global stages, which the U.S. government took very seriously. William Perry wrote:

> ... in 1989, when the North Koreans unloaded some of the fuel rods from the operating [5-MW] reactor, they did so without IAEA supervision. ... The size of the reactor told us that if all the unloaded fuel had been reprocessed, the North Koreans could have enough plutonium to make one and possibly two atomic bombs.
>
> By the fall of 1993, the operating reactor was nearing completion of its initial fuel cycle, and its entire load of fuel rods would be ready for reprocessing in a few months. If all of this fuel were to be reprocessed, it would yield enough plutonium for another five or six nuclear weapons. Moreover, if the reactor were to move into full-scale operation, it could yield enough plutonium for ten or twelve nuclear bombs a year. When the larger [50-MW and 200-MW] reactors were completed, their total capacity would amount to scores of bombs per year.
>
> We believed that such a development would create intolerable risks. ... We took a much more serious view of this proliferation issue ... because of the tense military situation on the Korean Peninsula, North Korea's history of extreme behavior, and our concern that North Korea might sell some of this plutonium to rogue nations or terrorists to get desperately needed hard currency.[84]

These different capabilities at different levels of development enabled the North Koreans to exercise continuous and phased pressure on the concerned countries and organizations over an extended period of time.

North Korea's deterrent capabilities

North Korea's deterrent capabilities played an indispensable role in the execution of their nuclear diplomacy. While exercising nuclear coercion *vis-à-vis* the United States, North Korea had to deter possible preventive attacks by the United States. Also, North Korea had to avoid being coerced into abandoning its nuclear development without obtaining meaningful "compensation."

By June 1994 the United States had developed a plan to attack North Korean nuclear facilities. According to the plan, the United States could execute such an attack with little or no risk of U.S. casualties and a low risk of North Korean casualties, as well as a very low risk of radiation release into the atmosphere.[85]

Moreover, the overall conventional military balance had been shifting in favor of the U.S.–ROK side. In fact, the United States was confident of a military victory in case of war. Gary Luck assessed in June 1994 that North Korea could be defeated even if it used the one or two nuclear weapons it might have possessed.[86] Since North Korea's capability to defend its nuclear-related facilities against such a preventive attack was limited and it would not be able to prevail in all-out war, it had to rely on "deterrence by punishment," or deterrence attained by the threat of causing unbearable damage to the opponent. In this context, it is worth noting that when Kang Sok Ju announced the withdrawal from the NPT on April 12, 1993, he emphasized that North Korea was capable of rejecting any international pressure or sanctions with "solidarity among the leader, the Party, and the people," "strong independent national economy," and "powerful military forces."[87]

In fact, by the time North Korea embarked on its nuclear diplomacy, it had already been taking steps to deal with possible counter-coercion from the United States and South Korea. In the early 1990s, North Korea significantly enhanced its offensive capabilities through an "intensive five-year campaign" with a 1995 completion date. There were several important developments during this period.[88] The first and the most important development was the deployment of a large number of long-range artillery and multiple-rocket launchers along the DMZ, and in particular on the western front near Seoul. North Korea reinforced its artillery capabilities in the forward areas since 1993, first in the central and western areas, and then in the eastern area.[89] North Korea was capable of delivering artillery shells and rockets to Seoul, making the North Korean threat to turn Seoul into a "sea of fire" a credible one. Second, North Korea strengthened its chemical warfare capability as stockpiles of chemical agents in the North Korean inventory dramatically increased. These steps seemed to have made chemical weapons an integral part of North Korea's warfighting strategy. Third, North Korea test-launched Scud and No Dong missiles in the opening phase of its nuclear diplomacy. This suggested that now North Korea might be able to bring the war not only to anywhere on the peninsula but also to Japan. Finally, although North Korea had continued to reduce the size of its military exercises since 1989, they started to pick up again in late 1993.[90]

In addition, according to the South Korean Ministry of National Defense, North Korea designated October 1992 through July 1993 as a war preparation period and separately established a war preparation command which directed the expansion of the production and stockpiling of war materials as well as the strengthening of underground facilities. At the same time, North Korea extended the age of citizens mobilized in wartime from 40 to 45, encouraged students to enlist, and requested those who had been discharged to rejoin the armed forces.[91]

Also important was North Korea's residual defensive capabilities. North Korea's defensive capabilities created since 1962 under the "military lines of the Party" seemed to have been another factor that deterred the United States and

South Korea from attempting to execute a short and decisive war against North Korea. With its entire population armed and the entire country fortified, offensive operations into North Korea would not have been an easy mission.[92]

The most important reason why the United States and, in particular, South Korea wanted to avoid a serious military clash was not the fear that the U.S.–ROK side might be defeated militarily but the large number of casualties and damages that would be suffered even if the war was won. Based on the U.S.–ROK combined Operation Plan (OPLAN) 5027, which envisaged offensive operations deep into North Korea, an all-out war on the peninsula would have caused gigantic human, material, and financial damage. Although it is still not clear how confident the North Koreans were of their ability to repel the U.S.–ROK side's offensive into their territory, it was quite clear that they were confident of their capability to impose unbearable costs on the U.S.–ROK side. The North Korean deterrent worked quite effectively.

Limits of the Nuclear Nonproliferation Regime

Both the existence and limits of the nuclear nonproliferation regime helped North Korea's nuclear diplomacy. First, the existence of a nuclear nonproliferation regime, in this case the NPT, and North Korea's membership in it enabled the country to attract significant international attention by announcing its decision to withdraw. The symbolism of the NPT and its relatively successful history gave weight to North Korea's announcement to withdraw from the regime since it was the first in history.

Second, the NPT gave the North Koreans two unique opportunities to exercise pressure on the United States. Of particular importance was Article X, which allows for member states to withdraw from the treaty if absolutely necessary and defines that the withdrawal will take effect three months after notification. In addition, Article X provides that a conference shall be convened 25 years after the treaty went into force to decide whether it shall continue in force indefinitely or shall be extended for an additional fixed period. This 25th anniversary happened to be 1995.[93] Thus, Article X-1 enabled North Korea to threaten withdrawal and still have a three-month lead-time during which it could effectively negotiate with the United States. Quite apart from the original intention of the provision, the three-month provision worked as a deadline for the U.S. negotiators.[94] Furthermore, Article X-2 set an additional quasi-deadline for the U.S. negotiators. The United States, which regarded nuclear non-proliferation as one of the most important post-Cold War security issues, was making an effort to indefinitely extend the NPT at the NPT Extension and Review Conference scheduled for 1995. The NPT's inability to stop North Korean nuclear development would have posed a serious challenge to the U.S. effort. Given the significant contribution of the nuclear non-proliferation regime in the past, it is obviously unfair to say that the existence of the regime was counterproductive. It must be acknowledged, however, that in the face of a determined international outlaw like North Korea, the international regime also allowed for certain negative developments.

Finally, the inherent limitation of the IAEA to enforce the NPT and the safeguards agreement in case its members balked proved serious in the North Korean nuclear case. The IAEA ended up demonstrating that it relied heavily on the United States in terms of intelligence collection and enforcement when it had to deal with uncooperative members. Although the United Nations discussed the imposition of economic sanctions against North Korea, the United States actually led the coordination effort.

Lack of transparency

The lack of transparency in the North Korean system seemed to have helped its conduct of nuclear diplomacy and the North Koreans seemed to have tried to manipulate the perceived risk involved in the nuclear crises by taking advantage of this opacity. First, the lack of transparency in the North Korean political system worked to encourage U.S. decision-makers to take the North Korean threats seriously and hedge against negative scenarios. William Perry wrote that he and General Shalikashvili thought that an attack on North Korean nuclear sites was "very likely" to incite military attack on South Korea, and that it would be irresponsible to "shrug off" the North Korean threat that it would regard the imposition of sanctions as an act of war.[95]

Second, the effectiveness of the North Korean threats was further reinforced by the perceived lack of rationality of the North Korean leadership, particularly that of Kim Jong Il, due to past actions such as the 1983 bombing in Rangoon and the 1987 bombing of a Korean Airliner. As Denny Roy suggested, the North Koreans seemed to have used "madman" tactics in that they depicted themselves as irrational and dangerous in order to keep the other side on the defensive and put themselves in an advantageous position.[96]

Characteristics

Location and timing

The most important part of North Korean nuclear development took place in Nyongbyon and Taechon, both located about 100 kilometers north of Pyongyang. There were other facilities spread throughout the country, but none were as important as these two locations.

The critical phase of North Korean nuclear diplomacy lasted for one year and seven months. More broadly, the North Korean nuclear issue surfaced in 1986 when the United States discovered "cylindrical craters" believed to be the residue of experimental high-explosive detonations, near the nuclear complex in Nyongbyon.[97] The North Koreans unloaded some of the fuel rods from the 5-MW reactor in 1989, and reprocessed some of the spent fuel, recovering weapons-grade plutonium. This was followed, however, by relative inactivity in terms of further development.

When North Korea announced its withdrawal from the NPT in 1993, however, it came as a total surprise. Few in the world anticipated that North Korea would take such a dramatic step. When North Korea initiated its nuclear diplomacy, the international environment was extremely negative. In September 1990, the Soviet Union established diplomatic relations with South Korea. In August 1992, China followed suit. In November, North Korea–Japan normalization talks broke down. In January 1993, Russia informed North Korea that it would no longer honor the military clause in the bilateral Treaty of Friendship, Cooperation, and Mutual Assistance of 1961.[98]

The nuclear diplomacy started just after new presidents were inaugurated in the United States and South Korea. This timing seems to have had two effects. First, North Korea's announcement to withdraw from the NPT took the new administrations aback and enabled the North Koreans to take the initiative in the affair. Second, it gave the North Koreans plenty of time to play the game to the finish. The new U.S. administration had four years to go, and the new South Korean government had five.

Forces involved and the type of use of force

North Korea's nuclear diplomacy did not involve actual application of force. What was involved was North Korea's actual and potential nuclear capabilities as well as demonstrations of force including the declaration of a "state of readiness for war" and the testing of missiles. This case vividly demonstrated the significance of nuclear weapons, for even largely potential capabilities had a tremendous impact on the behavior of the target states.

Intensity and targeting

What is particularly noteworthy of North Korea's nuclear diplomacy was the fact that despite the crises in 1993 and 1994 no casualties or physical damages were inflicted on the U.S.–ROK side. This was a departure from previous decades when a large number of casualties were inflicted by North Korean actions.

Although no actual use of force took place, the military threat was issued primarily against South Korea, and in particular Seoul. The most vivid threat came in March 1994 when the head of the North Korean delegation talked about turning Seoul into a "sea of fire." Although verbal threats were made against the United States, no real military threat was made against it. This was probably because North Korea was not able to pose a direct military threat against the continental United States since it was simply too far away. Second, by mainly targeting the South Koreans, North Korea tried to drive a wedge between the United States and South Korea. Finally, in order to improve relations with the United States, it was better to avoid attacking Americans.

Military-diplomatic coordination

North Korea's nuclear diplomacy was the first long, complex, and sophisticated military-diplomatic campaign conducted by Pyongyang. Although North Korea had used force for diplomatic purposes even before 1993, past experiences were nowhere near the nuclear diplomacy of 1993–94 in terms of complexity and level of sophistication. It therefore seems likely that North Korea had already prepared a more or less concrete game plan for its nuclear diplomacy by the time it announced its withdrawal from the NPT in March 1993.

According to defected former North Korean diplomats, a task force named "*Haeg Sangmujo*," or Nuclear Management Team, was organized sometime around 1991, bringing together some 20 officials from the MFA, MPAF, Workers' Party, the General Bureau of Atomic Energy, and other security agencies. Headed by Kang Sok Ju and reporting directly to Kim Jong Il, this task force played a critical policymaking role regarding the nuclear diplomacy. Among the different actors, the MFA took the lead and Kang led the North Korean delegation throughout the period. The MPAF and the KPA played supporting roles by backing verbal threats issued by the MFA with words and actions. The General Bureau of Atomic Energy seemed to provide technical support to the MFA.[99] Significant knowledge of legal and technological issues related to nuclear issues was demonstrated in the process, suggesting that the different organizations within the North Korean government were working closely together. On the other hand, the nuclear weapons program was managed by the "131 *Jidogug*," or Guidance Bureau No. 131, which served Kim Jong Il and was directed by the Ministry of Machine Industry, bringing together the Committee for Second Economy, the General Bureau of Atomic Energy, and nuclear specialists in universities and research institutions.[100]

Assessment

On October 12, 1993, North Korea presented a list of its demands to the U.S. side. According to the list, North Korea demanded that the United States fulfill the following requirements:

(a) Conclusion of a peace agreement (or treaty) that includes legally binding assurances to the DPRK against the U.S. threat or use of nuclear weapons;
(b) Provision of LWRs;
(c) Complete normalization of diplomatic relations between the DPRK and the United States to ensure respect for each other's sovereignty and non-interference in each other's internal affairs; and
(d) The U.S. promise to take balanced policies toward North and South Korea for the purpose of peaceful reunification.[101]

It is quite significant that North Korea proposed these items, all but one of which were eventually included in the Agreed Framework, as early as October 1993.

Peace agreement and negative nuclear assurances

North Korea first proposed the conclusion of a bilateral peace agreement with the United States in 1974. It made the same proposal in 1984, but also concurrently suggested the conclusion of a non-aggression agreement with South Korea. North Korea proposed the conclusion of a U.S.–DPRK peace agreement in 1993 for the third time, but this time on the basis that a "non-aggression agreement" had already been concluded with South Korea as stipulated in 1991 under the Basic Agreement. The U.S. position that South Korea must be included in any peace arrangement negotiations did not change during the nuclear talks, however, and the United States did not accept even the mention of a peace agreement in the Agreed Framework. North Korea's renewed effort to pursue the conclusion of a U.S.–DPRK peace agreement was once again not successful.

Despite the failure to conclude a peace agreement, North Korea obtained "formal assurances" against the threat or use of nuclear weapons by the United States. The North Koreans regarded this provision as highly important. When they proposed the conclusion of "non-aggression treaty" with the United States in 2002, they reiterated the American obligation to "give formal assurances to the DPRK against the threat or use of nuclear weapons."[102] Credibility of the negative security assurances later proved to be questionable, however. In March 2002, it was reported that the United States had decided to consider developing earth-penetrating nuclear weapons to be used against nations armed with weapons of mass destruction, including North Korea.[103]

Provision of light-water reactors and heavy fuel oil

In the Agreed Framework, the United States pledged to undertake to make arrangements for the provision to the DPRK of a LWR project with a total generating capacity of approximately 2,000 MW(e) by a target date of 2003. In March 1995, the Korean Peninsula Energy Development Organization (KEDO) was established accordingly. KEDO was set to build two 1,000-MW LWRs in Kumho on the east coast of North Korea and held a groundbreaking ceremony in August 1997. The turnkey contract went into effect in February 2000.[104] The entire project lagged behind schedule, however, due partly to lack of North Korean cooperation. In 2000, the LWRs were estimated to be completed in 2008 instead of 2003. North Korea demanded compensation for the delay, but KEDO did not respond positively.[105] Finally, KEDO decided in May 2006 to terminate the LWR project in response to the reemergence of the nuclear issue. North Korea failed to obtain LWRs as a result.

Related to the provision of the LWRs was the provision of alternative energy. According to the Agreed Framework, heavy fuel oil (HFO) for heating and electricity production was to be provided to North Korea. In 1995, the United States provided 50,000 tons of HFO. After that, the United States provided 500,000 tons of HFO annually, though with delays in 1997 and 1998.[106] After the nuclear issue was reignited in October 2002, however, KEDO decided to suspend the delivery of HFO.[107]

By 2005, KEDO had obtained approximately $2.5 billion from supporting countries and organizations, of which about $1.6 billion was earmarked for the LWR project and about $395 million for HFO. The largest contributor was South Korea, with a total amount of $1.5 billion; the second largest was Japan, with $498 million; and the third largest was the United States, with $405 million.[108] North Korea did not receive the LWRs and the HFO free of charge, though. In exchange, North Korea froze its graphite-moderated reactors and related reprocessing facilities and was obliged to eventually dismantle them. Moreover, expenditure for the LWRs was provided as a loan and not a grant. North Korea was obliged to repay KEDO for each LWR plant in equal, semi-annual installments, free of interest, over a 20-year term after completion of each LWR plant, including a three-year grace period beginning upon completion of that LWR plant.[109]

Normalization of relations with the United States

The Agreed Framework provided that the United States and the DPRK would "move toward full normalization of political and economic relations." It specified that:

(a) both sides would reduce barriers to trade and investment, including restrictions on telecommunications services and financial transactions;
(b) each side would open a liaison office in the other's capital following resolution of consular and other technical issues through expert level discussions; and
(c) as progress was made on issues of concern to each side, the United States and the DPRK would upgrade bilateral relations to the Ambassadorial level.

On the first point, the United States eased some economic sanctions against North Korea in January 1995, permitting direct telecommunications services, contracts for U.S. companies to import magnesite from the DPRK, and licenses for American firms to provide humanitarian goods to the North.[110] These measures, however, did not do much for the North Korean economy. Additional lifting of sanctions came only in June 2000.

On the second point, the United States and North Korea failed to open a liaison office in each other's capitals. After the KPA shot down a U.S. Army helicopter which had inadvertently intruded into the North Korean territory in December 1994, it refused to allow American diplomats to transit through Panmunjom from Seoul as the United States requested. Also, the North Koreans wanted the liaison office and living quarters to be in the same building for security reasons, but Washington, D.C. law prevented such an arrangement. Moreover, they thought the rent for offices was too expensive and the Trading with the Enemy Act made it illegal for Korean-Americans to donate money to North Korea. As a result, the two countries later agreed that North Korea open its liaison office at its Mission to the United Nations in New York and the United States arrange for the Swedish embassy in Pyongyang to represent U.S. interests.[111] According to a defected North Korean diplomat, Kim Jong Il was actually indecisive on this matter and changed his mind several times before finally deciding not to open the liaison offices in each other's capitals.[112]

Finally, the U.S. designation of North Korea as a "state sponsor of terrorism" remained an obstacle in achieving full normalization of political and economic relations between the two countries. Unless North Korea was removed from the list of state sponsors of terrorism, substantial improvement in U.S.–DPRK relations would not be possible.

Straining U.S.–ROK Relations

North Korea's demand for the United States to take "balanced policies" toward North and South Korea was simply ignored. Given the existence of the U.S.–ROK alliance treaty and the U.S. military presence in South Korea, it was unrealistic to expect such a policy change. Nevertheless, North Korea's nuclear diplomacy did result in a deterioration of U.S.–ROK relations. Friction between the United States and South Korea was created by a combination of North Korean efforts to consistently communicate with the Americans and sideline the South Koreans, lack of leverage on the part of South Korea, and confusion within the Kim Young Sam Administration.

After North Korea announced its withdrawal from the NPT, the nuclear issue was negotiated primarily by the United States and North Korea. Although under U.S. pressure North Korea paid some lip service to South Korea and the IAEA, its engagement with each always lacked substance. Until the South Koreans agreed to finance the KEDO operations, they did not have any useful leverage.

Although South Korea sought a negotiated settlement of the issue, it was reluctant to see improvement in U.S. and North Korean relations with Seoul on the sidelines. Kenneth Quinones, a former U.S. Department of State official, argued that in February 1994 Kim Young Sam seemed to have been more interested in preventing further improvement in U.S.–DPRK relations than in solving the North Korean nuclear issue.[113] Also, the South Korean policy lacked consistency, fluctuating between "soft" and "tough" extremes. In the course of Pyongyang's nuclear diplomacy, Kim Young Sam proved to be a volatile and insecure leader, incapable of carrying out a consistent and cohesive policy toward the North. Worse yet, Kim tended to change his position according to the changes in public opinion in his country.[114] Quinones wrote that when tensions rose, Kim sought salvage from the U.S.–ROK alliance; however, when the tension subsided, he tried to regain initiative in dealing with North Korea.[115]

U.S.–ROK relations were further strained by the military crisis in 1994. Kim Young Sam wrote that he almost quarreled with Clinton. According to Kim's memoir, Clinton said that he did not rule out going to war with North Korea in order to alter its behavior. Kim responded by saying, "You are trying to fulfill your objectives by fighting war in our country. ... You would never be allowed to be bombing on our soil."[116] Kim thought that if the United States bombed Pyongyang, all the artillery deployed near the Military Demarcation Line would open fire and Seoul, Busan, Gwangju, and Jeju would suffer heavy bombardment.[117]

Suspending Team Spirit

The North Korean indignation about Team Spirit can be inferred from Kim Il Sung's private remarks to East German Premier Erich Honecker in 1984:

> When Team Spirit exercise is conducted, we go on alert nationwide, workers are mobilized to the armed forces and, therefore, productive activities are stopped for more than a month. Due to this damage, the year's agricultural production is seriously hampered. Due to this military pressure, our people are all dying.[118]

Moreover, in April 1998, commenting on the "war manoeuvres of the enemy," North Korea's official Korean Central News Agency put the "resumption of the Team Spirit 93 joint war exercises" in parallel with the *Pueblo* incident, the EC-121 incident, the "Panmunjom incident" (Axe Murder incident), and the "'nuclear inspection' racket."[119] This shows the significance that the North Koreans put on the suspension of Team Spirit, which has not been held since 1993. Nevertheless, North Korea has not been totally satisfied. In 1998, it started to take issue with the Ulchi-Focus Lens exercise, a joint and combined U.S.–ROK simulation-supported command post exercise.[120] It called the Ulchi-Focus Lens a "replica of the Team Spirit," or the "second Team Spirit."[121]

Consolidation of Kim Jong Il's position

By the time North Korea embarked on its nuclear diplomacy, Kim Jong Il's position within the North Korean military establishment had been consolidated. The nuclear crisis was then used to further strengthen his position. Efforts to formalize his position in the military began in earnest in May 1990 when Kim was elected Vice Chairman of the DPRK National Defence Commission, soon followed by his election to the position of Supreme Commander of the KPA in December 1991. Kim was bestowed with the title of Marshal of the DPRK in April 1992.[122] In February 1992, he had a conversation with workers of the Party Central Committee in which he stressed the importance of "fomenting the social character of strengthening the People's Army and emphasizing the military affairs."[123]

It was against this backdrop that Kim enunciated his plan for nuclear diplomacy by ordering the army and all civilians to be placed on a semi-wartime footing in March 1993. Once the crisis started, yet another important step was taken. On April 9, Kim Jong Il was elected chairman of the National Defence Commission.[124] According to the Constitution of the DPRK, partially revised in April 1992, the Chairman of the National Defence Commission was now entitled to command and direct all the armed forces.[125] Then on July 19, Kim Jong Il issued Supreme Commander Directive No. 0040, with which he promoted 85 KPA officers who had participated in the Korean War.[126]

North Korea's nuclear diplomacy might also have worked to divert people's attention away from domestic difficulties. Prior to the beginning of its nuclear diplomacy, there had been signs that the North Korean leadership had serious concerns about domestic stability. On March 1, just 11 days prior to the announcement of withdrawal from the NPT, Kim Jong Il reportedly said in his talk entitled, "Abuses of Socialism Are Intolerable":

> At a time when the imperialists and reactionaries are resorting to unprecedentedly vicious schemes against socialism, many misleading statements are being made about socialism. …
>
> This slander against socialism is absurd. But, it has caused ideological confusion among the people, mainly because they are not fully equipped with the socialist idea. …
>
> . … Our socialism is unshakable, whatever the storm. This is because the single-hearted unity of the leader, the Party and the people has been realized and the people are building a new life in conformity with their independent demands under the guidance of the Party and the leader.[127]

In March 1993, it was reported that there had been a coup attempt by the commander and about 30 officers of the KPA Seventh Infantry Division, but the attempt was detected by the State Security Department before it was actually implemented.[128] The economic situation was also difficult during this period. The communiqué released at the 21st Plenary Meeting of the Sixth Central Committee of the Workers' Party in December 1993 tacitly acknowledged that the Third Seven-Year Plan (1987–93) had failed as it designated the following two to three years as an adjustment period.[129]

Although it is hard to measure how effective the diversionary tactics and the domestic propaganda were in consolidating Kim Jong Il's position and alleviating domestic instability, they seem to have served as more help than harm. After the Agreed Framework was concluded, the North Korean authority started to use the nuclear episode to glorify Kim Jong Il and praise his ability. For instance, the book entitled, *Gen. Kim Jong Il's Policy of Giving Priority to the Army*, published in Pyongyang in 2000, contended:

People do not forget that when the United States threatened the North with "special inspections" and "collective sanctions" under an excuse of "suspected nuclear development" in early 1993, by declaring the state of war readiness and announcing the withdrawal from the NPT (Nuclear Nonproliferation Treaty), Gen. Kim Jong Il made the United States surrender and agree to come to the negotiating table, and thereby successfully obtained the DPRK–U.S. Agreed Framework and a letter of assurance from Clinton.[130]

Chapter 7

MISSILE DIPLOMACY, 1998–2000

In the 1990s, North Korea used its missile capabilities and exports as diplomatic tools, first implicitly but then explicitly. When it launched the Taepo Dong missile in August 1998, missiles became a focus of attention in U.S.–DPRK talks, and in 1999 the United States undertook a major review of its policy toward North Korea.[1] The new policy called for a comprehensive approach to relations with Pyongyang and as a result the United States and North Korea took significant steps for normalization toward the end of 2000. Nevertheless, U.S. President William Clinton announced his decision not to visit Pyongyang in December 2000. North Korea's missile diplomacy ultimately failed to produce a diplomatic breakthrough.

Missile exports, flight-testing, and talks

Early signs of missile diplomacy[2]

At first, missile diplomacy was not a North Korean creation. Diplomatic deals based on missile development were first sought by the Israelis, who approached the North Koreans in 1992 in order to stop their missile-related exports to Arab countries in the Middle East and Iran. Israeli officials reportedly visited Pyongyang in 1992 and offered a deal whereby Israel would provide economic assistance to North Korea in return for its suspension of missile sales.[3] Also in 1993, an Israeli official met multiple times with North Korean officials in Beijing to prevent a reported North Korea–Iran deal of 150 No Dong missiles for oil and cash. The North Koreans demanded that the Israelis provide them with cash for compliance. The Israeli effort thus continued into 1994, but then the United States demanded that the Israel–North Korea missile talks stop.[4]

Although no successful deal was reached, the Israel–North Korea talks on missiles might well have been a learning experience for the North Korean policymakers. It was later reported that Israel had offered a package worth an estimated one billion dollars, which included buying a North Korean gold mine and supplying thousands of trucks in return for the cessation of missile exports to the countries in the Middle East.[5]

Missiles for influence

No Dong and Scud flight-tests[6]

North Korea showed the first signs of using missiles as a diplomatic tool in 1993. On May 29–30, it test-launched three Scud missiles and one indigenously designed medium-range No Dong missile in its most extensive flight-testing program ever. Present at the test site were Iranian and Pakistani observers.[7] At the time, North Korea was under pressure from the international community since it had announced its withdrawal from the Treaty on the Non-Proliferation of Nuclear Weapons (NPT) just two months earlier. U.S.–DPRK bilateral talks began shortly after the missile tests, and the first-ever joint statement between the two countries was announced on June 11. Although it seems that the missile tests did not have much impact on the U.S.–DPRK talks, it is reasonable to think that the North Koreans had diplomatic considerations in addition to other technological and monetary considerations in mind when they decided to conduct missile tests.

Preparations for a No Dong flight-test

In May 1994, there were indications that North Korea was preparing for flight-testing a No Dong missile.[8] On May 31 and June 2, North Korea actually test-fired anti-ship missiles in the Sea of Japan.[9] On June 14, North Korea conducted a burn test of an engine thought to be for the Taepo Dong missile.[10] On June 9, North Korean Foreign Minister Kim Yong Nam remarked that North Korea would continue missile testing, adding that they had the will and sufficient capability to defend itself from sanctions. He further stated:

> Missile launches occur in any country regularly, and the United States and Japan do this most often. Until now no one ever mentioned anything about our launches of experimental missiles. We do not understand why there is so much noise about it now.[11]

During this period, North Korea's steps toward nuclear development were creating a major crisis. It was under such circumstances that preparations for the flight-testing of the No Dong missile were initiated and eventually cancelled. These developments suggest that North Korea used the possible flight-test of the No Dong as part of its brinksmanship strategy, later deciding to use reduce tensions by canceling the flight test.

Diplomacy sets in: U.S.–DPRK missile talks

Once the nuclear issue was settled, the United States started to pay more attention to the missile issue, making it one of the most important agenda items in U.S.–DPRK relations. In early 1995, a U.S. State Department team visited North Korea and proposed that U.S.–DPRK missile talks begin February 20 in Beijing.[12] In the meantime, North Korea reportedly started selling No Dong technology to Iran.[13] In January 1996, Thomas Hubbard, Deputy Assistant Secretary of State for East Asian Affairs, once again proposed talks to discuss missile proliferation issues. The North Korean side demanded that economic sanctions be eased before a date and venue for the talks were scheduled. It subsequently accepted the U.S. proposal, partly in response to the U.S. decision to provide emergency food aid to the country.[14]

The first round

The first round of missile talks took place in Berlin in April 1996. Robert Einhorn, Deputy Assistant Secretary for Nonproliferation in the State Department's Political-Military Affairs Bureau, and Ri Hyong Chol, Director of the DPRK Foreign Ministry's U.S. Affairs Department, led the talks. The U.S. side saw the talks as an effort to bring North Korea into the international system of nonproliferation agreements, an outgrowth of the Agreed Framework.[15]

During the talks, the U.S. side gave the North Korean delegation a tutorial on the Missile Technology Control Regime (MTCR) and expressed its willingness to lift sanctions if North Korea agreed to terminate its missile production and export programs.[16] After the talks, the U.S. side described the talks as useful;[17] the North Korean side affirmed that the talks would continue.[18]

Shortly after the talks, however, the United States imposed sanctions on North Korea's Changgwang Sinyong Corporation. In June, the Korean Central News Agency (KCNA) reported that the media in Western countries, including the United States, were lambasting the DPRK for exporting missiles to countries in the Middle East even though the DPRK was holding talks to address this issue.[19] The momentum that had been building seemed under threat.

Preparations for the missile flight-test

In September 1996, a North Korean special operations submarine was found aground off the South Korean east coast. South Korean President Kim Young Sam reacted strongly,[20] suspending South Korea's participation in the Korean Peninsula Energy Development Organization (KEDO) and thus delaying progress on the light-water reactor (LWR) project.[21] Under tense circumstances, North Korea began preparations for a No Dong missile flight-test.[22] The United States informed the North Korean side that it would strongly oppose a missile test.[23] On October 23, the North Korean Ministry of Foreign Affairs (MFA) issued a statement of defiance.[24]

Despite the statement, however, North Korea eventually cancelled the missile test. The cancellation seemed to have been related to ongoing U.S.–DPRK talks during that period. North Korea indicated its concern over what had been discussed during U.S.–ROK meetings when Winston Lord, Assistant Secretary of State for East Asian and Pacific Affairs, visited Seoul in October. The MFA denounced the United States for letting the South Koreans to delay the LWR project. It also said that the United States was trying to use the submarine incident as a bargaining chip by associating it with the implementation of the Agreed Framework.[25] When it was reaffirmed in subsequent U.S.–DPRK talks that the United States remained committed to the Agreed Framework, the MFA expressed its satisfaction in early November.[26] Five days later, the U.S. Department of State announced that the North Korean missile test had been cancelled.[27]

The second round

The second round of U.S.–DPRK missile talks was held in New York in June 1997. The United States demanded that North Korea not deploy No Dong missiles and end the sales of Scud missiles and their components. North Korea did not respond positively and the talks ended without any meaningful results.[28] Also, it canceled the third round of talks scheduled for August after the North Korean ambassador to Egypt defected to the United States.[29] In August, the United States imposed sanctions on two additional North Korean firms – the Korea Pugang Trading Corporation and the Lyongaksan General Trading Corporation – for missile-proliferation activities. As a result, the missile talks stagnated.

Full-fledged missile diplomacy

It was only in March 1998, just after the Kim Dae Jung administration came into office, that the United States and North Korea agreed to resume missile talks, with North Korea showing a positive attitude. In these talks, North Korea started to explicitly demonstrate its willingness to use missiles as a diplomatic bargaining chip. On June 16, the KCNA broadcast a commentary:

> The discontinuation of our missile development is a matter which can be discussed after a peace agreement is signed between the DPRK and the United States. ... Our missile export is aimed at obtaining foreign money we need at present. As the United States has pursued economic isolation of the DPRK for more than half a century, our resources of foreign money have been circumscribed. So, missile export is the option we could not but take. If the United States really wants to prevent our missile export, it should lift the economic embargo as early as possible and make a compensation for the losses to be caused by discontinued missile export.[30]

In August, Vice Foreign Minister Kim Kye Gwan told a U.S. Congressional delegation visiting Pyongyang that North Korea would stop exporting missiles if the United States agreed to pay $500 million every year as compensation.[31] Behind these moves might have been an expectation that the benefit from the missile sales would likely stagnate now that North Korea had already sold much of what it could sell to the major trading partners like Syria, Iran, and Pakistan.[32] Or it might have been that North Korea desperately wanted hard currency because of its serious domestic economic crisis.

Underground site at Kumchangri

While missiles were emerging as the next big issue to be discussed between the United States and North Korea, the nuclear issue came back to center. In August 1998, the *New York Times* reported that U.S. intelligence agencies had detected a huge secret underground complex related to nuclear development in Kumchangri, 40 kilometers northeast of Nyongbyon.[33] This site was thought to house a new nuclear reactor or a reprocessing plant.

The discovery of the underground site quickly became a major issue. In U.S.–DPRK talks held between August 21 and September 5 in New York, the U.S. side, led by Charles Kartman, U.S. Special Envoy for the Korean Peace Talks, probed the North Korean side, led by Kim Kye Gwan, DPRK Vice Foreign Minister, in order to find out the nature of North Korean underground construction activities. Kartman informed the North Korean side that verbal assurances would not suffice to meet U.S. concerns.[34] With this, the missile issue was now bundled with the nuclear issue.

Launching the Taepo Dong 1

To the surprise of many, on August 31, 1998, North Korea launched a missile based on the Taepo Dong 1. Japan was shocked because part of the missile flew over its main island. The United States was shocked because it came at a time when they were engaging in talks with North Korea. The flight-test proved that the North Korean missile program was much more advanced than the U.S. intelligence community had previously estimated, proving that the Taepo Dong could enter a third stage, fueled by solid fuel, that would extend the range of the missile significantly.[35] Although the third stage exploded in the flight, its debris traveled to a point approximately 4,000 kilometers away from the launching pad. It suggested that North Korea might be capable of delivering a small chemical or biological warhead to the continental United States with the longer-range Taepo Dong 2 if it was equipped with a hard fuel-propelled third stage.[36] Arguably, the South Koreans were the least affected by the missile launch because they had already been under direct threat from Scud missiles which could reach the entirety of their territory. Nevertheless, the missile launch had the potential of frustrating Kim Dae Jung's accommodative engagement or sunshine policy toward North Korea, which was initiated just several months prior to the missile launch.

The Japanese government, faced with a missile launch over its territory without prior notification, lodged a strong protest against North Korea and took measures including suspension of Japan's financial contribution to KEDO.[37] Despite their verbal condemnation of the missile launch, however, the United States and South Korea did not take meaningful punitive measures. By the time of the Taepo Dong launch, the United States and South Korea had already agreed on implementing the sunshine policy toward North Korea and had reaffirmed that KEDO was central to such a policy. Because of this, Japan's strong reaction was regarded as unhelpful.[38] Under pressure from the two friends, the Japanese government agreed to resume its financial contribution to KEDO on October 21.[39]

After the Taepo Dong launch, North Korea made it even clearer that it was set on its missile diplomacy. For example, an article in the *Rodong Sinmun* stated that the world opinion evaluated that the development of the satellite launch vehicle was equivalent to the "development of the intercontinental ballistic missile," suggesting that the North Koreans understood the military implications of launching such a rocket.[40] Another article in the *Rodong Sinmun* reported that building a launching pad and facilities related to the control of and communication with the satellite was estimated to cost more than $300 million.[41] Finally, another commentary issued a blunt threat, contending, "Whether the DPRK's launch of artificial satellite is used for military purposes or not entirely depends on the attitude of the U.S. and other hostile forces."[42]

For the Clinton administration, the Taepo Dong test was politically significant for two reasons. First, the test could undermine Congressional support for the administration's North Korea policy, making it difficult to fund KEDO and sustain the Agreed Framework. Second, the test shifted the debate on missile defense in favor of those who argued for early development and deployment of a national missile defense, to which the administration was opposed. The missile test therefore encouraged the administration to address the missile issue more seriously.[43]

Talks in New York

The August missile launch came at a time when U.S.–DPRK talks were underway in New York. Despite intelligence reports that North Korea was preparing for the flight-testing, Washington assumed that the missile would not be launched while the U.S.–DPRK talks were taking place. The psychological shock to the U.S. side was thus remarkable. In early September, there were indications that North Korea was preparing to flight-test a Scud or No Dong missile on its east coast.[44] North Korea was trying to put continued pressure on the United States.

Despite the Taepo Dong launch, U.S.–DPRK talks in New York proved to be successful. In these talks, the two sides discussed the complex in Kumchangri and agreed to abide by the Agreed Framework. The United States reaffirmed that it would make every effort to construct the LWRs according to schedule and provide heavy fuel oil to North Korea on time. Also, North Koreans reportedly demanded one billion dollars in exchange for suspension of its missile exports.[45] In addition to the nuclear talks, the two countries agreed to resume talks on missiles and on North Korea's inclusion the U.S. list of state-sponsors of terror- ism.[46] In other words, the United States and North Korea agreed to discuss all relevant issues in a comprehensive manner. The Taepo Dong launch worked as a catalyst, giving new momentum.[47] On September 21, the U.S. government announced its decision to contribute an additional 300,000 metric tons of wheat in response to the World Food Programme (WFP) appeal for food assistance to North Korea.[48]

The third round

The third round of U.S.–DPRK missile talks was held in New York in October. At these talks, the Americans made it clear to the North Korean side that further launches of long-range missiles or further exports of such missiles would have "very negative consequences" for U.S.–DPRK relations.[49] The United States also hinted at substantial loosening of economic sanctions against North Korea if North Korea stopped flight-testing, reduced exports, and gradually halted domestic production and development of the missiles in excess of the MTCR threshold. The North Korean side decided to play hardball and rejected the U.S. proposal, contending that the United States had already promised to loosen sanctions as part of the Agreed Framework.[50]

Preparing the Taepo Dong

In November, activities seemingly related to Taepo Dong missile flight-testing, such as construction of launch facilities and bunkers to store the missiles, started once again.[51] Concurrently, on December 2, the KPA General Staff issued a statement:

> It must be clearly known that there is no limit to the strike of our People's Army and that on this planet there is no room for escaping the strike. It must also be realized that the target of our strike in the war is not only the U.S. imperialist aggression forces who chiefly execute the "Operation Plan 5027" but also the South Korean puppets who are willing to serve as their bullet-shield and Japan and all others that offer bases or act [as] servants behind the scenes.[52]

123

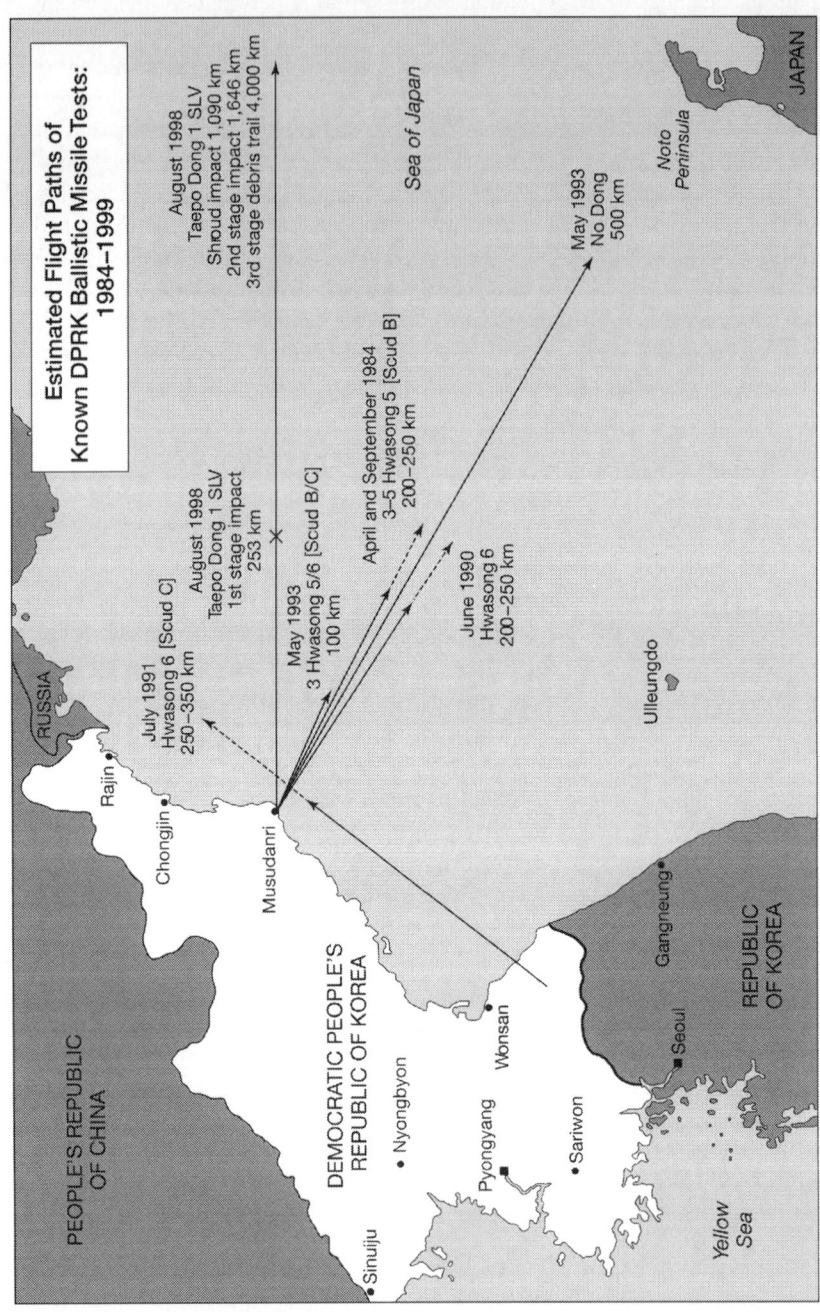

Map 7.1 Estimated flight paths of known DPRK ballistic missile tests
Source: Joseph S. Bermudez, "Estimated Flight Paths of Known DPRK Ballistic Missile Tests: 1984–99," obtained from and reprinted with permission of the copyright holder.

On December 9, North Korea suggested that the rocket development was part of its peaceful satellite program, adding that it could be re-launched anytime.[53] On the same day, it was reported that North Korea was moving parts of a missile from storage to a launch pad; estimates suggested that North Korea might launch another Taepo Dong 1 missile in December.[54]

At the same time, however, North Korea sent signals that it wanted to improve U.S.–DPRK relations. For example, a *Rodong Sinmun* commentary on December 18 stated that whether the "artificial satellite" would be launched and whether it would be used for military purposes depended on the attitude of the United States.[55] The United States issued warnings against a missile launch but continued talks with North Korea.[56] It was reported on December 31 that a U.S. intelligence official had concluded that the missile launch had been postponed.[57]

The fourth round

In the fourth round of U.S.–DPRK missile talks held in Pyongyang in March 1999, the North Koreans demanded that the United States provide one billion dollars each year for three years as compensation for stopping missile exports.[58] The U.S. side made it clear that the United States was not prepared to compensate North Korea for "stopping destabilizing missile sales it should not be making in the first place."[59]

Visiting Kumchangri

As bilateral talks continued into December 1998, North Korea dropped its demand for monetary compensation for allowing the U.S. to inspect the underground site at Kumchangri and started to demand food aid instead.[60] U.S.–DPRK talks were held between February 27 and March 15, 1999. As a result, North Korea agreed to invite a U.S. delegation for an initial visit to Kumchangri in May to be followed by subsequent visits to assuage U.S. concerns about the site's future use. In return, the United States agreed to take a step to improve political and economic relations between the two countries.[61] In April, the United States and North Korea reached an agreement on the details of a potato production project in North Korea. This agreement was significant in that this project represented the first bilateral U.S. assistance to the DPRK in history.[62]

In May, the U.S. team visited Kumchangri.[63] Based on the visit, the Department of State concluded in late June that the site at Kumchangri did not contain a plutonium production reactor or reprocessing plant and that the site was unsuitable for the installation of a plutonium production reactor or a reprocessing plant.[64]

Assuming a higher profile

The Perry Process

In the latter half of 1998, the U.S. government agreed that the policy toward North Korea needed a fundamental review in light of the suspicious Kumchangri site and the Taepo Dong missile launch. In this context, President Clinton named former Defense Secretary William Perry as the administration's North Korea Policy Coordinator in November 1998.[65] In close coordination with South Korean and Japanese officials, Perry drafted the "Review of United States Policy Toward North Korea," or so-called "Perry Report," and submitted it to the President and the Congress in September 1999.[66]

The report argued that the United States should not deal with nuclear and missile matters separately but instead should take a "comprehensive and inte-grated approach" toward both issues, pursuing a two-path strategy of "normal-ization" and "containment." In normalization, North Korea would: (a) assure that it did not have a nuclear weapons program; (b) stop the development, production, and deployment of missiles that exceeded the restrictions of the MTCR; and (c) cease exporting missiles, missile components, and related technology outside as stipulated by MTCR restrictions. The United States in return would strive to normalize economic and diplomatic relations with North Korea. If North Korea failed to pursue such relations with the United States, the latter would pursue containment instead.

Prior to the submission of the report, Perry visited Pyongyang in May 1999 and formally presented this new comprehensive package proposal to North Korea. It was a package of "incentives and disincentives," of "carrots and sticks," rather than a unilateral concession by the United States to North Korea. However, it was designed to be "attractive enough" for the North Koreans to respond positively.[67]

Taepo Dong 2 preparations[68]

In May 1999, North Korea resumed preparations for a flight-test of the Taepo Dong 2 missile. North Korea also conducted engine-burning and fueling tests.[69] In response to Perry's suggestion in May, North Korea had proposed a possible moratorium on missile flight-testing for the first time in the U.S.–DPRK talks in June.[70] By then, missile issues had become a major agenda item in the U.S.–DPRK relationship.[71] In other words, North Korea succeeded in enhancing the utility of the missile issue as an important diplomatic bargaining chip in its efforts to improve overall relations with the United States. Even after the June talks, though, North Korea continued the test preparations. By July, the launch-ing pad was almost complete. By early August, a Taepo Dong 2 missile had been assembled and stored in a site near the launching pad, just as another round of U.S.–DPRK talks convened in Geneva. In September, a National Intelligence

Council report assessed that North Korea was much more likely to weaponize the more capable Taepo Dong-2 than the three-stage Taepo Dong 1 as an intercontinental ballistic missile (ICBM).[72]

Freezing the test

North Korea's missile diplomacy bore fruit in September. In the U.S.–DPRK talks in Berlin, North Korea tacitly agreed to continue to refrain from testing long-range missiles while the United States and North Korea moved toward more normal relations.[73] In return, President Clinton announced his decision to unilaterally ease some sanctions against North Korea administered under the Trading With the Enemy Act, Defense Production Act, and the Department of Commerce's Export Administration Regulations.[74] On September 24, the DPRK formally announced that it would not launch missiles while talks with the United States were under way.[75]

Steps to fundamentally improve U.S.–DPRK relations

The United States and North Korea took steady steps toward normalization. On June 19, 2000, the United States announced it would substantially ease sanctions based on the September 1999 decision.[76] In July, the fifth round of the U.S.–DPRK missile talks was held in Kuala Lumpur.[77] Without talks at a higher level, however, it was impossible to substantially improve bilateral relations. After Perry visited Pyongyang in May 1999, the United States requested North Korea to dispatch a high-ranking official to Washington. North Korea did not respond, and the normalization process started to lose momentum.

Shortly thereafter, on October 9–12, Vice Chairman of the DPRK National Defence Commission (NDC) and Vice Marshal of the KPA Jo Myong Rok, visited the United States as a special envoy of Kim Jong Il, meeting with President Clinton, Secretary of State Madeleine Albright, and Secretary of Defense William Cohen. As a result of this visit, the two sides issued the U.S.–DPRK Joint Communiqué. In the Communiqué, the United States and DPRK agreed that resolution of the missile issue would make "an essential contribution to a fundamentally improved relationship. ..."[78]

In the meantime, both sides took an important step toward eliminating yet another obstacle in improving bilateral relations, issuing the Joint Statement on International Terrorism on October 6. In this Statement, North Korea affirmed that it opposed all forms of terrorism against any country or individual. In return, the United States noted that it would work toward removing North Korea from the list of state sponsors of terrorism if it satisfactorily addressed the requirements stipulated by U.S. law.[79]

Another major milestone came later that month, when Albright visited North Korea on October 23–24. The objective of the visit was to "convey directly to Chairman Kim Jong Il the views of President Clinton and to prepare for a possible visit by the President to the DPRK." During the official visit, Kim told Albright that the Taepo Dong launch in 1998 was North Korea's first and last satellite launch. Kim and Albright also discussed Kim's suggestion for the United States to sponsor satellites launches for North Korean use so that North Korea would not further its indigenous missile testing.[80]

During the Albright–Kim meetings, Kim (a) promised not to produce, test, or deploy missiles with a range of more than 500 kilometers, (b) offered to halt all missile exports, and (c) dropped the previous demand for cash, asking instead for one billion dollars worth of non-monetary assistance such as food or coal.[81] After these talks, however, several important issues remained unresolved, such as the issue of verification, the question of missiles already deployed, and the value of the non-monetary aid that North Korea should receive.[82]

Following the ministerial-level meeting, the sixth round of missile talks was held in November. During these talks, the U.S. delegation demanded that the North Korean side: (a) ban the production, testing, and deployment of all missiles with a range of over 300 kilometers that could carry a 500-kilogram payload; (b) accept verification measures, including a declaration of the numbers and types of missiles in its inventory; and (c) make a commitment to destroy its existing stocks.[83] In addition, the delegations explored in depth the idea of trading North Korean restraint on missile-related activities for U.S.-sponsored satellite launches for North Korea.[84] To this, North Korean delegates acknowledged that Kim's freeze proposal covered No Dong and Taepo Dong missiles, but they did not accept the freeze as applying to their Scud variants. They argued privately that limits on Scud forces could be considered only in the context of broader security issues. Also privately, they suggested that they could consider gradual elimination of No Dong and Taepo Dong missiles over an extended period of time in return for unspecified "compensation." On verification, the North Koreans agreed to establish cooperative mechanisms, but the details of these mechanisms were ostensibly left out. Finally, the North Koreans accepted food or oil as a means of "compensation," but the amount and nature of the "compensation" to be provided were not agreed upon.[85]

Despite all these talks and preparatory visits, the United States and North Korea failed to produce concrete results. On December 28, Clinton announced that he would not visit North Korea. North Korea's missile diplomacy came to a crashing halt.[86]

Critical factors

North Korea's ballistic missile capabilities[87]

North Korea's indigenous missile development dates back to the 1970s, but it wasn't until the early 1980s that the North Korean program found its stride.[88] North Korea's ballistic missiles, either existing or under development, fall largely into three categories: (a) Scud series; (b) No Dong series; and (c) Taepo

Dong series. Development of the Scud B missile began in earnest in the early 1980s, but its full-scale production didn't start until 1986. In the late 1980s, the North Korean leadership came up with specific requirements for its future missile programs based on the distance to the potential targets. On this basis, the No Dong and the Taepo Dong were developed. The Scud C had an extended range of 550 kilometers with a reduced payload of 770 kilograms and better accuracy thanks to an improved inertial guidance system.[89] Its first successful flight-test took place in June 1990. In 2000, the U.S. Forces Korea estimated that North Korea had more than 500 Scud missiles in its inventory.[90] The development of a No Dong capable of reaching major cities in Japan, including Tokyo, started in 1988.[91] The No Dong could fly 1,300 kilometers with a payload of 1,000 kilograms, carrying high explosive, cluster, chemical, and possibly nuclear and biological warheads. No Dong, like Scud, could be deployed on transporter-erector-launchers (TEL) and was thus hard to detect and destroy, as the great Scud hunt during the Gulf War demonstrated.[92] In 1999, North Korea was estimated to have 50–100 No Dong missiles in its inventory.[93]

The development of North Korea's first two-stage Taepo Dong missile began in the early 1990s. Its mockups were first identified in 1994. The Taepo Dong 1 was estimated to have a payload of 1,000 kilograms and a range of over 1,500 kilometers, which meant that it could reach almost all of Japan, including Okinawa. The Taepo Dong 2 had an estimated range of 3,500–6,000 kilometers with a 1,000-kilogram warhead. If completed, this missile could reach the Aleutian Islands (4,500 kilometers) and Alaska (5,000 kilometers).[94] In February 1999, the Director of Central Intelligence testified that with a third stage the Taepo Dong 2 would be able to deliver large payloads to the rest of the United States.[95] North Korea was estimated to have produced one to 10 Taepo Dong 1 and one or two Taepo Dong 2 prototypes by the end of 1999. Also, the U.S. Central Intelligence Agency estimated in 2000 that North Korea could build up to several Taepo Dong 2 missiles by 2005.[96] In the 1990s alone, North Korea successfully test-launched a medium-range No Dong and Taepo Dong 1 and was ready to test a Taepo Dong 2.[97]

The pace at which the North Korea expanded the variety and range of its missiles was impressive. Nevertheless, the U.S. intelligence community's estimates regarding North Korean missile developments were relatively low-key. The Department of Defense pointed out in 1997 that North Korea had no experience of testing multistage ballistic missiles or other related technologies, and noted that Taepo Dong missiles represented a significant technological departure from the proven Scud designs. The Department of Defense report thus concluded that this lack of test experience could complicate North Korea's ability to evaluate, improve, or repair flaws in its missile designs.[98] The impressive speed of North Korea's missile developments, combined with the relatively low-key estimates by leading intelligence agencies, helped enhance the psychological shock following the North Korean missile test. The only report which stood out as alarmist before the missile test was issued by the Commission to Assess the Ballistic Missile Threat to the United States, commonly referred to as the "Rumsfeld Commission," released in July 1998, just one and a half months before the Taepo Dong 1 launch.

International connections

By the end of the 1980s, North Korea had become one of the most active missile-exporting countries in the world, exporting not only missiles but also missile technology and missile-related facilities. North Korea and Iran concluded a $500-million missile contract in 1987, with North Korea exporting approximately 90–100 Scud B missiles and providing assistance to establish a missile assembly during the Iran–Iraq War.[99] The South Korean Ministry of Unification estimated in 1996 that North Korea produced approximately 100 Scud missiles annually, and had exported approximately 400 missiles to Iran and Syria. Arms exports accounted for more than 30 percent of the country's $20.4 billion in exports from 1980 to 1993.[100] In 2000, the U.S. government assessed that in the past 10 years, North Korea had received more than one billion dollars' worth of bartered goods and services and hard currency for its Scud missiles and production technology.[101] According to the U.S. Forces Korea, by early 2001, North Korea had exported at least 450 missiles to Iran, Iraq, Syria, Pakistan, and other countries.[102] Yet another source estimated that North Korea sold at least 540 missiles to countries like Iran, Iraq, Libya, and Egypt between 1985 and 2000. Among them were 50 No Dong missiles sold to Libya. Scuds were sold at $2–2.5 million dollars per unit and No Dongs were sold at about $7 million a unit.[103] Figures vary, but one thing was clear: missile exports constituted a significant part of North Korea's income.

Through international cooperation, Pakistan and Iran developed missile systems based on North Korea's No Dong. In April 1998, Pakistan flight-tested its *Ghauri* missile and in July Iran test-launched its *Shahab* 3, both based on No Dong technology. There was also a report that North Korea offered Taepo Dong 1 missiles to countries like Egypt, Libya, and Syria at $6 million a unit.[104] North Korean missile-related exports and technological cooperation were so extensive that they became a major international security concern. William Perry succinctly summarized the significance of the North Korean missile program coupled with nuclear, biological, and chemical capabilities when he wrote:

> The North's missiles are increasing in range. The so-called No Dong missile could reach Japan, and the so-called Taepo Dong could probably reach parts of the United States. With only high explosive warheads, such missiles pose a negligible military risk, but in tandem with a nuclear weapons program, they become a deadly threat.[105]

Characteristics

Location and timing

Most of North Korea's missile development efforts took place inside North Korean territory and all of its missile launches originated from within North Korea. All the ballistic missile flight-tests during this period took place on the east coast.

North Korea demonstrated its missile capabilities in several different forms, such as flight-tests and engine-burning tests. The most effective form was flight-testing. Missile flight-testing is a critical step in the process of any missile development and, therefore, had significant military, technological, and diplomatic implications. This was particularly true in the case of North Korea since Pyongyang tended to start deploying missiles after only one or two flight-tests. The Rumsfeld Commission Report asserted:

> North Korea's decision to deploy the No Dong after what is believed to be a single successful test flight is another example [of unexpected development patterns]. Based on U.S. and Russian experience, the Intelligence Community had expected that a regular test series would be required to provide the confidence needed before any country would produce and deploy a ballistic missile system. Yet North Korea deployed the No Dong.[106]

North Korea's nuclear diplomacy and missile diplomacy had chronological continuity. It was only four months after North Korea concluded the Supply Agreement with KEDO that North Korea held the first bilateral talks on missiles with the United States in 1996. However, this continuity arose more from the U.S. policy imperative than from North Korea.

It's important to note, however, that North Korea's missile-related activities were not driven solely by diplomatic considerations. Missile flight-testing also had much to do with technological and/or other imperatives such as the need to earn foreign currency, as well. For instance, even before the May 1993 No Dong launch, North Korea had already attempted flight-testing the No Dong on three occasions – in May 1990, November 1990, and June 1992 – without success. The need to generally improve military capabilities must have also played a role. However, taking into account the timing and the manner in which the missile tests were prepared, executed, or cancelled, it is clear that diplomatic needs were one of the critical factors that determined North Korea's missile-related activities.

Forces involved and the type of use of force

The May 1993 flight-test involved four missiles, by then the largest number of missiles launched on a single occasion. The Taepo Dong 1 missile launch took place without accompanying flight-tests, although there were signs that North Korea

131

was preparing additional missiles as well. On each occasion, there was no indication that North Korean armed forces were put on high alert.

In its missile diplomacy, North Korea demonstrated its missile capabilities by flight-testing them, in contrast to its nuclear diplomacy in 1993–94 in which it did not explode a nuclear device. This divergence might be due to North Korea's inability to actually explode a nuclear device, hesitation to waste the small amount of extracted plutonium it possessed, or an assessment that such a test might be counterproductive.

In its missile diplomacy, North Korea's deterrent capability did not matter too much because no punitive or preventive military and economic measures were seriously contemplated by other countries, especially the United States. Learning from the nuclear crises in the 1990s, by 1998 concerned countries had come to understand how difficult it was to take punitive or preventive measures against North Korea. As a result, positive incentives were preferred to negative ones.

Intensity and targeting

Missile flight-testing and other missile-related activities caused no physical damage or casualties despite the harsh rhetoric that the North Koreans sometimes employed. The apparent potential targets in the No Dong and Taepo Dong missile flight-tests were Japan and the United States. The No Dong missile flew in the direction of Tokyo. The Taepo Dong 1 flew over the Japanese main island in the direction of Hawaii. However, it is hard to tell whether Hawaii was a target because the flight path to the east was technically consistent with North Korea's contention that it was launching an artificial satellite. In any case, in terms of missile range and capabilities, the No Dong was designed for use against Japan and the Taepo Dong, or more specifically, the Taepo Dong 2 was designed for use against the United States.

Military-diplomatic coordination

North Korea's missile-related activities and diplomatic actions were extremely well coordinated, particularly after June 1998. Missile-related activities prior to that time also seemed to have reflected diplomatic considerations, but the connection between them was less apparent. Military-diplomatic maneuvers between June 1998 and September 1999 in particularly were quite impressive. The KCNA statement in June 1998 was followed by the Taepo Dong launch in August, which was carefully synchronized with the U.S.–DPRK talks in New York. Preparations for another Taepo Dong launch toward the end of 1998 were used to back active diplomatic campaigns to convince the United States to take the missile issue more seriously. Then in 1999, preparations for the Taepo Dong 2 launch were used to support the series of U.S.–DPRK talks in June, August, and September.

North Korea's missile-related activities seem to have been quite useful as a diplomatic tool for a number of reasons. First, missile-related activities were much more visible than obscure nuclear-related activities, as preparations for flight-testing or engine-burning testing, as well as actual flight-testing, could be identified easily by reconnaissance satellites or other means. Moreover, the Taepo Dong 1 launch had a spectacular psychological impact given the images of the launch widely disseminated across the world. In addition, it was relatively easy to synchronize missile tests with diplomacy since it did not take too much time to prepare and execute missile flight-testing. The Rumsfeld Commission estimated that even in case of the Taepo Dong 2, it would take less than six months after the decision was made to actually conduct the flight-test.[107]

Assessment

Normalizing relations with the United States

North Korea's most important objective was to improve and possibly normalize its relations with the United States. The Taepo Dong 1 launch served as a catalyst for comprehensive U.S.–DPRK talks on bilateral relations. The preparations for the Taepo Dong 2 launch induced the acceleration of the U.S.–DPRK talks, which culminated in the September 1999 simultaneous announcements by the United States regarding its decision to partially lift economic sanctions and by North Korea regarding its decision to freeze its missile flight-testing. The North Korean effort was also helped by South Korea's sunshine policy. Unlike Kim Young Sam, Kim Dae Jung advocated improved U.S.–DPRK relations. Moreover, the first inter-Korean Summit meeting was held in Pyongyang in June 2000.

As a result, the normalization process accelerated toward the end of the Clinton presidency. In the October 2000 joint communiqué, the United States and North Korea agreed to "take steps to fundamentally improve their bilateral relations" and "reduce tension on the Korean Peninsula and formally end the Korean War by replacing the 1953 Armistice Agreement with permanent peace arrangements." The United States did not accept the North Korean demand that the peace agreement be concluded bilaterally between the United States and North Korea, but the replacement of the Armistice Agreement with "peace arrangements" was clearly mentioned. Also important was the adoption of the "principles of respect for each other's sovereignty and non-interference in each other's internal affairs." To Pyongyang, this was tantamount to a U.S. guarantee of their regime survival.

Further details of the possible breakthrough were discussed during Secretary Albright's visit to Pyongyang and in the sixth round of the U.S.–DPRK missile talks. Wendy Sherman, special advisor to the president and policy coordinator on North Korea under the Clinton administration, later recalled that an agreement was "within reach."[108] This was an enormous achievement on the part of

North Korea given the status of the U.S.–DPRK relations just several years ago. In the end, however, the two sides failed to achieve a major breakthrough in their relationship.

Economic gains

Acquiring economic gains was yet another important objective for North Korea. In order to assess the effectiveness of its missile diplomacy, only the economic benefits that North Korea gained through the coercive use of missiles, not including revenues from missile sales, will be discussed in this section. A few important points stand out. First, North Korea failed to gain monetary rewards for its missile diplomacy, as the United States refused to accept its demand for monetary "compensation" for the discontinuation of missile exports and the long-range missile programs. Instead, North Korea obtained non-monetary aid from the United States. It is analytically difficult to determine how much of the non-monetary aid came as a direct result of the missile diplomacy, especially since the U.S. government stated on numerous occasions that its policy was not linking bilateral political issues to humanitarian aid.[109] In addition, the extent of aid offered seemed to be affected by a change in overall U.S. aid policy. For instance, in 1999, the United States made donations to North Korea as part of President Clinton's Food Aid Initiative, under which a record level of nearly 10 million tons of food was provided to the needy around the world.[110] Moreover, North Korea's economic and food situation also played a large role in determining the amount of aid offered, as demonstrated by the fact that the United States provided its first contribution of $25,000 in emergency assistance in the fall of 1995, just as the North Korean food situation began to deteriorate significantly.[111] For these reasons, the most we can say is that given the observed correlation between the timing of U.S.–DPRK talks and the U.S. decision to provide aid to North Korea, Pyongyang's missile diplomacy probably encouraged the United States to provide aid to North Korea, and that it affected the timing of that decision, but it's hard to quantify how much.

Second, the North Korean achievement of partial lifting of U.S. economic sanctions was clearly a result of its missile diplomacy.[112] The easing of the sanctions allowed for increases in bilateral trade in most consumer goods, personal and commercial fund transfers, and commercial air and sea transportation between the two countries. That said, there was also clearly a limit to these increases. For example, statutory restrictions such as U.S. missile sanctions and restrictions based on multilateral arrangements, such as the Wassenaar Arrangement – an international regime to control export of arms and dual-use technologies – remained in place.[113] North Korea's missile diplomacy apparently worked to compel the United States to ease part of its sanctions, but the volume of trade between the two countries remained negligible. Trade was $4.5 million, or .0031 percent of North Korea's total trade, in 1998; $11.3 million, or .0076 percent, in 1999; and $2.9 million, or .0015 percent, in 2000.[114] For this reason, the economic benefit that the easing of the sanctions would bring to the North was minimal.

Lastly, the October 2000 joint communiqué stated that the United States and North Korea agreed to "work together to develop mutually beneficial economic cooperation and exchanges," noting plans for "an exchange of visits by economic and trade experts at an early date." This was a significant step forward for North Korea. That said, it was not followed up after the end of the Clinton presidency.

Straining U.S.–ROK–Japan Relations

Regardless of whether it was an intended result, missile related-activities, particularly the missile flight-testing, highlighted differences among the United States, South Korea, and Japan, therefore complicating their relationship. The Taepo Dong launch in August 1998 strained relations between the United States and South Korea on the one hand and Japan on the other as differing threat perceptions and resulting policies toward North Korea rose to the surface. North Korea's missile diplomacy also put pressure on South Korea. This was particularly true after Kim Dae Jung came into office in February 1998 and started to implement his sunshine policy. Even after the 1998 Taepo Dong launch, Kim made it clear that the sunshine policy would be carried out despite the missile issue.[115] In July 1999, Kim said that he would not abandon the sunshine policy even if North Korea test-launched another ballistic missile.[116] As a consequence, the Kim Dae Jung administration was regarded as "soft" on North Korea and was subject to domestic criticism when North Korea behaved badly.

In addition, some quarters in South Korea were critical of the bilateral nature of the missile talks between the United States and North Korea since they excluded South Korea. For example, the South Korean daily *Kyunghyang Sinmun* wrote just after the first round of U.S.–DPRK missile talks started in April 1996 that South Korea felt alienated because the missile issue, though directly related to the security of South Korea, was being discussed in "exclusive talks between North Korea and the United States," and expressed the concern that the U.S.–DPRK talks in Berlin might impose "unreasonable financial burdens" on South Korea, as did the 1994 Agreed Framework.[117]

Consolidating Kim Jong Il's position

Although the connection between its missile-related activities and domestic politics is not clear, it is at least noteworthy that North Korea's missile-related activities, particularly flight-testing, tended to coincide with Kim Jong Il's steps to consolidate his power. For example, in May 1990, when the first attempt was made to flight-test a No Dong missile, Kim Jong Il was elected first vice chairman of the NDC at the first session of the ninth Supreme People's Assembly (SPA). In 1993, a No Dong missile was flight-tested one and a half months after

Kim was elected chairman of the NDC at the fifth session of the ninth SPA in April. Finally, Kim was reelected chairman of the NDC at the first session of the 10th SPA in September 1998, just after a Taepo Dong missile was launched.[118]

In particular, the Taepo Dong missile launch was used extensively for domestic propaganda purposes. The KCNA reported on September 4 that the "satellite" it launched was transmitting the melody of the "immortal revolutionary hymns 'Song of General Kim Il Sung' and 'Song of General Kim Jong Il' and the Morse signals 'Juche Korea,'" and concluded that the "successful launch of the first artificial satellite in the DPRK greatly encourages the Korean people in the efforts to build a powerful socialist state under the wise leadership of General Secretary Kim Jong Il."[119] On the next day, it was proposed that Kim Jong Il be reelected NDC chairman on the basis that the successful launch of the "first artificial satellite" during the "emotion-filled time of greeting the 50th anniversary of the National Day" had demonstrated the "inexhaustible potentials and the level of tremendous development of our republic which has advanced along the road of prosperity under the guidance of Kim Jong Il."[120] The reelection took place that day.[121]

Repercussions

Emergence of U.S.–ROK–Japan policy coordination

Although North Korea's missile diplomacy produced several positive results for Pyongyang, it also created negative repercussions as well. One of the most important diplomatic consequences of the Taepo Dong launch was the emergence of a U.S.–ROK–Japan trilateral policy coordination process. The North Korean missile diplomacy strained the relations among the three countries in the short run, but in the long run it actually encouraged these countries to coordinate their North Korea policies more closely than ever before.

North Korea Policy Coordinator Perry understood that close policy coordination with South Korea and Japan was indispensable to the successful execution of U.S. policy toward North Korea. During the policy review process, Perry visited the two countries three times and drafted his report in close cooperation with them. Moreover, policy coordination was further strengthened and institutionalized by the establishment of the Trilateral Coordination and Oversight Group (TCOG) in April 1999. As a result, when North Korea showed signs of preparing for missile flight-tests in mid-1999, the foreign ministers of the three countries demonstrated their solidarity by jointly issuing a warning statement before the tests were conducted.[122]

Increased efforts on ballistic missile defense programs

Another important consequence, both militarily and diplomatically, was renewed efforts by the United States and Japan on ballistic missile defense programs. The

Taepo Dong launch boosted the National Missile Defense (NMD) program in the United States. The realization that North Korea might soon have an ICBM capability strengthened the position of NMD advocates and accelerated the effort to develop an NMD system.

The Taepo Dong launch also encouraged Japan to work harder on Theater Missile Defense (TMD). In December 1998, Japan decided to formally participate in joint U.S.–Japan technological research on the Navy theater-wide sea-based upper-tier TMD system (later renamed Aegis Ballistic Missile Defense). Additionally, the Japanese government decided to procure four information-gathering satellites in direct reaction to the Taepo Dong launch.[123]

Having realized these negative outcomes, North Korea sought to cope with them. For instance, in January 2000, the MFA declared that the test of the NMD interceptor had "compelled the DPRK to take our moratorium into a serious consideration."[124] In February, the KCNA broadcast a commentary condemning the United States for using "North Korea's missile threat" to introduce its NMD and TMD systems.[125] A DPRK–Russia joint declaration signed in July contended that the "missile threat from some states" had been used as a pretext to justify the U.S. attempt to amend the Anti-Ballistic Missile Treaty, and warned that the deployment of TMD might seriously damage regional stability and security.[126] These efforts to minimize negative consequences notwithstanding, North Korea had already created a situation where U.S. and Japanese policymakers took missile proliferation challenges seriously, thus accelerating their efforts to develop missile defense systems.

Chapter 8

ASSAULTS ON THE KOREAN ARMISTICE, 1993–2002

In late 1993, North Korea undertook systematic assaults on the Korean Armistice by actively using force, both directly and indirectly, in the Joint Security Area (JSA), Demilitarized Zone (DMZ), and the offshore Northwest Islands area in the Yellow Sea, with the primary political objective of concluding a peace agreement with the United States. This series of actions has been arguably the longest and most elaborate military-diplomatic campaign that North Korea has ever undertaken. Despite the sophisticated nature of this campaign, however, these efforts produced only mixed results.

Military and diplomatic assaults on the Korean Armistice

Undermining the Military Armistice Commission

North Korea's diplomatic offensive to nullify the Korean Armistice started in earnest in October 1993 although early efforts had already begun in 1991. When the Commander in Chief of the United Nations Command (CINCUNC) appointed an ROK Army major general as a Senior Member of the United Nations Command (UNC) Military Armistice Commission (MAC), a position previously held by an American general officer, North Korea quickly rejected this appointment.[1] Since then, the Korean People's Army (KPA) has suspended MAC plenary sessions and MAC Senior Member-level communications, the central mechanisms of administering the Korean Armistice. It also adopted the position that the MAC process had been "paralyzed" by the March 25 appointment since the South Korean army was allegedly neither a signatory to the Armistice Agreement nor a member of the UNC and, therefore, could not represent it.[2] The UNC, however, contended that this North Korean argument was flawed because CINCUNC had signed the Armistice Agreement as commander of all UNC forces, including sixteen United Nations Member States and the ROK.[3] In 1992, the North Korean side, represented by the KPA/Chinese People's Volunteers (CPV) MAC, removed its Senior Member and did not appoint a new one.[4]

138

At the same time, North Korea further intensified its effort to undermine the Armistice and to open a high-level direct military channel with the United States in other venues as well. In October 1993, North Korea's Vice-Minister of Foreign Affairs stated at the United Nations General Assembly that the Armistice Agreement was out of date and the Armistice mechanism was virtually paralyzed. He then contended that the nuclear issue could be resolved, hostile relations between the North and the South could be removed, and peace on the Korean Peninsula could be realized only if the Armistice Agreement was replaced by a peace agreement and the UNC was dissolved.[5]

At the height of the nuclear crisis on the Korean Peninsula in 1994, North Korea played an interesting diplomatic sideshow between April and May. On April 28, the MFA proposed the establishment of a new peace mechanism to the United States.[6] On the same day, the KPA/CPV side notified the U.S.–ROK side that it would recall all remaining KPA/CPV MAC members, cease to participate in MAC activities, and no longer recognize the UNC representatives to the MAC as counterparts.[7] On the next day, the KPA performed a show of force by sending approximately 100 heavily armed soldiers into the JSA, in overwhelming excess of the 35 guards with small side arms permitted in the JSA by the Subsequent Agreements of the Armistice Agreement.[8] It was the first major demonstration of force in the JSA since the 1976 Axe Murder incident. Finally, North Korea announced the establishment of the KPA Panmunjom Mission on May 2 in order to "ease tension and ensure peace on the Korean Peninsula" through negotiations with the "U.S. army side."[9] When the UNC called for a MAC Secretary meeting, the KPA boycotted it.[10] In August, it was announced that China had decided to withdraw its delegation from the MAC.[11] The Chinese delegation left North Korea in December.[12]

In the meantime, North Korea seized the opportunity afforded by a helicopter accident in order to achieve its goal. On December 17, a U.S. Army helicopter inadvertently crossed the Military Demarcation Line (MDL) into the north and was shot down by the KPA. One of the crew was killed and the other was captured. Four days later, a meeting was held at Panmunjom between U.S. Marine Corps Maj. Gen. Ray Smith and KPA Maj. Gen. Ri Chan Bok. At the meeting, the two Major Generals agreed to the return of the remains. The KPA defined the meeting as a U.S.–DPRK general-officer meeting. The UNC said it was an UNC–KPA meeting.[13]

The North Korean effort to have bilateral U.S.–DPRK general-officer talks continued. On December 28, Thomas Hubbard, Deputy Assistant Secretary of State, visited North Korea. As a result of two-day negotiations, the two sides agreed that the surviving helicopter crewman would be returned. The memorandum of understanding, signed on December 29, stated that the two sides had agreed to continue military contacts in an "appropriate forum" to deflect the tension on the Korean Peninsula.[14] The two sides disagreed over what this "appropriate forum" meant, however. The North Korean side claimed that it meant bilateral military contacts between the United States and the DPRK in

Panmunjom.[15] The U.S. side contended that the two sides had agreed to maintain military contacts without reference to either the MAC meeting or the U.S.–DPRK military talks.[16]

Armed demonstrations, tentative agreements, and overreactions

On February 20 and 22, 1995, the KPA temporarily reinforced the JSA with approximately 80 KPA guards armed with load-bearing equipment and helmets, automatic rifles, mortars, and anti-tank weapons rather than the pistols and soft caps that they usually wore and in clear violation of the Armistice Agreement.[17] On February 23, the U.S. State Department issued a statement that North Korea was seriously mistaken if it thought it possible to force the United States to conclude a peace treaty on a bilateral basis by undermining the Armistice Agreement. It reiterated the U.S. position that South and North Korea should undertake that mission based on the Agreement on Reconciliation, Nonaggression, and Exchanges and Cooperation between North and South Korea, or Basic Agreement, signed in 1991.[18] The KPA then proposed negotiations to establish a U.S.–DPRK general-officer channel of communication.[19]

Although U.S.–DPRK general-officer talks were not realized, the UNC and the KPA subsequently started the talks.[20] In these talks, the KPA's objective was to establish a bilateral U.S.–KPA channel and to renegotiate the Armistice Agreement. The UNC, on the other hand, sought to reestablish a crisis management dialogue channel between the UNC and the KPA. On April 14, two KPA officers and three soldiers crossed the MDL, moved approximately 100 meters into the UNC portion of the DMZ, and remained there for about 30 minutes before moving back to the KPA side.[21] The ROK Ministry of National Defense (MND) later disclosed that between April 2 and 27 there had been 40 daytime and nighttime reconnaissance activities by the KPA in 18 different areas in the DMZ. The MND assessed that North Korea was trying to provoke a reaction from the South Korean side and heighten the tension in its effort to discredit the effectiveness of the Armistice.[22]

North Korean actions continued. On May 9, one KPA officer crossed the MDL, walked approximately 40 meters south into the UNC portion of the DMZ, and remained there for about four minutes. He then returned to the northern side following warnings by UNC DMZ police.[23] At this point, the UNC side suggested a compromise and proposed general-officer talks within the MAC framework. This proposal assumed American, South Korean, British, and Canadian officers as UNC members.[24] North Korea rejected it.[25]

On June 29, the MFA issued a memorandum demanding the withdrawal of U.S. Forces Korea (USFK) and the conclusion of a U.S.–DPRK peace agreement. It also said that if these demands were difficult to achieve, then at least the UNC should be dissolved. It suggested that the DPRK was willing to take a step-by-step approach to the eventual establishment of a new peace regime. Moreover, it mentioned the *Pueblo* incident of 1968 and the helicopter incident of 1994, highlighting that these incidents were resolved not through the Armistice system but through "direct DPRK–U.S. negotiations."[26] On July 5, the KPA Panmunjom Mission warned that unless an institutional mechanism was established, unforeseen incidents could continue to occur.[27]

Its prediction was certainly accurate. On the same day, the KPA temporarily inserted a platoon-sized force into the JSA. On August 15, it permitted a large demonstration of force in the JSA, and deployed more than 35 guards.[28] On August 22, one KPA officer and seven soldiers approached an MDL marker and removed it from its position. The KPA showed movements in the area again on September 4 and 7. On September 16, one KPA officer and five soldiers crossed the MDL and placed nine wooden stakes about five meters south of MDL Marker 1274.[29] When it became clear that the United States was not responding, North Korea took further steps to break the impasse. On February 15, 1996, six KPA soldiers equipped with automatic weapons and anti-tank rocket grenade launchers entered the JSA, and remained there for approximately 15 minutes.[30]

Then on February 22, the MFA officially made a three-point proposal to the United States, which included: signing a "tentative agreement"; organizing a U.S.–DPRK joint military body; and negotiating to discuss these two issues. The tentative agreement would replace the Armistice Agreement until a peace agreement was completed. The U.S.–DPRK joint military body would replace the MAC and be responsible for implementing the tentative agreement.[31]

After the MFA proposed the tentative agreement, North Korea mounted a major military-diplomatic offensive to nullify the Armistice. In a rare public announcement made by the First Vice Minister of People's Armed Forces, Kim Kwang Jin said that the status of the MDL and the DMZ could no longer be maintained.[32] On April 4, the KPA Panmunjom Mission declared that the KPA would relinquish its duties to maintain and control the MDL and the DMZ.

In the evening on April 5, 6, and 7, the KPA reinforced its guard force in the JSA with more than 200 additional soldiers armed with assault rifles, heavy and medium machine guns, rocket grenade launchers, and recoilless rifles. These soldiers remained in the JSA for several hours each time, constructing defensive positions.[33] On April 9, Kim Kwang Jin reiterated that the southern area of the DMZ had lost its meaning as a buffer zone, and said that the question was not whether a war would break out, but when.[34] On April 11, seven armed KPA soldiers crossed the MDL, intruded 300 meters into the south, and remained in the area for 45 minutes. On the same day, 10 KPA soldiers occupied hills 200 and 300 meters south of the MDL, and stayed there until 0230 hours on the next day.[35] On April 19, two North Korean patrol boats crossed the Northern Limit Line (NLL) – a quasi-maritime borderline separating the North and the South in the Yellow Sea.

The South Korean government reacted strongly to the armed demonstrations in the JSA. On April 5, the U.S.–ROK Combined Forces Command (CFC) raised the Watch Condition (WATCHCON) from three to two at the demand of the South Korean side. The next day, the ROK government summoned an emergency National Security Council (NSC) meeting.[36] On April 9, the ROK Army Chief of Staff issued an order for his men to immediately take measures according to the rules of engagement against the North Korean intrusions into the southern portion of the DMZ.[37]

Behind the scenes, there was an important perception gap between the ROK government and the U.S.-led UNC. While the ROK government took the incidents very seriously, the UNC did not view the North Korean actions as particularly alarming.[38] In fact, when a similar incident occurred in February 1995, the South Korean government regarded it as an attempt by the North Koreans to further their diplomatic goals.[39] The U.S. side viewed this response differently, assessing that the South Koreans wanted to prevent, or at least slow down, the improvement of U.S.–DPRK relations, which appeared to be taking place at Seoul's expense.[40] Washington also assessed that the general election scheduled in South Korea for April 11 likely influenced the behavior of the South Korean government, causing President Kim Young Sam to play up the seriousness of the military confrontation in order to marshal domestic support for his conservative platform.[41]

While the North Korean activities on the ground increased, similar harassments took place at sea. On April 19, two weeks after the armed demonstrations occurred in the JSA, two North Korean high-speed patrol boats crossed the NLL into a position about nine nautical miles southwest of Yeonpyeongdo islands and stayed there for one and a half hours. When the ROK Navy dispatched several vessels to the spot, the patrol boats returned to the north of the NLL.[42] On May 23, five North Korean patrol boats crossed the NLL and proceeded about four nautical miles south near Yeonpyeongdo. The ROK Navy and ROK Air Force quickly sent high-speed boats and fighters to the scene. The North Korean boats returned north after staying in the area for one and a half hours.

Unintended consequences of the submarine incident

On September 17, 1996, a North Korean *Sang-o*-class special-purpose midget submarine ran aground 200 meters off the east coast of South Korea while approaching the coast to recover infiltrators. Consequently, 24 crew members were killed and one was captured.[43] After a pause, the North Korean Ministry of People's Armed Forces announced that the submarine was on a routine training mission and seemed to have drifted down the South Korean coast due to engine trouble. The ministry demanded the return of the submarine and the crew, both deceased and living.[44] North Korea did not miss the opportunity to make its case even on this inadvertent situation. The KPA demanded that the "U.S. side" return the submarine and personnel, and increased pressure for holding general-officer-level talks.[45]

Although the incident was settled by the end of the year with both Koreas making concessions, U.S.–ROK relations deteriorated further in the process. While the South Korean government took a tough position, the United States

tried to resolve the issue in a more subdued manner. The South Korean government demanded a "clear apology" and assurance that no such incident would be
repeated. It also suspended its support for the Korean Peninsula Energy Development Organization (KEDO) light-water reactor construction project.[46]
Reportedly, President Kim Young Sam even contemplated a retaliatory air strike
against a North Korean submarine base in Wonsan.[47] The United States, on the
other hand, was focused on preventing North Korea from resuming its nuclear
development and further complicating the situation.[48] What was worse, just after
the submarine was discovered, U.S. Secretary of State Warren Christopher urged
"all parties" – not only North Korea but also South Korea – to exercise restraint.
President Kim was infuriated by these remarks.[49] The mishandling of the situation on the U.S. part, combined with Kim's high-handed and rigid attitude,
brought U.S.–ROK relations to one of its lowest points in history. In November,
a *New York Times* correspondent wrote that some U.S. officials seemed to feel
that their biggest headache on the peninsula was "the government in the
South."[50]

Escalations on the ground and at sea

In February 1997, the KPA softened its position and accepted the UNC demand
that all participants on the UNC side have equal voice in discussions. It also
agreed that only Armistice-related issues would be discussed in the General-
Officer Talks (GOT) and that the GOT would be held in the MAC conference
room.[51] This arrangement was rejected by the ROK government, however.[52] By
then, President Kim's attitude had become extremely rigid. Faced with South
Korea's rejection of the GOT, North Korea started to raise tensions on the
peninsula once again. From March through June, KPA personnel repeatedly
intruded deep into the south across the MDL. On April 10, South Korean troops
exchanged warning shots with North Korean counterparts across the MDL.
The incident occurred approximately 90 minutes before U.S. Defense Secretary
William Cohen arrived at Panmunjom.[53]

Pyongyang's escalation was also seen at sea. On June 5, a North Korean high-
speed patrol boat, together with nine fishing boats, crossed the NLL near Yeonpyeongdo. When three ROK Navy fast boats approached the North Korean
patrol boat, the patrol boat fired three gun rounds into the water. A South Korean
fast boat responded by shooting two rounds from a 40-millimeter gun as a
warning. The North Korean boats returned to their side about one and a half
hours after crossing the NLL.[54]

After a number of near clashes, a serious firefight finally broke out just one
month later. On July 16, a 14-man KPA patrol team crossed the MDL in
mountainous Cheorwon, Gangwon-do, advancing about 100 meters into the
southern DMZ. Ignoring repeated verbal warnings and warning shots from the
UNC guard post, the KPA patrol continued its activity. Then, almost immediately after a UNC guard post fired directly at the vicinity of the KPA patrol, the

KPA patrol returned fire. Two KPA guard posts in the area fired about 80 aimed rifle and machine-gun shots at two UNC guard posts. South Korean guards opened machine-gun fire, and the North Koreans responded by firing one 107-millimeter recoilless shell and a score of mortar shells to the southern side. In response, South Korean soldiers fired scores of rifle shots and one 57-millimeter round from a recoilless gun. The firefight lasted approximately one hour. While there were no casualties on the UNC side, some KPA soldiers appeared to have been injured or killed.[55]

The military significance of this incident was that the North Koreans went so far as to use mortars and recoilless guns, and the South Koreans fired directly at a KPA patrol for the first time in years. The direct shots from the South Koreans seemed to have taken the North Koreans by surprise.[56] After the armed clash, the North Koreans began to give advance notice of reconnaissance activities within the DMZ. The July 16 incident made it clear that not only the North Koreans but also the South Koreans were prepared to escalate. A spokesman of the ROK Joint Chiefs of Staff said that the clash was a "good lesson for the North Koreans."[57]

This incident made Americans even more concerned about a possible escalation and, therefore, more interested in confidence-building and tension-reduction measures than before.[58] Despite the military failure, North Korea was quick in taking the opportunity to make its point. The KPA Panmunjom Mission claimed that the United States was partially responsible for the incident since it had ignored the proposal for a tentative agreement and left the management of the DMZ to the "south Korean puppets."[59]

After Kim Dae Jung was inaugurated as president, the South Korean government eased its position and let the UNC and the KPA formally agree on the establishment of the GOT. In February 1998, the UNC suggested that the GOT replace the MAC plenary, while adding that the four UNC representatives from South Korea, the United States, Britain, and another UNC member country have "equal voice" within these talks. The KPA side objected to the equal-voice arrangement, and questioned who would be the head of delegation for the UNC.[60]

In the process, the North Koreans resorted to force again. Twelve KPA soldiers crossed the MDL and intruded 40–50 meters into the southern DMZ on March 12. On May 18, North Korea warned that it would no longer allow UNC helicopter flights over the JSA. On June 11, a KPA soldier fired an automatic rifle from his guard post into a UNC guard post and at the top of an observation tower.[61] The UNC and the KPA finally signed the agreement for procedures for the GOT on June 8.[62] North Korea never fully accepted the interpretation that the GOT would be the forum held between the UNC and the KPA, however. The North Korean media characterized these talks as ones between the KPA and the "International Allied Forces."[63] The KPA subsequently proposed in a general-officer informal meeting a tripartite agreement between the DPRK, the United States, and the ROK to establish a Joint Military Mechanism. The

KPA claimed that the ROK Army would be included in the new scheme only because they had a large army. The UNC regarded this proposal as an attempt by the KPA to undermine the UNC and the Armistice Agreement, and therefore rejected it.[64]

The Battle of Yeonpyeong and the "Military Demarcation Line at the West Sea"[65]

In June 1999, North Korea embarked on yet another military-diplomatic offensive to nullify the Armistice Agreement by rekindling the dispute surrounding the status of the waters around the Northwest Islands and the NLL. In the morning of June 7, North Korean patrol boats began crossing the NLL to the south, and continued doing so until June 15 when a major exchange of fire took place between the two navies.

The first sign of this new North Korean offensive was seen on June 6. On this day, the North Korean Central News Agency (KCNA) reported that South Korean combat vessels had crossed the "sea boundary line" and intruded deep into the "territorial waters" of the DPRK.[66] North Korean maritime operations began in earnest on June 7. At 0910 hours, a North Korean patrol boat crossed the NLL, about 5.6 nautical miles northeast of Yeonpyeongdo. Later, two more boats joined in the operation, and 12 fishing boats operated in the area. The fishing boats belonged to the Korean People's Navy and, therefore, were practically part of it. The ROK Navy sent a total of five fast boats and four patrol ships to the area, and conducted maneuvers to prevent the North Korean vessels from crossing the NLL.

On June 8, seven North Korean patrol boats repeatedly crossed the NLL between 0555 hours and 2320 hours, and 17 North Korean fishing boats operated in the area. The South Korean side deployed 12 fast boats and four patrol ships to the area. At 1145 hours, South Korean fishing boats operating in the area were ordered to return home.[67] At 1645 hours, the JCS issued Operation Directive No. 99–5, ordering the South Korean forces to react boldly against the North Korean provocations according to the rules of engagement. The next day, on June 9, six North Korean patrol boats together with five fishing boats crossed the NLL to the south once again. The South Korean side maintained local military superiority by dispatching 12 fast boats and four patrol boats. At 0635 hours, a North Korean patrol boat veered toward one of the ROK Navy fast boats, slightly damaging it. At this point, the UNC proposed that they hold a GOT meeting, and the MND issued a statement calling on North Korea to stop provocative activities. On June 10, South Korean fast craft lightly clashed with four North Korean patrol boats in an attempt to stop the NLL crossings. There were approximately 20 North Korean fishing boats fishing in the area. Having determined that the NLL crossings were deliberately executed, the ROK government summoned the NSC Standing Committee, and decided to firmly defend the NLL.

On June 11, ROK Navy fast boats conducted "tail-pushing operations" and a "bumping offensive" against North Korean vessels based on the decision the previous day to push Northern intruders back to the north of the NLL. This was the first offensive measure that South Korea took in this confrontation. As a result, two of the middle-sized North Korean patrol boats were severely damaged in the tail, and another two slightly damaged. One of the South Korean fast craft suffered a punctured hull, and three others were slightly damaged. North Korean actions further escalated on June 12. The North Korean vessels penetrated deeper into the south of the NLL, and attempted to bump into the South Korean vessels. The South Korean vessels avoided the bumping attempts and maneuvered to encircle the North Korean vessels. On June 13 and 14, North Korea increased the pressure on the South Korean side by mobilizing three torpedo boats. Under such circumstances, President Kim Dae Jung emphasized both the need to defend the NLL and the need to avoid becoming the first to open fire, escalating the situation.[68] On June 14, the ROK Navy deployed two *Pohang*-class corvettes equipped with *Exocet* anti-ship missiles and 76-millimeter guns in the area.

All told, between June 7 and 14, North Korean patrol boats crossed the NLL 52 times, while fishing boats crossed 62 times. Moreover, the North Korean side at one point deployed a buoy with a white flag between Socheongdo and Yeonpyeongdo on the 12-nautical-mile line from its coastline.[69]

Then on June 15, the "Battle of Yeonpyeong" broke out. At the time, there were seven North Korean and 13 South Korean vessels in the theater, with 20 North Korean fishing boats operating about one nautical mile south of the NLL. At 0845 hours, four North Korean patrol boats started to cross the NLL into the south and conducted bumping operations against five South Korean fast craft. Each side tried to outmaneuver the other. At 0904 hours, three North Korean torpedo boats joined in, and quickly approached five South Korean fast craft. The South Korean fast craft outmaneuvered them, however, and responded by beginning to conduct their own "bumping offensive." Five of them hit six North Korean vessels in the tail. At 0928 hours, severely bumped by a South Korean fast craft in the tail and pushed by another in the side, one of the North Korean patrol boats, PT 381, started to fire machine guns and 25-millimeter guns at two South Korean fast craft. The South Korean side responded by firing a 20-millimeter Gatling gun as well as 40-millimeter and 76-millimeter guns. The battle lasted for 14 minutes with the South Korean side firing a total of 4,584 rounds of ammunition. The South Korean side then exercised restraint, stopping short of imposing further damage on the North Korean vessels.[70] By the time the battle ended, at least one 40-ton North Korean torpedo boat was sunk with its crew, one 420-ton patrol craft was severely damaged, two 215-ton patrol boats were crippled, and two 70-ton patrol boats were slightly damaged. The MND estimated that 17–30 or more North Korean crew members were killed,[71] but other estimates suggested that the actual number was more than 100.[72] On the South Korean side, one patrol ship and four fast craft were damaged, and nine sailors were slightly injured. By 1100 hours, all the North Korean vessels had returned north and the NLL crossings had ceased.

Meanwhile, the defense readiness level of the South Korean armed forces in the theater was raised a notch given the possible resumption of hostilities and the U.S.–ROK Military Committee Meeting Steering Session decided to raise the WATCHCON to level two.[73] The North Korean air force put its fighters on alert with their engines burning.[74] The North Korean official news agency acknowledged the damage that the Korean People's Navy had suffered. The KCNA denounced the South Korean "armed provocation" and praised the restraint that the North Korean side had exercised.[75]

Despite the military defeat in the battle, North Korea boldly initiated a diplomatic offensive *vis-à-vis* the United States and South Korea at the next GOT. In the sixth GOT held on June 15, the KPA side claimed that South Korea had fired on their ships first. It denounced the South Korean naval vessels for intruding into what it called the "coastal waters," or the waters "contiguous ... to the land area of Korea" under the jurisdiction of the KPA Supreme Commander as defined in Paragraph 13b of the Armistice Agreement. This claim was similar to the one North Korea put forward in December 1973. The KPA side also contended that the NLL had been established unilaterally by the UNC and that the KPA had neither been informed nor recognized the line.

In the seventh GOT held on June 22, the KPA chief delegate claimed that according to the Armistice Agreement, the Northwest Islands were within the North Korean territorial waters. In order to claim that the NLL did not fit in well with the Armistice Agreement and to highlight the difference between the U.S. and South Korean positions on the status of the NLL, the KPA chief delegate said, "So, I think you should make clear that you are giving up the subparagraph 13b of the Armistice Agreement by insisting on the Northern Limit Line. I await your clear answer concerning this issue." The South Korean delegate responded by suggesting that the North and the South could discuss a new non-aggression separation line to replace the NLL in the inter-Korean Joint Military Commission in accordance with the 1991 North–South Basic Agreement.[76]

In the eighth GOT on July 2, the KPA presented a long and elaborate explanation and justification of its position, touching on international law, debate within South Korea, statements made by the U.S. government, and remarks by a South Korean minister.[77] Though self-serving, the discussion was highly articulate. The KPA delegate stated:

> The international Maritime Law clearly provides that the territorial waters of each nation includes the waters within twelve miles of starting line for reckoning. The International Law stipulates that in those countries like our country that is under the special situation of the Armistice, the issue of the waters of the islands which is inside of

the opponent's territorial waters shall be agreed upon by both sides on the basis of the existing Armistice Agreement.

Having unilaterally established the so-called [Northern] Limit Line without any consultation in advance with us, you, however, are violating our right over territorial waters. ... Unlike South Korea's position that the waters in question is its territorial waters, Spokesman of the U.S. Department of State, mentioning about the West Sea incident on June 17 last, announced that the so-called Northern Limit Line has [sic] never been officially recognized and, therefore, North Korean combat vessels could not be construed to have violated territorial waters of South Korea.

A Minister of Foreign Affairs and Trade of South Korea admitted that here existed a forum in connection with Northern Limit Line in the West Sea and proposed that this issue be discussed between the North and South. ... At a forum for the peaceful solution of the belligerence in the West Sea held in South Korea on June 18 last, a South Korean professor maintained that the crossing over of the Northern Limit Line by the North's patrol boats is [sic] hardly to be seen as an intrusion of the territorial waters, since the Northern Limit Line was a unilateral line. ... [W]hich part of the [North–South] agreement admits the Northern Limit Line? Article 20 of Chapter 5 of the Supplementary Agreement of the North–South Agreement stipulates that the North and South shall earnestly abide the present Armistice Agreement until durable peace is achieved between the North and the South. ... As for the past practice, our side has no knowledge of it [the NLL], and has never recognized it. We have set up some sea lanes for ourselves, for our vessels, as was required by our side, and it has nothing to do with your side.[78]

The South Korean member of the UNC delegation and KPA representatives exchanged harsh words during the talks.

In the ninth GOT held on July 21,[79] the KPA proposed a "maritime demarcation line at the West Sea" and insisted that this issue be settled on the basis of the Armistice Agreement and international law. The line extended about 90 nautical miles southwest from the western end of the boundary between Hwanghae-do and Gyeonggi-do provinces on the west coast, located far to the south of the NLL.[80] In response, the UNC proposed implementing confidence-building measures, and stated that the North–South Joint Military Commission was the correct forum for negotiating maritime boundaries. In the 11th GOT on September 1, the KPA asked for UNC's final position on the North Korean proposal.[81] The UNC rejected it.

On September 2, the KPA General Staff declared the establishment of the "Military Demarcation Line at the West Sea of Korea." It announced that the waters north of the line already proposed by the KPA would be waters under its military control, and that its "self-defensive right" to the line would be exercised by "various means and methods."[82] The ROK government refused to accept this declaration and stressed the validity of the NLL.[83] The UNC's reaction to the North Korean announcement was to just ignore it. The UNC decided that: (a) there was no legal basis for the North Korean decision; and (b) the North Koreans did not have the capability to militarily enforce the announced provisions.[84]

Peaceful means of undermining the Northern Limit Line[85]

After a lull, North Korea resumed its campaigns to alter the maritime order. On June 2, 2001, three North Korean cargo ships separately sailed through the Jeju Strait off the southwestern tip of the Korean Peninsula. When ROK Navy vessels contacted the North Korean ships via radio communications, they replied and revealed their destinations, the contents of their cargo, and the number of the crew. The South Korean navy vessels conducted low-key maneuvers to prevent the North Korean ships from passing the Jeju Strait. The North Korean ships ignored the South Korean demand to move out of its territorial waters, however, reported that as foreign ships they had chosen the route, and requested the South Korean side to help them navigate safely. They also added that they could not change course because they were "under the orders from above."[86] The South Korean government convened the NSC Standing Committee meeting and decided that the North Korean ships' passage through its territorial waters would be allowed this time, but that South Korea would take strong measures next time it happened. The decision was conveyed to the North Korean side. On June 3, the MND notified the North Korean side of the intrusion into South Korea's territorial waters by three North Korean ships. The North Korean side denied the allegation.

On June 4, one of the North Korean ships that had sailed through the Jeju Strait crossed the NLL from the south between Daecheongdo and Yeonpyeongdo at 1105 hours and entered the North Korean port of Haeju. This ship was carrying the rice provided by the United Nations World Food Programme as humanitarian aid, making it difficult for the South Korean authority to take strong measures against it. On the same day, another North Korean cargo ship intruded into South Korean territorial waters off the southwest coast of the Korean Peninsula en route from China to a North Korean port on the east coast at 1425 hours. As the ship headed for the Jeju Strait, the South Korean navy ordered one destroyer, one large transport ship, four corvettes, and three fast boats to prevent it from entering the strait. The North Korean ship still managed to sail through the strait. After these events, South Korea's minister of unification warned North Korea that stronger measures would be taken next time the same type of incident happened. At the same time, however, he proposed the conclusion of an inter-Korean maritime agreement for the purpose of preventing similar events from happening in the future.

On June 5, two other North Korean cargo ships, one travelling from Japan to the west coast and the other sailing from the west to the east coast, reported to the South Korean side that they would use the route south of Jeju Island and would not pass South Korea's "territorial waters." They sailed accordingly. The South Korea government later explained that the North Korean ships did not have the right of innocent passage through the Jeju Strait since the relationship between the North and the South was regulated by Armistice Agreement and, therefore, the provisions on the right of innocent passage in the United Nations Convention on the Law of the Sea did not apply.

The 2002 West Sea incident[87]

On June 29, 2002, two North Korean patrol boats separately crossed the NLL in the Yellow Sea. The first boat crossed the line at 0954 hours about seven nautical miles west of Yeonpyeongdo and the second boat at 1001 hours about 14 nautical miles west of the island. In response, two separate groups of two South Korean patrol boats were dispatched to confront them. At about 1025 hours, while the South Korean boats were sending warning signals with loudspeakers and sirens, one of the North Korean boats suddenly opened fire with an 85-millimeter gun, a 35-millimeter auxiliary gun, and hand-carried rockets at the distance of about 500 yards. The 85-millimeter gun hit the South Korean boat in the engine room. The South Korean boats quickly returned fire. About 10 minutes later, four other South Korean patrol boats and two corvettes joined in and started shooting. At this point, North Korean missile craft floating near the Sagot naval base turned its targeting radar on. At 1043 hours, one of the North Korean patrol boats went up in flames. At 1050 hours, the North Korean patrol boats returned north, and the South Korean side stopped firing at 1056 hours. As a result of the battle, one patrol boat was sunk, six sailors were killed, and 18 others were injured on the South Korean side. On the North Korean side, one patrol boat was damaged, and approximately 30 sailors were estimated to have been killed or injured.

Later on that day, the South Korean defense minister denounced the North Korean action and demanded an apology and the punishment of those who were responsible for the action. The Commander of the UNC described the North Korean action as a serious violation of the Armistice Agreement.[88] On July 25, the head of the North Korean delegation to the inter-Korean ministerial talks sent a telephone message to the south, which read, "Feeling regretful for the unforeseen armed clash that occurred in the West Sea recently, we are of the view that both sides should make joint efforts to prevent the recurrence of similar incidents in future."[89] This North Korean message was significant in that it was the second such apology since the Axe Murder incident and the first public expression of apology. However, North Korea neither took responsibility nor punished those who were responsible for the clash.

Critical factors

Koreanization of the defense of South Korea

Taking into account the end of the Cold War and the power shift between the two Koreas, the United States and South Korea started Koreanizing the defense of South Korea in the early 1990s. In 1990, the United States announced a three-stage plan to reduce U.S. forces in East Asia, including South Korea. In 1991, it was announced that there were no U.S. nuclear weapons deployed in South Korea. In 1992, the U.S.–ROK Combined Field Army was dissolved. In 1994, the Armistice or peacetime operational control (hereafter referred to as peacetime OPCON) over designated South Korean units exercised by the Commander in Chief of the U.S.–ROK Combined Forces Command (CINCCFC), a U.S. Army general, was transferred to the ROK JCS Chairman.[90] Against this backdrop, the United States and South Korea initiated Koreanization of the Armistice mechanism as well. In March 1991, ROK Army Maj. Gen. Hwang Won Tak was appointed Senior Member of UNC MAC.[91] Furthermore, in October 1991, the ROK Army took full responsibility for guarding the entire DMZ except for the JSA.[92]

The Koreanization efforts had several important consequences. First, the transfer of the peacetime OPCON created a situation in which the United States and South Korea could seriously disagree over how and what kind of military actions should be taken, particularly in response to North Korean provocations. When the CINCCFC had peacetime OPCON over both U.S. and ROK forces, disagreements between the United States and South Korea could not become too serious because the American general had the ultimate authority for making decisions. After the transfer, however, disagreements between the United States and South Korea could actually create serious tension between the two over how to use force. Second, the transfer also created a situation in which the North Koreans could militarily harass the South Koreans without directly confronting the Americans. Now that the South Koreans controlled the ROK forces in low-intensity conflicts like the naval battle in 1999, North Korea could highlight the disagreements between the United States and South Korea over the NLL by militarily engaging the ROK Navy without offending the Americans. Third, the transfer of the peacetime OPCON, which had eliminated the need to undergo a complex combined decision-making process, enabled the South Koreans to act more flexibly, swiftly, and effectively than before.[93] Finally, the Koreanization of the defense of the DMZ made the JSA practically the only place on land where the North Koreans could directly harass the Americans.[94]

Debate over the Northern Limit Line

While the North Korean government rejected the validity of the NLL, the South Korean government strongly argued for it, basing its argument mainly on the 1991

North-South Basic Agreement and the 1994 United Nations Convention on the Law of the Sea (UNCLOS).[95] According to the *Defense White Paper 1999*, the South Korean argument can be summarized as follows:[96]

(a) The NLL has worked effectively as a maritime boundary for the last 46 years, and North Korea has tacitly accepted and abided by it. Therefore, the principles of effectiveness and consolidation validate the NLL;

(b) According to the UNCLOS, the use of the median line in determining territorial seas does not apply "where it is necessary by reason of historic title or other special circumstances;"[97]

(c) The Basic Agreement specified that the "South–North demarcation line and the areas for nonaggression shall be identical with ... the areas that each side has exercised jurisdiction over until the present time."[98] The NLL has demarcated the areas of jurisdiction until the present time and, therefore, it is deemed to be a legitimate demarcation line; and

(d) The validity of NLL is not an issue to be discussed at the GOT. Until North and South Korea finalize the sea demarcation line through a separate agreement, the ROK government will continue to enforce the NLL as the sea demarcation line.

The South Korean position was not without weaknesses, however. First, South Korea contended that North Korea had tacitly accepted and abided by the NLL, but in fact North Korea had officially challenged it since 1973 both militarily and diplomatically. Also, when the UNC created the NLL, it did not inform the North Koreans of the line. Moreover, although North Korea abided by the NLL most of the time, it had done so not necessarily because it recognized the NLL but because it understood that the crossings of it would be countered militarily by the South Korean side. If North Korean behavior was affected by South Korea's military force, the principle of consolidation might not apply.[99]

Second, the name "Northern Limit Line" was not mentioned in the Basic Agreement. In fact, even South Koreans distinguished between the NLL and the "sea demarcation line." From the reading of South Korean official pronouncements, it could be inferred, on the one hand, that the NLL was a line whose existence was justified by the requirements of the Armistice Agreement, and was administered by the military for control purposes. The sea demarcation line, on the other hand, was a conceptual line defined in the Basic Agreement and administered by the Ministry of Unification.[100]

Third, the South Koreans were confused as to whether the area to the south of the NLL was their territorial sea or not. The South Korean defense minister said in June 1999 that South Korea would defend the areas to the south of the NLL as its "territorial sea." But a JCS representative asserted that the buffer zone, located to the south of the NLL, was not "territorial sea," and that the JCS simply called it *"haeyeog* (sea area)."[101]

Finally, some of the MND materials justified the NLL by claiming that the NLL approximately connected the median points between Hwanghae-do's coastline and the Northwest Islands and, therefore, the NLL reflected the principles of international law.[102] However, if the contemporary international law of the sea is used to define territorial waters, part of the area to the south of the NLL between Socheongdo and Yeonpyeongdo would become North Korean territory.

Moreover, there were some important differences between the United States and South Korea. First, the United States regarded the area in which the naval battle occurred in 1999 as international waters.[103] Also, the U.S. position was that there was a dispute over the territories and jurisdictions in the area.[104] Based on such an interpretation, the U.S. Department of State explained why the North Koreans should still refrain from crossing the NLL as follows:

> ... the Northern Limit Line was and still is demarcated by the UN [United Nations] command as a practical way to separate forces. ... We believe it's been an effective means to prevent military tension between North and South Korean military forces for 46 years, since 1953. So it's served a useful purpose that has benefited both sides.
>
> We continue to urge the DPRK to recognize this practicality by keeping its craft north of the line. In 1953, the area was a zone of conflict, you'll recall – a war zone; and territorial jurisdictions, they remain in dispute today. Therefore, we believe this is a practical measure, or a practical mechanism that has allowed there to be a reduction in tensions or the means of diffusing tensions.[105]

The U.S. argument in support of the NLL was not based on law but on practicality.[106]

Second, while the ROK was a signatory to the Basic Agreement, the United States was not and therefore interpretation of the status of the NLL would inevitably differ between the two allied partners. South Korea could reasonably claim the status of the NLL as the demarcation line of the "nonaggression areas of the sea" defined in the Basic Agreement. Neither the UNC nor the United States, however, had a legal basis to do the same.

Developments in the International Law of the Sea

Developments in international law, and in particular the adoption of the UNCLOS, seemed to have encouraged the North Koreans to renew their territorial claims and their military-diplomatic raid on the NLL. Having entered into force in November 1994, the UNCLOS provided that every state had "the right to establish the breadth of its territorial sea up to a limit not exceeding 12 nautical miles, measured from baselines determined in accordance with this Convention." By formalizing the 12-nautical-mile territorial sea demarcation – the claim long upheld by the North Korean side – the Convention seemed to have given the

153

North Koreans ammunition.[107] *Minju Joson*, a DPRK government daily, wrote in June 1999 that the waters at issue in the Northwest Islands area unquestionably belonged to the DPRK "in the light of the international convention" defining each country's water line within 12 nautical miles.[108]

The North Korean contention could backfire on itself, nevertheless, for contemporary international law allows an island to enjoy "the territorial sea, the contiguous zone, the exclusive economic zone and the continental shelf."[109] According to this principle, the Northwest Islands could have their own territorial waters as the UNC side contended. Finally, while South Korea ratified the UNCLOS in 1995, North Korea had yet to do so.[110]

Local military balance in the Northwest Islands Area

In 1999, the military balance in the Northwest Islands area was as follows. The Korean People's Navy had some 70 vessels including 23 torpedo boats and four fast missile boats deployed in the naval base at Sagot under the Eighth Naval Squadron. These were relatively small vessels, however. There were also 76-millimeter and 122-millimeter coastal guns and *Silkworm* surface-to-ship missiles deployed in the southern tip of the Ongjin Peninsula about seven nautical miles to the north of Yeonpyeongdo. MiG-17s/19s as well as An-2s were deployed in airbases in Onchon and Taetan.[111] South Korea's Second Fleet Command in Incheon possessed a much smaller number of ships in the theater, but they included corvettes, frigates, and destroyers with much larger displacement than the North Korean counterparts.[112] One marine brigade as well as coastal guns and radar sites were deployed in Baengnyeongdo; fast craft and one marine regiment were deployed in Daecheongdo and Yeonpyeongdo.[113] In June 1999, the South Korean side maintained 21 vessels comprised of 14 fast boats, four corvettes, one rescue ship, and two transport ships in the theater during the period of tension.[114]

By 1999, the local military balance in the Northwest Islands area had shifted in favor of South Korea. Learning lessons from the West Sea incident in the early 1970s, South Korea procured new fast boats and corvettes in the 1970s and the 1980s as part of the Force Improvement Program. These vessels played the central role in the Battle of Yeonpyeong. South Korea's victory resulted in large part from the superiority in speed and maneuverability as well as firepower and fire control system. The better speed and maneuverability made it possible for the South Korean boats to successfully execute "tail-pushing operations" and "bumping offensives" against the North Korean patrol boats and torpedo boats. The superior firepower and fire control system enabled the South Korean vessels to overwhelm their counterparts. In addition, by 1999, South Korea had acquired a number of ships equipped with anti-ship missiles, compromising North Korea's superiority in this category. The South Korean side could, therefore, credibly deter North Korea from escalating the situation. The Korea Naval Tactical Data System, introduced to the ROK Navy in late 1995, also played an important role in the operations in June 1999. This system enabled the navy command to instantaneously acquire tactical data such as location, speed, and direction of ships and aircraft in the theater.[115]

Characteristics

Location and timing

North Korea's military actions took place primarily in the JSA, DMZ, and in the Northwest Islands area. The JSA and the Northwest Islands area were particularly important stages for the North Korean armed demonstrations. Incidents in the Northwest Islands area often took place west of Yeonpyeongdo where the validity of the NLL was most contentious. The naval battles took place about six nautical miles west of Yeonpyeongdo in 1999 and 14 nautical miles west of the island in 2002.

Systematic military-diplomatic operations began in earnest in April 1994 at the height of the nuclear crisis. Major armed demonstrations in the JSA were performed repeatedly between 1994 and 1996. Hostile NLL crossings started to take place in 1996, escalated in 1997, and culminated in the 1999 naval battle. The North Korean navy achieved a perfect surprise in 2002 when it attacked the South Korean navy in an apparent act of revenge for the 1999 defeat. The surprise attack took place when the Korea/Japan World Cup soccer games were successfully convened.

Forces involved and the type of use of force

Conventional ground and naval forces played the central role in the attacks during this period. The use of commercial vessels as part of the broader military-diplomatic campaigns was an action of ingenuity. The use of force was in most cases indirect and coercive in nature. The North Korean actions in the JSA and the Yellow Sea were all highly visible, often occurring in broad daylight, and there was no attempt made by the North Korean side to conceal or hide what they were doing. The purpose of the armed demonstrations in the JSA was diplomatic and by no means simply military.

In the past, North Korea tended to use force where it had a local military advantage. In June 1999, it did not have that advantage. North Korea still instigated the action, nonetheless. This may have been because the North Koreans might have judged that military victory was not necessary, and that military confrontation and limited military skirmishes would be enough to achieve its policy objectives. The 2002 naval clash was an aberration from the prevailing tendency. In this case, military victory itself was one of the most important objectives and therefore physical destruction rather than coercion was its main goal.

Intensity and targeting

Despite the harsh rhetoric, North Korean actions were carefully controlled and limited at first. The intensity of its actions gradually heightened from July 1997, and serious shooting incidents occurred in 1999 and 2002. The North Koreans did not seek to escalate the situation excessively, though. During the 1990s, no Americans or South Koreans were killed. The 2002 naval clash was an aberration, as serious harm was inflicted on the South Koreans. Direct military attacks did not continue after this incident, however.

The physical target of North Korean actions during this period was predominantly South Korean. When the North Koreans provoked confrontation in the DMZ and the Northwest Islands area, it was always South Koreans that became their target. Although there were live fire exchanges in the DMZ and the Northwest Islands area, there was no live fire exchange in the JSA where U.S. forces were deployed. Although one U.S. Army helicopter was shot down in December 1994, this was the result of an accidental intrusion by the U.S. helicopter.

Military-diplomatic coordination

North Korea's military and diplomatic actions were extremely well coordinated. Major military actions almost always preceded or followed important diplomatic moves. The basic pattern was: (a) harass and provoke South Koreans; (b) argue that the tension was rising and that the situation could not be managed by the North and the South; and (c) propose talks with Americans to establish a new bilateral peace mechanism.

The organizations involved, such as the KPA, the KPA Panmunjom Mission, and the MFA, were very well coordinated. In fact, the KPA Panmunjom Mission (formerly the KPA/CPV MAC) was controlled and managed jointly by the Workers' Party's Organisation and Guidance Department, the KPA and the MFA.[116]

Assessment

Improving relations with the United States

The North Korean actions were part of a broader strategy to improve relations with the United States, executed in conjunction with Pyongyang's nuclear and missile diplomacy. More specifically, these actions were an attempt to create a direct military-to-military channel between the United States and the DPRK and, upon that basis, to conclude a bilateral peace agreement.

North Korea achieved several gains from its actions. First, the KPA Panmunjom Mission practically became a counterpart of the UNC. Second, the North Koreans succeeded in having the UNC agree to the creation of the GOT. Although they failed to establish exclusive U.S.–DPRK General-Officer Talks or U.S.–DPRK–ROK tripartite military talks, they succeeded in essentially replacing the MAC plenary meeting with the GOT. Also, they succeeded in keeping a mechanism in which an American – not a South Korean – general officer was the chief interlocutor. Finally, North Korea managed to frustrate the U.S.–ROK effort to establish peace on the Korean Peninsula through a multilateral forum. In 1996, Clinton and Kim Young Sam proposed the Four Party talks featuring the two Koreas, the United States and China, and its plenary talks were held six times between December 1997 and August 1998. Nevertheless, North Korea continued to insist on the conclusion of a bilateral peace agreement with the United States. As a result, the United States secretly proposed to South Korea the conclusion of three separate peace agreements in July 1999 – one between the United States and North Korea, one between the two Koreas, and one among the participants of the Four Party talks. South Korea rejected this proposal.[117]

Despite these tactical gains, however, North Korea failed to achieve its most important objective. After years of concentrated effort, Pyongyang ultimately failed to conclude a peace agreement with the United States. A U.S. defense official involved in the negotiations with the North Koreans in Panmunjom concluded that North Korea's provocative actions did not have much impact on the U.S. position or behavior.[118]

Complicating U.S.–ROK relations

Another North Korean objective in this prolonged military-diplomatic campaign was to complicate U.S.–ROK relations and diplomatically separate the two countries. The North Koreans tried to achieve this by creating situations where the differences between the two countries were highlighted. North Korean actions proved to be quite successful, particularly in the late years of the Kim Young Sam presidency.

Having witnessed the exceptionally strong reaction of South Korea to the April 1996 incident in the JSA and the September 1996 submarine incident, the United States became increasingly concerned about the possibility of escalation. For this reason, in the meeting between President Clinton and President Kim after the submarine incident, Clinton went so far as to bluntly seek to obtain "an ironclad commitment" that South Korean forces would not initiate military action against the North without American consent. Although a senior South Korean official later said that he believed Clinton had been reassured by Kim's response, an American official thought Kim's reaction had "still left room for doubt."[119] The July 1997 incident fueled the already high level of mutual suspicion between the two countries. As a result, the United States became more willing to establish a mechanism for building confidence and reducing tension between North and South Korea. The tension between the United States and South Korea lasted until the Kim Dae Jung administration came into office in 1998.

After the inauguration of the Kim Dae Jung administration, the U.S.–ROK relationship improved greatly. Although some disagreements remained, such as the status of the NLL, they were generally technical rather than substantive political issues. The two countries firmly shared the understanding that they should not play into North Korea's hand.

North Korean actions also sometimes worked against Pyongyang's interests. As a South Korean Defense Ministry official pointed out, the North Korean military pressure actually made it more difficult for the United States to agree to North Korean proposals even when these proposals were relatively reasonable. The United States was worried that doing so might give the North the wrong impression that its tactics were working and the U.S.–ROK alliance was in disarray.[120]

Undermining the South Korean position

Related to the previous point, undermining the South Korean position was another important objective of the North Korean military-diplomatic campaign. There were several positive outcomes for the North Koreans in this regard. First, North Korea succeeded in slowing down the Koreanization of the Armistice. The Koreanization of the South Korean defense would have undermined the North Korean position by weakening its contention that South Korea had been "colonized" by the United States and that the South Koreans were "puppets of American imperialists." In this sense, keeping the South Korean members subordinate to or at least equal to an American general officer in the GOT, for example, provided the North Koreans with a good propaganda asset.

Second, North Korea succeeded in undermining the South Korean claims on the NLL. The sustained crossings of the NLL and the naval battles made it clear that the South Korean position on the status of the NLL was not without weaknesses and inconsistencies. When the South Korean foreign minister said after the 1999 naval battle that he was "open to discussing" the sea demarcation line, he was facing a dilemma. On the one hand, not discussing the sea demarcation line would prolong the conflict over the issue. On the other hand, starting the discussion to establish the sea demarcation line might undermine the legitimacy of the NLL.[121] The North Korean actions in 1999, 2001, and 2002 stimulated a heated and sometimes politically divisive debate in South Korea regarding the legal status of the NLL and how to deal with North Korea's provocations. The NLL was no longer something "sacrosanct" and "inviolable" as it was several years ago.[122]

Although a tactical success, the 2002 naval battle also produced negative results for North Korea. The deaths of six young South Korean sailors and their families' expression of deep sorrow cemented the feeling in South Korea that they would have to firmly defend what the young sailors had sacrificed their lives for, the NLL. North Korea's naval action in 2002 made it even more difficult politically for South Korean leaders to make any concessions on the NLL.[123] The North Korean actions thus backfired in this regard.

In the fourth Inter-Korean General-level Military Talks in May 2006, the North Korean delegation proposed a new military demarcation line in the Yellow Sea.[124] The line mostly overlapped the NLL in the eastern and western ends, but expanded deep into the south in the area between Socheongdo and Yeonpyeongdo. This line indeed represented what the UNCLOS, under a peacetime situation, would require North and South Korea to draw, as it was the median line in the areas where the distance between the North Korean coastline and the Northwest Islands was less than 24 nautical miles and a 12-nautical-mile line where there was no South Korean island off the North Korean coast.[125] The South Korean side rejected the proposal, however.

Obtaining economic gains

The waters around the Northwest Islands were lucrative fishing areas, with the areas to the south of the NLL four times as productive as the northern side. For this reason, some believed that the active crossings of the NLL by North Korea in June 1999 had much to do with economic imperatives, and in particular the need to acquire foreign currency. In fact, North Korea had exported $2.8 million of blue crabs to Japan in 1998,[126] and the NLL crossings tended to increase during the blue crab season.[127] South Korean Defense Minister Cho Seong Tae speculated that, given the fact that KPA personnel manned fishing boats operating in the area, the KPA might have been busy fulfilling its required foreign currency acquisition quota.[128] Also, North Korea wanted to use this area as a shortcut for its maritime traffic, as it did back in the 1970s. By crossing the NLL, North Korean ships could dramatically shorten the sailing mileage to and from the Haeju port. North Korea ultimately failed to achieve this objective with its military actions, as well, though.

In an indirect and subtle way, however, North Korea's military actions helped to bring about some gains for Pyongyang over time. In June 2004, two years after the second naval clash in the Yellow Sea, North Korea and South Korea signed the Inter-Korean Maritime Agreement and its Subsequent Agreement. These agreements enabled commercial ships of both Koreas to sail directly to the other side's ports by using newly designated sea routes.[129] In August 2005, South Korea agreed to allow North Korean commercial vessels to sail through the Jeju Strait.[130] In the inter-Korean Summit meeting in October 2007, the two sides agreed to establish a "special peace and cooperation zone in the West Sea," which envisioned the creation of a joint fishing zone and passage of commercial vessels via direct routes to and from Haeju across the NLL. Although this agreement has not been implemented yet, it included some of the outcomes that the North Koreans had sought to obtain through its military-diplomatic campaign.[131] The North Korean actions in 2001 and 2002 seem to have worked as a catalyst in accelerating the process leading up to these agreements because they created the feeling in South Korea that conflict-prevention measures must be established as soon as possible to avoid future military crises.[132] In the final analysis, however, South Korea's desire to engage North Korea and bolster wide-ranging North–South interactions has played a much more important role in bringing about these new agreements than the North Korean military actions.[133]

Consolidating Kim Jong Il's position

North Korea might also have used the military actions in the JSA, the DMZ, and the Northwest Islands area for domestic political purposes, namely to consolidate Kim Jong Il's position. Several indications support such a possibility. First, in April 1996, just three days after the armed demonstrations took place in the JSA, in a program celebrating the third anniversary of Kim Jong Il's election as the Chairman of the DPRK National Defence Commission, the KCNA boasted that he had successfully frustrated "the enemy plot" in August 1976 with his boldness and intellectual ability when the "enemies perpetrated the Panmunjom [Axe Murder] incident."[134] This seemed to have been an attempt not only to enhance the effectiveness of the ongoing military-diplomatic maneuvers by reminding the Americans and the South Koreans of the brutal axe killings in the JSA but also to praise Kim Jong Il as a new military leader.

Second, on June 16, 1999, one day after the exchange of fire took place in the Yellow Sea, the Workers' Party daily *Rodong Sinmun* and journal *Kulloja* jointly carried an editorial entitled, "WPK's [Workers' Party of Korea's] policy of giving priority to the army is invincible."[135] The release of this very important editorial in the midst of the military-diplomatic campaign in the Yellow Sea suggested the North Korean intention to use the occasion to further glorify Kim Jong Il and justify the military-first policy adopted by the nation's leadership.

Finally, the June 2002 incident was most likely aimed partly at degrading the festive and successful World Cup games co-sponsored by South Korea and Japan. The success of the World Cup games was doubly problematic to the North Korean leaders since they had just failed to attract international attention to their first Arirang Festival, a two-month gymnastics and artistic festival to celebrate Kim Il Sung's birthday held in Pyongyang from April 29 until June 29, the day of the naval attack. It was yet another case in which North Korea attempted to frustrate successful international sports events held in South Korea since the bombing of the Korean Air passenger aircraft before the Seoul Olympic Games in 1988. Despite Pyongyang's aims, the June 29 attack only marginally affected the World Cup games.[136]

Repercussions

Enhanced U.S.–ROK coordination in dealing with North Korean provocations

Although the sustained military actions taken by North Korea did result in some victories for Pyongyang, it also produced a number of negative consequences such as strengthening U.S.–ROK political and military cooperation in dealing with North Korean military provocations. Two examples stand out. First, at the 20th Military Committee Meeting held in January 1999, the United States and South Korea agreed to establish a mechanism under which USFK would participate in operations dealing with North Korea's local provocations such as the infiltration of spy boats.[137] As has already been pointed out, the December 1994 transfer of the peacetime OPCON had made it easier for the North Koreans to drive a wedge between the United States and South Korea in times of crisis. The January 1999 agreement partly alleviated this problem and strengthened military cooperation between the two countries even in peacetime.[138] It was on the basis of this new mechanism that the USFK provided "immediate support" to the South Korean side in the naval crisis in June 1999.[139]

Second, the June 1999 naval clash prompted the United States and South Korea to seek to narrow their differences over the status of the NLL. As a result, the Joint Communiqué of the 31st U.S.–ROK Security Consultative Meeting issued in November 1999 mentioned the NLL for the first time. It read:

> With regard to the June naval clash, both Ministers urged the North to accept the practical value of, and abide by, the Northern Limit Line, which has been an effective means of separating South and North Korean military forces and thus preventing military tension for forty-six years.[140]

Although the U.S. position on the NLL had not changed, it was politically significant that for the first time the two sides agreed to officially declare the importance of upholding the NLL in the ministerial-level Security Consultative Meeting.

The widening gap in military balance

The July 1997 clash in the DMZ and the June 1999 naval clash openly demonstrated that the military balance had and was continuing to change in favor of South Korea. The July 1997 incident shocked the KPA because for the first time South Korean soldiers and weapons clearly excelled their Northern counterparts. In the naval battle in June 1999, furthermore, North Korea demonstrated that its conventional military assets were outdated and no match for South Korea.[141] The change in the military balance was undercutting North Korea's ability to effectively use force for political purposes. Donald Gregg, former U.S.

ambassador to South Korea, wrote that the naval battle had taught the North Koreans a "lesson," commenting:

> My own experience goes back to 1968 when they seized the (USS) *Pueblo*. I was with the CIA [Central Intelligence Agency] and part of my job was to find a way to retaliate and we couldn't. We did nothing. We did nothing after the Blue House raid, the Rangoon bombing and the blowup of a Korean Air flight. Last June was the first time North Koreans were given a punch in the nose.[142]

The June 1999 naval battle prompted South Korea to deploy its newly procured indigenous K-9 155-millimeter self-propelled long-range artillery batteries with a range of over 40 kilometers on Baengnyeongdo and Yeonpyeongdo.[143] This deployment strengthened South Korean long-range firepower and solidified the local military balance in the Northwest Islands area.[144]

South Korea's defense posture was further strengthened as a result of the 2002 naval clash. The rules of engagement (ROE) governing South Korea's actions were simplified from five stages to three. Before the clash, South Korean naval boats gave warnings, engaged in demonstration and interdiction maneuvers, fired warning shots, and then fired direct shots. After the ROE were revised, the sequence became demonstration maneuvers, followed by firing warning shots and then finally by firing direct shots at the intruding vessels. The purpose of the revision was to avoid exposing patrol boats to enemy surprise attacks.[145]

Chapter 9

NUCLEAR DIPLOMACY, ROUND TWO, 2002–08

In December 2002, North Korea set in motion a second round of nuclear diplomacy by announcing that it was resuming the operation and construction of nuclear facilities. Faced with Washington's financial sanctions imposed in 2005 and refusal to engage in serious dialogue, North Korea launched multiple ballistic missiles in July 2006 and conducted a nuclear test in October of the same year. In this military-diplomatic campaign, North Korea's bold calculated adventurism worked. After the nuclear test, the United States shifted its policy toward North Korea, stopped applying the Trading with the Enemy Act to it, and rescinded its designation as a State Sponsor of Terrorism. However, the two countries have yet to establish diplomatic relations.

Twists and turns

Initiation of the new round of nuclear diplomacy

In the U.S.–DPRK meeting held in Pyongyang on October 3, 2002, Assistant Secretary of State James Kelly informed Kim Kye Gwan, North Korea's Vice Minister of Foreign Affairs, that the United States had acquired information about North Korea's covert enriched uranium nuclear program, in violation of the 1994 Agreed Framework as well as other related agreements. On the next day, Kang Sok Ju, First Vice Foreign Minister and Kim Jong Il's right-hand man, asked, "What is wrong with us having our own uranium enrichment program? We are entitled to possess our own HEU [highly-enriched uranium], and we are bound to produce more powerful weapons than that."[1] Kang also said that North Korea considered the Agreed Framework nullified, and stated that the DPRK would resolve this issue if the United States: (a) concluded a nonaggression treaty with the DPRK; (b) lifted the embargo on North Korea and stopped interfering with Japan–DPRK normalization; (c) normalized relations with the DPRK; and (d) compensated North Korea for the delay in the construction of a light-water reactor (LWR). He also suggested that these issues could be solved through a summit meeting between the leaders of the two countries. Kelly did not respond positively, and the U.S. delegation left the negotiating table.[2]

On October 16, the U.S. government announced that in the U.S.–DPRK talks, North Korean officials had acknowledged that they had a program to enrich uranium for nuclear weapons.[3] This became a point of contention, however, when the North Koreans later claimed that they had never acknowledged the existence of the HEU program. The initial North Korean response was to propose a new negotiated settlement.[4] The United States did not respond positively. Rather, it brought the HEU issue to the Korean Peninsula Energy Development Organization (KEDO). KEDO decided in November that delivery of heavy fuel oil (HFO) under the 1994 Agreed Framework be suspended and that future shipments be dictated by North Korea's willingness to dismantle its nuclear program.[5] Furthermore, the United States pressured the North by temporarily seizing its cargo ship carrying components for Scud missiles off the coast of Yemen in December.[6]

At this point, North Korea decided to get tough, and quickly escalated the situation. On December 12, the Ministry of Foreign Affairs (MFA) announced that the DPRK would resume the operation and construction of its nuclear facilities.[7] In late December, North Korea ousted International Atomic Energy Agency (IAEA) inspectors. Moreover, on January 10, 2003, North Korea declared its withdrawal from the Treaty on the Non-proliferation of Nuclear Weapons (NPT) once again. After the announcement, it engaged in a series of military demonstrations. In late January, the North Koreans moved canned spent fuel away from the five-megawatt (MW) reactor in Nyongbyon (Yongbyon).[8] In February, the MFA suggested that the DPRK was operating its nuclear facilities "for the production of electricity."[9] It was reported that North Korea was also getting ready to resume the operation of the reprocessing facility.[10]

On February 17, the Korean People's Army (KPA) Panmunjom Mission issued a statement contending that if the U.S. side continued "violating and misusing the Armistice Agreement," the DPRK would no longer remain bound to it.[11] After the statement, a MiG-19 fighter flew over the Northern Limit Line (NLL) on February 20. Four days later, an anti-ship missile was fired toward the Sea of Japan for the first time in three years.[12] On March 2, four North Korean fighters, including two MiG-29s, approached a U.S. Air Force RC-135S Cobra Ball intelligence-gathering aircraft flying over the Sea of Japan. One of them came within 50 feet, and a North Korean pilot sent internationally recognized hand signals to the American flight crew to follow him, presumably to North Korean territory. The American crew members simply ignored the signals. After the event, a U.S. official said, "Clearly, it appears their intention was to divert the aircraft to North Korea, and take it hostage."[13] On March 7, North Korea announced that its nuclear facilities had resumed operation. Three days later it once again fired an anti-ship missile toward the Sea of Japan. In the meantime, the United States entered the war in Iraq on March 20. After the war began, Kim Jong Il did not appear in public for two months.

Declaration of nuclear weapons development

In April 2003, the MFA issued a statement noting that only a "physical deterrent force" could avert a war and protect the security of the country.[14] On June 9, North Korea declared that if the United States kept "threatening the DPRK with nukes," it would have no option but to build up a nuclear deterrent force.[15] As before, North Korea escalated tension by engaging in confrontations to back up its threats. In the early morning of July 17, for example, North Korean servicemen fired four machinegun shots toward the South Korean side and damaged its guard post in the DMZ. The South Korean side returned 17 shots but did not escalate further.[16]

In May, the United States and Japan agreed to take measures including economic sanctions if North Korea continued to escalate. In July, it was reported that Secretary of Defense Donald Rumsfeld had ordered U.S. military commanders to devise a new war plan called Operation Plan 5030, which would give commanders in the region authority to "conduct maneuvers – before a war has started – to drain North Korea's limited resources, strain its military, and perhaps sow enough confusion that North Korean generals might turn against the country's leader, Kim Jong Il."[17]

Initiation of multilateral talks

Even after North Korea declared its withdrawal from the NPT, the concerned countries insisted on solving the problem through diplomacy. In January, James Kelly commented that, "once we can get beyond nuclear weapons, there may be opportunities … to help North Korea in the energy area."[18] Also, President George W. Bush said that this issue would be solved in a peaceful way, adding that if North Korea abandoned its nuclear program, the United States would reconsider a "bold initiative."[19]

As a result, the three-party talks between the United States, North Korea, and China were held in Beijing in April. North Korea took the position that the talks would take place between the United States and North Korea with China merely playing the role of host.[20] While the talks were continuing, the head of the North Korean delegation, Ri Kun, informally told his U.S. counterpart, James Kelly, that North Korea had nuclear weapons and that it could demonstrate or sell them.[21]

In parallel with diplomatic responses, the concerned countries also stepped up non-diplomatic pressure on North Korea. In May, the United States proposed the Proliferation Security Initiative (PSI) to check the proliferation of weapons of mass destruction (WMD) and related materials, and urged other countries to participate. The Japanese police searched the premises of a trading company run by a Korean on suspicion of having illegally exported machine parts that could be used for the development of nuclear weapons, and vigorously inspected the North Korean passenger ferry *Mangyongbong-92* that entered the port of Niigata.

After the three-party talks, the countries concerned set out to explore the possibility of holding broader multilateral talks.[22] As a result, the first round of Six-Party Talks, featuring North Korea, the United States, China, South Korea, Japan, and Russia, was held in Beijing in late August 2003. In the talks, North Korea proposed that reciprocal actions would be taken simultaneously in four stages. First, the United States would resume the supply of HFO and sharply increase humanitarian food aid while North Korea would declare its intention to scrap its nuclear program. Second, when the United States concluded a non-aggression treaty with the DPRK and compensated it for the loss of electricity caused by the delay in providing the LWRs, North Korea would refreeze its nuclear facilities and nuclear substances and allow monitoring and inspection of such facilities and substances. Third, when diplomatic relations were established between the United States and the DPRK and between Japan and the DPRK, North Korea would resolve the missile issue. Finally, when the construction of the LWRs was completed, North Korea would dismantle its nuclear facilities.[23] China released a host country summary at the end of the talks, which stated that North Korea's "reasonable concern over its security" must be considered and resolved, adding that the nuclear issue should be resolved "in a manner that is phased and synchronized or parallel in implementation."[24]

Frustrated by the lack of progress after the talks, however, North Korea took steps to raise tensions. On October 2, the MFA announced that the DPRK had decided that its pursuit of a nuclear program was no longer for producing electricity but instead for strengthening its "nuclear deterrent force."[25] In late October, North Korea tested anti-ship missiles in the Sea of Japan on three occasions. KEDO decided to suspend the LWR project in November for a one year period.[26]

In the meantime, there were also some positive developments. In October, Bush said that the United States would consider providing written security assurances to North Korea in the context of the Six-Party Talks.[27] In December, the MFA announced that it was ready to accept "written security assurances" in lieu of a non-aggression treaty and proposed "first-phase action" in which North Korea would freeze its nuclear activities while the United States would remove the DPRK from its list of terrorism-sponsoring states, lift its political, economic and military sanctions and blockade, and provide energy aid.[28] The United States did not respond positively, however. Three days later, Vice President Dick Cheney reportedly said, "We don't negotiate with evil; we defeat it."[29] In January 2004, North Korea invited American nuclear scientists and area specialists including Siegfried Hecker, a senior fellow at the Los Alamos National Laboratory, to Nyongbyon to review its nuclear facilities. During the visit, the North Koreans even presented them with what they characterized as plutonium.[30]

In the second round of Six-Party Talks in February 2004, although the parties agreed to establish a working group and convene another round of the talks, North Korea refused to accept the goal of the talks as defined by the United States: "complete, verifiable, and irreversible dismantlement of all of

North Korea's nuclear programs (CVID)."[31] James Kelly suggested that when the nuclear issue was resolved, the six parties might be able to replace the armistice agreement on the Korean Peninsula with a "permanent peace mechanism."[32]

In the third round of the Six-Party Talks in June, the United States stopped using the term "CVID," and instead started to use the term "comprehensive dismantlement," while conceptually keeping CVID as the underlying principle. More importantly, under pressure from Japan to engage with North Korea more proactively, the United States made its first concrete proposal to North Korea when it suggested that as the DPRK dismantled its nuclear programs, the other parties would take corresponding steps such as providing HFO and provisional multilateral security assurances to North Korea.[33] The North Koreans thought it was "noteworthy" that the U.S. had proposed phased and reciprocal actions, but they also complained that the U.S. intention was to discuss what it would do only when the DPRK had completed the unilateral dismantlement of its nuclear program.[34] North Korea responded by putting forth its own proposal in which it would freeze all the facilities related to nuclear weapons and refrain from producing, transferring, and testing nuclear weapons in return for a U.S. commitment to lift its sanctions and blockade against the DPRK, energy assistance of 2,000 MW through the supply of heavy oil and electricity, and removal of the DPRK from the list of terrorism-sponsoring states.[35] The Chairman's Statement noted that the parties had stressed the need for a step-by-step reciprocal process of "words for words" and "action for action."[36]

In the meantime, as before, the North Koreans did not forget to show force. It was later reported that North Korea had test-fired a missile in the Sea of Japan a few days before the opening of the Six-Party Talks in June.[37] In September, North Korea started preparing for a No Dong ballistic missile launch. On November 1, several North Korean patrol boats crossed the NLL in the Yellow Sea on three separate occasions. South Korean patrol boats fired warning shots, but there was no direct clash between the two sides.[38] During this period, the U.S. side also took action. In October, the U.S. Congress passed the North Korean Human Rights Act, and Bush signed it. The act was designed to encourage private organizations to promote human rights in North Korea and increase the availability of information inside North Korea, thereby putting the pressure on the North Korean regime. In November, KEDO decided to prolong the suspension of the LWR Project in North Korea for another year.[39]

At this point, Pyongyang decided to suspend its operations as it waited to find out the result of the 2004 presidential election in the United States. When Bush was reelected in December, the MFA announced that it would "wait a bit longer" to find out what kind of North Korea policy the second Bush Administration might adopt.[40] A month later, Condoleezza Rice, Secretary of State-Designate, characterized North Korea as one of the "outposts of tyranny," however.[41] A few days later, in his inaugural address, Bush said the U.S. goal was to end "tyranny in our world."[42]

The threat of a nuclear test and the resumption of talks

On February 10, 2005, about three weeks after Bush entered his second term, North Korea declared itself a nuclear weapon state. Recognizing that U.S. policy had not changed after Bush's reelection, the MFA declared that the DPRK would suspend its participation in the Six-Party Talks for an indefinite period and that it had manufactured "nukes for self-defence." At the same time, it reiterated its willingness to solve the issue through dialogue.[43]

In this period, important personnel reshuffling took place within the U.S. Administration. In January, Rice was appointed Secretary of State. In the following month, Christopher Hill was named as the head of the U.S. delegation to the Six-Party Talks on the North Korean nuclear issue, and in April he became Assistant Secretary of State for East Asian and Pacific Affairs. During this period, Rice and Hill started to consider having serious bilateral talks with North Korea. In late March, Rice said that the United States recognized North Korea as a "sovereign state," adding that it did not have any intention to attack the North.[44]

In April, North Korea started to raise tensions once again. A senior North Korean official reportedly told an American specialist that his country had plans to unload its nuclear reactor in order to force Bush to negotiate on terms more favorable to North Korea.[45] In April, Kim Yong Chun, Chief of the KPA General Staff, warned that America's "hostile policy" would only prompt Pyongyang to "bolster its self-defensive nuclear deterrent under the banner of *Songun* [army-first policy]."[46] The MFA stated that to resume the Six-Party Talks, the United States must withdraw its "outpost of tyranny" remarks. The MFA also declared that the DPRK would regard sanctions imposed by the United Nations Security Council (UNSC) as a "declaration of war."[47] Rather than complying with the demand, Bush responded by calling Kim Jong Il "a tyrant."[48]

On May 1, North Korea reportedly fired a KN-02 short-range ballistic missile in the Sea of Japan after a failed test on April 29.[49] On May 5, it was reported that the United States had identified preparations for a nuclear test since October near Kilchu in the northeast of North Korea and that activity had accelerated in the past weeks.[50] On May 11, the MFA claimed that the DPRK had recently finished the unloading of 8,000 spent fuel rods from the 5-MW reactor and declared that it would resume the construction of 50-MW and 200-MW reactors.[51] In late May, the United States deployed 15 F-117 stealth bombers in South Korea.[52] In parallel with these escalatory moves, North Korea also showed a willingness to talk. On May 8, the MFA expressed its intention to find out whether the United States was prepared to hold bilateral talks within the framework of the Six-Party Talks.[53]

On the U.S. side, a North Korea policy review was taking place during this period. From the spring to the summer, the U.S. government developed and adopted a two-track policy toward North Korea in which both diplomacy and so-called "defensive measures," or pressure, would be used.[54] As a result, Rice and

Hill took steps to have serious bilateral talks with North Korea.[55] On May 9, Rice reiterated her position to recognize North Korea as "sovereign."[56] In May and June, Joseph DeTrani, Hill's deputy, met North Korean representatives at the United Nations. On June 17, Kim Jong Il expressed his willingness to return to the Six-Party Talks possibly in July if the United States "respected" his country. Kim also suggested that he would eliminate all medium- to long-range ballistic missiles if U.S.–DPRK diplomatic relations were normalized.[57] In late June, it was reported that North Korea had resumed construction of the 50-MW and 200-MW reactors.[58] In the July meeting with Hill, Kim Kye Gwan agreed to return to the Six-Party Talks.[59]

Activities in Nyongbyon, the Joint Statement, *and "Defensive Measures"*

On July 26, 2005, the first session of the fourth round of the Six-Party Talks convened in Beijing. In this session, the United States loosened its position on HEU in an attempt to break the deadlock and the focus of disagreement became whether North Korea should be entitled to LWRs or not.[60] In August 2005, Hecker visited North Korea again, and met Ri Hong Sop, the director of the Nuclear Scientific Research Centre in Nyongbyon. Ri told the visitors that: (a) the 5-MW reactor had operated from February 2003 to the end of March 2005 at the 25-MWth full power; (b) fuel rods were unloaded in April in part to extract the plutonium; (c) the reactor was reloaded with the last batch of fresh fuel produced prior to 1994, and operations resumed in mid-June; (d) reprocessing to extract plutonium from the unloaded 8,000 spent fuel rods had begun in late June and was almost finished in late August; and (e) the fuel fabrication facility was being refurbished to make more fuel.[61] The North Koreans were playing a game of coercion with the Americans. The same month, Bush appointed Jay Lefkowitz as special envoy for human rights in North Korea.

Against this backdrop, the fourth round of the Six-Party Talks was reconvened in September. The North Korean side again demanded LWRs. The U.S. side did not accept the demand. Finally, the United States suggested its own compromise. It accepted LWRs in the words of the joint statement, but decided to qualify its support later. The six-point Joint Statement adopted on September 19 thus stated that:

- The DPRK was committed to abandoning all nuclear weapons and existing nuclear programs and returning, at an early date, to the NPT and to IAEA safeguards;
- The United States had no intention to attack or invade the DPRK with nuclear or conventional weapons;
- The DPRK and the United States would take steps to normalize their relations;
- The DPRK and Japan would take steps to normalize their relations;

169

- The non-North Korea parties were willing to provide energy assistance to the DPRK and were wiling to discuss, at an appropriate time, the provision of LWRs to the DPRK; and
- The directly related parties would negotiate a permanent peace regime on the Korean Peninsula at an appropriate separate forum.[62]

The Joint Statement was significant in that it clearly spelled out the end scenario in which all parties would be satisfied. Nevertheless, disagreements remained. Just after the Joint Statement was adopted, Hill issued a statement, drafted primarily by Undersecretary of State for Arms Control and International Security Robert Joseph.[63] It stated that the "appropriate time" for providing LWRs to the DPRK would only come when the DPRK had eliminated all nuclear weapons and all nuclear programs, and come into full compliance with the NPT and IAEA safeguards. The statement also said that the United States supported a decision to terminate KEDO by the end of 2005.[64] North Korea was quick to respond. On the next day, the MFA declared that the United States "should not even dream of the issue of the DPRK's dismantlement of its nuclear deterrent before providing LWRs, a physical guarantee for confidence-building."[65]

Further complicating matters, on September 15, while the Six-Party Talks were proceeding, the U.S. Department of the Treasury decided to designate the Macao-based Banco Delta Asia (BDA) as a "primary money laundering concern" in an attempt to freeze the North Korean account in the bank.[66] This action was taken as a part of the "defensive measures," or coercive element, in the U.S. government's two-track policy. "Defensive measures," including PSI as well as economic and financial actions, were designed to deter, disrupt, and prevent North Korea's proliferation and other illicit activities.[67] After the September 15 announcement, banks all over the world started to shut down their dealings with North Korea. In October, the U.S. government for the first time publicly accused North Korea of manufacturing high-quality counterfeit $100 "supernotes."[68] The U.S. Treasury Department also announced that it was freezing the assets in the United States of eight North Korean enterprises involved in activities related to WMD.[69] The United States was taking these more aggressive tactics in the hope of enhancing its bargaining power.[70]

In the first session of the fifth round of the Six-Party Talks in November 2005, North Korea called for implementing the joint statement in phases and refused to discuss the nuclear issue unless the financial sanctions were lifted.[71] The session ended without meaningful results. In the same month, the U.S. Agency for International Development announced that it would cease to provide food aid to North Korea, and KEDO began discussing the termination of the LWR project. Moreover, the United States co-sponsored a resolution before the United Nations General Assembly that condemned North Korea's poor human rights record.[72] The General Assembly passed the resolution in December.[73]

Faced with strong protests from North Korea on the sanctions and continuing demands for bilateral talks, Hill offered a briefing session on the sanctions to the

North Koreans. The briefing did not work as planned, though, and in December, the MFA denounced the United States while linking prospects for resuming the Six-Party Talks to the U.S. attitude.[74] In January 2006, KEDO completed the withdrawal of all workers from the LWR project site. Bush said the United States would not lift sanctions unless North Korea stopped faking U.S. dollars. In February, while criticizing the United States, the MFA claimed that the DPRK government opposed "all sorts of illegal acts in the financial field" and would "actively join the international actions against money laundering."[75] In March, a U.S.–DPRK meeting was held in New York in which the North Korean side reiterated that lifting the financial sanctions were a prerequisite for North Korea's return to the Six-Party Talks.[76] On the next day, North Korea fired two anti-ship missiles in the Sea of Japan.[77] On March 30, the U.S. Department of the Treasury added a Swiss company and individual to the list of designees supporting the pro-liferation of WMD for their involvement with North Korea.[78]

Faced with the execution of a series of the "defensive measures," North Korea showed a strong attitude of defiance. In May, it was reported that preparations for a missile test were sighted.[79] Shortly thereafter, KEDO decided to terminate the LWR project. On June 1, the MFA declared that the "escalated hostile policy and increasing pressure" would only compel the DPRK to take the "strongest measures to protect its right to existence and sovereignty." At the same time, however, it also extended an invitation for Hill to visit Pyongyang once again.[80] The U.S. government rejected the invitation.

Multiple missile launches

After midnight on July 5, or in the afternoon of July 4, Independence Day by U.S. time, North Korea began launching Scud, No Dong, and Taepo Dong 2 missiles, defying strong international warnings against such an action. The mis-siles were launched at approximately 0333 hours, 0404 hours, 0501 hours, 0712 hours, 0731 hours, 0732 hours, and 1720 hours. The first, fourth, and sixth missiles were assessed as Scud D, Scud C, and Scud ER missiles, respectively; the second, fifth and seventh as No Dong; and the third as Taepo Dong 2.[81] While the Scud and No Dong missiles were successfully launched in the north-eastern direction between the Russian Far East and Japan's Hokkaido island, the Taepo Dong 2 launch failed disastrously. The missile disintegrated in the air several tens of seconds after the launch.[82]

On July 6, the MFA issued a statement noting that (a) the missile launches had been part of routine military exercises to increase defense capacity, (b) the KPA would go on with missile launch exercises in the future, and (c) the DPRK would take "stronger physical actions of other forms" if they faced more pres-sure from the international community.[83] On July 15, the UNSC unanimously adopted Resolution 1695, requiring member states to prevent the transfer and procurement of missiles and missile-related items, materials, goods and technol-ogy to and from North Korea, as well as the transfer of any financial resources in relation to North Korea's missile or WMD programs.[84] Although the resolution did not approve the use of force, China's support was nevertheless significant. On the next day, the MFA proclaimed that the United States had sought to "describe the issue between the DPRK and the U.S. as an issue between the DPRK and the UN [United Nations] and form an international alliance against the DPRK," adding that the DPRK would "bolster its war deterrent for self-defence in every way by all means and methods."[85] North Korea's diplomatic target was the United States and the United States only. On July 26, the Department of State acknowledged that the Bank of China had frozen some North Korean assets in its Macau branch.[86]

The October 9 nuclear test

In mid-August, unnamed U.S. officials suggested that North Korea might be preparing for a nuclear test. Suspicious vehicle movement was observed at a suspected test site and wire bundles used to monitor an underground test were identified.[87] On September 21, Hill revealed that he had suggested a bilateral working group to discuss financial sanctions on the condition that the North Koreans came back to the Six-Party Talks.[88] On October 3, the MFA issued a three-point statement, noting that: (a) the DPRK would conduct a nuclear test; (b) the DPRK would never use nuclear weapons first and strictly prohibit any threat of nuclear weapons transfer; and (c) Pyongyang would do its utmost to realize the denuclearization of the peninsula and give momentum to worldwide nuclear disarmament and ultimate denuclearization.[89]

At 1035 hours on October 9, the DPRK conducted a nuclear test near Punggye in Kilchu in the country's northeast. On October 11, the MFA issued a statement:

> Although the DPRK conducted the nuclear test due to the U.S., it still remains unchanged in its will to denuclearize the peninsula through dialogue and negotiations.
> ...The DPRK's nuclear test does not contradict the September 19 joint statement under which it committed itself to dismantle nuclear weapons and abandon the existing nuclear program. On the contrary, it constitutes a positive measure for its implementation.
> ...If the U.S. increases pressure upon the DPRK, persistently doing harm to it, it will continue to take physical countermeasures, considering it as a declaration of a war.[90]

In response to the nuclear test, the UNSC unanimously adopted Resolution 1718 on October 14. The resolution called upon all member states to take measures to make it difficult for North Korea to acquire (a) major conventional weapon systems, (b) all items, materials, equipment, goods, and technology which could contribute to nuclear-related, ballistic missile-related, or other WMD related programs, and (c) luxury goods.[91] The resolution mentioned Chapter VII and

Article 41 of the United Nations Charter, which allowed for such measures as interruption of economic relations and the severance of diplomatic relations, but did not mention Article 42, which provided for use of military force.

About-face: a major shift in the U.S. policy

Rather than acting on the resolution, the United States decided to change course.[92] On October 31, 2006, a U.S.–DPRK bilateral meeting was held in Beijing. In the high-level bilateral talk, Hill suggested a willingness to resolve the BDA issue separately from the Six-Party Talks.[93] Against this backdrop, the MFA announced that the DPRK would return to the Six-Party Talks on November 1.[94] In late November, additional U.S.–DPRK bilateral meetings were held in Beijing in which a so-called "early harvest" proposal was presented to Kim Kye Gwan. The proposal required North Korea to stop activities at Nyongbyon, allow IAEA inspectors back, present the list of its nuclear-related programs and facilities, and shut down its nuclear test sites by 2008. If North Korea fulfilled these requirements, it would receive food and energy aid and the United States would discuss ways to end the sanctions against BDA, normalize diplomatic relations, and establish a peace regime on the Korean Peninsula. The North Korean side responded by insisting that the BDA issue be addressed first.[95] In any case, after a 13-month intermission, the second session of the fifth round of the Six-Party Talks convened on December 18. In the meeting, Kim Kye Gwan warned that the implementation of the Joint Statement would be possible only after the BDA sanctions were lifted.[96] While the talks were proceeding, U.S. and North Korean officials separately had working-level talks on the BDA issue. After this round of talks, Kim Kye Gwan criticized the United States for having failed to lift the sanctions; U.S. intelligence identified renewed activities in the North Korean nuclear test site.[97]

In the meantime, an important political change took place in the United States. In the mid-term elections in November, the Democrats won a majority in both the House and the Senate, putting the Republicans in a difficult position. Moreover, as a result, important personnel changes followed this upset victory. U.S. Ambassador to the United Nations John Bolton, Secretary of Defense Rumsfeld, and Undersecretary of State for Arms Control Robert Joseph, all advocates of a tough policy toward North Korea, resigned between late 2006 and early 2007. After these personnel changes, the United States decisively shifted its approach toward engagement with North Korea.

In January 2007, U.S.–DPRK talks were held in Berlin. Hill and Kim Kye Gwan agreed that the DPRK would shut down nuclear facilities in Nyongbyon within 60 days and it would receive HFO in return. This "Berlin Agreement" was to be formalized at the next session of the Six-Party Talks.[98] Later in the same month, U.S. and North Korean officials again met to discuss issued related to financial sanctions.

Implementing the Joint Statement

On February 13, the third session of the fifth round of the Six-Party Talks ended with the adoption of an action plan for implementing the 2005 Joint Statement. The action plan had two phases. In the 60-day initial phase, the DPRK would shut down and seal for the purpose of eventual abandonment the Nyongbyon nuclear facility, including the reprocessing facility, and invite back IAEA personnel; and the other parties would provide emergency energy assistance equivalent to 50,000 tons of HFO. In the next phase, the DPRK would provide a complete declaration of all nuclear programs, and all existing nuclear facilities would be disabled. In return, the other parties would provide North Korea with economic, energy, and humanitarian assistance up to the equivalent of one million tons of HFO, including the initial shipment equivalent to 50,000 tons.[99] In the meantime, the United States assured its North Korean counterpart that that it would begin talks to end the BDA sanctions within 30 days.[100]

In March, the Department of the Treasury allowed North Korea to transfer the roughly $25 million frozen in BDA, in effect lifting its financial sanction.[101] On June 15, the Macau authorities announced the completion of the transfer. On the next day, the Director General of North Korea's General Department of Atomic Energy invited an IAEA working-level delegation to North Korea once more.[102] In July, North Korea shut down the 5-MW and 50-MW reactors, reprocessing facility, nuclear fuel fabrication plant in Nyongbyon, and the 200-MW reactor in Taechon.[103] Two days after South Korea began providing HFO, North Korea informed the United States that the facilities had been shut down.[104]

Following the second session of the sixth round of the Six-Party Talks, the agreement on "Second Phase Actions for the Implementation of the Joint Statement" was announced on October 3. In the agreement, North Korea pledged to disable the 5-MW reactor, the reprocessing plant, and the nuclear fuel rod fabrication facility in Nyongbyon by December 31, 2007. It also agreed to provide a "complete and correct declaration of all its nuclear programs" by the year's end. In return, the other parties reaffirmed the provision of assistance to North Korea. More importantly, the United States suggested it would remove North Korea from the list of State Sponsors of Terrorism as well as lift sanctions imposed under the Trading with the Enemy Act.[105] Although North Korea failed to meet the deadline, most of the agreed disablement tasks at the three core facilities were completed prior to February 2008, and North Korea provided over 18,000 pages of operating records from Nyongbyon in early May. In late June, it presented a list of allegedly all of its nuclear programs to the Chinese government. Bush responded by announcing that the Trading with the Enemy Act would no longer be applied to North Korea and notified Congress of his intent to rescind North Korea's designation as a State Sponsor of Terrorism.[106] Later in the month, a cooling tower for the 5-MW reactor in Nyongbyon was demolished. In July, the six parties agreed to establish a verification mechanism within the Six-Party Talks framework whose measures included visits to facilities,

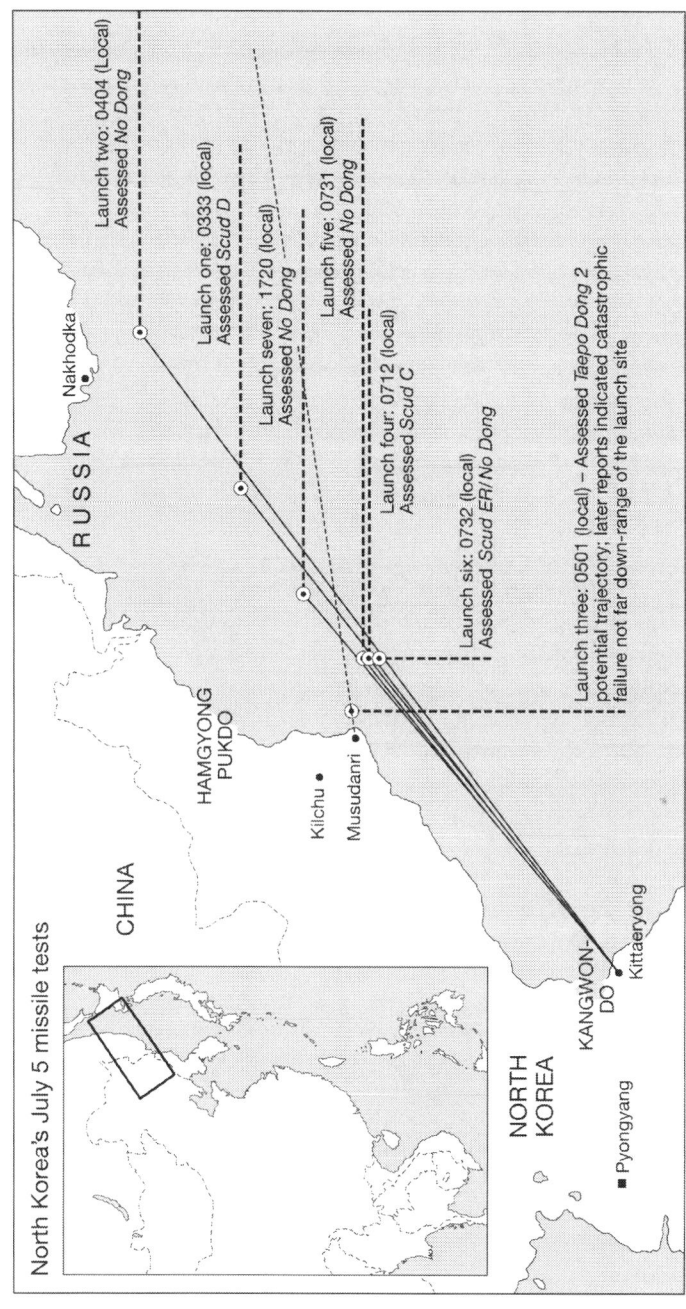

Launch two: 0404 (Local)
Assessed *No Dong*

Launch one: 0333 (local)
Assessed *Scud D*

Launch seven: 1720 (local)
Assessed *No Dong*

Launch five: 0731 (local)
Assessed *No Dong*

Launch four: 0712 (local)
Assessed *Scud C*

Launch six: 0732 (local)
Assessed *Scud ER/No Dong*

Launch three: 0501 (local) – Assessed *Taepo Dong 2*
potential trajectory; later reports indicated catastrophic
failure not far down-range of the launch site

RUSSIA

Nakhodka

HAMGYONG
PUKDO

Kilchu

Musudanri

CHINA

North Korea's July 5 missile tests

NORTH
KOREA

Pyongyang

KANGWON-
DO

Kittaeryong

Map 9.1   North Korea's July 5 missile tests
Source: Adam Ward, ed., "North Korea's 5 July Missile Tests," *Strategic Comments*, vol. 12, issue 6 (London: Taylor & Francis Ltd.,
July 2006), reprinted with permission of the publisher.

review of documents, interviews with technical personnel and other measures unanimously agreed by the six parties.[107]

However, when the United States failed to remove North Korea from the list of State Sponsors of Terrorism on the ground that they had not yet agreed to verification measures, North Korea announced in late August that it had decided to consider restoring its nuclear facilities in Nyongbyon.[108] In September, it removed IAEA seals and surveillance from the reprocessing plant.[109] In the meantime, North Korea reportedly conducted a Taepo Dong missile engine burn test as well as other missile launch tests and appeared to be preparing for another nuclear test.[110]

On October 1–3, however, a U.S. negotiating team visited Pyongyang for talks on verification measures, but on October 9, North Korea informed IAEA inspectors that it would no longer grant them access to facilities at Nyongbyon and stated that it was preparing to restart the nuclear facilities there.[111] Just two days later, on October 11, the United States announced that North Korea had finally agreed to the terms of verification: experts from all Six Parties would be allowed to have access to all declared facilities and, based on mutual consent, to undeclared sites; scientific procedures, including sampling and forensic activities, would be used; and all measures contained in the Verification Protocol would apply to both plutonium-based and uranium enrichment activities.[112] Based upon the bilateral agreement, the United States rescinded the designation of the DPRK as a State Sponsor of Terrorism on the same day.[113] It was reported that a key factor influencing this decision was the growing concern that North Korea could "test a nuclear weapon in the final 100 days of Bush's presidency."[114] On October 13, North Korea granted the IAEA access to the facilities at Nyongbyon.[115]

However, during the meeting of the Heads of Delegation of the Six-Party Talks in December, North Korea refused to agree to terms for verification. It turned out that the United States had removed North Korea from the list of State Sponsors of Terrorism, based on "oral understandings" that they had agreed on a verification plan.[116] North Korea's official media reported that there was "no paragraph referring to the collection of samples" in the U.S.–DPRK agreement of early October.[117]

Critical factors

Iraq, internal division, and the election

In a peculiar way, the twists and turns in the second nuclear episode were not primarily driven by North Korean factors but rather by other factors such as developments in Iraq, internal division within the U.S. government, and the U.S. midterm election. First, the most important U.S. foreign policy priority – Iraq – put North Korea on the backburner. Deputy Secretary of State Richard Armitage later argued that the U.S. government was not willing to be involved in North

Korean issues when Afghanistan and Iraq were policy priorities.[118] As a result, Washington defined North Korean nuclear development "not as a dispute between the United States and North Korea but one between North Korea and the rest of the world," and insisted that this issue be dealt with within a multilateral framework.[119] In the multilateral framework, China was expected to take the lead.[120] Moreover, U.S. leaders thought that the success in Iraq would be the most effective pressure on North Korea.[121]

Second, the Bush Administration long remained internally divided over North Korea. Vice President Cheney continued to block any policy to engage North Korea, and the hardliners within the administration seemed to favor regime change in North Korea as the ultimate goal of U.S. policy.[122] By contrast, moderates attempted to use engagement combined with pressure to encourage North Korea to make a "strategic decision" to dismantle its nuclear programs. Until the Vice President's position was weakened and the hardliners left office, neither the President nor the National Security Advisor provided coherence in North Korea policy.[123]

Finally, as the situation in Iraq deteriorated, the Republican party fared disastrously in the midterm election held in November 2006. When it became clear that the Bush Administration could not afford any more foreign policy debacles, it decided to use North Korea to score desperately needed diplomatic points.[124]

Weakness as strength

In a paradoxical way, North Korea's weakness worked as its strength. North Korea's collapse was anathema not only to South Korea but also to China. As a result, South Korea and China continued to reject any policy which pressured North Korea too much and helped stabilize the country whenever possible.

By 2003, South Korea's policy had decidedly become that of maintaining the status quo, i.e. division of the Korean Peninsula, in the foreseeable future. In order to achieve its goal of moderating North Korea's behavior and maintaining the status quo at the same time, South Korea opted for proactive engagement. As a result, inter-Korean trade grew from $642 million in 2002 to $1.35 billion in 2006.[125] The South Korean government provided official aid to North Korea in the amount of $93.77 million in 2003, $123.62 million in 2004, $135.88 million in 2005, and $193.77 million in 2006. Non-governmental aid fluctuated, but still remained high, at $45.77 million in 2002, $63.86 million in 2003, $132.50 million in 2004, $76.66 million in 2005, and $80.48 million in 2006.[126] The two Koreas were also engaged in joint development projects such as reconnection of railways and roads, tourism in Mt. Geumgang and development of the Gaeseong (Kaesong) Industrial Complex in North Korea.[127]

The sea change in South Korean politics also helped North Korea. In 2002, liberal Roh Moo-hyun was unexpectedly elected president, and he strongly promoted a proactive and accommodative engagement policy toward North Korea. In November 2004, President Roh even stated that the North Korean contention that their nuclear weapons and missiles constituted a means of safeguarding their security by deterring threats from the outside was "understandable."[128] According to a high-ranking U.S. official, Roh's policy orientation made it difficult to consider military options against North Korea.[129] In addition, South Korea was concerned about the negative impact of rising tension on its economy, with Moody's Investors Service changing the outlook for long-term ratings of South Korea from positive to negative in February 2003.[130] South Korean leaders were quite conscious of the negative impact this would have and therefore wanted to minimize political instability on the peninsula.

With a rapidly growing economy, China also played an important role in sustaining the North Korean regime. In the 2000s, China continued to provide assistance equivalent to about $200 million annually. In the China–North Korea Summit meetings in 2005 and 2006, China reportedly agreed to provide a 50–100-million-dollar aid package to North Korea.[131] Moreover, North Korea's trade with China totaled $1.7 billion in 2006, up from $488 million in 2000 and from $1.3 billion in 2005, despite its missile launch and nuclear test. This figure amounted to about 40 percent of North Korea's total trade. Between 2000 and 2005, bilateral trade grew on average by 30 percent annually, contributing to an estimated 3.5 percent annual growth for the North Korean economy.[132] In April 2005, Hill suggested that China shut down its oil pipeline to North Korea to pressure it to come back to talks. But China simply rejected this.[133] On this point, Charles Pritchard has correctly pointed out:

> Any conclusion that Beijing does not hold significant leverage over Pyongyang is not quite accurate. However, Beijing may avoid applying too much leverage on Pyongyang for what is only a second-tier national security priority for China (North Korea's nuclear weapons program) because it fears that doing so could have a negative impact on its top national security priority (regional security).[134]

Finally, partly due to the large amount of humanitarian assistance that the international community provided to North Korea, its economy recorded positive growth between 1999 and 2005 after experiencing an average 4.3 percent negative growth between 1990 and 1998.[135] Its grain production had grown for five years until 2005 though it marked negative growth in 2006.[136] Consequently, North Korea could conduct nuclear diplomacy within a relatively favorable domestic and regional environment and therefore survive pressure coming from the United States.

Nuclear capabilities

Although there were many similarities between North Korea's first and second round of nuclear diplomacy, one of the new factors in the second nuclear episode was the maturity of North Korea's nuclear program. Since the Agreed

Framework did not prohibit the development of a detonator, the miniaturization of nuclear devices, or the development of delivery means, North Korea could continue to work on these projects even after 1994. The yield of the October 2006 nuclear explosion was less than one kiloton, much smaller than the four kilotons that the North Koreans had predicted, and thus the test was not a clear-cut success.[137] That said, it was still significant that North Korea detonated a nuclear device.[138] At the time of the test, North Korean nuclear scientists and engineers must have been extremely nervous given the disastrous failure of the Taepo Dong 2 test in July. Kim Jong Il, the scientists, and the engineers took a chance, and produced a reasonably successful result.

The Institute for Science and International Security, a U.S. think tank, estimated that at the time of the 1994 nuclear crisis, there was 0–10 kilograms of separated plutonium (0–2 bombs equivalent) in North Korea's possession and that in 2006, there were 33–55 kilograms (6–13 bombs equivalent).[139] This estimate was reinforced by the declaration North Korea presented in June 2008, in which it stated that it had produced 38 kilograms of plutonium, 26 kilograms of which had been used to produce nuclear weapons.[140] Moreover, at the time of the test, the fuel fabrication facility was in the final stages of refurbishment, and would begin new fuel fabrication in 2007. This meant that within about a year, an entire reactor core of fresh fuel rods would have been fabricated.[141] This development seems to have worked as a significant pressure on the United States.

Another path in North Korea's nuclear development was a uranium enrichment program. North Korea made a secret deal with Pakistan in 1996 with which Pakistan would provide uranium enrichment technology to North Korea, and North Korea began its uranium enrichment program in earnest in the late 1990s.[142] Pakistan provided nearly a dozen first- and second-generation Pakistani centrifuges to North Korea together with blueprints and a shopping list of necessary components with which North Korean scientists could construct their own centrifuge production infrastructure. In 2000, North Korea decided to acquire materials for a uranium-enrichment facility with several thousand centrifuges. In November 2002, the U.S. Central Intelligence Agency estimated that North Korea was constructing a plant that could produce enough weapons-grade uranium for two or more nuclear weapons per year when fully operational – which could happen as soon as mid-decade.[143] In April 2003, a 22-ton shipment of high-strength aluminum tubes acquired by a German firm was intercepted en route to North Korea. The dimensions of those tubes matched the technical requirements for vacuum castings for a Urenco centrifuge, and authorities then discovered that this shipment was to be followed by another 200 tons of tubes.[144]

North Korea's improved nuclear capabilities seem to have done two things. First, the 2006 nuclear test worked as a catalyst in bringing about a change in U.S. policy. The nuclear test made it clear that the U.S. policy in the past had failed, and that unless the United States decided to engage with North Korea, there would be more and possibly bigger tests in the future.[145] Moreover, North

Korea's threat to conduct another nuclear test encouraged the United States to remove the country from the list of terrorism-sponsoring states. Second, North Korea's nuclear capabilities worked as a deterrent. As a high-ranking U.S. official pointed out, the advancement that the North Korean nuclear development had achieved since 1994 was one of the reasons why the United States regarded the use of force as a difficult option to take.[146]

Missile capabilities

During the second round of nuclear diplomacy, furthermore, North Korea's missile capabilities were also more advanced. By 2003, North Korea had deployed some 175–200 No Dong missiles capable of covering almost the entire territory of Japan.[147] As it was difficult to spot No Dong missiles mounted on mobile launchers, of which North Korea reportedly possessed about 30, a preemptive strike would not be effective.[148] Additionally, by 2006, North Korea had also developed a Taepo Dong 2 missile. In 2007, the U.S. government estimated the range of a two-stage Taepo Dong 2 to be 10,000 kilometers, and that of the three-stage version to be 15,000 kilometers.[149] By July 2006, the missile had become ready for a flight-testing, although the test ended in failure.[150]

In late 1999, the KPA established the Missile Training Guidance Bureau, and all ballistic missile units were subsequently subordinated to this bureau. Since the 2001–02 training cycle when the KPA started to conduct ballistic missile exercises at battalion level instead of battery level, annual exercises with Scud and No Dong units had expanded and many ballistic missile units had been redeployed.[151]

The increased number and types of the missiles combined with improved operational skills seem to have given North Korean leaders the option to undertake the missile launching spree of July 2006. These missile launches demonstrated the level of sophistication that the North Korean's missile forces had achieved. Seven missiles were launched within a relatively short period of time. Some of them were launched at night from mobile launchers, and made impact in a narrow target area despite the differences in their operational ranges.[152] A high-ranking U.S. official argued that the increased missile arsenal played a role in deterring U.S. use of force against North Korea.[153] Experts agree, however, that the July 2006 missile tests did not affect U.S. policy much.[154]

Deterrence vs. "preemption"

The basic deterrent structure in the second nuclear crisis was not much different from the one in 1994. North Korea's deterrent capabilities continued to come mainly from its conventional forces. The United States officially adopted "preemption" as its national security strategy in 2002. However, the United States and, in particular, South Korea were reluctant to use force for fear that a large number of casualties and damage would be suffered if North Korea retaliated. The number of North Korea's

170-millimeter artillery pieces had reportedly grown from about 200 in the early 1990s to over 600 by 2001, and the number of 240-millimeter multiple rocket launchers had increased to 430.[155] If chemical weapons were loaded on artillery shells, the expected number of casualties would shoot up dramatically. In fact, despite the public argument that all options were on the table, decision-makers at the U.S. Department of Defense were overwhelmingly pessimistic about taking military action against North Korea.[156]

Characteristics

Location and timing

As in the 1990s, a major part of North Korea's nuclear activities took place within its territory. The second round of nuclear diplomacy was conducted in more diverse fronts than in the first, however. For one, international nuclear-related transactions played a more important role in the 2000s both in terms of procurement of nuclear-related equipment and in terms of potential sales of nuclear devices. North Korea also took military actions in the Yellow Sea and the Sea of Japan in this episode.

The second round of nuclear diplomacy began in December 2002, and has lasted for six years as of December 2008. Rising tensions were at least tenta-tively eased with the signing of the February 2007 action plan, but the major issues of contention have not yet been resolved. It's important to note that the timing of the commencement of the second round of nuclear diplomacy was not of North Korea's own choosing. When North Korea decided to embark on its second nuclear diplomacy, it did so only after the United States had found out about its covert uranium enrichment program. From Pyongyang's perspective, therefore, North Korea had been suddenly forced to take strong action in the face of international pressure.

When the North Korean leaders decided to conduct missile and nuclear tests, they took a chance. There was no technological assurance that the sys-tems would actually work. In fact, neither of them were clear-cut successes. However, their psychological impact was not insignificant. North Korea sur-prised the world at least three times by quickly deciding to withdraw from the NPT in 2003, launching missiles in 2006, and conducting a nuclear test in the same year.

Forces involved and the type of use of force

Both actual and potential nuclear forces played an important role in this episode of nuclear diplomacy. Fighter aircraft, patrol boats, anti-ship missiles, and bal-listic missiles were also employed to enhance the nuclear coercion. In many ways, past episodes such as the *Pueblo* and EC-121 incidents, the West Sea incident, and missile diplomacy were replayed in the second round of nuclear diplomacy. It is quite interesting that the missile issue did not become a major topic in the Six-Party Talks although the North Korean side actually suggested it be one.[157]

The North Korean strategy was composed of two major elements: deterrence and compellence. Through deterrence, it achieved the most fundamental goal: regime survival. Through compellence, it attempted to encourage the United States to normalize relations with and provide economic assistance to the country. In order to make these coercive tools effective, the North Koreans invited American specialists such as Siegfried Hecker to visit their country on multiple occasions. When this indirect and implicit approach failed to produce results, they went ahead with missile and nuclear tests.

Intensity and targeting

As in 1993–94, the second round of nuclear diplomacy did not involve the actual application of force and it did not cause any casualties or physical damage to the concerned countries. The only difference between the first and second round was that an actual nuclear explosion was involved in the second one. As in the first round of nuclear diplomacy, North Korea refrained from causing human or material damage on any of the target countries, particularly the United States, most likely because it wanted to extract economic assistance from or improve relations with them.

Military-diplomatic coordination

Nuclear diplomacy in the 2000s within North Korea was reportedly managed by the task force called "*Yugja Hoedam Sangmujo*," or the Six-Party Talks Management Team.[158] Military actions and diplomacy were very well coordinated, as in most of the cases military actions were preceded or followed by diplomatic moves to give meaning to them.

It is also important to note that the MFA might not have been aware of the existence of the HEU program when the U.S. side challenged North Korean diplomats on the issue in 2002. On this point, Kang Sok Ju reportedly said that "we in the Foreign Ministry were surprised that there was indeed this program: we did have this program, and the military was running it."[159] As in the 1990s, it seems that nuclear diplomacy and nuclear weapons development were managed by different organizations: the Six-Party Talks Management Team and the "131 *Jidogug*," or Guidance Bureau No. 131.[160]

Assessment

For all its provocative actions, North Korea's political objectives in the 2000s were not any different from those in the first nuclear episode in the 1990s. North Korea was still seeking to ensure regime survival by improving relations with the United States and, to a lesser extent, Japan. North Korea repeatedly clarified this point in the early stages of this round of the nuclear diplomacy. For example, North Korea presented a "proposal for a package solution to the nuclear issue and the order of simultaneous actions" in 2003. According to the proposal, the United States was to (a) conclude a non-aggression treaty with North Korea, (b) establish diplomatic relations with it, (c) guarantee economic cooperation between the DPRK and Japan, and between the two Koreas, and (d) compensate North Korea for the loss of electricity caused by the delayed provision of LWRs and complete their construction.[161] In essence, North Korea was demanding security assurances and a new peace mechanism, normalization with the United States, economic benefits, and energy assistance. In this section, the effectiveness of the second round of nuclear diplomacy will be assessed against these policy objectives as well as other possible domestic political objectives.

Security assurances and a new peace mechanism

In the 2005 Joint Statement, the United States affirmed that it had no nuclear weapons on the Korean Peninsula and that it had "no intention to attack or invade the DPRK with nuclear or conventional weapons." This was a big step forward for North Korea. The North Korean leaders seemed to have been concerned about the U.S. decision to consider developing earth-penetrating nuclear weapons to be used against nations armed with WMD, including North Korea, coupled with its adoption of "preemption" as official strategy.[162] For example, the North Korean media reported in June 2005 that the United States had deployed missiles capable of penetrating underground in an attempt to bring about "regime change."[163] The U.S. pledge was thus doubly meaningful since it provided conventional security assurances in addition to nuclear-related negative security assurances that the Agreed Framework had already provided. However, from the North Korean perspective, no assurance without actual military movement to support it would be enough. From Pyongyang's perspective, the written security assurance in the Joint Statement was only part of the answer.

Regarding the replacement of the Korean Armistice with a new peace mechanism, the Joint Statement called on the directly related parties to negotiate a "permanent peace regime" on the Korean Peninsula, repeated in the 2007 action plan. Although Hill said in 2007 that the talks to sign a formal peace treaty could begin "next year," it was a rather open-ended commitment without any target date.[164] In any case, it was at least moderately meaningful to North Korea because Pyongyang had repeatedly demanded the replacement of the Armistice Agreement with a new peace mechanism since 1993 and the establishment of a peace mechanism would certainly contribute to the survival of Kim Jong Il's regime and to the normalization of U.S.– DPRK relations.

Normalization of relations with the United States

The United States stopped applying the Trading with the Enemy Act to North Korea in June 2008 and rescinded its designation as a State Sponsor of Terrorism in October the same year. Although the Bush Administration emphasized that these actions were largely symbolic and that most sanctions, including those related to the October 2006 nuclear test, proliferation activities, and human rights violations, would continue, this was a major about-face in the administration's North Korea policy.[165] North Korea responded cautiously, welcoming the U.S. actions but warning that the successful implementation of the verification agreement would depend on whether the delisting of the DPRK as a state sponsor of terrorism would actually take effect and economic rewards be provided.[166] Nevertheless, given that the application of the Trading with the Enemy Act and designation as a State Sponsor of Terrorism had been regarded as two of the most important stumbling blocks to the fundamental improvement of U.S.–DPRK relations, the steps that the United States took in June and October 2008 at least paved a way for substantial improvement of diplomatic relations between the two countries.

In addition, these U.S. actions had important potential implications for U.S.–DPRK economic relations. For one, by no longer applying the Trading with the Enemy Act, the United States removed the requirement for licenses on all imports from North Korea.[167] With the delisting of North Korea as a State Sponsor of Terrorism, a ban on arms-related exports and sales, controls over exports of dual-use items, prohibitions on economic assistance, and the imposition of financial and other restrictions imposed by U.S. law were technically lifted. Most significantly, the United States was now no longer required to oppose loans by the World Bank and other international financial institutions to North Korea.[168] Despite these major changes, however, the United States and North Korea failed to fully normalize diplomatic relations.

Provision of light-water reactors and heavy oil

In July 2007, South Korea provided 50,000 tons of HFO to North Korea in return for the nuclear freeze. In October, the parties agreed in the second phase of the action plan to provide 450,000 tons of HFO as well as materials and equipment for producing energy equivalent to 500,000 tons of HFO.[169] By early February 2008, it was informally agreed that materials and equipment related to refurbishing coal mines and thermal and hydro power plants would be provided to North Korea as non-HFO assistance.[170] By the end of July 2008, North Korea had received approximately 420,000 tons of HFO and equivalent assistance.[171] The 50,000 tons of HFO that South Korea procured from SK Energy were valued at $22 million.[172] By simple calculation, one million tons of HFO would cost about $440 million.

North Korea did not obtain nearly as much direct material benefit as it had in its first nuclear diplomacy, though. The 1994 Agreed Framework offered North Korea an annual provision of 500,000 tons of HFO for about eight years, or some four million tons of HFO, about four times as much as offered in the 2007 action plan. Ironically, suppliers of HFO will have to spend about the same amount of money, however, due to rising oil prices. In addition, although the 2005 Joint Statement mentioned the possible provision of LWRs to North Korea, no concrete decision has yet been made.

Moreover, North Korea's nuclear development came at a price. According to the ROK Ministry of National Defense, North Korea has probably spent \$290–764 million for its nuclear program, including \$57–170 million to construct the 5-MW reactor, \$20–59 million for the reprocessing facility, \$24–73 million for the plutonium production needed for one nuclear device, and \$33–106 million for designing and producing nuclear weapons.[173]

Economic cooperation with Japan and South Korea

North Korea's nuclear diplomacy also negatively affected its relationship with Japan, and bilateral economic cooperation between the two has not yet been realized. In July 2002, just months before the onset of the second round of nuclear diplomacy, North Korea started to take a series of measures to improve its economic management. If economic reform were to gather momentum, Pyongyang would have to introduce a large amount of foreign capital goods and funds into the country. It was in this context that Japanese Prime Minister Junichiro Koizumi visited Pyongyang to meet with Kim Jong Il in September. The two leaders agreed that Japan would provide economic assistance to North Korea after normalization. The bilateral Pyongyang Declaration specified that the economic assistance would include grant aid, loans and credits, and humanitarian assistance, with the total amount expected to be several billion dollars at the minimum.[174] The onset of tension over the nuclear issue as well as the revelation that North Korea had actually abducted Japanese citizens and that some of them were already dead, however, stalled the normalization process. Furthermore, the Japanese government imposed unilateral sanctions on North Korea shortly after the nuclear test in October 2006, making it even harder for the two countries to improve relations.[175] As a result, Japan refused to provide not only the economic assistance specified in the Pyongyang Declaration but also the relatively small amount of energy aid based on the six-party agreements in February and October 2007.

By contrast, inter-Korean economic cooperation continued despite the nuclear crisis. The South Korean government provided an average \$136.76 million annually as official aid to North Korea between 2003 and 2006, and joint development projects also proceeded. North Korea's nuclear diplomacy did not cause this outcome, however, as warming relations between North and South were a result of South Korea's proactive sunshine policy of engagement. In fact,

North Korea's diplomacy of brinkmanship significantly slowed down the development of inter-Korean economic cooperation, which could have advanced much more rapidly had it not been for the nuclear issue.[176]

Maintaining domestic stability

North Korean leadership extensively used the nuclear test for domestic propaganda purposes. After the nuclear test, words of celebration appeared in every corner of the nation. A few weeks after the test, reportedly more than 100,000 people including party, army, and state cadres were mobilized in Pyongyang to celebrate the "historic successful nuclear test" in an army–people rally held at Kim Il Sung Square.[177] On January 1, 2007, the New Year's special editorial said, "The army and people of Korea, under the unfurled banner of *Songun* [army-first policy], have won victory after victory in the showdown with the United States and in safeguarding socialism." It also said, "That we have come to possess a nuclear deterrent was an auspicious event in our national history, a realization of our people's centuries-long desire to have a national strength no one could dare challenge."[178]

Repercussions

Significantly, the 2006 nuclear test has deprived North Korea of plausible deniability, as the test clearly demonstrated that North Korea actually possessed nuclear weapons and had the ability to explode them. Before the test, while the United States was convinced that North Korea had nuclear weapons, China was doubtful. North Korea often took advantage of this gray zone in its diplomatic maneuvers. After the test, however, this plausible deniability was lost and North Korean diplomatic flexibility was undermined. The hurdle for the United States and Japan to fundamentally improve relations with North Korea is now higher than before.

CONCLUSION

North Korea's changing policy objectives

North Korea's policy objectives have changed significantly over time. In the 1960s, they were ambitious, aggressive, and hostile. Forcibly stopping U.S. intelligence activities, diverting U.S.–ROK strategic focus away from the Vietnam War, and attempting to overthrow the South Korean government are but a few examples. North Korea's policy objectives in the 1970s were not as grandiose as in the 1960s but they were still quite ambitious. Examples from this decade include making maritime territorial claims, concluding a peace agreement with the United States, getting the United States to withdraw its forces from South Korea, and destabilizing South Korea. In the 1980s, North Korea took extremely aggressive actions. It attempted to assassinate the South Korean president and undermine the Seoul Olympic Games by bombing a Korean Air civilian passenger airliner. Despite the expressed aggressiveness, however, these actions, and particularly the bombing of a passenger aircraft, reflected a sense of anxiety and desperation, as North Korea's policy objectives were becoming increasingly defensive. South Korea's economy was pulling ahead of the North as it prepared to make its debut on the international stage by hosting the Olympic Games. Concerned with preserving the balance, North Korea felt like it had to stop these developments. By the early 1990s, North Korea's policy objectives had become more decidedly defensive. Regime survival and acquisition of economic assistance had become the most important objectives. North Korea attempted to achieve these goals by trying to normalize relations with the United States and Japan. Military crises notwithstanding, North Korea's policy objectives since the 1990s have been minimalist.

While North Korea's policy objectives were predominantly hostile in the 1960s, cooperative elements began to appear in the 1970s. In 1974, North Korea proposed the conclusion of a peace agreement with the United States primarily for the purpose of getting rid of the U.S. presence in South Korea. North Korea's goal was to change the status quo on the Korean Peninsula by improving its relations with the United States. The important difference between the 1970s and the 1990s was that while the North Koreans tried to change the status quo by improving its relations with the United States in the 1970s, they tried to maintain the status quo by doing the same in the 1990s.

Purely military objectives diminished in importance while diplomatic and economic objectives loomed larger over time. The primary objectives involved in the seizure of the *Pueblo* and the shooting down of the EC-121 in the 1960s, stopping U.S. intelligence operations, were military in nature. The 1970s were a transitional period. North Korea's policy objectives in the West Sea incident were primarily diplomatic and legal, and secondarily economic. North Korea's objective in the Axe Murder incident was definitely more diplomatic than military. Since the 1990s, North Korea's military-diplomatic campaigns have been about trading military capabilities for diplomatic and economic gains.

Patterns of military-diplomatic actions

Patterns of North Korea's military-diplomatic actions have changed in conjunction with its changing policy objectives, particularly in terms of their intensity and targeting. First, the intensity and the number of casualties associated with its military actions diminished over time. North Korea in the 1960s was extremely ambitious, and used force in a variety of ways – to coerce, control, and subvert. It used force directly and aggressively and caused a large number of casualties for both the United States and South Korea. Then in the 1970s, as a more cooperative approach emerged, North Korea used force in a limited, indirect, and coercive manner, with explicit coordination between military and diplomatic activities. As a result, the number of casualties caused by North Korean actions diminished significantly. The number of casualties temporarily increased in the 1980s due to the surge in terrorism-type subversive actions in North Korea's desperate attempt to derail the turn in domestic and international support in favor of South Korea. In the 1990s, as North Korea's policy objectives became more defensive, it started to engage in a show of force for coercive purposes instead of physically applying force, as it had done in earlier periods. As a consequence, North Korea only inflicted limited damage and casualties, especially against the United States, despite the long and high-profile nature of its military-diplomatic campaigns in the decade.

The number of casualties caused by North Korea decreased from a high of 507 in the 1960s to 94 in the 1970s to more than 140 in the 1980s to zero in the 1990s and then to six between 2000 and 2007.[1] There seem to have been two important reasons for these numbers. One is that the need to actually resort to brute force diminished once North Korea came to have military capabilities of significant strategic importance, such as nuclear and longer-range missile forces. The other is that the emergence of cooperative policy objectives, such as normalizing relations with the United States and obtaining economic assistance from the neighbors, has made it diplomatically unwise for the North Koreans to inflict significant physical damage on others. Killing Americans, and South Koreans to a lesser extent, would certainly be detrimental to the normalization of U.S.–DPRK relations.

Another indication that the North Koreans tailored their military actions to their policy objectives is seen in the shift in targeting patterns. In the 1960s, North Korea exercised no target discrimination; in the sustained attacks along the Demilitarized Zone (DMZ), both U.S. and South Korean servicemen became targets. In 1968, the *Pueblo* incident and the Blue House raid took place simultaneously. In the 1970s, however, the North Koreans started to distinguish between U.S. and South Korean targets. In the Axe Murder incident, for example, U.S. servicemen were specifically targeted. This target discrimination became clearer in the 1980s. The attempted attack against the U.S. SR-71, for example, was North Korea's last direct use of force against U.S. personnel and assets. After the incident, North Korea stopped attacking Americans, a trend which has continued to this day. Moreover, after the Rangoon incident in 1983, North Korea stopped attacking the South Korean leadership.

Assessing effectiveness

Some of North Korea's military actions were very successful in achieving its policy objectives while others were only moderately successful. Still others were simply counterproductive. The *Pueblo* incident and the first round of nuclear diplomacy were highly successful while the assaults along the DMZ in the 1960s, the West Sea incident in the 1970s, and North Korea's missile diplomacy in the 1990s were moderately so. The attempt to undermine the Korean Armistice in the 1990s did not produce positive results. The Axe Murder incident and other unconventional attacks such as the bombing of the Korean airliner were disastrously counterproductive. The second round of nuclear diplomacy has produced fairly positive, if inconclusive, results.

However rational the North Koreans might be, they do make mistakes. At the time of the Axe Murder incident, for example, the international environment had been very favorable to North Korea. The tactical mistake of killing American servicemen in an extremely brutal manner turned the whole venture into a disastrous failure. In June 1999, furthermore, the North Koreans underestimated the South Korean reaction. As a result of the Battle of Yeonpyeong, North Korea lost lives, naval vessels, and their reputation for military prowess. Other unconventional actions also failed. Assassination attempts on South Korean presidents have never succeeded; neither have guerrilla infiltrations. The bombing of a Korean airliner in 1987, furthermore, decisively shifted the attitude of the international community against North Korea.

Taken as a whole, North Korean leaders have been highly rational and moderately successful high-risk takers with idiosyncratic policy objectives. The claim that the North Koreans have always been highly effective in using force and that Kim Il Sung and Kim Jong Il are "military geniuses" is not true. They have been voracious users of force, but they have not been any better at using it than others.

Military balance and patterns of military action

Military advantage as an enabling factor

North Korea's propensity to use or threaten force has been high, particularly when a fresh opportunity was created by the acquisition of new military capabilities. Examples abound. North Korea's assaults along the DMZ, the *Pueblo* incident, and the shooting down of the EC-121 in the late 1960s were all preceded by a major military buildup based on the "Party military lines" adopted in 1962.[2] The naval actions around the Northwest Islands (NWI) in the early 1970s were made possible by the procurement of fast guided-missile boats from the Soviet Union in the preceding decade. North Korea's nuclear and missile diplomacy in the 1990s was made possible by the development of nuclear and missile capabilities which had accelerated in the 1980s. Some years after North Korea froze its plutonium-based nuclear program in 1994, it embarked on a uranium-based nuclear program. When the United States uncovered the secret program in 2002, North Korea attempted to use it as a new bargaining chip.

It is noteworthy that North Korea became relatively inactive in using its conventional military force in the 1980s. The changing military balance on the Korean Peninsula explains this period of relative calm. By 1986, South Korea had finished its second mid-term Force Improvement Program and the United States and South Korea had adopted more offensive elements into their defense strategy.[3] South Korea had been outspending North Korea on defense since 1976 and the overall military balance was shifting in favor of the U.S.–ROK side.[4] Moreover, North Korea was beginning to devote a larger share of its resources to ballistic missile and nuclear development with a diminishing emphasis on conventional forces.

Military advantage and the choice of location

North Korea's preferred location for military actions changed over time in line with the changing military balance. At first, North Korea was active along the DMZ. When the DMZ was fortified in the late 1960s, however, the North Koreans shifted their attention to the NWI area in the Yellow Sea where they had a local military advantage. South Korea then fortified the NWI and strengthened its naval forces. When this happened, the North Koreans moved their attention away from the NWI area to the JSA, where it enjoyed local military superiority. In the 1990s, North Korea's major military-diplomatic campaigns – nuclear and missile diplomacy – were based in sustained activities inside the North Korean territory, which served as a sanctuary. North Korea tended to use force where it enjoyed local military superiority. Put differently, as North Korea lost local military advantages as a result of U.S.–ROK countermeasures, its room for action diminished accordingly. By the

1990s, North Korea's military actions had been largely confined to its own territory as well as small areas such as the JSA and the NWI area in the Yellow Sea.

Unconventional attacks followed the same pattern. In the 1960s, the majority of North Korean infiltrators came to the south across the DMZ. When the DMZ was fortified in the late 1960s, the North Koreans started to dig tunnels beneath the DMZ in order to get around the fortified DMZ, and increased seaborne infiltrations. Then after South Korea strengthened its naval power, North Korea started to put an emphasis on submerged infiltration methods. The submarine incidents of 1996 and 1998 were partly the results of such a shift. In the 1980s, North Korea resorted to terrorism, and two of the three major terrorist plots – the Rangoon incident and the bombing of the Korean Airliner passenger plane – were executed outside of the Korean Peninsula. This, too, seems to have reflected the shift in military balance in and around the peninsula. In short, the North Koreans have continued to look for new frontiers for possible action as the military balance changed over time.

Military advantage as a determinant of success

The single most important determinant of success in North Korea's military-diplomatic campaigns has been the presence—or absence—of a military advantage during the campaign. When the North Koreans had a military advantage, the chance that their actions would succeed was high. In other words, relevant military advantages, not skilled negotiation tactics, played the decisive role in determining the outcome of North Korea's military-diplomatic campaigns. As examples, while the first round of nuclear diplomacy resulted in the Agreed Framework and North Korea's missile diplomacy almost produced a significantly improved relationship with the United States, the same North Koreans failed to obtain any meaningful diplomatic or economic benefit from their military actions in the JSA, the DMZ, and the NWI area in the 1990s even though they expended just as much military-diplomatic effort. What distinguished these two sets of cases was the existence of actual and potential nuclear and missile capabilities in the former, which generated a tremendous compellent effect on the target countries. In terms of strategic significance and compellent value, the armed demonstrations in the JSA, the skirmishes in the DMZ, and the naval clash in the NWI area were nowhere near as significant as the nuclear and missile capabilities in the other examples cited above. This does not mean that tactical factors did not matter.[5] Sophisticated diplomatic actions were always indispensable in translating military action into meaningful policy results. It does mean, however, that tactical factors such as negotiation skills were at best secondary determinants of the effectiveness of North Korea's military-diplomatic campaigns.

Learning from the past

North Korean skill in using military force in conjunction with diplomatic action has become more sophisticated over time. As a result, they have demonstrated an ability to conduct highly sophisticated and elaborate military-diplomatic campaigns since the 1990s. For example, the North Koreans seem to have learned lessons from the *Pueblo* incident as demonstrated in their conduct of nuclear diplomacy in the 1990s. In both cases, they acquired what the Americans cared very much about – the *Pueblo* and its crew in the former, and nuclear capabilities in the latter – and used them as a bargaining chip. The only difference was that the military-diplomatic campaign was rather incidental in the *Pueblo* case while its nuclear diplomacy was a result of a deliberate and premeditated action. It is quite suggestive, therefore, that the North Koreans have actually characterized these two incidents as examples of Kim Jong Il's "war of brains" and "war of wisdom" against the United States. The negotiations resulting from the seizure of the *Pueblo* seem to have made the North Koreans realize that diplomatic interactions with the Americans, accompanied by appropriate military action, could produce positive results.

Also, since the 1990s, North Korea has started to recycle old tricks. The multiple armed demonstrations of force in the JSA in the mid-1990s were a modified version of the Axe Murder incident without blood. The actions in the NWI area in 1999, 2001, and 2002 had much in common with those in the first half of the 1970s. In 2002, furthermore, North Korea started to replay its nuclear diplomacy, this time incorporating slightly different ingredients than the previous era.

North Korea's military-diplomatic coordination in the 1960s was at best rudimentary. The assaults along the DMZ were not followed up by diplomatic action. In the *Pueblo* and EC-121 incidents, Kim Il Sung's thinking was simple: shoot them if they came close. The U.S.–DPRK talks following the capture of the *Pueblo* were an unexpected result rather than a premeditated outcome. The shooting down of the EC-121 in 1969 was not followed by any meaningful diplomatic action. In the 1970s, North Korea's military-diplomatic coordination became a bit more sophisticated. In the West Sea incident, a series of military actions were taken specifically to back the demands that the North Koreans made at meetings in Panmunjom. The Axe Murder incident could have served North Korea's policy objectives had it not been for the tactical mistakes committed on the ground, namely the excessively brutal nature of the attack. Diplomatic coordination thus had to work to minimize the damage rather than to exploit the opportunity created by the military action.

After a long pause in the 1980s, North Korea returned in the 1990s with a surprising ability to conduct long, multi-phased, and highly sophisticated military-diplomatic campaigns. Its nuclear and missile diplomacy are cases in point. They were both based on actual and potential military capabilities of regional and global significance. In both cases, the North Koreans made effective use of the element of surprise. Both of them brought about high-level bilateral talks between the United States and North Korea. In both cases, many of the objectives spelled out by the North Koreans were quite realistic. North Korea's military-diplomatic campaigns to undermine the Korean Armistice in the 1990s are often forgotten, but they were also highly sophisticated and complex in terms of how military actions were coordinated with diplomatic moves.

One problem for North Korea is that its sophisticated coordination between military actions and diplomatic moves sometimes makes its military-diplomatic campaigns less effective. This is because when military and diplomatic actions are so apparently coordinated, the target nations can easily figure out that the military actions are simply a part of the demonstration of force and, therefore, will not develop into an actual military clash. Military coercion tends to work better when the coercer's intention or the consequences of the situation is not entirely clear. This is why coercers tend to manipulate risk by reducing transparency. In this sense, it is rational for the North Koreans to maintain a certain level of ambiguity in their policy and intensions.

Deterrence as a crucial ingredient

Despite the tendency to focus on the offensive aspect of North Korean military strategy, effective deterrence has been a critical enabling factor in North Korea's military actions. For North Korea's military-diplomatic campaigns to succeed, North Korea had to prevent strong reactions from the U.S.–ROK side.

The United States and/or South Korea seriously considered military actions in response to the North Korean raid on the Blue House, the seizure of the *Pueblo*, the shooting-down of the EC-121, the Axe Murder incident, and its nuclear development. In 2002, the United States even talked about "preemption." In all cases, however, they eventually dropped the military option. There have been several different sources of North Korea's deterrent capabilities. One of them was the "Party military lines" adopted in 1962. Kim Il Sung presented two of the four major elements of the Party military lines – arming of the entire population and the fortification of the entire country – as "the most powerful defence system from the military strategic point of view, a system which is capable of thwarting any enemy attack."[6] One of the most important reasons why the United States and South Korea could not take punitive military actions was the realization that fighting a war with the highly militarized, fortified nation in arms would be costly and futile.

The characteristics of North Korea's deterrent, however, changed over time. Until the 1980s, its deterrent largely originated from its ability to defend itself in case of a major military clash, or deterrence by denial. By the early 1990s, however, it had become clear that North Korea's ability to inflict unbearable damage on the United States and South Korea, or deterrence by punishment, had become the most important source of its deterrent. In the 1990s, North Korea deployed a large number of long-range artillery and multiple rocket launchers along the DMZ. By forward-deploying a total of 12,000 long-range artillery and rocket systems, North Korea made it possible to fire 500,000 rounds per hour against South Korea by 2001.[7] Despite the confidence that the U.S.–ROK side had in militarily defeating North Korea in case of war, North Korea successfully deterred preventive and/or counter-coercive actions with its ability to "punish."[8]

Extensive use of legal issues

Legal issues were prime considerations in North Korea's military actions. North Korean policymakers have proved to be extremely knowledgeable about legal issues and versed in exploiting them to their advantage, although they have done poorly in abiding by international law and agreements. Quite frequently, North Korea's military-diplomatic campaigns involved legal issues in important ways. In the West Sea incident of the 1970s, for example, North Korea exploited the failure of the Armistice Agreement to define maritime boundaries, and challenged the validity of the Northern Limit Line (NLL). Later, the North Koreans took advantage of provisions in the Non-Proliferation Treaty (NPT) in putting a time pressure on American negotiators. In another example, North Korea undertook sustained actions in the JSA and the DMZ as well as around the NWI in the 1990s in order to undermine the Armistice Agreement by highlighting its defects. In particular, North Korea's naval operations in June 1999 aimed to exploit the defects of the Armistice Agreement and the weakness in the North–South Basic Agreement of 1992.

Sometimes, legal factors were extremely important. In June 1999, North Korean naval vessels started crossing the NLL systematically even though North Korea did not have a local military advantage, as the outcome of the naval clashes in this period suggest. The North Koreans still took these actions, however, because they hoped that they could exploit legal problems pertaining to the status of the NLL. In other words, North Korea has used or threatened force where it could plausibly, though not necessarily persuasively, claim legal justice even when it lacked a local military advantage. In fact, North Korea's legal argument regarding the NLL was much more sophisticated in 1999 than in the 1970s. Also, the maritime demarcation line North Korea proposed in 2006 was consistent with the contemporary peacetime international law of the sea.

North Korea's ability to make use of legal factors seems to come partly from the nature of its political system, in which a small number of specialists tends to stay in the same position for a long time, resulting in a deep understanding of technical issues and the effective retention of organizational memory.[9] Former North Korean diplomats who defected to South Korea have revealed that there were many aged officials in the Ministry of Foreign Affairs and that almost 90 percent of the officials in the ministry stayed in the same bureau throughout their careers.[10] Such a personnel management system certainly creates rigidity. However, it also guarantees consistency, continuity, and a significant level of professionalism.

The element of surprise

An element of surprise has almost always been an important ingredient in North Korea's military actions. The seizure of the *Pueblo*, the shooting down of the EC-121, the Axe Murder incident, the announcement of withdrawal from the NPT, the launch of the Taepo Dong missile, the multiple ballistic missile launches, and the nuclear test all came as surprises to North Korea observers.

It also appears that in recent years the North Koreans have taken into account political developments in both the United States and South Korea while deciding when to initiate an action. North Korea's nuclear and missile diplomacy commenced shortly after new administrations came into office in the United States and/or South Korea. By doing so, the North Koreans put U.S. and South Korean policymakers off balance. The element of surprise was used effectively.

Underlying its effective use of surprise is the nature of North Korea's political system, military capabilities, and tactical skills. What is significant is not necessarily the fact that the North Koreans used the element of surprise quite often but that they have been able to actually plan, prepare, and execute actions to surprise the target countries. That said, frequent use of the element of surprise has come at a price. North Korea is no longer trusted by anyone, and its reputation in the international community is at rock bottom.

Domestic politics

Domestic political objectives have also played a role in some of North Korea's military-diplomatic campaigns, but they have been of secondary importance. Kim Il Sung used the *Pueblo* incident to justify his "dual-track development policy" and the purging of his political rivals. He decided to shoot down the EC-121 partly to strengthen his position within the military establishment. The Axe Murder incident occurred when Kim Jong Il was trying to consolidate his position as heir to Kim Il Sung, defying criticism from within the North Korean political system. Military actions in the 1990s were taken when Kim Jong Il was finishing his attempt to establish his positions both in the party and in the military establishments. The Taepo Dong missile was launched in 1998 just before Kim Jong Il was reelected chairman of the National Defence Commission. The nuclear test in 2006 was also used to glorify Kim's leadership.

That said, the contention that North Korean leaders resort to force only when they face domestic difficulties is not true. In the period directly following the end of the Korean War in 1953, North Korea did not undertake many military actions as its attention was focused on a number of serious domestic power struggles. North Korea's use of force actually increased when Kim Il Sung's position was consolidated in the 1960s. Furthermore, when Kim Jong Il formalized his position in the Workers' Party in the early 1980s, North Korea continued to undertake provocative actions, such as the Rangoon incident.

North Korea's military actions could have worked against domestic political objectives because as history shows some of the actions actually failed. The Axe Murder incident, for example, was a major failure. In the 1999 naval battle, the North Korean navy was defeated. Unconventional attacks such as the Rangoon bombing and the bombing of the Korean airliner also failed disastrously. These cases would have given ammunition to Kim Jong Il's domestic rivals, if they actually existed. We can therefore conclude that military actions have not always helped Kim Il Sung and Kim Jong Il domestically.

The international environment

The contention that North Korea undertakes military action only when faced with a negative international environment is similarly not true. History shows that North Korea initiated military actions both when the international environment was favorable as well as when it was not. Actions in the late 1960s, for example, were taken in a mixed international environment in which the Sino-Soviet split was a negative factor but the Vietnam War had rather positive implications for North Korea. The Axe Murder incident took place in an environment most favorable to North Korea. Its nuclear diplomacy began twice when the international situation was extremely negative, but the Taepo Dong launch occurred when the international environment was quite favorable due to the adoption of the engagement and sunshine policies on the part of the United States and South Korea, respectively. The 1999 naval clash, what is more, took place shortly after William Perry visited Pyongyang.

As these cases also suggest, the international environment has not necessarily determined the outcome of the episodes, either. The Axe Murder failed disastrously despite a highly favorable international environment, while both nuclear diplomacy initiatives turned out to be a success despite a highly unfavorable international environment.

Repercussions

Despite short-term successes, in some cases North Korea's military-diplomatic campaigns have produced negative mid- to long-term repercussions by provoking unintended reactions in other countries. In the 1960s, sustained assaults along the DMZ caused the U.S.–ROK side to fortify the DMZ. In the 1970s, North Korean naval and air activities provoked South Korea to fortify the NWI and build up and modernize its naval forces deployed in the area. The local military balance in the area had become decisively favorable to the South Korean side by the time the naval vessels of North and South Korea engaged in battle in 1999. Additionally, the launch of a Taepo Dong missile in 1998 encouraged the United States and Japan to renew their ballistic missile defense programs.

These cases have demonstrated the importance of paying attention to mid- to long-term repercussions in assessing the effectiveness of North Korea's military-diplomatic campaigns. Short-term success could turn into mid- to long-term disadvantages. Military responses or other countermeasures can make an important difference in assessments of the longer-term effectiveness of North Korea's military-diplomatic campaigns.

Looking into the future

Since 1966, North Korea has used force in a highly calculated but often dangerously provocative manner, bringing the situation to the brink of war. No matter how calculated its actions were, they have indeed been military adventures. After more than 40 years, North Korea's calculated adventurism has come to full maturity. Or, put differently, North Korea's calculated adventurism has come to the limit of its life. Over time, North Korea's policy objectives have become extremely conservative and limited. With all of its military-diplomatic campaigns, what North Korea now seeks to achieve is simply regime survival, normalization of relations with other countries, and obtaining economic aid.

The North Korean leaders are bold in taking negative, hostile actions but extremely cautious in taking positive, conciliatory steps. They risked war in the *Pueblo* incident, the Axe Murder incident, and during the first round of nuclear diplomacy, but they did not allow the Americans to have an office in Pyongyang. They would "disable" part of their nuclear program but not go any further.

From Pyongyang's perspective, this might actually be the optimal strategy. Since the late 1990s, North Korea's military-diplomatic campaigns have been executed in a half-hearted manner and have produced commensurately mediocre results. The reason behind this is the dilemma that North Korea faces. It could obtain large gains if it were to abandon its nuclear and missile programs, but if it did so, it would be left with no effective policy leverage. Nobody knows better than Kim Jong Il what his portfolio of policy options looks like and how solid or fragile his regime might be. It is perfectly natural that North Korean leaders try to play some cards but keep others back. Up to now, North Korea has used every possible conventional and unconventional tool in its military-diplomatic campaigns.

The life of a singer ends when he starts singing his old songs. Tellingly, the most interesting characteristics of North Korea's second nuclear initiative – fighter aircraft, patrol boats, anti-ship missiles, nuclear bombs, and ballistic missiles – are actually all stars from past episodes. In a similar vein, the challenge against the U.S. RC-135S in 2003 was a modified repeat of the *Pueblo* and EC-121 incidents. In 2003, just as in the 1970s, North Korean MiG-19 and patrol boats crossed the NLL. In 2006, the No Dong and Scud flew once again after an absence of 13 years. The Taepo Dong also reappeared, now as the Taepo

197

Dong 2, and yet again anti-ship missiles were fired. In 2006, even the nuclear bomb came up again, and this time it exploded. Given all this, perhaps the second round of nuclear diplomacy should be entitled, "The Final Episode of Calculated Adventurism." That said, however, one should always remember that, more often than not, the "final" episode is never final. There is always the possibility of reruns.

APPENDIX A

Casualties suffered due to hostilities

	US		ROK				DPRK	
Year	*Killed*	*Wounded*	Killed		*Wounded*		*Killed*	*Wounded*
1964	0	1	1		0		3	1
1965	0	0	21	(19)	6	(13)	4	51
1966	6	1	29	(4)	28	(5)	43	19
1967	16	51	115	(22)	243	(53)	228	57
1968	18	54	145	(35)	240	(16)	321	13
1969	35	5	10	(19)	39	(17)	55	6
1970	0	0	9	(7)	22	(17)	46	3
1971	0	0	18	(4)	28	(4)	22	2
1972	0	0	0		0		0	0
1973	0	0	2		1		2	1
1974	1	4	1	(38)	2	(16)	5	0
1975	0	1	0		0		0	0
1976	2	4	4		10		3	5
1977	3	1	1		1		0	0
1978	0	0	1		4		23	0
1979	1	2	2		1		7	0
1980	0	0	5	(1)	11	(1)	19	1
1981	0	0	0		2		1	0
1982	0	0	0		0		1	0
1983	0	0	0		0		16	2
1984	0	0	0		0		0	0
1985	0	0	0		0		0	0
1986	0	0	0		0		0	0
1987	0	0	0	(11)	0		0	0
1988	0	0	0		0		0	0
1989	0	0	0		0		0	0
1990	0	0	0		0		0	0
1991	0	0	0		0		0	0
1992	0	0	0		2		3	0
1993	0	0	0		0		0	0
1994	0	0	0		0		0	0
1995	0	0	0		0		0	0
1996	0	0	0		0		24	0
1997	0	0	0		0		1	14
1998	0	0	0		0		15	0
1999	0	0	0		9		17-30+	Many
2000	0	0	0		0		0	0
2001	0	0	0		0		0	0

(continued on next page)

(continued)

	US		ROK		DPRK	
2002	0	0	6	18	About 30 (killed and wounded)	
2003–2007	0	0	0	0	0	0

*Figures in parentheses denote civilian casualties.
**Casualties suffered due to the terrorist attacks are not included.
Source: Lee Mun Hang, *JSA-Panmunjeom, 1953–1994* (Seoul: Sohwa, 2001), p. 373 (for the 1953–1992 period); and the data obtained from the ROK Ministry of National Defense, August 29, 2002 (for the 1993–2000 period) and February 29, 2008 (for the 2001–2007 period).

APPENDIX B

North Korea's infiltrations into South Korea

Year	Total	By Land	By Sea (Number of Cases/Infiltrators)
1960	86 / 157	26 / 38	51 / 99
1961	81 / 115	28 / 32	54 / 79
1962	58 / 104	14 / 26	39 / 71
1963	36 / 57	16 / 27	19 / 29
1964	47 / 96	17 / 33	29 / 62
1965	60 / 142	20 / 49	40 / 93
1966	91 / 210	21 / 62	68 / 146
1967	184 / 694	96 / 359	82 / 311
1968	141 / 601	104 / 386	35 / 202
1969	144 / 429	97 / 254	46 / 172
1970	86 / 245	59 / 156	27 / 89
1971	52 / 198	23 / 83	29 / 115
1972	20 / 58	8 / 25	12 / 33
1973	24 / 62	2 / 6	22 / 56
1974	21 / 66	4 / 17	17 / 49
1975	26 / 78	5 / 6	21 / 72
1976	7 / 36	1 / 3	6 / 33
1977	6 / 24	2 / 5	4 / 19
1978	8 / 36	3 / 10	5 / 26
1979	5 / 33	3 / 11	2 / 22
1980	15 / 69	9 / 27	6 / 42
1981	3 / 9	3 / 9	0 / 0
1982	4 / 7	0 / 0	4 / 7
1983	5 / 37	1 / 3	4 / 34
1984	1 / 1	0 / 0	1 / 1
1985	1 / 5	0 / 0	1 / 5
1986	0 / 0	0 / 0	0 / 0
1987	0 / 0	0 / 0	0 / 0
1988	0 / 0	0 / 0	0 / 0
1989	0 / 0	0 / 0	0 / 0
1990	6 / 30	0 / 0	6 / 30
1991	3 / 14	0 / 0	3 / 14
1992	5 / 16	4 / 12	1 / 4
1993	4 / 11	1 / 3	3 / 8
1994	3 / 9	2 / 6	1 / 3
1995	2 / 5	1 / 3	1 / 2
1996	1 / 25	0 / 0	1 / 25
1997	2 / 10	0 / 0	2 / 10
1998	5 / 29	0 / 0	5 / 29
1999–2007	0 / 0	0 / 0	0 / 0

Source: National Defense Military History Research Institute, *Daebijeonggyujeonsa II, 1961–1980* (History of the Counter-Unconventional Warfare II) (Seoul: Gugbang Gunsa Yeonguso, 1998), pp. 359–360 (for the 1960–1985 period); and the data obtained from the ROK Ministry of National Defense, August 29, 2002 (for the 1986–2000 period) and February 29, 2008 (for the 2001–2007 period).

APPENDIX C

Crossings of the Northern Limit Line

Year	Times	Vessels
1973	137	184
1974	320	341
1975	643	362
1976	779	294
1977	714	212
1978	427	199
1979	282	152
1980	375	131
1981–1988	n.a.	n.a.
1989	29	n.a.
1990	21	n.a.
1991	12	n.a.
1992	38	n.a.
1993	25	n.a.
1994	30	n.a.
1995	26	n.a.
1996	16	n.a.
1997	6	n.a.
1998	48	n.a.
1999	71	n.a.
2000	25	n.a.
2001	20	n.a.
2002	19	n.a.
2003	21	n.a.
2004	19	n.a.
2005	14	n.a.
2006	21	n.a.
2007	28	n.a.

*Figures between 1989 and 2007 are official numbers given by the ROK Ministry of National Defense. Others are not official.

**Counting method might have changed over time and that there have been cases where the ROK Navy did not report Northern Limit Line crossings by North Korean vessels. These factors have made the figures not perfectly reliable. These figures are useful in identifying "trends," however. Stephen Tharp, interview by author, Seoul, ROK, March 14, 2001.

Source: Park Ung Seo and et al., *Bughan Gunsa Jeongchaegron* (On North Korean Military Policy) (Seoul: Gyeongnam Daehaggyo Geugdong Munje Yeonguso, 1983), p. 342; and the data obtained from the ROK Ministry of National Defense, August 29, 2002 (for the 1989–2000 period) and February 29, 2008 (for the 2001–2007 period).

NOTES

Introduction

1 Dae-Sook Suh, *Kim Il Sung: The North Korean Leader* (New York: Columbia University Press, 1988), pp. 137–57, 212–37.

2 For compellence, see Gary Schaub, Jr., "Compellence: Resuscitating the Concept," in Lawrence Freedman, ed., *Strategic Coercion: Concepts and Cases* (Oxford: Oxford University Press, 1998).

3 For the distinction between "controlling" and "coercive" use of force, see Lawrence Freedman, "Strategic Coercion," in Freedman, ed., *Strategic Coercion*, pp. 16, 20–23; and Lawrence Freedman, *Deterrence* (Polity Press, 2004), pp. 84–89. For "subversion," see U.S. Department of Defense, *Dictionary of Military and Associated Terms*, Joint Publication 1–02, April 12, 2001, p. 416.

4 Kim Nam Jin et al., *Hyangdo-ui Taeyang Gim Jeong Il Janggun* (Gen. Kim Jong Il: The Leading Sun) (Pyongyang: Pyeongyang Chulpansa, 1995), pp. 397–402. The English edition of this book is *Kim Jong Il: The Lodestar of the 21st Century*, vol. 2 (Tokyo: Gwang Myeongsa, 1997), pp. 40–45.

5 Kim, *Hyangdo-ui Taeyang*, pp. 399–402; and Kim, *Kim Jong Il*, pp. 42–45.

6 "Uri Dang-ui Seongun Jeongchi-neun Pilseungbulpaeida," a joint article of *Rodong Sinmun* and *Kulloja*, June 16, 1999, in *Rodong Sinmun*, June 16, 1999; and "WPK's policy of giving priority to army is invincible," *KCNA*, June 16, 1999.

Chapter 1

1 James P. Finley, *The US Military Experience in Korea, 1871–1982: In the Vanguard of ROK–US Relations* (San Francisco: Command Historian's Office, HQ USFK/ EUSA, 1983), p. 114.

2 Ministry of National Defense (MND), Republic of Korea, *Defense White Paper 1991–1992* (Seoul: Korea Institute for Defense Analyses, 1992), p. 358; and James Lee, "'Panmunjeom San Jeungin' Jeimseu Ri Yugseong Jeung-eon (1) ('A Living Witness of Panmunjom,' Oral Testimony of James Lee)," *Sindong-a*, December 1997, http://www.donga.com/docs/magazine/new_donga/9712/nd97120100.html.

3 For the EC-121 incident, see U.S. Congress, House, Hearings before the Special Subcommittee on the U.S.S. *Pueblo* of the Committee on Armed Services, *Inquiry into the U.S.S. Pueblo and EC-121 Plane Incidents*, 91st Congress, First Session, March 4, 5, 6, 10, 14, 17, 19, 20, April 25, and 28, 1969, H.A.S.C. no. 91–101 (Washington, DC: U.S. Government Printing Office, 1969), pp. 889–91; Richard Nixon, *The Memoirs of Richard Nixon*, vol. 1 (New York: Warner Books, 1979),

pp. 472–76; Henry A. Kissinger, *White House Years* (Boston, MA: Little, Brown and Company, 1979), pp. 312–21; Daniel P. Bolger, *Scenes from an Unfinished War: Low-Intensity Conflict in Korea, 1966–1969* (Washington, DC: U.S. Government Printing Office, 1991), pp. 101–9; Public Affairs Office, UNC/CFC and USFK/EUSA, Yongsan Army Garrison, Seoul, Korea, "Serious Incidents in the DMZ," USFK Backgrounder, no. 16, current as of June 1993, http://www.korea.army.mil/PAO/backgrounder/bg16.htm (accessed on July 12, 2002); Joseph S. Bermudez, Jr., *North Korean Special Forces*, 2nd edn (Annapolis, MD: Naval Institute Press, 1998), p. 94; Lee Mun Hang, *JSA-Panmunjeom, 1953–1994* (Seoul: Sohwa, 2001); and "North Koreans Down Navy Recon Plane," *Pacific Stars and Stripes*, April, 17, 1969.

4 Kissinger, *White House Years*, p. 320.

5 "The Korean Situation," Telegram From the Commander in Chief, Pacific (McCain) to the Chairman of the Joint Chiefs of Staff (Wheeler), Honolulu, November 16, 1968, in U.S. Department of State, *Foreign Relations of the United States, 1964–1968*, vol. 29, part 1, *Korea* [hereafter *FRUS, 1964–1968*] (Washington, DC: U.S. Government Printing Office, 2000), pp. 447–48; and "Mr. Bundy's Meeting with Mr. Colby, June 22, 1967," Memorandum of Conversation, Washington, DC, June 22, 1967, in *FRUS, 1964–1968*, pp. 180–81.

6 Telegram From the Commander in Chief, United Nations Command, Korea, *FRUS, 1964–1968*, p. 264.

7 Bermudez, *North Korean Special Forces*, pp. 86–88.

8 Lee, *JSA-Panmunjeom*, p. 373.

9 Taik-young Hamm, *Arming the Two Koreas: State, Capital and Military Power* (London: Routledge, 1999), p. 100.

10 "Conflict & Tension on the Korean Peninsula! A Chronology (28 Jul 53-Aug 98)," obtained from the Secretariat, United Nations Command, Military Armistice Commission (UNCMAC) on July 18, 2001, p. 58.

11 Bermudez, *North Korean Special Forces*, pp. 116–17.

12 Hamm, *Arming the Two Koreas*, p. 100.

13 Joseph S. Bermudez, Jr., *Terrorism: The North Korean Connection* (New York: Crane Russak, 1990), p. 43.

14 Bermudez, *North Korean Special Forces*, pp. 133–36.

15 Ibid., pp. 136–39.

16 According to Kim Hyeon Hui, a Research Department for External Intelligence staffperson stated that the objectives of bombing the Korean Airliner Flight 858 were to (a) damage South Korea by disrupting the Olympic Games and (b) frustrate the "two-Korea policy" plot of the "South Koreans puppets." Cho Gab Je, *Kitachousen Onna Himitsu Kousakuin-no Kokuhaku: Daikankoukuuki Bakuhajiken-no Kakusareta Shinjitsu* (Confession of a North Korean Female Agent: Hidden Truth of the Bombing Incident of the Korean Airliner), trans. by Kikutoshi Ikeda (Tokyo: Tokuma Bunko, 1997), p. 56.

17 *Pyongyang Times*, June 18, 1994, p. 2.

18 MND, *Defense White Paper 1998* (Seoul: Korea Institute for Defense Analyses, 1999), p. 304; and MND, *Defense White Paper 1999* (Seoul: Ministry of National Defense, 1999), p. 246.

Chapter 2

1 Kim Il Sung, "The Present Situation and the Tasks of Our Party," Report to the Conference of the Workers' Party of Korea, October 5, 1966, in *Kim Il Sung Works*, vol. 20 (Pyongyang: Foreign Languages Publishing House, 1984), p. 322.

2 "Armed Incidents Along the Korean DMZ," Intelligence Memorandum, no. 1620/66, Washington, November 8, 1966, in U.S. Department of State, *Foreign Relations of the United States, 1964–1968*, vol. 29, part 1, *Korea* [hereafter *FRUS, 1964–1968*] (Washington, DC: U.S. Government Printing Office, 2000), pp. 209–10.

3 Daniel P. Bolger, *Scenes from an Unfinished War: Low-Intensity Conflict in Korea, 1966–1969* (Washington, DC: U.S. Government Printing Office, 1991), pp. 37–38; and Lee Mun Hang (James M. Lee), *JSA-Panmunjeom, 1953–1994* (Seoul: Sohwa, 2001), pp. 16 and 374.

4 Bolger, *Scenes from an Unfinished War*, p. 39.

5 "Armed Incidents Along the Korean DMZ," in *FRUS, 1964–1968*, p. 210.

6 Ibid., pp. 209–10.

7 Ibid.

8 *Pyongyang Times*, November 10, 1966, pp. 1–2.

9 *Pyongyang Times*, June 29, 1967, pp. 1–2.

10 *Pyongyang Times*, April 20, 1967, p. 1.

11 Central Intelligence Agency (CIA), "Kim Il-Sung's New Military Adventurism," Intelligence Report, November 26, 1968, p. 35, in ESAU papers, no. 39, "Cold War Era Hard Target Analysis of Soviet and Chinese Policy and Decision Making, 1953–73," Central Intelligence Agency Information Management Services, http://www.foia.cia.gov/CPE/ESAU/esau-39.pdf.

12 "Situation in Korea as of mid-July 1967," Telegram From the Commander in Chief, United Nations Command, Korea and the Commander of United States Forces, Korea (Bonesteel) to the Commander in Chief, Pacific (Sharp), Korea, July 21, 1967, in *FRUS, 1964–1968*, p. 265.

13 Bolger, *Scenes from an Unfinished War*, p. 42; and Joseph S. Bermudez, Jr., *North Korean Special Forces*, 2nd edn (Annapolis, MD: Naval Institute Press, 1998), p. 77.

14 Lee, *JSA-Panmunjeom*, p. 16.

15 Kim Il Sung, "Let Us Embody the Revolutionary Spirit of Independence, Self-Sustenance and Self-Defence More Thoroughly in All Branches of State Activity," Political Programme of the Government of the Democratic People's Republic of Korea, Announced at the First Session of the Fourth Supreme People's Assembly of the DPRK, December 16, 1967, in *Kim Il Sung Works*, vol. 21 (Pyongyang: Foreign Languages Publishing House, 1985), pp. 425–26.

16 "Armed Incidents Along the Korean DMZ," in *FRUS, 1964–1968*, p. 209.

17 Ibid.

18 Notes of the President's Meeting With Cyrus R. Vance, Washington, February 15, 1968, in *FRUS, 1964–1968*, pp. 380–82; and "The Objectives of My Mission," Memorandum From Cyrus R. Vance to President Johnson, Washington, DC, February 20, 1968 in *FRUS, 1964–1968*, pp. 384–91.

19 "The Objectives of My Mission," p. 387.

20 Ibid., p. 386.

21 Ibid., pp. 386 and 389.

22 Notes of the President's Meeting With Cyrus R. Vance, in *FRUS, 1964–1968*, p. 378.

23 "The Objectives of My Mission," in *FRUS, 1964–1968*, p. 385.

24 Notes of the President's Meeting With Cyrus R. Vance, in *FRUS, 1964–1968*, p. 378.

25 Ibid., pp. 381–82.

26 Quoted in CIA, "Kim Il-Sung's New Military Adventurism," p. 10.

27 "Situation in Korea as of mid-July 1967," in *FRUS, 1964–1968*, p. 263.

28 "The Likelihood of Major Hostilities in Korea," Special National Intelligence Estimate, SNIE 14.2–68, Washington, DC, May 16, 1968, in *FRUS, 1964–1968*, p. 429.

29 Telegram From the Department of State to the Embassy in Korea, Washington, DC, February 12, 1968, in *FRUS, 1964–1968*, p. 372.

30 *Pyongyang Times*, April 20, 1967, p. 3.

31 "Situation in Korea as of mid-July 1967," in *FRUS, 1964–1968*, p. 264.

32 Telegram From the Commanding General, United States Eighth Army, Korea, and the Commander in Chief, United Nations Command, Korea (Bonesteel) to the Chairman of the Joint Chiefs of Staff (Wheeler), Seoul, November 10, 1966, in *FRUS, 1964–1968*, pp. 213–14.

33 Chin O. Chung, *Pyongyang between Peking and Moscow: North Korea's Involvement in the Sino-Soviet Dispute, 1958–1974* (Alabama: University of Alabama Press, 1976), pp. 57–58.

34 Record of Conversation between A.A. Gromyko and Deputy Chairman of the Cabinet of Ministers, Minister of Foreign Affairs of the DPRK Comrade Pak Song-ch'ol, November 20, 1967, in Bernd Schaefer, "North Korean 'Adventurism' and China's Long Shadow, 1966–72," Working Papers Series #44, Cold War International History Project, Woodrow Wilson International Center for Scholars (October 2004), pp. 42–45.

35 Memorandum to Holders of Special National Intelligence Estimate Number 14.2–67, Washington, February 29, 1968, in *FRUS, 1964–1968*, p. 398.

36 National Defense Military History Research Institute, *Geongun 50-nyeonsa* (Fifty-Year History since the Foundation of the Armed Forces) (Seoul: Gugbang Gunsa Yeonguso, 1998), pp. 232–33.

37 Telegram From the Embassy in Korea to the Department of State, Seoul, May 14, 1968, in *FRUS, 1964–1968*, pp. 425–26.

38 Telegram From the Embassy in Korea to the Commander in Chief, Pacific (Sharp), Seoul, April 16, 1968, in *FRUS, 1964–1968*, p. 418.

39 "U.S. Policy toward Korea," Paper Prepared by the Policy Planning Council of the Department of State, Washington, June 15, 1968, in *FRUS, 1964–1968*, p. 436.

40 Lee, *JSA-Panmunjeom*, p. 370.

41 Bermudez, *North Korean Special Forces*, 2nd edn, pp. 76–77.

42 Lee, *JSA-Panmunjeom*, p. 373.

43 Kim, "The Present Situation and the Tasks of Our Party," p. 322.

44 "Notes of the President's Meeting With the National Security Council," Notes of Meeting, Washington, DC, January 24, 1968, in *FRUS, 1964–1968*, p. 480; and Schaefer, "North Korean 'Adventurism' and China's Long Shadow," p. 12.

45 CIA, "Kim Il-Sung's New Military Adventurism," p. 6.

46 *Pyongyang Times*, December 8, 1966, pp. 1–2.

47 "Record of Conversation between Soviet Politburo member Nikolai Podgorny and Kim Chung-wong, 20 January 1967," in Sergey S. Radchenko, "The Soviet Union and the North Korean Seizure of the USS *Pueblo*: Evidence from Russian Archives," Cold War International History Project, Woodrow Wilson International Center for Scholars, Working Papers Series #47, p. 59.

48 Telegram From the Embassy in Korea to the Department of State, Seoul, November 22, 1966, in *FRUS, 1964–1968*, pp. 216–20.

49 Editorial Note, in *FRUS, 1964–1968*, p. 273.

50 Telegram From the Embassy in Korea to the Department of State, Seoul, September 19, 1967, in *FRUS, 1964–1968*, p. 276.

51 "Additional ROK Troop Contribution to Vietnam," Telegram From the Embassy in Korea to the Department of State, Seoul, November 25, 1967, in *FRUS, 1964–1968*, pp. 291–92.

52 Summary of Conversations Between President Johnson and President Pak, Honolulu, April 17, 1968, in *FRUS, 1964–1968*, pp. 419–21. The civilians were supposed

to replace one South Korean combat group numbering 5,000–6,000 men in rear areas in South Vietnam so that it could be sent to other locations.

53 Central Intelligence Agency, Directorate of Intelligence, "North Korean Tactics Against South Korea: 1968," *Weekly Summary Special Report*, January 24, 1969, p. 1, in CIA Records Search Tool, Archives II Library, The U.S. National Archives and Records Administration.

54 "Vice President's Meeting with Prime Minister of Korea," Telegram From the Embassy in Vietnam to the Department of State, Saigon, October 31, 1967, in *FRUS, 1964–1968*, pp. 286–87.

55 "North Korean Harassment and U.S. Commitments," Memorandum of Conversation, Washington, November 13, 1967, footnote no. 2, in *FRUS, 1964–1968*, p. 289.

56 Memorandum to Holders of Special National Intelligence Estimate Number 14.2–67, Washington, February 29, 1968, in *FRUS, 1964–1968*, pp. 397–98.

57 *Pyongyang Times*, November 10, 1966, pp. 1–2.

58 Telegram From the Embassy in Korea to the Department of State, Seoul, November 29, 1966, in *FRUS, 1964–1968*, p. 222. The U.S. Ambassador also mentioned that North Korea might attempt to exploit the fact that a ROK unit landed in Vietnam, carrying a UN flag, and that the Soviets could point out that the UNC exercising the operational control over the ROK forces, a non-UN nation, went beyond the authority of the UN resolution. Furthermore, the ambassador noted that the UN resolution adopted during the Korean War called only for a unified command and the phrase "United Nations Command" never appeared in any UN resolutions. Ibid., p. 223.

59 Footnote no. 7, in *FRUS, 1964–1968*, p. 272.

60 CIA, "Kim Il-Sung's New Military Adventurism," p. 11.

61 Ibid., p. 19. Also, see Masayuki Suzuki, *Kitachousen: Shakaishugi-to Dentou-no Kyoumei* (North Korea: Resonance between Socialism and Tradition) (Tokyo: Tokyo Daigaku Shuppankai, 1992), pp. 56–59.

62 CIA, "Kim Il-Sung's New Military Adventurism," pp. 2–5.

63 *Granma*, April 24, 1966, as quoted in CIA, "Kim Il-Sung's New Military Adventurism," p. 9.

64 Bolger, *Scenes from an Unfinished War*, p. 47.

65 Ibid., pp. 47–55.

66 "Conflict & Tension on the Korean Peninsula! A Chronology (28 Jul 53-Aug 98)," obtained from the Secretariat, United Nations Command, Military Armistice Commission (UNCMAC) on July 18, 2001, p. 17; and Ministry of National Defense, *Gugbang Baegseo 1999* (Defense White Paper 1999) (Seoul: Gugbangbu, 1999), p. 286.

67 Bolger, *Scenes from an Unfinished War*, pp. 52 and 54.

68 Ibid., pp. 58–59.

69 *Geongun 50-nyeonsa*, p. 241.

70 Bolger, *Scenes from an Unfinished War*, pp. 47–48, and 78.

71 Ibid., p. 108.

Chapter 3

1 Description of the *Pueblo* Incident is based on the following sources: U.S. Congress, House, Hearings before the Special Subcommittee on the U.S.S. *Pueblo* of the Committee on Armed Services, *Inquiry into the U.S.S. Pueblo and EC-121 Plane Incidents*, 91st Congress, First Session, March 4, 5, 6, 10, 14, 17, 19, 20, April 25, and 28, 1969, H.A.S.C. no. 91–101 (Washington, DC: U.S. Government Printing Office, 1969); Trevor Armbrister, *A Matter of Accountability* (New York: Coward-McCann,

1970); Donald S. Zagoria and Janet D. Zagoria, "Crisis on the Korean Peninsula," in Barry M. Blechman, Stephen S. Kaplan et al., *Diplomacy of Power: Soviet Armed Forces as a Political Instrument* (Washington, DC: The Brookings Institution, 1981); Ralph McClintock, "*Pueblo* Incident: AGER Program Background," http://www.uss*Pueblo*.org/v2f/background/agerback.html; Harry Iredale, "*Pueblo* Incident: Attacked by North Korean Military Forces," http://www.uss*Pueblo*.org/v2f/attack/attacked.htm.

2 Iredale, "*Pueblo* Incident."

3 Marine Corps Intelligence Activity, *North Korea Country Handbook*, MCIA-2630-NK-016-97, pp. A-176 and A-181, http://www.globalsecurity.org/military/library/report/1997/nkor.pdf.

4 "Notes of the President's Meeting With the National Security Council," Notes of Meeting, Washington, January 24, 1968, in U.S. Department of State, *Foreign Relations of the United States, 1964–1968*, vol. 29, part 1, *Korea* [hereafter *FRUS, 1964–1968*] (Washington, DC: U.S. Government Printing Office, 2000), p. 479.

5 Gekkan Chousen (Wolgan Chosun), ed., *Kin Shounichi: Sono Shougeki-no Jitsuzou* (Kim Jong Il: The Shocking Reality), trans. by Hwang Min Gi (Tokyo: Kodansha, 1994), p. 209.

6 James Bamford, *Body of Secrets: Anatomy of the Ultra-Secret National Security Agency* (New York: Anchor Books, 2002), p. 251.

7 In fact, North Koreans privately remarked to the Soviets that in principle they regarded the whole East Korean Bay as the inland sea of the country, stating that the territorial waters should be measured from the boundary of this inland sea rather than from the shore. "Report, Embassy of Hungary in the Soviet Union to the Hungarian Foreign Ministry," January 30, 1968, obtained from James Person, Program Associate, North Korea International Documentation Project (NKIDP), Woodrow Wilson International Center for Scholars [unpublished].

8 *Pyongyang Times*, February 1, 1968, p. 10; and Chuck Downs, *Over the Line: North Korea's Negotiating Strategy* (Washington, DC: The AEI Press, 1999), p. 125.

9 Song Hyo Sun, *Buggoe Dobal 30-nyeon* (Thirty Years of North Korean Provocations) (Seoul: Bughan Yeonguso, 1978), p. 61.

10 "Notes of the President's Luncheon Meeting," Notes of Meeting, Washington, January 25, 1968, in *FRUS, 1964–1968*, p. 510; "On the current problems of the international situation and on the struggle of the CPSU for the unity of the international communist movement," Excerpt from a speech by Leonid Brezhnev at the April (1968) CC CPSU Plenum, April 9, 1968, in Sergey S. Radchenko, "The Soviet Union and the North Korean Seizure of the USS *Pueblo*: Evidence from Russian Archives," Cold War International History Project, Woodrow Wilson International Center for Scholars, Working Papers Series #47, p. 64.

11 Telegram From the Embassy in Korea to the Department of State, Seoul, January 27, 1968, in *FRUS, 1964–1968*, p. 536.

12 Kim Il Sung, "On the 20th Anniversary of the Founding of the Korean People's Army," Speech at a Banquet Given in Honour of the 20th Anniversary of the Founding of the Heroic Korean People's Army, February 8, 1968, in *Kim Il Sung Works*, vol. 22, 2nd edn (Pyongyang: Foreign Languages Publishing House, 1992), p. 6.

13 "Summary Minutes of *Pueblo* Group," Summary Minutes of Meeting, Washington, DC, January 24, 1968, in *FRUS, 1964–1968*, p. 469.

14 Zagoria and Zagoria, "Crises on the Korean Peninsula," p. 359.

15 Ibid., p. 360.

16 "Notes of the President's Breakfast Meeting," Notes of Meeting, Washington, DC, January 25, 1968, in *FRUS, 1964–1968*, p. 502.

17 Central Intelligence Agency, Center for the Study of Intelligence, "Looking for the *Pueblo*," https://www.cia.gov/library/center-for-the-study-of-intelligence/csi-publications/books-and-monographs/a-12/finding-a-mission.html.

18 James Lee, "'Panmunjeom San Jeungin' Jeimseu Ri Yugseong Jeung-eon (2) ('A Living Witness of Panmunjom,' Oral Testimony of James Lee)," *Sin Dong-a*, January 1998, http://www.donga.com/docs/magazine/new_donga/9801/nd98010260.html.

19 "Notes of the President's Breakfast Meeting," in *FRUS, 1964–1968*, pp. 500–501.

20 "Notes on the President's Thursday Night Meeting on the *Pueblo* Incident," Notes of Meeting, Washington, January 25, 1968, in *FRUS, 1964–1968*, p. 519.

21 Report on Meeting of the Advisory Group, Washington, January 29, 1968, in *FRUS, 1964–1968*, p. 559.

22 Editorial Note, in *FRUS, 1964–1968*, pp. 570–71.

23 The Commander in Chief, U.S. Pacific Command (CINCPAC) privately argued in June 1968 that retention of U.S. influence and control at each major echelon over the ROK Army, the exercise of U.S. restraint upon its actions in periods of tension, and the maintenance of U.S. advisory role during the post-*Pueblo* force add-on and modernization were "of the utmost importance." Historical Branch, Office of the Joint Secretary, Headquarters CINCPAC, *Commander in Chief Pacific: Command History 1968*, vol. II (Hawaii: Camp H.M. Smith, 1969), p. 61.

24 "Briefing of ROK Minister of Defense on *Pueblo* incident," Telegram From the Commander in Chief, United Nations Command, and Commander of United States, Korea (Bonesteel) to the Commander in Chief, Pacific (Sharp), Seoul, January 23, 1968, in *FRUS, 1964–1968*, p. 463.

25 Notes of the President's Meeting With Cyrus R. Vance, Washington, February 15, 1968, in *FRUS, 1964–1968*, pp. 376–77; and "The Objectives of My Mission," Memorandum From Cyrus R. Vance to President Johnson, Washington, DC, February 20, 1968 in *FRUS, 1964–1968*, p. 385.

26 Daniel P. Bolger, *Scenes from an Unfinished War: Low-Intensity Conflict in Korea, 1966–1969* (Washington, DC: Government Printing Office, 1991), p. 49.

27 Telegram From the Department of State to the Embassy in Korea, Washington, DC, January 23, 1968, in *FRUS, 1964–1968*, p. 466.

28 Telegram From the Embassy in Korea to the Department of State, Seoul, January 28, 1968, in *FRUS, 1964–1968*, p. 541.

29 Telegram From the Embassy in Korea to the Department of State, Seoul, February 4, 1968, in *FRUS, 1964–1968*, pp. 324–25.

30 Telegram From the Embassy in Korea to the Department of State, Seoul, February 6, 1968, in *FRUS, 1964–1968*, pp. 331–34.

31 "Mission of Cyrus R. Vance," Special Instruction, Paper Prepared in the Department of State, Washington, undated, in *FRUS, 1964–1968*, pp. 355–56.

32 "The Objectives of My Mission," in *FRUS, 1964–1968*, p. 385.

33 "Next Korean Moves," Memorandum From Alfred Jenkins of the National Security Council Staff to the President's Special Assistant (Rostow), Washington, DC, February 2, 1968, in *FRUS, 1964–1968*, p. 584.

34 "*Pueblo* – Policy Issues Raised at Second Meeting of Senior Representatives," Memorandum From the Director of the Korean Task Force (Berger) to Secretary of State Rusk, Washington, February 4, 1968, in *FRUS, 1964–1968*, p. 602.

35 "Summary of Panmunjom Meeting February 4," Telegram From the Embassy in Korea to the Department of State, Seoul, February 4, 1968, in *FRUS, 1964–1968*, p. 598; Telegram From the Department of State to the Embassy in Korea, Washington, DC, February 4, 1968, in *FRUS, 1964–1968*, p. 605; "Summary of Panmunjom Meeting, Feb. 5," Telegram From the Embassy in Korea to the

Department of State, Seoul, February 5, 1968, in *FRUS, 1964–1968*, p. 608; and Lee, *JSA-Panmunjeom*, pp. 31, 33, and 41.

36 "Panmunjom Talks – Next Steps," Action Memorandum From the Director of the Korean Task Force (Berger) to Secretary of State Rusk, Washington, February 7, 1968, in *FRUS, 1964–1968*, p. 616.

37 Footnote no. 6, in *FRUS, 1964–1968*, p. 618.

38 "5th Closed Senior MAC Members Meeting Feb 10," Telegram From the Embassy in Korea to the Department of State, Seoul, February 10, 1968, in *FRUS, 1964–1968*, p. 621.

39 "Sixth Closed Meeting at Panmunjom," Action Memorandum From the Director of the Korean Task Force (Berger) to Secretary of State Rusk, Washington, February 15, 1968, in *FRUS, 1964–1968*, p. 624.

40 *Pyongyang Times*, February 22, 1968, p. 6.

41 Telegram From the Department of State to the Embassy in Korea, Washington, DC, February 7, 1968, in *FRUS, 1964–1968*, p. 338.

42 "USS *Pueblo*," Memorandum From Secretary of State Rusk to President Johnson, Washington, DC, March 14, 1968, in *FRUS, 1964–1968*, p. 666.

43 "*Pueblo*," Telegram From the Embassy in the Soviet Union to the Department of State, Moscow, March 26, 1968, in *FRUS, 1964–1968*, p. 675.

44 "*Pueblo*," Memorandum of Conversation, Washington, DC, August 13, 1968, in *FRUS, 1964–1968*, p. 694.

45 "Eleventh Senior MAC Members Meeting at Panmunjom, March 9, 1968," Telegram From the Embassy in Korea to the Department of State, Seoul, March 9, 1968, in *FRUS, 1964–1968*, p. 656.

46 "Summary of Sixteenth Senior MAC Members Meeting at Panmunjom, May 8, 1968," Telegram From the Embassy in Korea to the Department of State, Seoul, May 8, 1968, in *FRUS, 1964–1968*, p. 684.

47 Action Memorandum From the President's Special Assistant (Rostow) to President Johnson, Washington, May 19, 1968, in *FRUS, 1964–1968*, p. 688.

48 "Status of *Pueblo* Talks at Panmunjom," Action Memorandum From the Deputy Assistant Secretary of State for East Asian and Pacific Affairs (Brown) to Secretary of State Rusk, Washington, September 4, 1968, in *FRUS, 1964–1968*, p. 698.

49 "22nd Senior MAC Members Closed Mtg and Panmunjom Sep 30, 1968," Telegram From the Embassy in Korea to the Department of State, Seoul, September 30, 1968, in *FRUS, 1964–1968*, pp. 707–8, 711.

50 "Instructions for Twenty-Sixth Meeting," Telegram From the Department of State to the Embassy in Korea," Washington, December 11, 1968, in *FRUS, 1964–1968*, p. 734.

51 Editorial Note, in *FRUS, 1964–1968*, pp. 740–41.

52 Ibid., pp. 742–44.

53 "U.S. urged to properly judge Koreans' will," *KCNA*, December 7, 1999.

54 Editorial Note, in *FRUS, 1964–1968*, p. 461; and "Notes of the President's Breakfast Meeting," in *FRUS, 1964–1968*, p. 501.

55 Benjamin Welles, "North Korean Military Linked to 1966 Meeting," *New York Times*, February 1, 1968, as quoted in Seung-Hwan Kim, *The Soviet Union and North Korea: Soviet Asian Strategy and Its Implications for the Korean Peninsula, 1964–1968* (Seoul: Research Center for Peace and Unification of Korea, 1988), p. 155.

56 "North and South Korean Forces," Annex to "The Likelihood of Major Hostilities in Korea," Special National Intelligence Estimate, SNIE 14.2–68, Washington, DC, May 16, 1968, in *FRUS, 1964–1968*, p. 432.

57 "Summary Minutes of *Pueblo* Group," in *FRUS, 1964–1968*, p. 475; and "Notes of the President's Meeting With the National Security Council," in *FRUS, 1964–1968*, p. 477; and Armbrister, *A Matter of Accountability*, p. 239.

58 "Notes of the President's Meeting with the Joint Chiefs of Staff," Notes of Meeting, Washington, January 29, 1968, in *FRUS, 1964–1968*, p. 560; and U.S. Congress, *Inquiry*, p. 916.

59 Central Intelligence Agency, "Kim Il-Sung's New Military Adventurism," Intelligence Report, November 26, 1968, in ESAU papers, no. 39, "Cold War Era Hard Target Analysis of Soviet and Chinese Policy and Decision Making, 1953–73," Central Intelligence Agency Information Management Services, p. 41, http://www.foia.cia.gov/CPE/ESAU/esau-39.pdf.

60 "Notes of the President's Meeting With the National Security Council," in *FRUS, 1964–1968*, p. 477.

61 "Meeting on Korean Crisis Without the President," in *FRUS, 1964–1968*, p. 489.

62 Radchenko, "The Soviet Union and the North Korean Seizure of the USS Pueblo," p. 20.

63 Record of Conversation between Soviet Deputy Foreign Minister Vasily Kuznetsov and the North Korean Ambassador to the Soviet Union Kim Pyong-chik, 21 May 1965, in Radchenko, "The Soviet Union and the North Korean Seizure of the USS Pueblo," p. 44.

64 Telegram From the Department of State to the Embassy in the Soviet Union, Washington, DC, February 6, 1968, in *FRUS, 1964–1968*, pp. 609–11.

65 "Notes of the President's Foreign Affairs Luncheon," Notes of Meeting, Washington, January 30, 1968, in *FRUS, 1964–1968*, p. 574.

66 Radchenko, "The Soviet Union and the North Korean Seizure of the USS Pueblo."

67 "On the current problems of the international situation," pp. 65–66.

68 Record of Conversation between Chairman of the Council of Ministers of the USSR Aleksei Kosygin and North Korean Ambassador in the USSR Chon Tu-hwan, May 6, 1968, in Radchenko, "The Soviet Union and the North Korean Seizure of the USS Pueblo," pp. 70–71.

69 "Panmunjom Talks – Next Steps," in *FRUS, 1964–1968*, p. 616.

70 "Notes of the President's Breakfast Meeting," in *FRUS, 1964–1968*, p. 502.

71 Robert R. Simmons, *The Pueblo, EC-121, and Mayaguez Incidents: Some Continuities and Changes*, Occasional Papers/Reprints Series in Contemporary Asian Studies, no. 8 (School of Law, University of Maryland, 1978), p. 12.

72 "Notes of the President's Luncheon Meeting With Senior American Advisors," Notes of Meeting, Washington, January 29, 1968, in *FRUS, 1964–1968*, p. 567.

73 Simmons, *The Pueblo, EC-121, and Mayaguez Incidents*, p. 3.

74 "North Korean Intentions," Memorandum From Director of Central Intelligence Helms to Secretary Defense McNamara, Washington, DC, January 23, 1968, in *FRUS, 1964–1968*, p. 465.

75 *Jane's Fighting Ships, 1987–88* (London: Jane's Publishing Company, no publication year indicated), pp. 330–31.

76 "Summary of Fourteenth Senior MAC Members Meeting at Panmunjom, April 11, 1968," Telegram From the Embassy in Korea to the Department of State, Seoul, April 11, 1968, in *FRUS, 1964–1968*, p. 678.

77 "Eighteenth *Pueblo* Meeting," Telegram From the Embassy in Korea to the Department of State, Seoul, June 27, 1968, in *FRUS, 1964–1968*, p. 693.

78 U.S. Congress, *Inquiry*, pp. 922–23.

79 Editorial Note, in *FRUS, 1964–1968*, p. 744.

80 Ibid., pp. 742–44.

81 Footnote no. 3, in *FRUS, 1964–1968*, p. 629.

82 Footnote no. 4, in *FRUS, 1964–1968*, p. 480.

83 Editorial Note, in *FRUS, 1964–1968*, p. 743.

84 Ibid.; and Bamford, *Body of Secrets*, pp. 276–77.

85 Bamford, *Body of Secrets*, p. 277.

86 "Notes of the President's Meeting With the National Security Council," in *FRUS, 1964–1968*, p. 480.

87 "Summary Minutes of Pueblo Group," in *FRUS, 1964–1968*, p. 470; and "Notes of the President's Breakfast Meeting," in *FRUS, 1964–1968*, p. 501.

88 "Summary Minutes of Pueblo Group," in *FRUS, 1964–1968*, p. 471.

89 Central Intelligence Agency, "Confrontation in Korea," January, 24, 1968, in CIA Records Search Tool, Archives II Library, The U.S. National Archives and Records Administration, p. 2.

90 "Thirteenth senior MAC members meeting at Panmunjom," Telegram From the Embassy in Korea to the Department of State, Seoul, March 28, 1968, in *FRUS, 1964–1968*, p. 676.

91 "On the Immediate Tasks of Socialist Economic Construction," Summary of the Report Delivered by Comrade Kim Il, First Vice Premier of the Cabinet of the Democratic People's Republic of Korea, at the Conference of the Workers' Party of Korea on October 10, 1966, in *Pyongyang Times*, Supplement (2), October 13, 1966, p. 2.

92 Kim Il Sung, "On Making Good Preparations for War so as to Cope with the Prevailing Situation," March 21, 1968, in *Kim Il Sung Works*, vol. 22, 2nd edn (Pyongyang: Foreign Languages Publishing House, 1992), pp. 46–47.

93 Korean Central Intelligence Agency, ed., *Buggoe Gunsa Jeonryag Jaryojib* (Collection of Materials on north Korean Military Strategy) (Seoul: Jungang Jeongbobu, 1974), p. 330.

94 Kim Il Sung, "Congratulations to Officers and Men of Unit 447 of the Korean People's Army on Shooting Down the Heavy Reconnaissance Aircraft of the US Imperialist Aggressive Forces which Illegally Intruded into the Northern Half of the Republic for Reconnaissance Purposes," April 16, 1969, in *Kim Il Sung Works*, vol. 23 (Pyongyang: Foreign Languages Publishing House, 1985), pp. 423–24.

Chapter 4

1 Both North and South Koreans call the Yellow Sea the "West Sea." Description of the incident is based on the following materials unless otherwise specified. "Bughan Seohaean 5-gae doseo Jeobsog Suyeog Chimbeom Sageon (An Incident involving North Korea's Intrusion into the Contiguous Waters of the Five Islands off the West Coast)," November 19–December 19, 1973, 2 vols, V. 1 Gibon Munseo (Basic Documents), classification no. 729.55, registration no. 6128 and V.2 Jaryojib (Materials), classifications no. 729.55, registration no. 6129, Diplomatic Archives, Seoul, ROK (hereafter referred to as "ROK Diplomatic Archives"); *Gughoe Hoewirog* (Proceedings of the Plenary), no. 17, 88th National Assembly, ROK, December 2, 1973, pp. 36–37; *Gugbang Wiwonhoe Hoewirog* (Proceedings of the National Defense Committee), no. 16, 88th National Assembly, ROK, December 10, 1973, pp. 10–17; *Gugbang Wiwonhoe Hoewirog* (Proceedings of the National Defense Committee), no. 1, 91st National Assembly, ROK, March 13, 1975, pp. 2–4; Kim Chang Sun et al., ed., *Bughan Chongram* (A General Survey of North Korea) (Seoul: Bughan Yeonguso, 1983), p. 1657; Kang In-duk (Institute for East Asian Studies), ed., *Bughan Jeonseo, 1945–1980* (North Korean Handbook) (Seoul: Geugdong Munje Yeonguso, 1980), p. 761; Ministry of National Defense (MND), Republic of Korea, *Defense White Paper 1991–1992* (Seoul: Korea Institute for Defense

Analyses, 1992), pp. 361–63; Lee Ki-Tak, "Hanbando-ui Saeroun Gunsa Hwan-gyeong-gwa Haeyang-eseoui Anbo (New Military Environment on the Korean Peninsula and Security of the Seas)," *Strategy 21*, no. 1 (1998); Kim Yong Sam, "Hangug Haegun-ui Jeolchibusim: 56-ham Chimmol hu 32-nyeon man-e Bughan-e Bogsuhanda (Struggle of the ROK Navy: Revenge against North Korea 32 Years After the Sinking of the ROK Navy Ship No. 56)," *Wolgan Joseon*, July 1999; Lee Ki-Tak, "Seohae-ui Jeonryagjeog-in Jungyoseong-gwa Munjaejeom-deul: Gugbang Jeonryag Damdangja-deul-ege Alrinda (Strategic Importance and Problems of the Yellow Sea: Informing the Defense Policy-Makers)," *Gunsa Segye*, no. 75 (August 1999), pp. 27–30; and James M. Lee, "History of Korea's MDL & Reduction of Tension along the DMZ and Western Sea through Confidence Building Measures between North and South Korea," in Chae-Han Kim, ed., *The Korean DMZ: Reverting beyond Division* (Seoul: Sowha, 2001), pp. 87–97.

2 The South Koreans usually refer to these islands as "Seohae O-do (Five Islands in the West Sea)." The "Northwest Islands" is the term used by the UNC.

3 Military Armistice Commission (MAC), United Nations Command (UNC) Component, "Three Hundred and Forty-Sixth Meeting of the Military Armistice Commission," December 1, 1973, pp. 8–9 and 15; and *Korea Times*, December 2, 1973, p. 1; and *Korea Herald*, December 2, 1973, p. 1.

4 National Unification Board, *Seohae 5-gae Doseo-wa Geu Gwanryeonmunje-e Gwanhan Yeongu* (A Study on the Five Islands in the West Sea and the Related Issues), Nambuggwangye Daebibangan Yeongu (A Study on the Reaction Plans on South-North Relations) (Seoul: Gugto Tongilwon, 1977), serial no. 77-1-1136, p. 11.

5 Description of the discussions at the 346th MAC meeting is based on the following materials unless otherwise indicated. MAC, UNC Component, "Three Hundred and Forty-Sixth Meeting"; and "Summary 346th Military Armistice Commission Meeting," Telegram from CINCUNC to JCS, December 1, 1973.

6 Lee, "History of Korea's MDL & Reduction of Tension along the DMZ and Western Sea," p. 89.

7 MAC, UNC Component, "Three Hundred and Forty-Sixth Meeting," pp. 5–6.

8 "Summary 346th Military Armistice Commission Meeting."

9 *Korea Times*, December 8, 1973, p. 1.

10 *Korea Times*, December 11, 1973, p. 1.

11 MAC, UNC Component, "Three Hundred and Forty-Seventh Meeting of the Military Armistice Commission," December 24, 1973, p. 10

12 Ibid., pp. 9–10; and *Korea Herald*, December 25, 1973, p. 1.

13 Description of the discussions at the 347th MAC meeting is based on the following materials unless otherwise indicated. MAC, UNC Component, "Three Hundred and Forty-Seventh Meeting"; and "Summary 347th Military Armistice Commission Meeting," Telegram from CINCUNC to JCS, December 24, 1973.

14 "Fishing Boat Incident," Joint Embassy/UNC Message from U.S. embassy in Seoul to Secretary of State, February 19, 1974, Electronic Telegrams, 1/1/1974–12/31/1974 (ET 1974), Central Foreign Policy Files, created, 7/1973–12/1975, documenting the period 1973?[sic]-12/1975 (CFPF), Record Group 59 (RG 59), Access to Archival Databases (ADD), The U.S. National Archives and Records Administration (NARA); "Conflict & Tension on the Korean Peninsula!" p. 42; Office of the South–North Dialogue, *South–North Dialogue In Korea*, no. 4 (December 1973–February 1974), http://dialogue.unikorea.go.kr/bbs/filedn.asp?file=edialogue/04.hwp; and *Korea Times*, February 16, 1974, p. 1.

15 "Fishing Boat Incident."

16 "June 28 ROK Maritime Police Boat Incident," from U.S. embassy in Seoul to Secretary of State, June 28, 1974, ET 1974, CFPF, RG 59, ADD, NARA; MAC,

UNC Component, "Three Hundred and Fifty-Second Meeting of the Military Armistice Commission," July 1, 1974, pp. 2–7; and "Summary 352d Military Armistice Commission Meeting," Telegram from CINCUNC to JCS, July 1, 1974; "Conflict & Tension on the Korean Peninsula!" p. 43; Lee Mun Hang (James M. Lee), *JSA-Panmunjeom, 1953–1994* (Seoul: Sohwa, 2001), pp. 103–4; James Lee, "'Panmunjeom San Jeungin' Jeimseu Ri Yugseong Jeung-eon (1) ("A Living Witness of Panmunjom," Oral Testimony of James Lee)," *Sindong-a*, December 1997; and Office of the South–North Dialogue, *South–North Dialogue In Korea*, no. 5 (February 1974–July 1974), http://dialogue.unikorea.go.kr/bbs/filedn.asp?file=edialogue/04.hwp.

17 Before the February 26 incident occurred, a North Korean vessel was sunk by the South Korean side after intruding into the "contiguous" waters off the South Korean east coast on February 15. MAC, UNC Component, "Three Hundred and Fifty-Nineth [*sic*] Meeting of the Military Armistice Commission," February 21, 1975, pp. 5–6; and "Summary 359th Military Armistice Commission Meeting," Telegram from CINCUNC to JCS, February 21, 1975.

18 MAC, UNC Component, "Three Hundred and Sixtieth Meeting of the Military Armistice Commission," March 3, 1975, pp. 5–6; "Gugbangbu Daebyeon-in Palpyomun (Statement by MND Spokesperson)," February 26, 1975, in "Bughan Seonbag Seohae Chimmul Sageon, 2.26 (Incident of the Sinking of a North Korean Ship in the West Sea on February 26)," in "Bughan-ui Dobal Sageon, 1973–75 (North Korea's Provocation Incidents, 1973–75)," classification no. 729.55, registration no. 8359 (11265), ROK Diplomatic Archives, p. 23; a retired South Korean defense official, interview by author, Seoul, ROK, December 12, 2007; a retired South Korean defense official, interview by author, Seoul, ROK, December 18, 2007 and January 17, 2008; *Korea Herald*, February 27, 1975, p. 1; and "U. S. Sends Up Planes in Korean Clash," *Associated Press*, February 27, 1975. For North Korea's account of the event, see *Rodong Sinmun*, March 5, 1975, p. 8. The South Korean side claimed that the boat had an estimated displacement of 50 tons while the North Korean side claimed it was a 200-ton ship. Though technically a novel, the following book tells an interesting story of what happened in February 1975. Choi Sun-Jo, *Seohae Haejeon* (Naval Battle in the West Sea) (Seoul: Jiseong-ui-saem, 2007), pp. 48–49.

19 Testimony by Yu Byeong Hyeon, *Gugbang Wiwonhoe Hoewirog*, no. 1, p. 3.

20 MAC, UNC Component, "Three Hundred and Sixtieth Meeting," pp. 6–7; "U.S. Sends Up Planes in Korean Clash;" *Joseon Ilbo*, February 28, 1975, p. 1; and *Korea Herald*, February 28, 1975, p. 1.

21 *Pyongyang Times*, March 8, 1975, p. 4.

22 "U.S. Sends Up Planes in Korean Clash."

23 MAC, UNC Component, "Three Hundred and Sixtieth Meeting," pp. 3–4, 10, 15, and 23–24.

24 "Gugbangbu Daebyeon-in Palpyomun."

25 "Seohae Satae (West Sea Incident)," March 4, 1975, in "Bughan Seonbag Seohae Chimmul Sageon, 2.26," p. 37.

26 "Summary 360th Military Armistice Commission Meeting," Telegram from CINCUNC to JCS, March 3, 1975.

27 "Summary Public Affairs Aspects of North Korea Boat/Aircraft Incident," Joint State/DOD Message, from Secretary of State to U.S. embassy in Seoul, February 28, 1975, Electronic Telegrams, 1/1/1975–12/31/1975 (ET 1975), CFPF, RG 59, ADD, NARA.

28 "Press Coverage of Yellow Sea Incident," Telegram from U.S. embassy in Seoul to Secretary of State, February 28, 1975, ET 1975, CFPF, RG 59, ADD, NARA.

29 *Korea Herald*, March 26, 1975, p. 1; and *Seoul Sinmun*, March 25, 1975, p. 1.

30 *Korea Herald*, March 26, 1975, p. 1; and MAC, UNC Component, "Three Hundred and Sixty-Second Meeting of the Military Armistice Commission," May 27, 1975, pp. 25–26 and 51–52.

31 Lee, "Hanbando-ui Saeroun Gunsa Hwangyeong-gwa Haeyang-eseoui Anbo," p. 269.

32 *Seohae 5-gae Doseo-wa Geu Gwanryeonmunje-e Gwanhan Yeongu*, p. 17.

33 Kwon Yeong Gi, "Seohae 5-do-neun 'Hwayaggo' Hanbando-ui Noegwan (The West Sea Five Islands are "Powder Keg" and a Detonator)," *Wolgan Joseon*, July 1999, p. 650.

34 MAC, UNC Component, "Three Hundred and Sixty-Second Meeting," p. 26.

35 MAC, UNC Component, "Three Hundred and Sixty-Third Meeting of the Military Armistice Commission," June 11, 1975, p. 4.

36 *Korea Herald*, June 11, 1975, p. 1; and *Seoul Sinmun*, June 11, 1975, p. 1.

37 MAC, UNC Component, "Three Hundred and Sixty-Sixth Meeting of the Military Armistice Commission," July 30, 1975, p. 7.

38 MAC, UNC Component, "Three Hundred and Seventy-First Meeting of the Military Armistice Commission," February 26, 1976, p. 13; and *Habdong Yeongam 1977* (Seoul: Habdong Yeongamsa, 1977), p. 91.

39 *Seohae 5-gae Doseo-wa Geu Gwanryeonmunje-e Gwanhan Yeongu*, p. 11.

40 Kim Il Sung had already suggested the conclusion of a U.S.–DPRK peace agreement to his colleagues in December 1973. Kim Il Sung, "On the Review of This Year's Work and the Direction of Next Year's Work," Speech at a Meeting of the Political Committee of the Workers' Party of Korea, December 31, 1973, in *Kim Il Sung Works*, vol. 28 (Pyongyang: Foreign Languages Publishing House, 1986), p. 536.

41 *Pyongyang Times*, March 30, 1974, p. 3.

42 Ibid.

43 Ibid., p. 1.

44 Je Seong Ho, *Hanbando Pyeonghwa Cheje-ui Mosaeg: Beobgyubeobjeog Jeobgeun-eul Jungsim-euro* (Search for a Peace Regime on the Korean Peninsula: Focusing on a Legal-Normative Approach) (Seoul: Jipyeong Seowon, 2000), pp. 110–11.

45 "Agreement between the Commander-in-Chief, United Nations Command, on the one hand, and the Supreme Commander of the Korean People's Army and the Commander of the Chinese People's Volunteers, on the other hand, Concerning a Military Armistice in Korea," Panmunjom, Korea, July 27, 1953.

46 *Seohae 5-gae Doseo-wa Geu Gwanryeonmunje-e Gwanhan Yeongu*, p. 9.

47 Ibid., pp. 10, 119, and 122–25.

48 The UNC position is discussed in detail in the following document. "Questions Regarding Northern Limit Line," Telegram from Secretary of State to U.S. embassy in Seoul, December 22, 1973, Electronic Telegrams, 1/1/1973–12/31/1973 (ET 1973), CFPF, RG 59, ADD, NARA. Although North Korea had not publicly claimed the 12-nautical-mile "contiguous" waters, its statements and practices suggested that it had such a claim.

49 *Seohae 5-gae Doseo-wa Geu Gwanryeonmunje-e Gwanhan Yeongu*, p. 133.

50 Kim Yeong Gu, *Hanguk-gwa Bada-ui Gugjebeob* (The Republic of Korea and the International Law of the Sea) (Seoul: Hangug Haeyang Jeonryag Yeonguso, 1999), p. 114.

51 *Seohae 5-gae Doseo-wa Geu Gwanryeonmunje-e Gwanhan Yeongu*, p. 100. The coverage would change depending on how the baseline is drawn.

52 Hugo Caminos, *The Legal Régime of Straits in the 1982 United Nations Convention on the Law of the Sea* (The Hague: Kluwer International, 1987), p. 82.

53 Kim, *Hanguk-gwa Bada-ui Gugjebeob*, p. 15.

54 "Developments along Northern Limit Line," Joint Embassy/UNC Message from U.S. embassy in Seoul to Secretary of State, December 1, 1973, ET 1973, CFPF, RG 59, ADD, NARA, p. 2.
55 "Questions Regarding Northern Limit Line."
56 "Northern Limit Line: Defining Contiguous Waters," Joint Embassy/UNC Message from Secretary of State to U.S. embassy in Tokyo, January 7, 1974, ET 1974, CFPF, RG 59, ADD, NARA.
57 "Seohaean Satae-e gwanhan Beobjeog gochal (Legal Examination of the Situation in the West Sea)," December 1973, in "Bughan Seohaean 5-gae doseo Jeobsog Suyeog Chimbeom Sageon," V. 1, ROK Diplomatic Archives, serial pp. 78–80.
58 United Nations, "Territorial Sea Law No. 3037 of 31 December 1977," http://www.un. org/Depts/los/LEGISLATIONANDTREATIES/PDFFILES/KOR_1977_Law.pdf; and United Nations, "Enforcement Decree of the Territorial Seas Act, promulgated by Presidential Decree No. 9162, 20 September 1978," http://www.un.org/Depts/los/ LEGISLATIONANDTREATIES/PDFFILES/KOR_1978_Decree.pdf.
59 "United Nations Convention on the Law of the Sea," http://www.un.org/Depts/los/ convention_agreements/texts/unclos/closindx.htm.
60 Lee, "History of Korea's MDL & Reduction of Tension along the DMZ and Western Sea," p. 88. See the Korean text, "Joseon Inmingun Choego Saryeonggwan Mich Junggug Inmin Jiwongun Saryeongwon-eul Ilbang-euro hago Ryeonhabguggun Chongsaryeonggwan-eul Dareun Ilbang-eurohaneun Joseon Gunsa Jeongjeon-e Gwanhan Hyeobjeong (Agreement between the Supreme Commander of the Korean People's Army and the Commander of the Chinese People's Volunteers, on the One Hand, and the Commander-in-Chief, United Nations Command, on the Other Hand, Concerning a Military Armistice in Korea)," in *Joseon Jungang Nyeongam 1953* (Pyongyang: Joseon Jungang Tongsinsa, 1953), p. 149.
61 Heo Man Ho, "Hyujeon Cheje-ui Deungjang-gwa Byeonhwa (Emergence and Transformation of the Armistice Regime)," in Hangug Jeongchi Waegyo Haghoe, ed., *Hangug Jeonjaeng-gwa Hyujeon Cheje* (The Korean War and the Armistice Regime) (Seoul: Jibmundang, 1998), pp. 167–68.
62 Ministry of Unification, "Seohae Haesang Gyeonggyeseon Munje (Question of the sea demarcation line in the West Sea)," June 14, 1999.
63 The coordinates of the NLL were: (37°42'45"N, 126°06'40"E) (37°39'30"N, 126° 01'00"E) (37°42'53"N, 125°45'00"E) (37°41'30"N, 125°41'52"E) (37°41'25"N, 125°40'00"E) (37°40'55"N, 125°31'00"E) (37°35'00"N, 125°14'30"E) (37° 38'15"N, 125°02'50"E) (37°46'00"N, 124°51'00"E) (38°00'00"N, 124°51'00"E) (38°03'00"N, 124°38'00"E) (38°03'00"N, 124°25'00"E). "Northern Limit Line (NLL)," CINCUNC OPLAN 5027A, February 15, 1973, in "Bughan Seohaean 5-gae doseo Jeobsog Suyeog Chimbeom Sageon," V. 1, ROK Diplomatic Archives, p. C-9, serial p. 20.
64 "Seohae Gyojeon Gwanryeon, Uri-ui Ibjang (Our Position on the Battle in the West Sea)," *Gugbang Sosig*, September 1999, no. 107.
65 MND, *Defense White Paper 1999* (Seoul: Ministry of National Defense, 1999), pp. 81–82; and Lee, "History of Korea's MDL & Reduction of Tension along the DMZ and Western Sea," p. 88.
66 *Seohae 5-gae Doseo-wa Geu Gwanryeonmunje-e Gwanhan Yeongu*, pp. 131–32.
67 Yu Jae Min, "Nambughan Bulgachimseon Hyeobsang-gwa Hangye (Negotiations for the Demarcation Line for Nonaggression between South and North Korea and their Limits)," *Gugbang Daehagwon Anbo Gwajeong Usu Nonmunjib* (Collection of Excellent Articles of the National Defense University Security Course) (Seoul: Gugbang Daehagwon, 1998), pp. 12, 15, and 37.

68 Central Intelligence Agency (CIA), *Korean Fishing Areas in the Yellow Sea – Spawning Ground for Maritime Conflict*, GCR-RP 75–20, May 1975, CIA Records Search Tool (CREST), Archives II Library, The U.S. National Archives and Records Administration, p. 2.

69 Ibid., pp. 3–4.

70 *Seohae 5-gae Doseo-wa Geu Gwanryeonmunje-e Gwanhan Yeongu*, p. 90; and Lee, "History of Korea's MDL & Reduction of Tension along the DMZ and Western Sea," pp. 96–97.

71 "North Korean Activities In Yellow Sea: ROK Request to Convey Firm Message to DPRK," Telegram from U.S. embassy in Seoul to Secretary of State, December 2, 1973, ET 1973, CFPF, RG 59, ADD, NARA.

72 "ROKG Legal Memorandum on Northwest Coastal Incidents," Joint State/Defense Message from Secretary of State to U.S. embassy in Seoul, December 22, 1973, ET 1973, CFPF, RG 59, ADD, NARA.

73 *Korea Times*, February 16, 1974, p. 1.

74 *JungAng Ilbo*, October 6, 1996, p. 22.

75 MAC, UNC Component, "Three Hundred and Second Meeting of the Military Armistice Commission," June 9, 1970, pp. 5–6; and Lee, "History of Korea's MDL & Reduction of Tension along the DMZ and Western Sea," p. 89.

76 International Institute for Strategic Studies, *The Military Balance, 1973–1974* (London: International Institute for Strategic Studies, 1973), p. 53.

77 *Jane's Fighting Ships, 1986–87* (London: Jane's Publishing Company, no publication year indicated), p. 328.

78 Office of the South–North Dialogue, *South–North Dialogue in Korea*, no. 5; and *Seohae 5-gae Doseo-wa Geu Gwanryeonmunje-e Gwanhan Yeongu*, p. 65.

79 Joseph S. Bermudez, Jr., *North Korean Special Forces*, 2nd edn (Annapolis, MD: Naval Institute Press, 1998), p. 113; and *Seohae 5-gae Doseo-wa Geu Gwanryeonmunje-e Gwanhan Yeongu*, p. 113.

80 Gordon Jacobs, "The Korean People's Navy: Further Perspectives," *Jane's Intelligence Review*, July 1993, p. 316.

81 *Seohae 5-gae Doseo-wa Geu Gwanryeonmunje-e Gwanhan Yeongu*, p. 101.

82 An Seung Beom, ed., *2000 Hanguggun Jangbi Yeongam* (ROK Armed Forces Equipment Annual 2000) (Seoul: Gunsa Jeongbo, 1999), pp. 127–28; and *Seohae 5-gae Doseo-wa Geu Gwanryeonmunje-e Gwanhan Yeongu*, p. 190.

83 Kim, "Hangug Haegun-ui Jeolchibusim," p. 659.

84 An, ed., *2000 Hanguggun Jangbi Yeongam*, pp. 138–39.

85 "Reinforcement of Garrisons of ROK-held Islands," Telegram from U.S. embassy in Seoul to Secretary of State, February 13, 1974, ET 1974, CFPF, RG 59, ADD, NARA.

86 Comments by Han Yeong Su, *Gugbang Wiwonhoe Hoewirog* (Proceedings of the National Defense Committee), no. 16, p. 15.

87 Lee, "'Panmunjeom San Jeungin' Jeimseu Ri Yugseong Jeung-eon (1)."

88 Lee, "Seohae-ui Jeonryagjeog-in Jungyoseong," p. 27.

89 In December 1967, the East German embassy already predicted this would happen in the future. The Extraordinary and Plenipotentiary Ambassador of the GDR in the DPRK, Pyongyang to State Secretary and First Deputy Minister of Foreign Affairs Comrade Hegen, December 8, 1967, in Bernd Schaefer, "North Korean 'Adventurism' and China's Long Shadow, 1966–72," Working Papers Series #44, Cold War International History Project, Woodrow Wilson International Center for Scholars (October 2004), p. 48.

218

90 North Korean claims were widely reported in the South Korean press. For example, see *Korea Times*, December 2, 1973, p. 1; and *Korea Times*, December 8, 1973, p. 1. Also, see Kim Tae Seo, "Bughan-ui Seohae Dobal-gwa Geu Chimryagjeog Jeoui (North Korea's Provocations in the West Sea and its Aggressive Intensions)," *Bughan*, vol. 3, no. 1, serial no. 25 (January 1974), p. 65.

91 "Discussion with ROKs on Northwest Coast Questions," Joint Embassy/UNC Message from U.S. embassy in Seoul to Secretary of State, January 9, 1974, ET 1974, CFPF, RG 59, ADD, NARA.

92 Ibid.

93 CIA, *Korean Fishing Areas in the Yellow Sea*, p. 4. Also, see "ROK/NK Fishing Pattern in Yellow Sea," Telegram from U.S. embassy in Seoul to Secretary of State, March 13, 1975, ET 1975, CFPF, RG 59, ADD, NARA. This latter report said, "There are no areas where the NK and ROK fishing fleets intermingle. This is due to the vigorous patrol actions by each side taken to preclude this situation from occurring."

94 Lee, "'Panmunjeom San Jeungin' Jeimseu Ri Yugseong Jeung-eon (1)." Another possible interpretation is that while the North Koreans tried to undermine the legal status of the NLL, they actually tried to encourage the tighter enforcement of the NLL in order to prevent South Korean fishing boats from coming north.

95 Between November 3 and December 1, 1973, 12 foreign commercial vessels entered the port of Haeju through the waters near Yeonpyeongdo. *Korea Times*, December 2, 1973, p. 1.

96 Memorandum from South Korean ambassador in Sweden to the Foreign Minister, December 23, 1973, in "Bughan Seohaean 5-gae doseo Jeobsog Suyeog Chimbeom Sageon," V. 2, ROK Diplomatic Archives, serial p. 129.

97 "346th MAC Meeting: North Korean Territorial Waters Claim," Joint Embassy/UNC Message from U.S. embassy in Seoul to Secretary of State, December 6, 1973, ET 1973, CFPF, RG 59, ADD, NARA, p. 2.

98 *Pyongyang Times*, March 30, 1974, p. 1.

99 Department of State, "Secretary's Meeting with Romanian Special Emissary – US–North Korean Contacts," Memorandum of Conversation, August 26, 1974, Digital National Security Archive (DNSA), document no. 01310.

100 "Memcon of Your Conversations with Chou En-lai," Memorandum for Henry A. Kissinger from Winston Lord, July 29, 1971, in William Burr, ed., "Henry Kissinger's Secret Trip to China, The Beijing-Washington Back-Channel, September 1970–July 1971," National Security Archive Electronic Briefing Book, no. 66, February 27, 2002, http://www.gwu.edu/~nsarchiv/NSAEBB/NSAEBB66/ch-34.pdf.

101 Department of State, Memorandum for Mr. Henry A. Kissinger, The White House, "NSSM 154 – United States Policy Concerning the Korean Peninsula," April 3, 1973, DNSA, document no. 01071, pp. vii–viii. For Kissinger plans, see Hideya Kurata, "Chousenhantou Heiwataisei Juritsumondai-to Beikoku (The United States and the Issue of Establishing a Peace Regime on the Korean Peninsula)," in Yoshinobu Yamamoto, ed., *Ajia Taiheiyou-no Anzenhoshou-to America* (Security in the Asia-Pacific and the United States) (Tokyo: Sairyuusha, 2005).

102 National Security Council, "Termination of the U.N. Command in Korea," National Security Decision Memorandum 251, March 29, 1974, DNSA, document no. 00205.

103 The White House, "Secretary's Dinner for the Vice Foreign Minister of the People's Republic of China," Memorandum of Conversation, Secretary's Suite, Waldorf Towers, New York City, October 2, 1974, DNSA, document no. 00310.

104 "Termination of the U.N. Command in Korea."

105 Corrected Copy, Joint Embassy/UNC Message from U.S. embassy in Seoul to Secretary of State, December 1, 1973, ET 1973, CFPF, RG 59, ADD, NARA, p. 2.

106 Ibid., p. 3.
107 "North Korean Activities In Yellow Sea."
108 "Reinforcement of Garrisons of ROK-held Islands."
109 "Gugje Jeongchi-neun Seon-ida. NLL-eun Sasuhaeya Handa (The International Politics is about the Line. The NLL must be Defended Unconditionally)," a speech by Professor Lee Ki-Tak, *Wolgan Joseon*, July 2001, p. 169.
110 Kim, "Hangug Haegun-ui Jeolchibusim," p. 660.
111 The ROK Marine Corps Headquarters were disbanded in October 1973, and the Marine Corps was subordinated to the ROK Navy Headquarters.
112 Lee Seon Ho, *Hanbeon Haebyeongdae-neun Yeongwonhan Haebyeongdae* (Once You are a Marine, You Will Always be) (Seoul: Doseo Chulpan Jeongudang, 1997), p. 367; and ROK Navy, "Jajugugbang – Jeonryeog Jeongbi mich Budae Baljeon: Haebyeong Budae (Self-Reliant National Defense – Improvement of the Forces and Development of Units: Marine Corps Units)," ROK Navy homepage, http://www. navy.mil.kr/sub_guide/sub_data.jsp?menu=3&smenu=1.
113 *Seohae 5-gae Doseo-wa Geu Gwanryeonmunje-e Gwanhan Yeongu*, pp. 119–20.
114 A retired South Korean defense official, interview by author, Seoul, ROK, June 1, 2001.
115 Lee, "Hanbando-ui Saeroun Gunsa Hwangyeong-gwa Haeyang-eseoui Anbo," p. 267.
116 An, ed., *2000 Hanguggun Jangbi Yeongam*, pp. 138–39; and ROK Navy, "Jaju-gugbang – Jeonryeog Jeongbi mich Budae Baljeon: Gugsan-ham Geonjo (Self-Reliant National Defense – Improvement of the Forces and Development of Units: Building Indigenous Ships)," ROK Navy homepage, http://www.navy.mil.kr/ sub_guide/sub_data.jsp?menu=3&smenu=1.
117 ROK Navy, "Jajugugbang – Jagjeon/Hunryeon: Yudotan Sisa (Self-Reliant National Defense – Operations/Training: Test-firing of Guided Missiles)," ROK Navy homepage, http://www.navy.mil.kr/sub_guide/sub_data.jsp?menu=3&smenu=1.

Chapter 5

1 The description of the incident is based on the following sources. U.S. Congress, House, Hearing before the Subcommittees on International Political and Military Affairs and on International Organization of the Committee on International Relations, *Deaths of American Military Personnel in the Korean Demilitarized Zone*, 94th Congress, Second Session, September 1, 1976 (Washington, DC: U.S. Government Printing Office, 1976); Richard G. Head, Frisco W. Short, and Robert C. McFarlane, *Crisis Resolution: Presidential Decision Making in the Mayaguez and Korean Confrontations* (Boulder, CO: Westview Press, 1978); Wayne A. Kirkbride, *DMZ: A Story of the Panmunjom Axe Murder*, 2nd edn (Seoul: Hollym, 1984); Park Hee-do, *Doraoji Anhneun Dari-e Seoda* (Standing in the Bridge of No Return) (Seoul: Saemteo, 1988); Kim Chung Yum, *Hangug Gyeongje Jeongchaeg 30-nyeonsa: Gim Jeong Ryeom Hoegorog* (Thirty Years' History of South Korean Economic Policy) (Seoul: JungAng Ilbosa, 1995); Tae-Young Yoon, "Crisis Management on the Korean Peninsula: South Korea's Crisis Management towards North Korea within the Context of the South Korea–U.S. Alliance, 1968–83," Ph.D. Dissertation, Department of Politics and Philosophy, Faculty of Humanities and Social Science, The Manchester Metropolitan University, October 1997; and "Shipwreck of North Korea's 'Axe Diplomacy'," in Office of the South–North Dialogue, *South–North Dialogue In Korea*, no. 11 (March 1976–November 1976), http://dialogue. unikorea.go.kr/bbs/filedn.asp?file=edialogue/11.hwp.
2 *Pyongyang Times*, August 21, 1976, p. 1.

3 "Panmunjom Incident: Press Guidance," Secretary of State, August 19, 1976, in
   Korea Information Service on Net (KISON), *DMZ Axe Incident (1976)*, Korean
   Security Archive, The Special Collections (Washington, DC: International Center,
   2000).

4 Jo Seong Gwan, "1976-nyeon 8-wol 21-il Gaeseong Jingyeog Jagjeon Gyehyoeg
   (Operation Plan to Advance into Kaesong, August 21, 1976)," *Wolgan Joseon*,
   October 1992, pp. 214–28.

5 Yoon, "Crisis Management on the Korean Peninsula," p. 272.

6 "Destruction of Korean Peoples Army Border Guard Barrack Located in Joint
   Security Area," undated, and "JCS Assessment," undated, and "Addendum," undated, in *DMZ Axe Incident*.

7 "Panmunjom Incident and Situation in Pyongyang," Telegram from USLO Peking to
   Secretary of State, August 21, 1976, in *DMZ Axe Incident*.

8 "Situation in Pyongyang," Telegram from USLO Peking to Secretary of State,
   August 22, 1976, in *DMZ Axe Incident*.

9 Jung Chang-Hyun, *Gyeot-eseo Bon Gim Jeong Il*, rev. and enl. edn (Kim Jong Il
   Seen from the Side) (Seoul: Gimyeongsa, 2000), pp. 202–4.

10 *Pyongyang Times*, March 13, 1976, p. 1.

11 "Government Memorandum of Democratic People's Republic of Korea," *Pyongyang
    Times*, August 17, 1976, p. 3.

12 U.S. Congress, *Deaths of American Military Personnel*, p. 28.

13 "Statement to NAM Summit by North Korean Foreign Minister," Telegram, August
    20, 1976, in *DMZ Axe Incident*.

14 *Pyongyang Times*, August 21, 1976, p. 1.

15 Military Armistice Commission, United Nations Command Component
    (UNCMAC), "Three Hundred and Seventy-Ninth Meeting of the Military Armistice
    Commission," August 19, 1976, p. 2.

16 "Three Hundred and Seventy-Ninth Meeting of the Military Armistice Commis-
    sion," pp. 7–12.

17 "August 19 Armistice Commission Meeting – Further Observations," August 20,
    1976, in *DMZ Axe Incident*.

18 "Meeting with President Park," August 19, 1976, in *DMZ Axe Incident*.

19 Presidential Secretariat, *Bag Jeong Hui Daetongryeong Yeonseolmunjib* (Speeches
    of President Park Chung Hee), January–December 1976 (Seoul: Daetongryeong
    Biseosil, 1977), p. 150.

20 Park, *Doraoji Anhneun Dari-e Seoda*, p. 187.

21 Ibid., p. 149.

22 Don Oberdorfer, *The Two Koreas: A Contemporary History* (Reading, MA: Addison-
    Wesley, 1997), p. 81.

23 *Pyongyang Times*, August 28, 1976, p. 3.

24 "21 August 1976 Informal Meeting between the Military Armistice Commission
    (MAC) Senior Members (SM)," Telegram from CINCUNC to JCS, August 22,
    1976, p. 3, in *DMZ Axe Incident*.

25 Head et al., *Crisis Resolution*, pp. 200–201.

26 "ROK Criticism of U.S. Actions," August 25, 1976, in *DMZ Axe Incident*.

27 "North Korean August 25 Proposal Re[garding] JSA Security Procedures," August
    25, 1976, and "Tentative Analysis KPA Proposal 380th MAC Meeting 25 August,"
    August 25, 1976, in *DMZ Axe Incident*.

28 "North Korean August 25 Proposal Re[garding] JSA Security Procedures."

29 Yoon, "Crisis Management on the Korean Peninsula," p. 290.

30 "381st MAC Meeting," August 28, 1976, in *DMZ Axe Incident*.

31 William H. Gleysteen Jr., *Massive Entanglement, Marginal Influence: Carter and Korea in Crisis* (Washington, DC: Brookings Institution Press, 1999), pp. 12–15.

32 Oberdorfer, *The Two Koreas*, pp. 84–86.

33 Description of this section is based on the following sources unless otherwise indicated. Ministry of Foreign Affairs, *Hangug Oegyo 30-nyeon, 1948–1978* (Thirty Years of the Diplomacy of the ROK, 1948–78) (Seoul: Oegyobu, 1979), pp. 220–24; Ministry of Foreign Affairs and Trade, *Hangug Oegyo 50-nyeon, 1948–1998* (Fifty Years of the Diplomacy of the ROK, 1948–98) (Seoul: Oegyotongsangbu, 1999), pp. 205–17; Se-Jin Kim, ed., *Korean Unification: Source Materials with an Introduction* (Seoul: Research Center for Peace and Unification, 1976); B. K. Gills, *Korea Versus Korea: A Case of Contested Legitimacy* (London: Routledge, 1996), pp. 121–44 and 190–96; and Chi Young Park, "Korea and the United Nations," in Youngnok Koo and Sung-joo Han, eds, *The Foreign Policy of the Republic of Korea* (New York: Columbia University Press, 1985), pp. 262–84; and Office of the South–North Dialogue, *South–North Dialogue in Korea*, no. 9 (March 1975–December 1975), http://dialogue.unikorea.go.kr/bbs/filedn.asp?file=edialogue/09.hwp.

34 "DPRK Foreign Ministry Issues Statement," November 23, 1973, in *Pyongyang Times*, December 1, 1973, p. 1.

35 U.S. Congress, *Deaths of American Military Personnel*, pp. 8–9.

36 *Pyongyang Times*, August 28, 1976, p. 2.

37 National Unification Board, *Seohae 5-gae Doseo-wa Geu Gwanryeonmunje-e Gwanhan Yeongu* (A Study on the Five Islands in the West Sea and the Related Issues), Nambuggwangye Daebibangan Yeongu (A Study on the Reaction Plans on South–North Relations) (Seoul: Gugto Tongilwon, 1977), serial no. 77-1-1136, p. 52.

38 U.S. Central Intelligence Agency, "DMZ Incident: Korea, 18 August 1976,"undated, in *DMZ Axe Incident*.

39 Ministry of National Defense, Republic of Korea, *Defense White Paper 1990* (Seoul: Korea Institute for Defense Analyses, 1991), pp. 75–79.

40 "Destruction of Korean Peoples Army Border Guard Barrack Located in Joint Security Area."

41 U.S. Congress, *Deaths of American Military Personnel*, p. 32.

42 "Memorandum of Conversation," The White House, September 15, 1976, in *DMZ Axe Incident*.

43 "Update JSA Incident," August 18, 1976, in *DMZ Axe Incident*.

44 "Agreement on the Military Armistice Commission Headquarters Area, Its Security and Its Construction," in "Subsequent Agreements," UNCMAC, revised October 1, 1976, Tab "D" (1)-2.

45 UNCMAC Component, "Three Hundred and Seventy-Seventh Meeting of the Military Armistice Commission," June 28, 1976, pp. 11–12.

46 U.S. Congress, *Deaths of American Military Personnel*, p. 26; and MAC, UNC Component, "Three Hundred and Sixty-Fifth Meeting of the Military Armistice Commission," July 12, 1975, pp. 2–4 and 9–12

47 "Three Hundred and Seventy-Seventh Meeting," p. 11; and "Conflict & Tension on the Korean Peninsula! A Chronology (28 Jul 53–Aug 98)," obtained from the UNCMAC Secretariat on July 18, 2001.

48 "Summary 377th Meeting of the Military Armistice Commission (MAC)," Telegram from CINCUNC to JSC, June 28, 1976.

49 "Three Hundred and Seventy-Seventh Meeting," pp. 11–12.

50 The North Korean side actually discussed the August 6 incident at the MAC meeting on August 19. "Three Hundred and Seventy-Ninth Meeting of the Military Armistice Commission," p. 6; and *Rodong Sinmun*, August 20, 1976, p. 4.

51 "Summary 379th Meeting of the Military Armistice Commission (MAC)," Telegram from CINCUNC to JSC, August 19, 1976.

52 Oberdorfer, *The Two Koreas*, p. 83.

53 United Nations Command (UNC)/United States Forces Korea (USFK)/Eighth United States Army (EUSA), *The 1976 Annual Historical Report*, p. 15, in file 350.018–3, "Axe Murder, 1976 (assorted)," United Nations Command, Combined Forces Command and United States Forces Korea, Command History Office.

54 Jung, *Gyeot-eseo Bon Gim Jeong Il*, pp. 201–2.

55 Pak Chol, then a guard at the JSA, had already once provoked a scuffling incident against a UNC guard on March 3, 1974. UNC/USFK/EUSA, *The 1976 Annual Historical Report*, p. 12, footnote 4. Lt. Pak Chol disappeared from the JSA immediately after the Axe Murder incident, came back about a week later, left the area, and did not return until late September. Then he left again and has not been seen by UNC personnel since. Head, et al., *Crisis Resolution*, p. 204. According to a defected former KPA officer, Pak Chol's true name is Pak Jong Nam. Sim Sin Bok, interview by author, Seoul, ROK, May 14, 2002.

56 Sim Sin Bok, interview by author, Seoul, ROK, May 14, 2002.

57 Defense Intelligence Agency, *National Intelligence Situation Report* (Korea), NISR 7–76, August 26, 1976 (1000 hours), CIA Records Search Tool (CREST), Archives II Library, The U.S. National Archives and Records Administration.

58 Jung, *Gyeot-eseo Bon Gim Jeong Il*, pp. 201–2.

59 Ibid., p. 203.

60 Kim Il Sung, "Talk with the Chief Editor of the Japanese Political Magazine *Sekai*," March 28, 1976, in *Kim Il Sung Works*, vol. 31 (Pyongyang: Foreign Languages Publishing House, 1987), pp. 57–58.

61 *Pyongyang Times*, August 28, 1976, p. 1.

62 Ministry of Foreign Affairs, *Hangug Oegyo 30-nyeon*, pp. 223–24.

63 "Memorandum of Conversation," The White House, September 15, 1976.

64 Central Intelligence Agency, "North Korea Politics," November 16, 1976, CREST, pp. 2–3; and Ministry of Foreign Affairs and Trade, *Hangug Oegyo 50-nyeon*, p. 217.

65 "Secretary's Meeting with Republic of Korea Foreign Minister Pak Tong-chin," Department of State, Memorandum of Conversation, September 27, 1976, Digital National Security Archive (DNSA), document no. 02089, pp. 1–2.

66 U.S. Congress, *Deaths of American Military Personnel*, p. 11.

67 Ibid., p. 12.

68 James M. Lee, "History of Korea's MDL & Reduction of Tension along the DMZ and Western Sea through Confidence Building Measures between North and South Korea," in Chae-Han Kim, ed., *The Korean DMZ: Reverting beyond Division* (Seoul: Sowha, 2001), p. 111.

69 Kim, *Hangug Gyeongje Jeongchaeg 30-nyeonsa*, p. 347.

70 Head, et al., *Crisis Resolution*, pp. 206–8.

71 After the withdrawal of the U.S. Seventh Infantry Division from Korea in 1971, only U.S. forces stationed in the DMZ were security forces in support of the JSA.

72 "Memorandum of Conversation," The White House, September 15, 1976.

73 U.S. Congress, *Deaths of American Military Personnel*, p. 8.

74 Choi Zoo Hwal, "Gim Jeong Il 30-nyeon Noryeog Kkeut-e Gunbu Wanjeonjangag (Kim Jong Il Perfectly Consolidated his Position in the Military after 30 Years of Efforts)," *Win*, June 1996, pp. 163–64.

75 Sin Gyeong Wan, "Gyeot-eseo Bon Gim Jeong Il (Kim Jong Il Seen from the Side)," *Wolgan JungAng*, June 1991, pp. 404–5.

76 Jung, *Gyeot-eseo Bon Gim Jeong Il*, p. 201.

Chapter 6

1 "DPRK Government declares its withdrawal from NPT to defend its supreme interests," Pyongyang, March 12, 1993, *Pyongyang Times*, March 20, 1993, p. 1; and "7th Meeting of 9th DPRK Central People's Committee decides to withdraw from NPT," *Pyongyang Times*, March 20, 1993, p. 2.

2 For evaluations of North Korea's nuclear program, see International Atomic Energy Agency, "In Focus: IAEA and DPRK," http://www.iaea.org/NewsCenter/Focus/ IaeaDprk/index.shtml; Federation of American Scientists (FAS), "Nuclear Weapons Program," updated on November 16, 2006, http://www.fas.org/nuke/guide/dprk/ nuke/index.html; Larry A. Niksch, *North Korea's Nuclear Weapons Program*, CRS Issue Brief for Congress, updated October 5, 2006, http://fpc.state.gov/documents/ organization/74904.pdf; Office of the Secretary of Defense (OSD), *Proliferation: Threat and Response* (Washington, DC: U.S. Government Printing Office, January 2001), http://fas.org/irp/threat/prolif00.pdf; David Albright and Kevin O'Neill, eds., *Solving the North Korean Nuclear Puzzle* (Washington, DC: The Institute for Science and International Security, 2000); U.S. General Accounting Office (GAO), *Nuclear Nonproliferation: Difficulties in Accomplishing IAEA's Activities in North Korea*, Report to the Chairman, Committee on Energy and Natural Resources, U.S. Senate (Washington, DC: GAO, July 1998); OSD, *Proliferation: Threat and Response*, (Washington, DC: U.S. Government Printing Office, November 1997); Joseph S. Bermudez, Jr., "North Korea's Nuclear Infrastructure," *Jane's Intelligence Review*, vol. 6, no. 2 (February 1994), pp. 74–79; and Arms Control Association (ACA), "Background Information on North Korea's Nuclear Program," May 5, 1994.

3 Detailed description of the events is based on the following materials unless otherwise indicated: International Atomic Energy Agency, *The Annual Report for 1994*, http://www.iaea.org/Publications/Reports/Anrep94/index.html; Joel S. Wit, Daniel B. Poneman, and Robert L. Gallucci, *Going Critical: The First North Korean Nuclear Crisis* (Washington, DC: Brookings Institution Press, 2004); Center for Strategic and International Studies (CSIS), "Nuclear Confrontation with North Korea: Lessons of the 1994 Crisis for Today," March 20, 2003, Seoul, Korea, http://www.nautilus. org/archives/pub/ftp/napsnet/special_reports/CSIS-seoul.txt; C. Kenneth Quinones, *Kitachousen: Bei-Kokumushou Tantoukan-no Koushou Hiroku* (North Korea's Nuclear Threat: "Off the Record" Memories) (Tokyo: Chuuoukouronsha, 2000); Leon V. Sigal, *Disarming Strangers: Nuclear Diplomacy with North Korea* (Princeton, NJ: Princeton University Press, 1998); Don Oberdorfer, *The Two Koreas: A Contemporary History* (Reading, MA: Addison-Wesley, 1997); Michael J. Mazarr, *North Korea and the Bomb: A Case Study in Nonproliferation* (New York: St. Martin's Press, 1995); and Mitchell Reiss, *Bridled Ambition: Why Countries Constrain Their Nuclear Capabilities* (Washington, DC: Woodrow Wilson Center Press, 1995).

4 Asagumo Shimbunsha Henshuusoukyoku, *Bouei Handobukku 2000* (Defense Handbook 2000) (Tokyo: Asagumo Shimbunsha, 2000), p. 471; and Oberdorfer, *The Two Koreas*, p. 279.

5 "Order No. 0034 of the KPA Supreme Commander," Pyongyang, March 8, 1993, in *Pyongyang Times*, March 13, 1993, p. 1. Also, see Asahi Shimbun *AERA* Henshuubu (Asahi Shimbun *AERA* Editorial Staff), *Kitachousen karano Boumeisha: 60-nin-no Shougen* (Defectors from North Korea: Testimony of Sixty of Them) (Tokyo: Asahi Shimbunsha, 1997), p. 95.

6 *Kitachousen Seisaku Doukou*, no. 203, April 30, 1993, p. 32.

7 Oberdorfer, *The Two Koreas*, p. 279.

8 *Pyongyang Times*, March 20, 1993, p. 1.

9 Gist of a Press Briefing by Spokesman Lee Kyung-Jai for President Kim Young Sam of the Republic of Korea, Upon Receiving a Briefing by the Deputy Prime Minister and Minister of National Unification Han Wan-Sang on the Work of the National Unification Board, Seoul, March 15, 1993, reprinted in *Korea and World Affairs*, vol. 17, no. 1 (Spring 1993), pp. 167–68.
10 Mazarr, *North Korea and the Bomb*, p. 116.
11 *Pyongyang Times*, April 3, 1993, p. 1.
12 Ibid., p. 8.
13 U.S. Department of State, Daily Press Briefing, April 22, 1993.
14 United Nations Security Council, "Resolution 825," S/RES/825, May 11, 1993.
15 "DPRK FM spokesman: N-problem cannot be solved by strongarm acts and pressure," *Pyongyang Times*, May 15, 1993, p. 3.
16 Wit, Poneman, and Gallucci, *Going Critical*, pp. 53–54.
17 "Joint Statement Following U.S.–North Korea Meeting," Text of U.S.–North Korean joint statement released by the Office of the Spokesman, U.S. Department of State, New York City, June 11, 1993; and *Pyongyang Times*, June 19, 1993, pp. 4 and 8.
18 "Head of DPRK delegation interviewed in New York," *Pyongyang Times*, June 19, 1993, p. 8.
19 Oberdorfer, *The Two Koreas*, p. 286.
20 *Pyongyang Times*, June 26, 1993, p. 3.
21 Wit, Poneman, and Gallucci, *Going Critical*, pp. 71–72.
22 "U.S.–North Korea Talks on the Nuclear Issue," Press Statement (text agreed by the D.P.R.K. and U.S. delegations), Text of statement by the U.S. delegation to the U.S.–D.P.R.K. talks on the nuclear issue, released in Geneva, July 19, 1993.
23 Wit, Poneman, and Gallucci, *Going Critical*, p. 79.
24 For example, see *Pyongyang Times*, September 20, 1993, p. 3; *Pyongyang Times*, February 5, 1994, pp. 1 and 3; and *Pyongyang Times*, February 19, 1994, p. 8.
25 United Nations, General Assembly, "Report of the International Atomic Energy Agency," A/RES/48/14, November 1, 1993.
26 *Rodong Sinmun*, November 4, 1993, p. 3; and "Answering dialogue with dialogue, war with war is our stand, declares Vice-Marshal Kim Kwang Jin," *Pyongyang Times*, November 6, 1993, p. 1.
27 *JungAng Ilbo*, November 4, 1993, p. 5; and Ministry of National Unification, *Tongil Baegseo 1995* (Unification White Paper 1995) (Seoul: Tongilwon, 1995), pp. 215–21.
28 *Gekkan Chousen Shiryou*, vol. 33, no. 11 (November 1993), pp. 10–12.
29 *Pyongyang Times*, October 9, 1993, p. 8.
30 *Washington Post*, November 6, 1993, p. A19.
31 *Pyongyang Times*, December 4, 1993, p. 1.
32 Oberdorfer, *The Two Koreas*, p. 295; and Reiss, *Bridled Ambition*, p. 261. By then, the United States and North Korean negotiations had reached a secret understanding that the term "special inspection" would not be used in future negotiations. C. Kenneth Quinones, e-mail message to author, February 20, 2008.
33 Reiss, *Bridled Ambition*, pp. 262–63.
34 Wit, Poneman, and Gallucci, *Going Critical*, pp. 100–107.
35 C. Kenneth Quinones, e-mail message to author, February 16, 2008.
36 *Pyongyang Times*, February 5, 1994, p. 3.
37 Wit, Poneman, and Gallucci, *Going Critical*, p. 127.
38 "Resumption of U.S.–North Korea Negotiations on Nuclear and Other Issues," Statement by Department Spokesman Michael McCurry, released by the Office of the Spokesman, U.S. Department of State, Washington, DC, March 3, 1994, including the text of the U.S.–North Korea agreed conclusions.
39 Quinones, *Kitachousen*, p. 290; and Reiss, *Bridled Ambition*, p. 266.

40 Tongilwon, *Tongil Baegseo 1995*, p. 227.
41 "Safeguards," in *The Annual Report for 1994*.
42 *Pyongyang Times*, March 26, 1994, pp. 1 and 3.
43 Quoted in "Statement by the President of the Security Council," March 31, 1994.
44 United Nations Security Council, "Statement by the President of the Security Council," S/PRST/1994/13, March 31, 1994; and IAEA, "Safeguards," excerpt from *The Annual Report for 1994*.
45 Wit, Poneman, and Gallucci, *Going Critical*, p. 160.
46 *Dong-A Ilbo*, March 23, 1994, p. 4.
47 *Joseon Ilbo*, April 20, 1994, p. 2; and Ministry of National Defense (MND), Republic of Korea, *Defense White Paper 1995–96* (Seoul: Korea Institute for Defense Analyses, 1996), p. 62. See the Korean edition for a more accurate description. MND, *Gugbang Baegseo 1995–1996* (Defense White Paper 1995–96) (Seoul: Gugbangbu, 1995), p. 64.
48 Joseph S. Bermudez, Jr., *The Armed Forces of North Korea*, The Armed Forces of Asia Series (London: I.B. Tauris, 2001), p. 146.
49 *Rodong Sinmun*, May 4, 1993, p. 6.
50 Wit, Poneman, and Gallucci, *Going Critical*, p. 175.
51 "IAEA Safeguards in the DPRK," IAEA, PR94/21, May 19, 1994; and Wit, Poneman, and Gallucci, *Going Critical*, p. 182.
52 United Nations Security Council, "Statement by the President of the Security Council," S/PRST/1994/28, May 30, 1994.
53 U.S. Department of State, Daily Press Briefing, June 3, 1994.
54 *Hangug Ilbo*, June 4, 1994, p. 2.
55 *Pyongyang Times*, June 11, 1994, p. 8.
56 *Rodong Sinmun*, June 8, 1994, p. 6.
57 IAEA, "Events in the Democratic People's Republic of Korea."
58 *Pyongyang Times*, June 18, 1994, p. 2.
59 *Joseon Ilbo*, July 2, 1994, p. 2.
60 *Sankei Shimbun*, December 2, 1997.
61 *Asahi Shimbun*, September 22, 1998; and C. Kenneth Quinones, e-mail message to author, February 16, 2008.
62 Wit, Poneman, and Gallucci, *Going Critical*, p. 205.
63 Ibid., p. 210.
64 Ibid., pp. 211–12.
65 Oberdorfer, *The Two Koreas*, p. 323.
66 Wit, Poneman, and Gallucci, *Going Critical*, pp. 180–81.
67 Ibid., pp. 186–87.
68 Ibid., p. 244.
69 Kim Young Sam, *Gim Yeong Sam Daetongryeong Hoegorog* (President Kim Young Sam's Memoir), vol. 1 (Seoul: Joseon Ilbosa, 2001), pp. 315–16.
70 For Carter's visit, see Marion V. Creekmore, Jr., *A Moment of Crisis: Jimmy Carter, the Power of a Peacemaker, and North Korea's Nuclear Ambitions* (New York: PublicAffairs, 2006).
71 President Clinton, "Opening statement at a news conference," Washington, DC, June 22, 1994.
72 *Pyongyang Times*, July 2, 1994, p. 1.
73 Wit, Poneman, and Gallucci, *Going Critical*, p. 249.
74 "4-Point Joint Statement Reached between the United States and North Korea," Geneva, August 12, 1994, reprinted in *Korea and World Affairs*, vol. 18, no. 3 (Fall 1994), pp. 576–77.
75 *Pacific Stars and Stripes*, September 22, 1994, pp. 1 and 6.

76 Ibid.
77 *Rodong Sinmun*, September 25, 1994, p. 4.
78 *Agence France Presse*, September 27, 1994.
79 *Pyongyang Times*, October 1, 1994, p. 1.
80 For example, see Secretary of Defense William J. Perry, Department of Defense News Briefing, October 5, 1994.
81 Sigal, *Disarming Strangers*, p. 188.
82 *Washington Times*, October 6, 1994, p. A14.
83 "Agreed Framework between the United States of America and the Democratic People's Republic of Korea," Geneva, October 21, 1994; and "Agreed Framework between the Democratic People's Republic of Korea and the United States of America," Geneva, October 21, 1994, http://www1.korea-np.co.jp/pk/011th_issue/971001genevaagreemet.htm; and *Pyongyang Times*, October 22, 1994, p. 8.
84 Ashton B. Carter and William J. Perry, *Preventive Defense: A New Security Strategy for America* (Washington, DC: Brookings Institution Press, 1999), p. 126.
85 Ibid., p. 128.
86 Ibid., p. 130.
87 *Rodong Sinmun*, March 13, 1993, p. 3.
88 Defense Intelligence Agency (DIA), *North Korea: The Foundations for Military Strength*, update 1995 (Washington, DC: U.S. Government Printing Office, 1996), p. 13.
89 MND, *Defense White Paper 1998* (Seoul: Korea Institute for Defense Analyses, 1999), p. 67.
90 MND, *Defense White Paper 1996–97* (Seoul: Korea Institute for Defense Analyses, 1997), p. 65.
91 MND, Republic of Korea, *Defense White Paper 1994–1995* (Seoul: Korea Institute for Defense Analyses, 1995), p. 72.
92 According to Kim Il Sung, the military lines ordered "to train the People's Army into a cadre army, to modernize armaments, fortify military positions, arm the entire people, and to garrison the whole country. … " Kim Il Sung, "Let Us Strengthen the Revolutionary Forces in Every Way so as to Achieve the Cause of Reunification of the Country," Concluding Speech Delivered at the Eighth Plenary Meeting of the Fourth Central Committee of the Workers' Party of Korea, February 27, 1964, in *Kim Il Sung Works*, vol. 18 (Pyongyang: Foreign Languages Publishing House, 1984), pp. 222–23.
93 "Treaty on the Non-Proliferation of Nuclear Weapons (1968)," INFCIRC/140, U.N. T.S. no. 10485, vol. 729, pp. 169–75, Entered into Force on March 5, 1970.
94 It is telling that the United States did not react to the same time pressure in 2003. It simply ignored the effectuation of North Korea's withdrawal from the NPT in April 2003.
95 Carter and Perry, *Preventive Defense*, pp. 128–29.
96 Denny Roy, "North Korea and the 'Madman' Theory," *Security Dialogue*, vol. 25, no. 3 (1994), p. 311.
97 Oberdorfer, *The Two Koreas*, p. 250.
98 Mazarr, *North Korea and the Bomb*, p. 96.
99 Hyun Seong Il, *Bughan-ui Guggajeonryag-gwa Pawo-elriteu: Ganbu Jeongchaeg-eul Jungsim-euro* (North Korea's National Strategy and its Power Elite: Focusing on the Leader Personnel Policies) (Seoul: Seon-in Doseochulpan, 2007), pp. 424–25; Hyun Seong Il, interview by author, Seoul, ROK, March 19, 2008; and A defected former North Korean diplomat, interview by author, Seoul, ROK, May 15, 2002.
100 Hyun, *Bughan-ui Guggajeonryag-gwa Pawo-elriteu*, p. 425; and Hyun Seong Il, interview by author, Seoul, ROK, March 19, 2008.

101 Quinones, *Kitachousen*, p. 259.
102 "Conclusion of non-aggression treaty between DPRK and U.S. called for," *KCNA*, October 25, 2002.
103 *New York Times*, March 10, 2002.
104 For details of KEDO activities, see KEDO homepage, http://www.kedo.org/.
105 "KCNA accuses U.S. of trying to evade its responsibility," *KCNA*, June 10, 2000; and "Spokesman for DPRK Foreign Ministry on compensation for loss of electricity," *KCNA*, July 1, 2000.
106 Albright and O'Neill, eds, *Solving the North Korean Nuclear Puzzle*, pp. 32–39 and 42–44.
107 "KEDO Executive Board Meeting Concludes," KEDO News, November 14, 2002.
108 KEDO, *2005 Annual Report*, p. 13, http://www.kedo.org/pdfs/KEDO_AR_2005.pdf.
109 "Agreement on Supply of a Light-Water Reactor Project to the Democratic People's Republic of Korea between the Korean Peninsula Energy Development Organization and the Government of the Democratic People's Republic of Korea," December 15, 1995.
110 "U.S. Policy Toward North Korea," Testimony of Mark Minton, Director of the Office of Korean Affairs, before the Senate Foreign Relations Committee, Subcommittee on East Asian and Pacific Affairs, Washington, DC, September 12, 1996.
111 C. Kenneth Quinones, e-mail message to author, February 20, 2008.
112 Hyun, *Bughan-ui Guggajeonryag-gwa Pawo-elriteu*, pp. 272 and 429.
113 Quinones, *Kitachousen*, p. 286.
114 U.S. Department of State, Bureau of Intelligence and Research, "ROK: Kim Hangs On," Brief, April 12, 1996, in The National Security Archive Korea Project, The National Security Archive, Washington, DC.
115 Quinones, *Kitachousen*, p. 334.
116 Hahm Sung Deuk, ed., *Gim Yeong Sam Jeongbu-ui Seonggong-gwa Silpae* (The Kim Young Sam Government: Its Successes and Failures) (Seoul: Nanam, 2001), p. 37.
117 Ibid., p. 38. The North Korean artillery could not reach Busan, Gwangju, and Jeju, but it is how Kim Young Sam recollected the situation.
118 Kim Chang Hui, "Bughan, 80-nyeondae jungban Seodog-eseo Haegmuljil Guib (North Korea Purchased Nuclear Material from West Germany in the mid-1980s)," *Sindong-a*, November 1995, p. 134.
119 "KPA, invincible revolutionary armed forces," *KCNA*, April 24, 1998.
120 "US Forces Korea – Exercises," GlobalSecurity.org, http://www.globalsecurity.org/military/ops/ex-usfk.htm.
121 "KPA will answer enemies' war of aggression with revolutionary war," *KCNA*, August 19, 1998; and "Prelude to second Korean war," *KCNA*, August 26, 1998.
122 *Pyongyang Times*, April 23, 1992, p. 1.
123 Kim Jong Il, *Gim Jeong Il Seonjib* (Kim Jong Il Selected Works), vol. 13 (Pyongyang: Joseon Rodongdang Chulpansa, 1998), pp. 1–9.
124 *Pyongyang Times*, April 10, 1993, p. 2.
125 "DPRK's Old Socialist Constitution (Full Text)," http://www1.korea-np.co.jp/pk/062nd_issue/98092413.htm.
126 *Kitachousen Seisaku Doukou*, no. 208 (August 1993), p. 40.
127 Kim Jong Il, "Abuses of Socialism Are Intolerable," Talk published in *Kulloja*, Organ of the Central Committee of the Workers' Party of Korea, March 1, 1993, in *Pyongyang Times*, March 6, 1993, pp. 2–4.
128 Joseph S. Bermudez, Jr., *North Korean Special Forces*, 2nd edn (Annapolis, MD: Naval Institute Press, 1998), p. 158.
129 *Pyongyang Times*, December 11, 1993, pp. 1 and 3.

130 Kim Cheol U, *Gim Jeong Il Janggun-ui Seongun Jeongchi: Gunsa Seonhaeng, Gun-eul Juryeoggun-euro Haneun Jeongchi* (Gen. Kim Jong Il's Policy of Giving Priority to the Army: Policy that Gives Priority to the Military Affairs and that Centers on the Army) (Pyongyang: Pyeongyang Chulpansa, 2000).

Chapter 7

1 Gary Samore, "U.S.–DPRK Missile Negotiations," *The Nonproliferation Review*, vol. 9, no. 2 (Summer 2002), p. 16.
2 Kenneth Katzman and Rinn-Sup Shinn, *North Korea: Military Relations with the Middle East*, CRS Report for Congress, 94–754F, September 27, 1994, pp. 12–13.
3 *Korea Times*, June 16, 1993, p. 2 and *Reuters*, November 4, 1992, in *Executive News Service*, November 4, 1992, as quoted in Center for Nonproliferation Studies, Monterey Institute of International Studies, "Chronology of North Korea's Missile Trade and Developments" [hereafter simply referred to as "Chronology"], http://cns.miis.edu/research/korea/chron.htm.
4 *Korea Times*, June 16, 1993, p. 2; *Reuters*, July 3, 1993; *Reuters*, August 17, 1993; *US–Korea Review*, September 1993, p. 3; Jon B. Wolfsthal, *Arms Control Today*, September 1993, p. 24; and Udi Segal, *IDF Radio* (Tel Aviv), March 22, 1994, in *JPRS-TND*-94-008, April 1, 1994, p. 34, all quoted in "Chronology." C. Kenneth Quinones, e-mail message to author, February 16, 2008; and David Wright, "Cut North Korea Some Slack," *Bulletin of the Atomic Scientists*, vol. 55, no. 2 (March/April 1999).
5 Wright, "Cut North Korea Some Slack."
6 For North Korea's missile testing, see Greg Gerardi and Joseph Bermudez, Jr., "An Analysis of North Korean Ballistic Missile Testing," *Jane's Intelligence Review*, vol. 7, no. 4 (April 1995), pp. 184–90; and *Aviation Week and Space Technology*, July 11, 1994, p. 55; and Joseph S. Bermudez, Jr., "North Korea's Musudan-ri Launch Facility," Missile News: Special Report, CDISS, http://www.cdiss.org/spec99aug.htm (accessed on July 18, 2002).
7 Joseph S. Bermudez, Jr., *A History of Ballistic Missile Development in the DPRK*, Occasional Paper no. 2, Monitoring Proliferation Threats Project (Monterey, California: Center for Nonproliferation Studies, Monterey Institute of International Studies, 1999), p. 21, http://cns.miis.edu/pubs/opapers/op2/op2.pdf.
8 *New York Times*, May 29, 1994, pp. 1 and 6; and *Aviation Week & Space Technology*, June 20, 1994, p. 19. *Yeonhab* (*Yonhap*), May 28, 1994, in FBIS-EAS-94-104, May 31, 1994, p. 47; and *Reuters*, May 28, 1994, quoted in "Chronology."
9 *Hangug Ilbo*, June 4, 1994, p. 2.
10 *Joseon Ilbo*, July 2, 1994, p. 2.
11 *KBS-1 Radio Network*, Seoul, June 9, 1994; *Reuters*, June 9, 1994, in *Executive News Service*, June 9, 1994, quoted in "Chronology."
12 "Liaison Office Site Survey in Pyongyang, 1/31–32/4," Telegram from U.S. embassy in Beijing to Secretary of State, February 6, 1995, in The National Security Archive Korea Project (NSAKP), The National Security Archive, Washington, DC.
13 Samore, "U.S.–DPRK Missile Negotiations," p. 17.
14 Evan S. Medeiros, "U.S., North Korea May Hold Talks On North's Missile Sales, MTCR Status," *Arms Control Today*, vol. 26, no. 1 (February 1996), p. 25.
15 DoS, Daily Press Briefing, April 19, 1996.
16 "Guidance for U.S. Delegation to DPRK Missile Talks," Cable, SecState to USMission USUN, June 10, 1997, in NSAKP; and *Washington Times*, June 5, 1996, p. A20.
17 DoS, Daily Press Briefing, April 22, 1996

18 *Pyongyang Times*, April 27, 1996, p. 8.

19 *KCNA*, June 28, 1996, in *Gekkan Chousen Shiryou*, no. 36, vol. 8 (August 1996), p. 20.

20 Remarks by President Kim Young Sam of the Republic of Korea at a Reception in Celebration of the 48th Armed Forces Day, Reconsidering South Korea's Assistance to North Korea and Endorsing the Defense Minister's Reinforcement Plan, Army Hall, Seoul, October 1, 1996, in *Korea and World Affairs*, vol. 20, no. 4 (Winter 1996), pp. 667–68.

21 Don Oberdorfer, *The Two Koreas: A Contemporary History* (Reading, MA: Addison-Wesley, 1997), p. 389.

22 DoS, "North Korea Missile Proliferation," Memorandum, April 16, 1997, NSAKP.

23 DoS, Daily Press Briefing, October 17 and 18, 1996.

24 *Pyongyang Times*, November 2, 1996, p. 1.

25 *Gekkan Chousen Shiryou*, no. 36, vol. 12 (December 1996), pp. 16–17.

26 "DPRK–US negotiations held in New York," *Pyongyang Times*, November 9, 1996, p. 1.

27 DoS, Daily Press Briefing, November 8, 1996.

28 Arms Control Association, "Chronology of U.S.–North Korean Nuclear and Missile Diplomacy," June 2003, http://www.armscontrol.org/factsheets/dprkchron.asp.

29 *Associated Press*, August 27, 1997.

30 "Nobody can slander DPRK's missile policy – *KCNA* commentary," *KCNA*, June 16, 1998.

31 *Associated Press*, August 19, 1998.

32 An official of the South Korean Ministry of Unification revealed that North Korean arms exports amounted to a total of $2.5 billion between 1980 and 1989, but that arms sales diminished precipitously in the 1990s and amounted only to $300 million between 1990 and 1995. The official pointed out that it was due to the difficulties in obtaining foreign currency through arms exports that North Korea started to demand that the United States provide "compensation" for the the cessation of the missile exports. *Yeonhab*, August 29, 1998. However, given the vastly different figures assigned to North Korea's arms exports depending on sources, it is hard to determine whether this interpretation is correct.

33 *New York Times*, August 17, 1998, p. A1.

34 DoS, "U.S.–D.P.R.K. Talks," Press Statement, September 10, 1998.

35 *Washington Post*, September 25, 1998, p. A31.

36 Bermudez, *A History of Ballistic Missile Development in the DPRK*, p. 30.

37 Government of Japan (GOJ), Comment by Chief Cabinet Secretary Hiromu Nonaka on North Korea's Test Missile Launch, August 31, 1998; and GOJ, Announcement by the Chief Cabinet Secretary on Japan's immediate response to North Korea's missile launch, September 1, 1998.

38 *Korea Times*, September 5, 1998.

39 GOJ, Announcement by Chief Cabinet Secretary Hiromu Nonaka concerning the Resumption of Japan's Cooperation with KEDO, October 21, 1998.

40 *Rodong Sinmun*, September 8, 1998, p. 3.

41 *Rodong Sinmun*, September 17, 1998, p. 3.

42 *Rodong Sinmun*, September 25, 1998, p. 6; and "U.S. hit for frantic anti-DPRK campaign," *KCNA*, September 25, 1998.

43 Samore, "U.S.–DPRK Missile Negotiations," p. 17.

44 *New York Times*, September 4, 1998, p. A3. There was also a report that North Korea was preparing for another *Taepo Dong* 1 launch. *Asahi Shimbun*, September 5, 1998.

45 *Korea Times*, September 4, 1998.

46 DoS, "U.S.–D.P.R.K. Talks."

47 Joel Wit, interview by author, Washington, D.C., July 22, 2002.
48 DoS, "North Korea: Additional Food Assistance," Press Statement, September 21, 1998.
49 DoS, "U.S.–DPRK Missile Talks," Press Statement, October 2, 1998.
50 Ibid.; Howard Diamond, "U.S., North Korea Meet on Missiles; Japan, S. Korea Press on Defense," *Arms Control Today*, vol. 28, no. 7 (October 1998); and *Jiji Tsuushin Nyusu Sokuhou*, October 2, 1998.
51 Osamu Eya, *Kin Shounichi Daizukan* (An Illustrated Book on Kim Jong Il) (Tokyo: Shougakkan, 2000), p. 11; *Washington Post*, November 20, 1998; and Greg Seigle, "Another N. Korean Missile Launch Near, Says USA," *Jane's Defence Weekly*, December 9, 1998, p. 1.
52 "KPA will answer U.S. aggression forces' challenge with annihilating blow," Statement of KPA general staff spokesman, *KCNA*, December 2, 1998.
53 *Sankei Shimbun*, December 10, 1998.
54 *Asahi Shimbun*, December 11, 1998, p. 8; Seigle, "Another N Korean missile launch near, says USA"; and *Times of India*, December 12, 1998, quoted in "Chronology."
55 *Rodong Sinmun*, December 18, 1998; and "We will watch U.S. attitude," *KCNA*, December 18, 1998.
56 DoS, Daily Press Briefing, December 2, 1998.
57 *Washington Times*, December 31, 1998, p. A4.
58 *Korea Herald*, April 1, 1999.
59 DoS, Daily Press Briefing, March 30, 1999.
60 DoS, "Conclusion of Third Round of U.S.–D.P.R.K. Bilateral Talks on Suspect Underground Construction," Press Statement, December 11, 1998; and *New York Times*, December 15, 1998, p. A3.
61 DoS, "Statement by Secretary of State Madeleine K. Albright," March 16, 1999; "U.S.–D.P.R.K. Joint Press Statement," New York, March 16, 1999; and "U.S.–DPRK Joint Statement," U.S. Mission, New York, March 16, 1999.
62 U.S. Agency for International Development (USAID), "Agreement Reached on Bilateral Assistance Project for North Korea," Press Release, April 22, 1999.
63 DoS, "North Korea – Site Access at Kumchangni," Press Statement, May 7, 1999; and DoS, Press Statement by James P. Rubin, May 27, 1999; and "Report of U.S. Delegation on May 20–21 Visit to Kumghang-Ri," Cable, Tokyo 4263, U.S. embassy in Tokyo to Secretary of State, May 27, 1999, in NSAKP.
64 DoS, "Report on the U.S. Visit to the Site at Kumchang-ni, Democratic People's Republic of Korea," Press Statement, June 25, 1999.
65 DoS, "Dr. William Perry Named North Korea Policy Coordinator," Press Statement, November 12, 1998.
66 William J. Perry, Special Advisor to the President and the Secretary of State, "Review of United States Policy Toward North Korea: Findings and Recommendations," October 12, 1999.
67 DoS, Remarks by Secretary of State Madeleine K. Albright and Hong Soon-Young, Minister of Foreign Affairs and Trade of the Republic of Korea in Joint Press Availability after Their Meeting, Washington, DC, May 17, 1999.
68 See following materials for North Korea's missile-related activities. "No-dong: N40–51'17" E129–39'58"," maintained by John Pike and Tim Brown, updated March 25, 2000, http://www.fas.org/nuke/guide/dprk/facility/nodong.htm; Center for Nonproliferation Studies, Monterey Institute of International Studies, "North Korea: A Second Taep'o-dong Test?" http://cns.miis.edu/research/korea/taep2.htm; *Washington Times*, June 17, 1999, p. A3; Bermudez, "North Korea's Musudan-ri Launch Facility"; DoD News Briefing, July 6, 1999; and *New York Times*, July 22, 1999, p. A8.
69 *Dong-A Ilbo*, June 21, 1999, p. 1; and *Asahi Shimbun*, June 24, 1999.

70 Joel Wit, interview by author, Washington, DC, July 27, 2002; and Robert Carlin, e-mail message to author, February 24, 2008.

71 *Korea Times*, August 9, 1999.

72 National Intelligence Council (NIC), "Foreign Missile Developments and the Ballistic Missile Threat to the United States Through 2015," September 1999, http://nunnturnerinitiative.org/e_research/official_docs/cia/9–99CIA.pdf.

73 The White House, "Easing Sanctions Against North Korea," Statement, September 17, 1999.

74 Ibid.; and The White House, "Fact Sheet: Easing Sanctions Against North Korea," September 17, 1999.

75 "DPRK not to launch missile," *KCNA*, September 24, 1999.

76 The White House, Statement by the President, June 19, 2000; and DoS, "Fact Sheet: Implementation of Easing of Sanctions Against North Korea," June 19, 2000.

77 Transcript of Remarks and Q&A with Assistant Secretary of State for Non-Proliferation Mr. Robert Einhorn at the Conclusion of the U.S.-DPRK Missile Talks, U.S. Embassy, Kuala Lumpur, July 12, 2000.

78 "U.S.–DPRK Joint Communiqué," Washington, DC, October 12, 2000.

79 DoS, "Joint U.S.–DPRK Statement on International Terrorism," Statement, Washington, DC, October 6, 2000.

80 Press Conference by Secretary of State Madeleine K. Albright, Koryo Hotel, Pyongyang, North Korea, October 24, 2000.

81 Madeleine Albright with Bill Woodward, *Madam Secretary* (New York: Miramax Books, 2003), p. 465; *New York Times*, March 6, 2001, pp. A1 and A8; and Chun Yong Taek, interview by Nam Mun Hui, "Bughan, No Dong misail gaebal pogi yagsoghaessda (North Korea promised to abandon No Dong missile Development)," *Sisa Jeonal*, no. 597, April 5, 2001.

82 *New York Times*, March 6, 2001.

83 Ibid.

84 Press Statement issued by Robert J. Einhorn, Assistant Secretary of State for Non-proliferation in Kuala Lumpur, Malaysia, November 3, 2000.

85 Samore, "U.S.–DPRK Missile Negotiations," pp. 18–19.

86 For the details leading up to the final decision, see Albright, *Madam Secretary*, pp. 468–70.

87 For the history, capability, production, and deployment of North Korea's missiles, see Federation of American Scientists, "Nuclear Forces Guide - Missiles," updated on March 17, 2008, http://www.fas.org/nuke/guide/dprk/missile/; Statement of General Thomas A. Schwartz, Commander in Chief, United Nations Command/Combined Forces Command, and Commander, United States Forces Korea before the Senate Armed Forces Committee, March 27, 2001, pp. 9–10; Office of the Secretary of Defense, *Proliferation: Threat and Response* (Washington, DC: Office of the Secretary of Defense, January 2001); Bermudez, *A History of Ballistic Missile Development in the DPRK*; Testimony of General John H. Tilelli, Commander-in-Chief of United States Forces in Korea, House Armed Services Committee Hearing, March 3, 1999; Joseph S. Bermudez, Jr, "Taepo-Dong Launch Brings DPRK Missiles Back into the Spotlight," *Jane's Intelligence Review*, vol. 10, no. 10 (October 1998), p. 30; The Commission to Assess the Ballistic Missile Threat to the United States, "Executive Summary of the Report of the Commission to Assess the Ballistic Missile Threat to the United States," July 15, 1998, [hereafter referred to as "The Rumsfeld Commission Report"]; David C. Wright, "An Analysis of the North Korean Missile Program," in Report of the Commission to Assess the Ballistic Missile Threat to the United States, Appendix III: *Unclassified Working Papers*, Pursuant to Public Law 201, 104th Congress, July 15, 1998, pp. 346–48; Defense

Intelligence Agency (DIA), *North Korea: The Foundations for Military Strength*, update 1995 (Washington, DC: U.S. Government Printing Office, 1995), pp. 11–12, and 21; Joseph S. Bermudez, Jr and W. Seth Carus, "The North Korean 'Scud B' Programme," *Jane's Intelligence Review*, vol. 1, no. 4 (April 1989), pp. 177–81; Defense Agency, Japan, *Defense of Japan 1999* (Tokyo: Urban Connections, year not indicated), pp. 202–8; and Chiaki Akimoto, "Inpa Kakujikken-no Shinso (Real Facts of Nuclear Experiments of India and Pakistan)," *Chuuoukouron*, August 1998, pp. 110–19.

88 Bermudez, *A History of Ballistic Missile Development in the DPRK*, pp. 1 and 4.

89 DIA, *North Korea*, p. 21.

90 Statement of General Thomas A. Schwartz, Commander in Chief, United Nations Command/Combined Forces Command, and Commander, United States Forces Korea before the Senate Armed Forces Committee, March 7, 2000, p. 6.

91 On November 6, 1998, South Korean Defense Minister Chun Yong Taek stated that North Korea would be able to deploy nine *No Dong* missiles launchers by the end of 1998. *Mainichi Shimbun*, November 7, 1998.

92 Thomas A. Keaney and Eliot A. Cohen, *Gulf War Air Power Survey*, Summary Report (Washington, DC: U.S. Government Printing Office, 1993), pp. 83–90; and Anthony H. Cordesman and Abraham R. Wagner, *The Lessons of Modern War*, Volume IV: *The Gulf War* (Boulder, CO: Westview Press, 1996), p. 856.

93 Bermudez, *A History of Ballistic Missile Development in the DPRK*, pp. 22–23.

94 NIC, "Foreign Missile Developments and the Ballistic Missile Threat."

95 Statement of the Director of Central Intelligence, George J. Tenet, As Prepared for Delivery Before the Senate Armed Services Committee Hearing on Current and Projected National Security Threats, February 2, 1999.

96 NIC, "Global Trends 2015: A Dialogue About the Future With Nongovernment Experts," NIC 2000–2002, December 2000.

97 Bermudez, *A History of Ballistic Missile Development in the DPRK*, p. 1.

98 Office of the Secretary of Defense, *Proliferation: Threat and Response* (Washington, DC: U.S. Government Printing Office, November 1997), p. 8.

99 Joseph S. Bermudez, Jr., "Ballistic Missiles in the Third World: Iran's Medium-Range Missiles," *Jane's Intelligence Review*, vol. 4, no. 4 (April 1992), p. 147; and Joseph S. Bermudez, Jr., "New Developments in North Korean Missile Programme," *Jane's Soviet Intelligence Review*, vol. 2, no. 8 (August 1990), p. 344.

100 *Korea Times*, September 26, 1996.

101 "DPRK Missile Program for Michael Rosenthal," Memorandum, Roe to Kaplan, February 10, 2000, NSAKP.

102 Statement of General Thomas A. Schwartz, March 27, 2001, p. 7.

103 *Joseon Ilbo* (Digital Chosunilbo), April 6, 2001; and *Yeonhab Nyuseu*, April 6, 2001. Bermudez has estimated that Scud B and C were priced at $1.5 to $2 million per unit. Bermudez, *A History of Ballistic Missile Development in the DPRK*, p. 19.

104 Bermudez, *A History of Ballistic Missile Development in the DPRK*, p. 31.

105 Ashton B. Carter and William J. Perry, *Preventive Defense: A New Security Strategy for America* (Washington, DC: Brookings Institution Press, 1999), p. 221.

106 "The Rumsfeld Commission Report."

107 Ibid.

108 *New York Times*, March 6, 2001, pp. A1 and A8.

109 Charles Kartman, Special Envoy for the Korean Peace Process and U.S. Representative to KEDO, "United States Policy Toward North Korea," Testimony before House Committee on International Relations, September 24, 1998.

110 U.S. Department of Agriculture, "United States to Provide 400,000 Tons of Food to North Korea," Release No. 0215.99, Washington, DC, May 17, 1999.

111 Mark Minton, Director of the Office of Korean Affairs, "U.S. Policy Toward North Korea," Testimony before the Senate Foreign Relations Committee, Subcommittee on East Asian and Pacific Affairs, Washington, DC, September 12, 1996.

112 The White House, Statement by the President, June 19, 2000.

113 The White House, "Easing Sanctions Against North Korea," September 17, 1999.

114 Korea Trade-Investment Promotion Agency, *Bughan-ui Daewoe Muyeog Donghyang, 1990–2000-nyeon* (Trends of North Korea's Foreign Trade, 1990–2000) (Seoul: Daehan Muyeog Tuja Jinheung Gongsa, 2001), p. 174.

115 *Korea Herald*, September 7, 1998.

116 Cheong Wa Dae (Blue House), "Teugpawon Gandamhoe (Informal Gathering for Correspondents)," Briefing and Press Release, July 6, 1999; *Washington Post*, June 24, 1999; *Korea Times*, July 7, 1999.

117 *Gyeonghyang Sinmun*, April 21, 1996, p. 3, cited in FBIS-EAS-96-078.

118 "Kim Jong Il elected Chairman of DPRK National Defence Commission," *KCNA*, September 5, 1998.

119 "Successful launch of first satellite in DPRK," *KCNA*, September 4, 1998.

120 "Kim Jong Il's election as NDC Chairman proposed," *KCNA*, September 5, 1998.

121 "Kim Jong Il elected Chairman of DPRK National Defence Commission," *KCNA*, September 5, 1998.

122 DoS, "Trilateral Meeting Joint Press Statement," Press Statement, July 27, 1999.

123 Defense Agency, *Defense of Japan 1999*, pp. 83 and 207.

124 "DPRK FM spokesman on U.S. missile interceptor test," *KCNA*, January 22, 2000.

125 "KCNA on U.S. Defense Secretary's remarks," *KCNA*, February 10, 2000.

126 "DPRK–Russia joint declaration released," *KCNA*, July 20, 2000.

Chapter 8

1 "Chronology of North Korea's Attempts to Neutralize the Armistice Agreement," in Ministry of National Defense (MND), Republic of Korea, *Defense White Paper 1996–1997* (Seoul: Korea Institute for Defense Analyses, 1997), p. 261; and Headquarters, United Nations Command (UNC), *Annual Historical Summary, 1 January 1991–31 December 1991*, compiled by the Command Historical Branch, UNC, Unit 15259, APO AP 96205–0032, p. 38.

2 UNC, "Report of the Activities of the United Nations Command for 1995," Annex, obtained from the UNC Military Armistice Commission (UNCMAC), 2001, p. 8; UNC, "Report of the Activities of the United Nations Command for 1999," Annex, obtained from the UNCMAC, 2001, p. 5; and Headquarters, UNC, *Command Historical Summary, 1 January 1992–31 December 1992*, compiled by the Command Historical Branch, UNC, Unit #15259, APO AP 96205–0032, p. 37.

3 UNC, "Report of the Activities of the United Nations Command for 1999," Annex, obtained from the UNCMAC, 2001, p. 6.

4 UNC, *Command Historical Summary 1992*, p. 41.

5 *Pyongyang Times*, October 16, 1993, p. 8.

6 *Pyongyang Times*, May 7, 1994, pp. 1 and 3.

7 Headquarters, UNC, *Command Historical Summary, 1 January 1995–31 December 1995*, compiled by the Command Historical Branch, UNC, Unit #15237, APO AP 96205–0010, p. 27.

8 UNC, *Command Historical Summary, 1 January 1994–31 December 1994*, compiled by the Command Historical Branch, UNC, Unit #15237, APO AP 96205–0010, p. 56; and "Agreement on the Military Armistice Commission Headquarters Area, Its Security and Its Construction," in "Subsequent Agreements," UNCMAC, revised October 1, 1976, Tab "D" (1)-2.

9 "List of the Members to the Korean People's Army Panmunjom Mission Entrusted by the Supreme Command of the Korean People's Army," reprinted in Lee Mun Hang (James M. Lee), *JSA-Panmunjeom, 1953–1994* (Seoul: Sohwa, 2001), pp. 401–2.

10 UNC, *Command Historical Summary 1994*, Appendix G.

11 *Pyongyang Times*, September 10, 1994, p. 8.

12 UNC, "Report of the Activities of the United Nations Command for 1999," p. 4.

13 *JungAng Ilbo*, December 22, 1994, p. 5.

14 *Joseon Ilbo*, December 31, 1994, p. 3.

15 *Rodong Sinmun*, December 31, 1994, p. 4.

16 *JungAng Ilbo*, December 30, 1994, p. 5.

17 UNC, "Report of the Activities of the United Nations Command for 1995," p. 14.

18 U.S. Department of State, "Korea: Neutral Nations Supervisory Commission," Statement, Washington, D.C., February 23, 1995.

19 UNC, *Command Historical Summary 1995*, Appendix G.

20 Ibid.

21 UNC, "Report of the Activities of the United Nations Command for 1995," p. 12.

22 *Segye Ilbo*, April 28, 1995, p. 2.

23 UNC, "Report of the Activities of the United Nations Command for 1995," p. 13.

24 *JungAng Ilbo*, May 22, 1995, p. 1.

25 *Hangug Ilbo*, May 26, 1995, p. 2.

26 *Rodong Sinmun*, June 30, 1995, p. 5.

27 *Rodong Sinmun*, July 6, 1995, p. 6; and UNC, *Command Historical Summary 1995*, p. 36.

28 UNC, "Report of the Activities of the United Nations Command for 1995," p. 15.

29 Ibid., pp. 13–14.

30 UNC, "Report of the Activities of the United Nations Command for 1996," Annex, obtained from the UNCMAC in April 2001, p. 13.

31 *Pyongyang Times*, March 2, 1996, p. 1.

32 *Pyongyang Times*, April 6, 1996, p. 1.

33 UNC, "Report of the Activities of the United Nations Command for 1996," pp. 14–15.

34 Radiopress, *Kitachousen Seisaku Doukou*, no. 246, May 31, 1996, p. 49.

35 UNC, "Report of the Activities of the United Nations Command for 1996," pp. 14–15.

36 *Korea Times*, April 7, 1996; and Kim Young Sam, *Gim Yeong Sam Daetongryeong Hoegorog* (President Kim Young Sam's Memoir), vol. 2 (Seoul: Joseon Ilbosa, 2001), pp. 194–96.

37 *Korea Times*, April 10, 1996; and Gang In Seon, "Inteobyu: Yuengun Saryeongbu Daebyeonin Jim Kolseu (Interview: UNC Spokesman Jim Coles)," *Wolgan Joseon*, June 1996, p. 431.

38 *Washington Post*, April 9, 1996, p. A1; *Korea Times*, April 10, 1996; and Gang, "Inteobyu," pp. 430–35. Also, see *Korea Times*, April 7, 1996.

39 Gang, "Inteobyu," p. 433.

40 *Korea Times*, April 9, 1996.

41 U.S. Department of State, Bureau of Intelligence and Research, "ROK: Kim Hangs On," Brief, April 12, 1996, The National Security Archive Korea Project.

42 *Korea Times*, April 22, 1996.

43 UNC, "Report of the Activities of the United Nations Command for 1996," p. 15; and Joseph S. Bermudez, Jr, *North Korean Special Forces*, 2nd edn (Annapolis, MD: Naval Institute Press, 1998), pp. 160–67. For an account by a captured North Korean agent, see Lee Gwang Su, *Senkoushirei: Shougen Kitachousen Sensuikan Gerira Jiken* (Order to Go Underwater: Testimony on the North Korean Submarine Guerrilla Incident) (Tokyo: Za Masada, 1998).

44 "Statement by a Spokesman for North Korea's Armed Forces Ministry, Demanding the Return of the Submarine and Its Crew, Including the Dead Bodies," Pyongyang, September 23, 1996, reprinted in *Korea and World Affairs*, vol. 20, no. 3 (Fall 1996), p. 516.

45 Headquarters, UNC, *Command Historical Summary, 1 January 1996–31 December 1996*, compiled by the Command History Office, UNC, Unit #15237, APO AP 96205–0010, Appendix G-5.

46 Hahm Sung Deuk, ed., *Gim Yeong Sam Jeongbu-ui Seonggong-gwa Silpae* (The Kim Young Sam Government: Its Successes and Failures) (Seoul: Nanam, 2001), p. 95; and *Washington Post*, November 9, 1996, p. A19.

47 *Sankei Shimbun*, November 24, 1999.

48 After the submarine incident, the U.S. Department of Defense reportedly requested South Korea not to respond independently to local aggression caused by North Korea. *JungAng Ilbo*, April 7, 1997.

49 Kim, *Gim Yeong Sam Daetongryeong Hoegorog*, vol. 2, pp. 255–56.

50 *New York Times*, November 17, 1996, p. 12.

51 Headquarters, UNC, *Command Historical Summary, 1 January 1997–31 December 1997*, compiled by the Command History Office, UNC, Unit #15237, APO AP 96205–0010, Appendix G.

52 A South Korean security expert, interview by author, Seoul, ROK, November 6, 2001; and Aaron Trimble, e-mail message to author, November 11, 2001.

53 *Korea Times*, April 11, 1997.

54 *Joseon Ilbo*, June 6, 1997, pp. 1–2; *Korea Times*, June 6, 1997; and Gwon Yeong Gi, "Seohae 5-do-neun 'Hwayaggo' Hanbando-ui Noegwan (The West Sea Five Islands are 'Powder Keg' and a Detonator)," *Wolgan Joseon*, July 1999, pp. 647–48.

55 UNC, "Report of the Activities of the United Nations Command for 1997," Annex, obtained from the UNCMAC, 2001, p. 15; Bruce Bechtol, Jr., interview by author, Seongnam-si, ROK, February 24, 2008, and *Korea Herald*, July 17, 1997.

56 Stephen Tharp, interview by author, Seoul, ROK, March 14, 2001.

57 *Korea Herald*, September 8, 1997.

58 Aaron Trimble, e-mail message to author, November 11, 2001.

59 *Pyongyang Times*, July 26, 1997, p. 1; and *Rodong Sinmun*, July 19, 1997, p. 6.

60 *Korea Herald*, February 20, 1998.

61 UNC, "Report of the Activities of the United Nations Command for 1998," Annex, obtained from the UNCMAC, 2001, p. 13.

62 UNCMAC, "We own the Zone," a briefing material, obtained from UNCMAC on March 14, 2001, p. 68.

63 "Talks between KPA, International Allied Forces to be held," *KCNA*, June 19, 1998.

64 UNC, "Report of the Activities of the United Nations Command for 1998," p. 18; and UNCMAC, "We own the Zone," p. 72.

65 Description of the naval actions of two Koreas is based on the following materials. MND, *Defense White Paper 1999* (Seoul: Ministry of National Defense, 1999), pp. 246–49; "Bughan Gyeongbijeong NLL Chimbeom Sageon-deung Hyeonan Bogo (Status Report on the Issues such as the Violation of the NLL by north Korean Patrol Boats)," *Gugbang Wiwonhoe Hoewirog* (Proceedings of the National Defense Committee), no. 1, 204th National Assembly, ROK, June 10, 1999; "Seohaesang Gyojeonsatae-e Gwanhan Bogo (Report on the Battle in the West Sea)," *Gughoe Bonhoeui Hoewirog* (Proceedings of the Plenary Session), no. 2, 204th National Assembly, ROK, June 16, 1999; "Seohaesang Gyojeonsatae Gwanryeon Hyeonan Bogo (Report on the Battle in the West Sea)," *Gugbang Wiwonhoe Hoewirog* (Proceedings of the National Defense Committee), no. 2, 204th National Assembly, ROK, June 17, 1999; "Bughan-ui Bugbang Hangyeseon Muhyoseoneon-e Daehan

Daechaeg-deung Hyeonan Bogo (Report on the Countermeasures to the North Korea's Declaration of Invalidation of the NLL)," *Gugbang Wiwonhoe Hoewirog* (Proceedings of the National Defense Committee), no. 1, 207th National Assembly, ROK, September 7, 1999; MND, "Seohae Gyojeon-gwanryeon Uri-ui Ibjang (Our Position on the Battle in the West Sea)," *Gugbang Sosig*, no. 107, September 1999; ROK Navy, "Yeonpyeong Haejeon (Battle of Yeonpyeong)," news video, http://www.navy.mil.kr/bbs/movie/movie_read.jsp?szCtgrID=10&szSeq=5&szSrchType=0&szKwd=&pg=16&pgrp=2; Kim Byeong Seog, "Eonron-i Milgo Gun-i Abjangseon NLL Sasujagjeon (An Operation to Defend the NLL without any Conditions: The Media Backed It and the Military Led It)," *Wolgan Joseon*, July 1999; UNC, "Report of the Activities of the United Nations Command for 1999," p. 12; Lee Jung Hoon, "Haegun 2-hamdae Yeonpyeong Haejeon-ui Juyeog Pilseunghaegun-ui Seonbong (Navy Second Fleet: The Main Actor of the Battle of Yeonpyeong and the Vanguard of the Navy of Certain Victory)," *Sindong-a*, February 2002; and Yun Gyeong Won, "'Yeonpyeong Haejeon' dangsi Saryeonggwan 'Chong Majeul Sigan Gidaryeossda (The Commander at the Time of the Battle of Yeonpyeong, "I was Waiting to be Shot)," An Interview with Park Jung Sung, *Deillian*, June 19, 2006.

66 "S. Korean warships intrude into north," *KCNA*, June 6, 1999.
67 "Bughan Gyeongbijeong NLL Chimbeom Sageon-deung Hyeonan Bogo."
68 "Hwaggohan Anbotaeseman-i Bug Dobal Jeoji (Only the Strong Security Posture Can Stop North's Provocations)," Address by Kim Dae Jung, *Gugbang Ilbo*, March 15, 2000.
69 A retired South Korean defense official, interview by author, Seoul, ROK, December 18, 2007.
70 A retired South Korean defense official, interview by author, Seoul, ROK, May 5, 2006.
71 The data obtained from the MND, February 29, 2008.
72 A retired South Korean defense official, interview by author, Seoul, ROK, May 5, 2006.
73 MND, *Defense White Paper 1996–1997*, p. 132.
74 A U.S. government official, interview by author, February 19, 2009.
75 "S. Korean warships fire at KPA navy warships," *KCNA*, June 15, 1999.
76 Proceedings of the Seventh General Officers Talks, June 22, 1999, provided by the UNCMAC.
77 Proceedings of the Eighth General Officers Talks, July 2, 1999, provided by the UNCMAC; and UNC, "Report of the Activities of the United Nations Command for 1999."
78 Ibid.
79 Proceedings of the Ninth General Officers Talks, July 21, 1999, provided by the UNCMAC; PAO, UNC/USFK/CFC/EUSA, "Ninth General Officer Talks Held," News Release, no. 990708, Seoul (UNC), July 21, 1999; UNC, "Report of the Activities of the United Nations Command for 1999," p. 9; "KPA urges U.S. and S. Korea to accept maritime demarcation line at West Sea," *KCNA*, July 21, 1999; and *Rodong Sinmun*, July 22, 1999, p. 5.
80 "KPA urges U.S. and S. Korea to accept maritime demarcation line at West Sea," *KCNA*, July 21, 1999.
81 Proceedings of the Eleventh General Officers Talks, September 1, 1999, provided by the UNCMAC; "KPA will take decisive step for defence of sovereignty," *KCNA*, September 1, 1999; and *Rodong Sinmun*, September 2, 1999, p. 5.
82 "Special communiqué of KPA general staff," *KCNA*, September 2, 1999.
83 *Korea Herald*, September 3, 1999.
84 Stephen Tharp, interview by author, Seoul, ROK, March 14, 2001.

85 Description of this section is based on the following documents. MND, "Bughan Seonbag-ui Yeonghae Chimbeom-gwa Urigun-ui Daeeung (Violation of the Territorial Waters by North Korean Ships and Our Armed Forces' Response)," June 9, 2001, in *Gugbang Ilbo*, June 10, 2001; and Ministry of Unification, Ministry of National Defense, and Government Information Agency, *Bughan Seonbag-ui Yeonghae Chimbeom, Ireohge Daecheohaesseumnida* (We Dealt with the Violations of [Our] Territorial Seas by North Korean Vessels This Way) (Seoul: Tongilbu, Gugbangbu, and Gugjeong Hongbocheo, June 2001).

86 "Bughan Seonbag-ui Yeonghae Chimbeom-gwa Urigun-ui Daeeung."

87 Description of this incident is based on the following documents. MND, "The Naval Clash on the Yellow Sea on 29 June 2002 between South and North Korea: The Situation and ROK's Position," July 1, 2002, http://www.globalsecurity.org/wmd/library/news/rok/2002/0020704-naval.htm; Bruce E. Bechtol, Jr., *Red Rogue: The Persistent Challenge of North Korea* (Virginia: Potomac Books, 2007), chapter 5; and *Hangug Ilbo*, July 5, 2002.

88 The title of the "Commander-in-Chief, United Nations Command" was changed to "Commander, United Nations Command" in 2002.

89 "Working contact for ministerial talks proposed to south side," *KCNA*, July 25, 2002.

90 The North Koreans continued to use this issue to demean South Korea even after the armistice/peacetime operational control was transferred. See *Pyongyang Times*, September 17, 1994, p. 8; and *Pyongyang Times*, March 4, 1995, p. 8.

91 "Chronology of North Korea's Attempts to Neutralize the Armistice Agreement," p. 261.

92 UNC, *Annual Historical Summary, 1 January 1991*, pp. 51 and 54.

93 Comments by Gwag Yeong Dal, former superintendent of the Air Force Academy, ROK Air Force, *Wolgan Joseon*, July 1999, p. 692.

94 Glenn Rice, e-mail message to author, February 5, 2004.

95 For the South Korean official position on the status of the NLL, see MND, *Defense White Paper 1999*, pp. 81–82; Arms Control Bureau, MND, "The Unjustness of North Korea's Claim on the West Sea Sea Demarcation Line and the Position of the Republic of Korea," September 1999; Arms Control Bureau, MND, ed., *The Republic of Korea Position regarding the Northern Limit Line* (Seoul: Ministry of National Defense, 2002); and MND, *Bugbang Hangyeseon (NLL)-e Gwanhan Uri-ui Ibjang* (Our Position regarding the Northern Limit Line) (Seoul: Gugbangbu, 2007).

96 A concise summary of the ROK position can be found in MND, *Gugbang Baegseo 1999* (Defense White Paper 1999) (Seoul: Gugbangbu, 1999), p. 66. The English version of the same summary is poorly translated. MND, *Defense White Paper 1999*, pp. 81–82.

97 "United Nations Convention on the Law of the Sea," adopted on December 10, 1982. The Convention came into force on November 16, 1994.

98 "Agreement on Reconciliation, Nonaggression, and Exchanges and Cooperation between South and North Korea," came into force on February 19, 1992; and "Protocol on the Implementation and Observance of Chapter II, Nonaggression, of the Agreement on Reconciliation, Nonaggression, and Exchanges and Cooperation between South and North Korea," came into force on September 17, 1992.

99 Lee Jang-Hie, interview by author, Seoul, ROK, June 27, 2001.

100 Ministry of Unification, "Seohae Haesang Gyeonggyeseon Munje (Question of the sea demarcation line in the West Sea)," June 14, 1999; and "Bughan Gyeongbijeong NLL Chimbeom Sageon-deung Hyeonan Bogo."

101 "Bughan Gyeongbijeong NLL Chimbeom Sageon-deung Hyeonan Bogo."

102 MND, "The Unjustness of North Korea's Claim on the West Sea Sea Demarcation Line and the Position of the Republic of Korea."

103 U.S. Department of State, Daily Press Briefing, June 16, 1999.

104 U.S. Department of State, Daily Press Briefing, June 17, 1999.

105 Ibid.

106 Stephen Tharp, interview by author, Seoul, ROK, March 14, 2001.

107 Lee Jang-Hie, "Bugbang Hangyeseon-ui Gugjebeobjeog Bunseog-gwa Jaehaeseog (Analysis and Reinterpretation of the NLL from the Perspective of International Law)," *Tongil Gyeongje*, no. 56 (August 1999), pp. 116–17, and 119.

108 "*Minju Joson* comments on armed conflict," *KCNA*, June 29, 1999.

109 Article 121-(2) of the United Nations Convention on the Law of the Sea.

110 MND, *Bugbang Hangyeseon (NLL)-e Gwanhan Uri-ui Ibjang*, p. 56.

111 "Seohaesang Gyojeonsatae Gwanryeon Hyeonan Bogo."

112 Lee, "Haegun 2-hamdae Yeonpyeong Haejeon-ui Juyeog Pilseunghaegun-ui Seon-bong."

113 Gwon, "Seohae 5-do-neun 'Hwayaggo' Hanbando-ui Noegwan," p. 649; Kim Yong Sam, "Hangug Haegun-ui Jeolchibusim: 56-ham Chimmol hu 32-nyeon man-e Bughan-e Bogsuhanda (Struggle of the ROK Navy: Revenge against North Korea 32 Years After the Sinking of the ROK Navy Ship No. 56)," *Wolgan Joseon*, July 1999, p. 667; and Osamu Eya, *Kin Shounich Daizukan* (An Illustrated Book on Kim Jong Il) (Tokyo: Shougakkan, 2000), pp. 72–73.

114 "Seohaesang Gyojeonsatae Gwanryeon Hyeonan Bogo."

115 Ibid.; An Seung Beom, ed., *2000 Hanguggun Jangbi Yeongam* (ROK Armed Forces Equipment Annual 2000) (Seoul: Gunsa Jeongbo, 1999), p. 121; and "Haegun Jeonsul Jihwitongje Chegye (The Korean Naval Tactical Data System)," http://www.roknavy.com/yptotal.htm; and a U.S defense official, interview by author, Seoul, ROK, April 18, 2001.

116 A U.S. defense official, interview by author, Seoul, ROK, March 25, 2008; Choi Zoo Hwal, interview by author, Seoul, ROK, November 9, 2001; and Ko Yeong Hwan, "Bughan Woegyo Jeongchaeg Gyeoljeonggigu mich Gwajeong-e Gwanhan Yeongu: Bughan-ui Dae-Jungdong/Apeurika Woegyo-reul Jungsim-euro (A Study on North Korea's Foreign Policy Decision-Making Organizations and Processes: Focusing on North Korea's Foreign Policy towards Middle East and Africa)," Master's Thesis, Kyunghee University, August 2000, p. 34.

117 Lee Jong-Seok, "Hanbando Pyeonghwacheje Guchug Nonui, Jaengjeom-gwa Daean Mosaeg (Debate on Establishing the Peace Regime on the Korean Peninsula: Issues and the Search for Alternatives)," *Sejong Jeongchaeg Yeongu* (Sejong Policy Research), vol. 4, no. 1 (2008), p. 20.

118 A U.S. defense official, interview by author, Seoul, ROK, April 18, 2001.

119 Oberdorfer, *The Two Koreas*, p. 392.

120 *Korea Times*, April 9, 1996.

121 Lee Sang Myeon, "Seohae Gyojeon-i Namgin Beobjeogmunje (Legal Issues that the West Sea Battle Left)," *Joseon Ilbo*, June 21, 1999, p. 6.

122 Jo Seong Sig, "Haegun Janggyo Chulsin Jo Seong Sig Gija-ui NLL Daehaebu (Detailed Anatomy of the NLL by Reporter Jo Scong Sig, a Former Naval Officer)," *Sindong-a*, January 2008.

123 Lee Jong-Seok, interview by author, Sejong Institute, ROK, January 28, 2008.

124 Ministry of Unification, "Je 4-cha Nambug Jangseonggeub Gunsahoedam (Fourth Inter-Korean General-level Military Talks)," Panmunjom, May 16–18, 2006, http://dialogue.unikorea.go.kr/sub2/sub2_2.asp?CL=111&SN=4&MSN=1.

125 *JungAng Ilbo*, May 18, 2006.

126 Ministry of Unification, "Bughan-ui Seohaean Kkochgejabi Siltae (Status of North Korea's Blue Crab Fishing)," June 25, 1999.
127 "Bughan Gyeongbijeong NLL Chimbeom Sageon-deung Hyeonan Bogo."
128 Ibid.
129 Ministry of Unification, "Official Signature and Exchange of the Inter-Korean Maritime Agreement and Subsequent Agreement (June 5, 2004)," Press Release, June 14, 2004.
130 Ministry of Unification, "Je 5-cha Nambug Haeun Hyeobryeog Silmujeobchog Gongdong Bodomun (Joint Press Release on the Fifth Working-Level Contact on South-North Maritime Cooperation)," August 10, 2005, http://dialogue.unikorea.go.kr/sub2/sub2_2.asp?CL=099&SN=5&MSN=1.
131 "Declaration on the Advancement of South–North Korean Relations, Peace and Prosperity," signed by Roh Moo-hyun and Kim Jong Il, Pyongyang, October 4, 2007.
132 Lee Jong-Seok, interview by author, Sejong Institute, ROK, January 28, 2008.
133 A South Korean government official, interview by author, Seoul, ROK, March 21, 2008.
134 *Kitachousen Seisaku Doukou*, no. 246 (May 1996), p. 69.
135 *Rodong Sinmun*, June 16, 1999; and "WPK's policy of giving priority to army is invincible," *KCNA*, June 16, 1999.
136 *Korea Times*, June 30, 2002; and *Korea Times*, July 1, 2002.
137 MND, *Defense White Paper 1999*, pp. 80–81.
138 A South Korean security expert, interview by author, Seoul, ROK, April 25, 2001.
139 MND, *Defense White Paper 1999*, pp. 80–81.
140 "31st Republic of Korea-United States Security Consultative Meeting Joint Communiqué," Washington, DC, November 23, 1999.
141 MND, *Defense White Paper 1999*, p. 70.
142 "Ex-US Envoy Interviewed by ROK News Agency," *Yonhap* (English), January 12, 2000, in FBIS-EAS-2000-0111.
143 *Gunji Kenkyuu*, April 2000, p. 134.
144 A South Korean security expert, interview by author, Seoul, ROK, April 25, 2001.
145 *Seoul Sinmun*, July 21, 2004; and *Korea Herald*, July 3, 2002.

Chapter 9

1 Yoichi Funabashi, *The Peninsula Question: A Chronicle of the Second Nuclear Crisis* (Washington, DC: Brookings Institution Press, 2007), p. 94.
2 Ibid., p. 95.
3 Department of State (DoS), "North Korean Nuclear Program," Press Statement, October 16, 2002.
4 "Conclusion of non-aggression treaty between DPRK and U.S. called for," *KCNA*, October 25, 2002.
5 "KEDO Executive Board Meeting Concludes," *KEDO News*, November 14, 2002.
6 *Washington Post*, December 11, 2002, p. A1.
7 "Operation and building of nuclear facilities to be resumed immediately," *KCNA*, December 12, 2002.
8 *New York Times*, January 31, 2003, p. A1.
9 "U.S. anti-DPRK international pressure campaign assailed," *KCNA*, February 5, 2003.
10 *Reuters*, February 27, 2003.
11 "Spokesman for Panmunjom mission of KPA issues statement," *KCNA*, February 18, 2003.

12 *New York Times*, March 4, 2003, p. A1.

13 *New York Times*, March 8, 2003, p. A1.

14 "Statement of fm [foreign ministry] spokesman blasts UNSC's discussion of Korean nuclear issue," *KCNA*, April 6, 2003.

15 "KCNA on DPRK's nuclear deterrent force," *KCNA*, June 9, 2003.

16 *New York Times*, July 17, 2003, p. A6.

17 Bruce B. Auster, Kevin Whitelaw, and Thomas Omestad, "Upping the Ante for Kim Jong Il: Pentagon Plan 5030, a new blueprint for facing down North Korea," *U.S. News & World Report*, July 21, 2003, p. 21.

18 Press Availability by James A. Kelly, Assistant Secretary of State for East Asian and Pacific Affairs, January 13, 2003, Ministry of Foreign Affairs [*sic*], Seoul, Korea.

19 "President Bush Discusses Iraq," Remarks by President Bush and Polish President Kwasniewski in Photo Opportunity, The Oval Office, January 14, 2003.

20 "Spokesman for DPRK Foreign Ministry on expected DPRK-U.S. talks," *KCNA*, April 18, 2003.

21 Charles L. Pritchard, *Failed Diplomacy: The Tragic Story of How North Korea Got the Bomb* (Washington, D.C.: Brookings Institution Press, 2007), p. 65; and *Washington Post*, April 25, 2003, p. A1.

22 "Joint Statement between the United States of America and the Republic of Korea," The White House, Office of the Press Secretary May 14, 2003.

23 "Keynote Speeches Made at Six-way Talks," *KCNA*, August 29, 2003.

24 Japan Ministry of Foreign Affairs, "Six-Party Talks on North Korean Issues (Overview and Evaluation)," September 2003.

25 "DPRK to Continue Increasing Its Nuclear Deterrent Force," *KCNA*, October 2, 2003.

26 KEDO, "KEDO Executive Board Meeting," November 21, 2003.

27 "Background Briefing by a Senior Administration Official on the President's Meeting with the President of China," Bangkok, Thailand, Office of the Press Secretary, The White House, October 19, 2003.

28 "Spokesman of DPRK Foreign Ministry on Issue of Resumption of Six-Way Talks," *KCNA*, December 9, 2003.

29 *Knight Ridder Newspapers*, December 20, 2003.

30 Hecker thought the sample to be plutonium metal. Siegfried S. Hecker, Senior Fellow, Los Alamos National Laboratory, Senate Committee on Foreign Relations Hearing on "Visit to the Yongbyon Nuclear Scientific Research Center in North Korea," University of California, January 21, 2004, p. 11.

31 For CVID, see James A. Kelly, "North Korea: Towards a New International Engagement Framework," Remarks to The Research Conference, Washington, DC, February 13, 2004.

32 "Chairman's Statement for The Second Round of Six-Party Talks," Beijing, February 28, 2004; and DoS, "North Korea – Kelly Remarks," Question Taken at the May 3, 2004 Press Briefing, May 3, 2004.

33 Glenn Kessler, *The Confidante: Condoleezza Rice and the Creation of the Bush Legacy* (New York: St. Martin's Press, 2007), p. 70; and James A. Kelly, "Dealing With North Korea's Nuclear Programs," Prepared Statement, Senate Foreign Relations Committee, July 15, 2004.

34 "DPRK Foreign Ministry Spokesman on Six-Party Talks," *KCNA*, June 28, 2004.

35 Ibid.; and Funabashi, *The Peninsula Question*, p. 359.

36 "Chairman's Statement of Third Round of Six-Party Talks," Beijing, June 26, 2004.

37 *Yomiuri Shimbun*, June 26, 2004.

38 *Korea Times*, November 1, 2004.

39 KEDO, "KEDO Extends Suspension of LWR Project," November 26, 2004.

40 "DPRK Remains Unchanged in Its Stand to Seek Negotiated Solution to Nuclear Issue," *KCNA*, December 4, 2004.
41 Opening Remarks by Secretary of State-Designate Dr. Condoleezza Rice, Senate Foreign Relations Committee, Washington, D.C., January 18, 2005.
42 "President Bush Sworn-In to Second Term," Inaugural Address, Washington, DC, January 20, 2005.
43 "DPRK FM on Its Stand to Suspend Its Participation in Six-party Talks for Indefinite Period," *KCNA*, February 10, 2005.
44 Kessler, *The Confidante*, p. 74.
45 *New York Times*, April 18, 2005, p. A4.
46 "Chief of KPA General Staff on DPRK's Intention to Bolster Its Nuclear Deterrent," *KCNA*, April 8, 2005.
47 "Spokesman for DPRK Foreign Ministry Assails Rice's Reckless Remarks," *KCNA*, April 25, 2005.
48 Press Conference of the President, Office of the Press Secretary, The White House, April 28, 2005.
49 Joseph S. Bermudez, Jr., "Proliferation in Pyongyang," *Jane's Defence Weekly*, May 25, 2005, p. 21; *Kyodo Tsuushin*, May 2, 2005; and *Mainichi Shimbun*, May 5, 2005.
50 *New York Times*, May 6, 2005, p. A1.
51 "Spent Fuel Rods Unloaded from Pilot Nuclear Plant," *KCNA*, May 11, 2005.
52 *New York Times*, May 30, 2005, p. A7; and *Asahi Shimbun*, June 8, 2005, p. 8.
53 "U.S. Assertion about DPRK's Call for DPRK–U.S. Talks Independent of Six-Way Talks Dismissed," *KCNA*, May 8, 2005.
54 A former U.S. government official, interview by author, September 11, 2007; and Philip Zelikow, "The Plan That Moved Pyongyang," *Washington Post*, February 20, 2007, p. A13.
55 Kessler, *The Confidante*, p. 75.
56 Interview on CNN With John King, Secretary Condoleezza Rice, Embassy Moscow, Moscow, Russia, May 9, 2005.
57 Ministry of Unification, "Results and Significance of Presidential Special Envoy Chung Dong-young's visit to North Korea," June 19, 2005; and *Financial Times*, June 21, 2005, p. 2.
58 *Nihon Keizai Shimbun*, evening edition, June 30, 2005.
59 Kessler, *The Confidante*, pp. 76–77.
60 *Financial Times*, July 28, 2005, p. 10.
61 Siegfried S. Hecker, "Technical summary of DPRK nuclear program," Center for International Security and Cooperation, Stanford University, 2005 Carnegie International Non-Proliferation Conference, Washington, DC, November 8, 2005, pp. 5 and 7.
62 "Joint Statement of the Fourth Round of the Six-Party Talks," Beijing, September 19, 2005.
63 Pritchard, *Failed Diplomacy*, p. 122.
64 Assistant Secretary of State Christopher R. Hill's Statement at the Closing Plenary of the Fourth Round of the Six-Party Talks, Beijing, September 19, 2005.
65 "Spokesman for DPRK Foreign Ministry on Six-Party Talks," *KCNA*, September 20, 2005.
66 U.S. Department of the Treasury, "Treasury Designates Banco Delta Asia as Primary Money Laundering Concern under USA PATRIOT Act," JS-2720, September 15, 2005.
67 A former U.S. government official, interview by author, September 11, 2007; and Robert G. Joseph, Under Secretary for Arms Control and International Security, "U.S. Strategy to Combat the Proliferation of Weapons of Mass Destruction,"

Written Statement to the Senate Armed Services Committee Subcommittee on Emerging Threats and Capabilities, Washington, DC, March 29, 2006.

68 *Washington Times*, October 12, 2005, p. A03.

69 U.S. Department of the Treasury, "Treasury Targets North Korean Entities for Supporting WMD Proliferation," Press Release, JS-2984, October 21, 2005.

70 *New York Times*, October 24, 2005, p. A7.

71 "Kim Kye Gwan Interviewed in Beijing," *KCNA*, November 12, 2005; *OhmyNews*, November 14, 2005; and Radiopress, *Kitachousen Seisaku Doukou*, no. 380, December 25, 2005, p. 2.

72 Jane Morse, "U.S. Intensifies Efforts To Promote Human Rights in North Korea: Search continues for 'durable solutions' for North Korean refugees," *USINFO* http://usinfo.state.gov/eap/Archive/2006/Apr/06–41288.html.

73 "Situation of human rights in the Democratic People's Republic of Korea," United Nations General Assembly, A/RES/60/173, December 16, 2005, GA/10437.

74 "FM Spokesman Blasts Virulent Outcries of U.S. Ambassador to S. Korea," *KCNA*, December 10, 2005.

75 "DPRK Foreign Ministry Spokesman Urges U.S. to Make Policy Switchover," *KCNA*, February 9, 2006.

76 *Washington Post*, March 9, 2006, p. A16.

77 *Yomiuri Shimbun*, March 9, 2006.

78 U.S. Department of the Treasury, "Swiss Company, Individual Designated by Treasury for Supporting North Korean WMD Proliferation," JS-4144, March 30, 2006.

79 *Daily Telegraph*, May 20, 2006, p. 12.

80 "DPRK Foreign Ministry; DPRK's Stand on Six-Party Talks Reclarified," *KCNA*, June 1, 2006.

81 Adam Ward, ed., "North Korea's 5 July Missile Tests," *Strategic Comments*, vol. 12, issue 6 (London: Taylor & Francis Ltd., July 2006); and "Dokusen! Kita-misairu Chakudan 'Zen Deta' (Scoop! The North's Missile Impacts 'Perfect Data')," *Yomiuri Weekly*, vol. 65, no. 34 (August 6, 2006), pp. 22–23.

82 Summary Press Meeting with Minister Nukaga, Japan Defense Agency, September 15, 2006.

83 "DPRK Foreign Ministry Spokesman on Its Missile Launches," *KCNA*, July 6, 2006.

84 United Nations Security Council, Resolution 1695, S/RES/1695 (2006), July 15, 2006.

85 "DPRK Foreign Ministry Refutes 'Resolution of UN Security Council,'" *KCNA*, July 16, 2006.

86 Tom Casey, Deputy Spokesman, Daily Press Briefing, DoS, Washington, DC, July 26, 2006.

87 *Los Angeles Times*, August 18, 2006, p. A10.

88 Christopher Hill, On-the-Record Briefing – 61st UN General Assembly, New York, September 21, 2006.

89 "DPRK Foreign Ministry Clarifies Stand on New Measure to Bolster War Deterrent," *KCNA*, October 3, 2006.

90 "DPRK Foreign Ministry Spokesman on U.S. Moves Concerning Its Nuclear Test," *KCNA*, October 11, 2006.

91 United Nations Security Council, Resolution 1718 (2006), S/RES/1718, October 14, 2006.

92 For how the U.S. policy shift occurred, see Philip Zelikow, "The Plan That Moved Pyongyang," p. A13; Robert B. Zoellick, "Long Division," *Wall Street Journal*, February 26, 2007; and Pritchard, *Failed Diplomacy*, p. 157.

93 Mike Chinoy, *Meltdown: The Inside Story of the North Korean Nuclear Crisis* (New York: St. Martin's Press, 2008), pp. 306–7; and *Joseon Ilbo*, December 13, 2006.

94 "Spokesman for DPRK Foreign Ministry on Resumption of Six-Party Talks," *KCNA*, November 1, 2006.

95 Chinoy, *Meltdown*, pp. 310–11; and *Korea Times*, December 11, 2006.

96 Chinoy, *Meltdown*, p. 315; and Pritchard, *Failed Diplomacy*, p. 157.

97 Chinoy, *Meltdown*, p. 316.

98 Ibid., p. 320; and *Yomiuri Shimbun*, February 8, 2007.

99 "Initial Actions for the Implementation of the Joint Statement," Beijing, China, February 13, 2007.

100 Chinoy, *Meltdown*, p. 326.

101 U.S. Department of the Treasury, "Statement by DAS Glaser on the Disposition of DPRK-Related Funds Frozen at Banco Delta Asia," HP-322, March 19, 2007.

102 "IAEA Working-level Delegation Invited to Visit DPRK," *KCNA*, June 16, 2007.

103 IAEA, "IAEA Team Confirms Shutdown of DPRK Nuclear Facilities," IAEA Press Release 2007/12, July 18, 2007.

104 DoS, "North Korea – Shutdown of Yongbyon Facilities," Press Statement, July 14, 2007. Also, see "CISAC's Lewis and Hecker visit North Korea, confirm shutdown of nuclear facilities," CISAC Press Release, August 13, 2007.

105 "Second-Phase Actions for the Implementation of the Joint Statement," October 3, 2007; and *Washington Post*, October 4, 2007, p. A17.

106 Christopher R. Hill, "Status of the Six-Party Talks for the Denuclearization of the Korean Peninsula," Statement Before the Senate Foreign Relations Committee, Washington, D.C., February 6, 2008; and DoS, "North Korea: Presidential Action on State Sponsor of Terrorism (SST) and the Trading with the Enemy Act (TWEA)," Fact Sheet, June 26, 2008.

107 "Press Communiqué of the Heads of Delegation Meeting of the Sixth Round of the Six-Party Talks," Beijing, July 12, 2008.

108 "Foreign Ministry's Spokesman on DPRK's Decision to Suspend Activities to Disable Nuclear Facilities," *KCNA*, August 26, 2008.

109 "IAEA Removes Seals from Plant in Yongbyon," IAEA Press Release, September 24, 2008.

110 *Joseon Ilbo*, September 16, 2008; *New York Times on the Web*, October 9, 2008; and *Washington Post*, October 12, 2008, p. A01.

111 "IAEA Inspectors No Longer Permitted Access to Yongbyon," IAEA Press Release, October 9, 2008.

112 DoS, "U.S.–North Korea Understandings on Verification," Fact Sheet, October 11, 2008.

113 DoS, "U.S.–DPRK Agreement on Denuclearization Verification Measures," Press Statement, October 11, 2008.

114 *Washington Post*, October 12, 2008, p. A01.

115 "DPRK Grants IAEA Access to Yongbyon Facilities," IAEA Press Release, October 13, 2008.

116 *Washington Post*, December 12, 2008, p. A22.

117 "KCNA Dismisses Misinformation about Verification Issue," *KCNA*, November 24, 2008.

118 Funabashi, *The Peninsula Question*, p. 156.

119 Under Secretary of State John R. Bolton NHK-TV Interview (2 parts), U.S. Embassy Tokyo, Japan, January 24, 2003.

120 Funabashi, *The Peninsula Question*, pp. 305–10.

121 Ibid., p. 157.

122 Ibid., especially pp. 138, and 144–47.

123 *Washington Post*, October 5, 2004, p. A1; and Funabashi, *The Peninsula Question*, pp. 148, and 150–51.

NOTES

124 *New York Times*, March 21, 2007, p. A1.
125 Ministry of Unification, *Tongil Baegseo 2008* (Unification White Paper 2008) (Seoul: Tongilbu, 2008), p. 314.
126 Ministry of Unification, "Yeondo-byeol Daebug Jiwon Chui (Changes in Assistance to North Korea by Fiscal Year)," http://www.unikorea.go.kr/kr/CMSF/CMSFBsub.jsp?topmenu=2&menu=3&sub=3&subtab=-1&act=&main_uid=&fullurl=%2Fkr%2FPLDT%2FPLDTIdata33&brd_cd=&page_n=(accessed on December 20, 2007).
127 Ministry of Unification, *Tongil Baegseo 2008*, pp. 121–62.
128 "Address at a Luncheon Hosted by the Los Angeles World Affairs Council," Cheong Wa Dae, Office of the President, Republic of Korea, November 12, 2004.
129 Funabashi, *The Peninsula Question*, p. 156.
130 "Rating Action: Moody's Changes South Korea's Rating Outlook to Negative," Moody's Investers Service, Hong Kong, February 11, 2003.
131 Jeong Hyeong-Gon, "Bug-Jung Gyeongje Hyeobryeog Ganghwa-ui Pageub Yeonghyang (Consequences of the Upgraded North Korea–China Economic Cooperation)," *KIEP Segye Gyeongje*, February 2006, p. 27.
132 Dick K. Nanto and Emma Chanlett-Avery, *The North Korean Economy: Overview and Policy Analysis*, CRS Report for Congress, April 18, 2007, p. 32; Lee Young Hun, "Bug-Jung Muyeog-ui Hyeonhwang-gwa Bughan Gyeongje-e Michineun Yeonghyang (Current Status of North Korea–China Trade and its Impact on North Korean Economy)," Institute for Monetary and Economic Research, February 13, 2006; Ministry of Unification, *Peace and Prosperity: White Paper on Korean Unification 2005* (Seoul: Tongilbul, 2005), p. 54; and Ministry of Unification, "Trade Volume between North Korea and Japan," March 2, 2006.
133 *Washington Post*, May 7, 2005, p. A11.
134 Pritchard, *Failed Diplomacy*, p. 91.
135 The Bank of Korea, "Gross Domestic Product of North Korea in 2004," May 31, 2005. The Bank of Korea assessed that the North Korean economy had grown steadily as energy supply improved somewhat and efforts were made to increase production capacity since the implementation of the Economic Management Improvement Measures in July 2002. See also Education Center for Unification, *Bughan Gyeongje, Eodikkaji wassna?* (What is the status of North Korean economy?) (Seoul: Tongil Gyoyugwon, 2005), p. 212.
136 Rural Development Administration, "2005 Bughan-ui Gogmul Saengsanryang Chujeong Balpyo (Assessment of North Korean Grain Production in 2005 Announced)," November 29, 2005; and The Bank of Korea, "2006-nyeon Bughan Gyeongje Seongjangryul Chujeong Gyeolgwa (Results of the Estimate of the North Korean Economic Growth Rate in 2006)," Press Release, August 17, 2007.
137 For details of the nuclear test, see Siegfried S. Hecker, "Report on North Korean Nuclear Program," Center for International Security and Cooperation, Stanford University, November 15, 2006, pp. 4–6.
138 Chinese nuclear specialists concluded, "If the DPRK aimed for 4 kilotons and got 1 kiloton, that is not bad for a first test. We call it successful, but not perfect." Hecker, "Report on North Korean Nuclear Program," p. 3.
139 David Albright and Paul Brannan, "The North Korean Plutonium Stock, February 2007," Institute for Science and International Security, February 20, 2007. Also, see Hecker, "Report on North Korean Nuclear Program," p. 4.
140 *Asahi Shimbun*, July 11, 2008, p. 1.
141 Hecker, "Report on North Korean Nuclear Program," pp. 4 and 7.
142 Funabashi, *The Peninsula Question*, pp. 119–20.

245

143 CIA estimate provided to Congress, November 19, 2002, http://www.fas.org/nuke/ guide/dprk/nuke/cia111902.html. Later this document became controversial, and the intelligence community had to reconfirm its position regarding the estimate in 2007. Statement by Joseph DeTrani, North Korea Mission Manager, Office of the Director of National Intelligence news release, March 4, 2007.

144 For the details of the program, see Mitchell B. Reiss, Robert Gallucci, et al., "Red-Handed," *Foreign Affairs*, March/April 2005; and The International Institute for Strategic Studies, *Nuclear Black Markets: Pakistan, A.Q. Khan and the Rise of Proliferation Networks – A Net Assessment*, IISS strategic dossier (London: The International Institute for Strategic Studies, 2007).

145 Don Oberdorfer, interview by author, Washington, DC, August 15, 2007; and Charles Pritchard, interview by author, Washington, DC, September 4, 2007.

146 Funabashi, *The Peninsula Question*, p. 156.

147 *Asahi Shimbun*, April 25, 2003, p. 2.

148 *Joseon Ilbo*, April 28, 2007.

149 "Missile Defense Program Overview for the Washington Roundtable on Science and Public Policy," presentation prepared by BG Patrick O'Reilly, U.S. Army, Deputy Director, Missile Defense Agency, January 29, 2007, p. 4, http://www.marshall.org/ pdf/materials/495.pdf.

150 For a detailed technical analysis of the Taepo Dong 2, see Charles P. Vick, "Taep'o-dong 2 (TD-2), NKSL-X-2," March 20, 2007, http://www.globalsecurity.org/wmd/ world/dprk/td-2.htm.

151 Joseph S. Bermudez, Jr, "Moving Missiles," *Jane's Defence Weekly*, August 3, 2005, p. 23.

152 Ministry of Defense, *Defense of Japan 2007* (Tokyo: Inter Group, 2007), pp. 38–39.

153 Funabashi, *The Peninsula Question*, p. 157.

154 Don Oberdorfer, interview by author, Washington, DC, August 15, 2007; Charles Pritchard, interview by author, Washington, DC, September 4, 2007; and James Foster, interview by author, Tokyo, Japan, November 22, 2007.

155 Hwang Il-do, "Bug Jangsajeongpo: Alryeojiji anhneun Daseos gaji Jinsil (North Korea's Long-Range Artillery: Five Unknown Facts)," *Sindong-a*, December 2004, http://www.donga.com/docs/magazine/shin/2004/11/23/200411230500004/20041123 0500004_1.html; and Yu Yong Won, "Sudogwon-eul Sajeonggeori An-e Neohgo Issneun Bughan-ui Dayeonjang Rokes Mich Jajupo Yeongu (Study on North Korean Multiple Rocket Launchers and Self-Propelled Artillery that Put Seoul Metropolitan Area within their Range)," *Wolgan Joseon*, March 2001.

156 *Asahi Shimbun*, June 8, 2005.

157 This might have been related to the Bush Administration's desire to accelerate the development of missile defense programs. Robert Carlin, e-mail message to author, February 24, 2008.

158 Hyun Seong Il, *Bughan-ui Guggajeonryag-gwa Pawo-elriteu: Ganbu Jeongchaeg-eul Jungsim-euro* (North Korea's National Strategy and its Power Elite: Focusing on the Leader Personnel Policies) (Seoul: Seon-in Doseochulpan, 2007), p. 425; and Hyun Seong Il, interview by author, Seoul, ROK, March 19, 2008.

159 Funabashi, *The Peninsula Question*, p. 105.

160 Hyun, *Bughan-ui Guggajeonryag-gwa Pawo-elriteu*, p. 425; and Hyun Seong Il, interview by author, Seoul, ROK, March 19, 2008.

161 "Keynote Speeches Made at Six-way Talks," *KCNA*, August 29, 2003.

162 *New York Times*, March 10, 2002.

163 "KCNA Blasts U.S. Attempt at 'Regime Change' in DPRK," *KCNA*, June 7, 2005.

164 *Daily Telegraph*, July 17, 2007, p. 16.

165 DoS, "North Korea: Presidential Action on State Sponsor of Terrorism (SST) and the Trading with the Enemy Act (TWEA)," Fact Sheet, June 26, 2008; and DoS, "Existing Sanctions and Reporting Provisions Related to North Korea," Fact Sheet, October 11, 2008.

166 "Foreign Ministry Spokesman on DPRK's Will to Cooperate in Verification of Objects of Nuclear Disablement," *KCNA*, October 12, 2008.

167 DoS, "North Korea: Presidential Action on State Sponsor of Terrorism (SST) and the Trading with the Enemy Act (TWEA)."

168 DoS, *Country Reports on Terrorism 2007*, April 2008, p. 171.

169 Minister's Weekly Press Briefing, H.E. Song Min-soon, Minister of Foreign Affairs and Trade (MOFAT), ROK, October 31, 2007; and "The Informal Heads of Delegations Meeting for the Six-party Economic and Energy Cooperation Working Group," Daily Press Briefing, MOFAT, December 10, 2007.

170 Hill, "Status of the Six-Party Talks for the Denuclearization of the Korean Peninsula."

171 Christopher Hill, "North Korean Six-Party Talks and Implementation Activities," Statement before the Senate Committee on Armed Services, Washington, DC, July 31, 2008.

172 Lee Jong-Heon, "Analysis: N. Korea's use of oil aid," *UPI*, July 12, 2007.

173 *JungAng Ilbo*, October 4, 2006.

174 "Japan–DPRK Pyongyang Declaration," Pyongyang, September 17, 2002.

175 "Tough measures taken against North Korea," Abe Cabinet E-mail Magazine, October 12, 2006.

176 Lee Jong-Seok, interview by author, Sejong Institute, ROK, February 19, 2008.

177 "Servicepersons and Pyongyangites Hail Successful Nuclear Test," *KCNA*, October 20, 2006.

178 *Pyongyang Times*, January 6, 2007, pp. 1–2.

Conclusion

1 Lee Mun Hang, *JSA-Panmunjeom, 1953–1994* (Seoul: Sohwa, 2001), p. 373 (for the 1953–92 period); and the data obtained from the ROK Ministry of National Defense, August 29, 2002 (for the 1993–2000 period) and February 29, 2008 (for the 2001–7 period).

2 According to Kim Il Sung, the military lines ordered "to train the People's Army into a cadre army, to modernize armaments, fortify military positions, arm the entire people, and to garrison the whole country. ... " Kim Il Sung, "Let Us Strengthen the Revolutionary Forces in Every Way so as to Achieve the Cause of Reunification of the Country," Concluding Speech Delivered at the Eighth Plenary Meeting of the Fourth Central Committee of the Workers' Party of Korea, February 27, 1964, in *Kim Il Sung Works*, vol. 18 (Pyongyang: Foreign Languages Publishing House, 1984), pp. 222–23.

3 Ministry of National Defense, ed., *Yulgogsaeob-ui Eoje-wa Oneul Geurigo Naeil* (Yesterday, Today, and Tomorrow of the *Yulgok* Project) (Seoul: Gugbangbu, 1994); National Defense Military History Research Institute, *Geongun 50-nyeonsa* (Fifty-Year History since the Foundation of the Armed Forces) (Seoul: Gugbang Gunsa Yeonguso, 1998), pp. 354–65; Chung Min Lee, *The Emerging Strategic Balance in Northeast Asia: Implications for Korea's Defense Strategy and Planning for the 1990s* (Seoul: Research Center for Peace and Unification of Korea, 1989), pp. 195 and 198; and Peter Hayes, *Pacific Powderkeg: American Nuclear Dilemmas in Korea* (Lexington: Lexington Books, 1991), pp. 91 and 93.

4 Taik-young Hamm, *Arming the Two Koreas: State, Capital and Military Power* (London: Routledge, 1999), p. 80.

5 For studies on North Korea's negotiation tactics, see Chuck Downs, *Over the Line: North Korea's Negotiating Strategy* (Washington, DC: The AEI Press, 1999); and Scott Snyder, *Negotiating on the Edge: North Korean Negotiating Behavior* (Washington, DC: United States Institute of Peace Press, 1999).

6 Kim Il Sung, "The Present Situation and the Tasks of Our Party," Report to the Conference of the Workers' Party of Korea, October 5, 1966, in *Kim Il Sung Works*, vol. 20 (Pyongyang: Foreign Languages Publishing House, 1984), p. 361.

7 Testimony of General Thomas A. Schwartz, Commander in Chief, United Nations Command/Combined Forces Command, and Commander, United States Forces Korea before the Senate Armed Forces Committee, March 27, 2001.

8 Ashton B. Carter and William J. Perry, *Preventive Defense: A New Security Strategy for America* (Washington, DC: Brookings Institution Press, 1999), pp. 128–29.

9 Jun Bong-Geun, interview by author, Seoul, ROK, May 16, 2002.

10 A defected former North Korean diplomat, interview by author, Seoul, ROK, May 15, 2002; and Hyun Seong Il, interview by author, Seoul, ROK, March 19, 2008.

SELECT BIBLIOGRAPHY

Archive collections

CIA Records Search Tool (CREST), U.S. National Archives and Records Administration.

Digital National Security Archive (DNSA).

Korea Information Service on Net (KISON), *DMZ Axe Incident (1976)*, Korean Security Archive, The Special Collections (Washington, DC: International Center, 2000).

National Security Archive Electronic Briefing Book.

National Security Archive Korea Project.

ROK Diplomatic Archives, "Bughan Seohaean 5-gae doseo Jeobsog Suyeog Chimbeom Sageon (Incident Involving North Korea's Intrusion into the Contiguous Waters of the Five Islands off the West Coast)," November 19–December 19, 1973, 2 vols., V. 1 Gibon Munseo (Basic Documents), classification no. 729.55, registration no. 6128 and V. 2 Jaryojib (materials), classification no. 729.55, registration no. 6129, Diplomatic Archives, Seoul, ROK.

—— "Bughan Seonbag Seohae Chimmul Sageon, 2.26 (Incident of the Sinking of a North Korean Ship in the West Sea on February 26)," in "Bughan-ui Dobal Sageon, 1973–75 (North Korea's Provocation Incidents)," classification no. 729.55, 1973–75, registration no. 8359 (11265), ROK Diplomatic Archives.

U.S. National Archives and Records Administration (NARA), Electronic Telegrams, Central Foreign Policy Files, Record Group 59 (RG 59), Access to Archival Databases (ADD).

Official publications and documents

Democratic People's Republic of Korea (North Korea)

Kim, Il Sung, "Let Us Strengthen the Revolutionary Forces in Every Way so as to Achieve the Cause of Reunification of the Country," Concluding Speech Delivered at the Eighth Plenary Meeting of the Fourth Central Committee of the Workers' Party of Korea, February 27, 1964, in *Kim Il Sung Works*, vol. 18 (Pyongyang: Foreign Languages Publishing House, 1984).

—— "The Present Situation and the Tasks of Our Party," Report to the Conference of the Workers' Party of Korea, October 5, 1966, in *Kim Il Sung Works*, vol. 20 (Pyongyang: Foreign Languages Publishing House, 1984).

—— "Let Us Embody the Revolutionary Spirit of Independence, Self-Sustenance and Self-Defence More Thoroughly in All Branches of State Activity," Political Programme of the Government of the Democratic People's Republic of Korea, Announced at the First Session of the Fourth Supreme People's Assembly of the DPRK, December 16,

1967, in *Kim Il Sung Works*, vol. 21 (Pyongyang: Foreign Languages Publishing House, 1985).

—— "On the 20th Anniversary of the Founding of the Korean People's Army," Speech at a Banquet Given in Honour of the 20th Anniversary of the Founding of the Heroic Korean People's Army, February 8, 1968, in *Kim Il Sung Works*, vol. 22, 2nd edn (Pyongyang: Foreign Languages Publishing House, 1992).

—— "On Making Good Preparations for War so as to Cope with the Prevailing Situation," March 21, 1968, in *Kim Il Sung Works*, vol. 22, 2nd edn (Pyongyang: Foreign Languages Publishing House, 1992).

—— "Congratulations to Officers and Men of Unit 447 of the Korean People's Army on Shooting Down the Heavy Reconnaissance Aircraft of the US Imperialist Aggressive Forces which Illegally Intruded into the Northern Half of the Republic for Reconnaissance Purposes," April 16, 1969, in *Kim Il Sung Works*, vol. 23 (Pyongyang: Foreign Languages Publishing House, 1985).

—— "On the Review of This Year's Work and the Direction of Next Year's Work," Speech at a Meeting of the Political Committee of the Workers' Party of Korea, December 31, 1973, in *Kim Il Sung Works*, vol. 28 (Pyongyang: Foreign Languages Publishing House, 1986).

—— "Talk with the Chief Editor of the Japanese Political Magazine *Sekai*," March 28, 1976, in *Kim Il Sung Works*, vol. 31 (Pyongyang: Foreign Languages Publishing House, 1987).

Kim, Jong Il, *Gim Jeong Il Seonjib* (Kim Jong Il Selected Works), vol. 1 (Pyongyang: Joseon Rodongdang Chulpansa, 1992).

—— *Gim Jeong Il Seonjip* (Kim Jong Il Selected Works), vol. 13 (Pyongyang: Joseon Rodongdang Chulpansa, 1998).

Kim, Nam Jin, et al., *Hyangdo-ui Taeyang Gim Jeong Il Janggun* (Gen. Kim Jong Il: The Leading Sun) (Pyongyang: Pyeongyang Chulpansa, 1995).

—— *Kim Jong Il: The Lodestar of the 21st Century*, vol. 2 (Tokyo: Gwang Myeongsa, 1997).

"Joseon Inmingun Choego Saryeonggwan Mich Junggug Inmin Jiwongun Saryeongwon-eul Ilbang-euro hago Ryeonhabguggun Chongsaryeonggwan-eul Dareun Ilbang-euro-haneun Joseon Gunsa Jeongjeon-e Gwanhan Hyeobjeong (Agreement between the Supreme Commander of the Korean People's Army and the Commander of the Chinese People's Volunteers, on the One Hand, and the Commander-in-Chief, United Nations Command, on the Other Hand, Concerning a Military Armistice in Korea)," in *Joseon Jungang Nyeongam 1953* (Pyongyang: Joseon Jungang Tongsinsa, 1953).

Kim, Cheol U, *Gim Jeong Il Janggun-ui Seongun Jeongchi: Gunsa Seonhaeng, Gun-eul Juryeoggun-euro Haneun Jeongchi* (Gen. Kim Jong Il's Policy of Giving Priority to the Army: Policy that Puts Priority to the Military Affairs and that Centers on the Army) (Pyongyang: Pyeongyang Chulpansa, 2000).

Republic of Korea (South Korea)

Arms Control Bureau, Ministry of National Defense, "The Unjustness of North Korea's Claim on the West Sea Sea [*sic*] Demarcation Line and the Position of the Republic of Korea," September 1999, http://www.mnd.go.kr/mnd/mnden/prg_file/1.htm (accessed on February 9, 2002).

—— ed., *The Republic of Korea Position regarding the Northern Limit Line* (Seoul: Ministry of National Defense, 2002).

—— *Bugbang Hangyeseon (NLL)-e Gwanhan Uri-ui Ibjang* (Our Position regarding the Northern Limit Line) (Seoul: Gugbangbu, 2007).

Bank of Korea, "Gross Domestic Product of North Korea in 2004," May 31, 2005.

Bank of Korea, "2006-nyeon Bughan Gyeongje Seongjangryul Chujeong Gyeolgwa (Results of the Estimate of the North Korean Economic Growth Rate in 2006)," Press Release, August 17, 2007.

Education Center for Unification, *Bughan Gyeongje, Eodikkaji wassna?* (What is the status of North Korean economy?) (Seoul: Tongil Gyoyugwon, 2005).

Korea Trade-Investment Promotion Agency, *Bughan-ui Daewoe Muyeog Donghyang, 1990–2000-nyeon* (Trends of North Korea's Foreign Trade, 1990–2000) (Seoul: Daehan Muyeog Tuja Jinheung Gongsa, 2001).

Korean Central Intelligence Agency, ed., *Buggoe Gunsa Jeonryag Jaryojib* (Collection of Materials on North Korean Military Strategy) (Seoul: Jungang Jeongbobu, 1974).

Ministry of Foreign Affairs, *Hangug Oegyo 30-nyeon, 1948–1978* (Thirty Years of the Diplomacy of the ROK, 1948-1978) (Seoul: Oegyobu, 1979).

Ministry of Foreign Affairs and Trade, *Hangug Oegyo 50-nyeon, 1948–1998* (Fifty Years of the Diplomacy of the ROK, 1948-1998) (Seoul: Oegyotongsangbu, 1999).

Ministry of National Defense, *Defense White Paper 1990* (Seoul: Korea Institute for Defense Analyses, 1991).

—— *Defense White Paper 1991–1992* (Seoul: Korea Institute for Defense Analyses, 1992).

—— *Yulgogsaeob-ui Eoje-wa Oneul Geurigo Naeil* (Yesterday, Today, and Tomorrow of the *Yulgok* Project) (Seoul: Gugbangbu, 1994)

—— *Defense White Paper 1994–1995* (Seoul: Korea Institute for Defense Analyses, 1995).

—— *Gugbang Baegseo 1995–1996* (Defense White Paper 1995-1996) (Seoul: Gugbangbu, 1995).

—— *Defense White Paper 1995–1996* (Seoul: Korea Institute for Defense Analyses, 1996).

—— *Defense White Paper 1996–1997* (Seoul: Korea Institute for Defense Analyses, 1997).

—— *Gugbang Baegseo 1999* (Defense White Paper 1999) (Seoul: Gugbangbu, 1999).

—— *Defense White Paper 1998* (Seoul: Korea Institute for Defense Analyses, 1999).

—— *Defense White Paper 1999* (Seoul: Ministry of National Defense, 1999).

—— "Seohae Gyojeon-gwanryeon Uri-ui Ibjang (Our Position on the Battle in the West Sea)," *Gugbang Sosig*, no. 107, September 1999.

—— "Bughan Seonbag-ui Yeonghae Chimbeom-gwa Urigun-ui Daeeung (Violation of the Territorial Waters by North Korean Ships and Our Armed Forces' Response)," June 9, 2001 (*Gugbang Ilbo*, June 10, 2001).

—— "The Naval Clash on the Yellow Sea on 29 June 2002 between South and North Korea: The Situation and ROK's Position," July 1, 2002.

Ministry of National Unification, *Tongil Baegseo 1995* (Unification White Paper 1995) (Seoul: Tongilwon, 1995).

Ministry of Unification, "Seohae Haesang Gyeonggyeseon Munje (Question of the sea demarcation line in the West Sea)," June 14, 1999.

—— "Bughan-ui Seohaean Kkochgejabi Siltae (Status of North Korea's Blue Crab Fishing)," June 25, 1999.

—— *Peace and Prosperity: White Paper on Korean Unification 2005* (Seoul: Ministry of Unification 2005).

—— "Je 5-cha Nambug Haeun Hyeobryeog Silmujeobchog Gongdong Bodomun (Joint Press Release on the Fifth Working-Level Contact on South–North Maritime Cooperation)," August 10, 2005.

—— "Je 4-cha Nambug Jangseonggeub Gunsahoedam (Fourth Inter-Korean General-level Military Talks)," Panmunjom, May 16-18, 2006.

—— *Tongil Baegseo 2008* (Unification White Paper 2008) (Seoul: Tongilbu, 2008).

Ministry of Unification, Ministry of National Defense, and Government Information Agency, *Bughan Seonbag-ui Yeonghae Chimbeom, Ireohge Daecheohaesseumnida* (We Dealt with the Violations of [Our] Territorial Seas by North Korean Vessels This Way) (Seoul: Tongilbu, Gugbangbu, and Gugjeong Hongbocheo, June 2001).

National Assembly, *Gughoe Hoewirog* (Proceedings of the Plenary), no. 17, 88th National Assembly, ROK, December 2, 1973.

—— *Gugbang Wiwonhoe Hoewirog* (Proceedings of the National Defense Committee), no. 16, 88th National Assembly, ROK, December 10, 1973.

—— *Gugbang Wiwonhoe Hoewirog* (Proceedings of the National Defense Committee), no. 1, 91st National Assembly, ROK, March 13, 1975.

—— *Gugbang Wiwonhoe Hoewirog* (Proceedings of the National Defense Committee), no. 1, 204th National Assembly, ROK, June 10, 1999.

—— *Gugbang Wiwonhoe Hoewirog* (Proceedings of the National Defense Committee), no. 2, 204th National Assembly, ROK, June 16 and 17, 1999.

—— *Gugbang Wiwonhoe Hoewirog* (Proceedings of the National Defense Committee), no. 1, 207th National Assembly, ROK, September 7, 1999.

National Defense Military History Research Institute, *Geongun 50-nyeonsa* (Fifty-Year History since the Foundation of the Armed Forces) (Seoul: Gugbang Gunsa Yeonguso, 1998).

—— *Daebijeonggyujeonsa II, 1961-1980* (History of the Counter-Unconventional Warfare II) (Seoul: Gugbang Gunsa Yeonguso, 1998).

National Unification Board, *Seohae 5-gae Doseo-wa Geu Gwanryeonmunje-e Gwanhan Yeongu* (A Study on the Five Islands in the West Sea and the Related Issues), Nambuggwangye Daebibangan Yeongu (A Study on the Reaction Plans on South–North Relations) (Seoul: Gugto Tongilwon, 1977), serial no. 77-1-1136.

Office of the South–North Dialogue, *South–North Dialogue in Korea*, no. 4 (December 1973–February 1974).

—— *South–North Dialogue in Korea*, no. 5 (February 1974–July 1974).

—— *South–North Dialogue in Korea*, no. 9 (March 1975–December 1975).

—— *South–North Dialogue in Korea*, no. 11 (March 1976–November 1976).

Presidential Secretariat, *Bag Jeong Hui Daetongryeong Yeonseolmunjib* (Speeches of President Park Chung Hee), January–December 1976 (Seoul: Daetongryeong Biseosil, 1977).

ROK Navy, "Jajugugbang — Jeonryeog Jeongbi mich Budae Baljeon: Haebyeong Budae (Self-Reliant National Defense — Improvement of the Forces and Development of Units: Marine Corps Units)," ROK Navy homepage.

—— "Jajugugbang — Jeonryeog Jeongbi mich Budae Baljeon: Gugsan-ham Geonjo (Self-Reliant National Defense — Improvement of the Forces and Development of Units: Building Indigenous Ships)," ROK Navy homepage.

—— "Jajugugbang — Jagjeon/Hunryeon: Yudotan Sisa (Self-Reliant National Defense — Operations/Training: Test-firing of Guided Missiles)," ROK Navy homepage.

—— "Yeonpyeong Haejeon (Battle of Yeonpyeong)," news video.

Rural Development Administration, "2005 Bughan-ui Gogmul Saengsanryang Chujeong Balpyo (Assessment of North Korean Grain Production in 2005 Announced)," November 29, 2005.

United States of America

Central Intelligence Agency, "Confrontation in Korea," January, 24, 1968, in CIA Records Search Tool, Archives II Library, The U.S. National Archives and Records Administration.

—— Directorate of Intelligence, "North Korean Tactics Against South Korea: 1968," *Weekly Summary Special Report*, January 24, 1969.

—— "Kim Il-Sung's New Military Adventurism," Intelligence Report, November 26, 1968, ESAU papers, no. 39, "Cold War Era Hard Target Analysis of Soviet and Chinese Policy and Decision Making, 1953–1973," Central Intelligence Agency Information Management Services.

—— *Korean Fishing Areas in the Yellow Sea – Spawning Ground for Maritime Conflict*, GCR-RP 75-20, May 1975, CIA Records Search Tool (CREST), Archives II Library, The U.S. National Archives and Records Administration.

—— "North Korea Politics," November 16, 1976, CREST.

Central Intelligence Agency, Center for the Study of Intelligence, "Finding a Mission," https://www.cia.gov/library/center-for-the-study-of-intelligence/csi-publications/books-and-monographs/a-12/finding-a-mission.html.

Defense Intelligence Agency, *North Korea: The Foundations for Military Strength*, update 1995 (Washington, DC: U.S. Government Printing Office, 1996).

Department of Defense, *Dictionary of Military and Associated Terms*, Joint Publication 1-02, April 12, 2001.

—— Office of the Secretary of Defense, *Proliferation: Threat and Response* (Washington, DC: U.S. Government Printing Office, November 1997).

—— Office of the Secretary of Defense, *Proliferation: Threat and Response* (Washington, DC: Office of the Secretary of Defense, January 2001).

Department of State, *Foreign Relations of the United States, 1964–1968*, vol. 29, part 1, *Korea* (Washington, DC, U.S. Government Printing Office, 2000).

Finley, James P., *The US Military Experience in Korea, 1871–1982: In the Vanguard of ROK–US Relations* (San Francisco, CA: Command Historian's Office, HQ USFK/EUSA, 1983).

National Intelligence Council, "Foreign Missile Developments and the Ballistic Missile Threat to the United States Through 2015," September 1999.

—— "Global Trends 2015: A Dialogue About the Future With Nongovernment Experts," NIC 2000-02, December 2000.

Pacific Command, Historical Branch, Office of the Joint Secretary, Headquarters CINC-PAC, *Commander in Chief Pacific: Command History 1968*, vol. II (Hawaii: Camp H. M. Smith, 1969).

Perry, William J., Special Advisor to the President and the Secretary of State, "Review of United States Policy Toward North Korea: Findings and Recommendations," October 12, 1999.

United Nations Command, Military Armistice Commission, "Three Hundred and Second Meeting of the Military Armistice Commission," June 9, 1970.

—— "Three Hundred and Forty-Sixth Meeting of the Military Armistice Commission," December 1, 1973.

—— "Three Hundred and Forty-Seventh Meeting of the Military Armistice Commission," December 24, 1973.

—— "Three Hundred and Fifty-Second Meeting of the Military Armistice Commission," July 1, 1974.

—— "Three Hundred and Fifty-Nineth [*sic*] Meeting of the Military Armistice Commission," February 21, 1975.

—— "Three Hundred and Sixtieth Meeting of the Military Armistice Commission," March 3, 1975.

—— "Three Hundred and Sixty-Second Meeting of the Military Armistice Commission," May 27, 1975.

—— "Three Hundred and Sixty-Third Meeting of the Military Armistice Commission," June 11, 1975.

—— "Three Hundred and Sixty-Fifth Meeting of the Military Armistice Commission," July 12, 1975.

—— "Three Hundred and Sixty-Sixth Meeting of the Military Armistice Commission," July 30, 1975.

—— "Three Hundred and Seventy-First Meeting of the Military Armistice Commission," February 26, 1976.

—— "Three Hundred and Seventy-Seventh Meeting of the Military Armistice Commission," June 28, 1976.

—— "Three Hundred and Seventy-Ninth Meeting of the Military Armistice Commission," August 19, 1976.

—— "Agreement on the Military Armistice Commission Headquarters Area, Its Security and Its Construction," in "Subsequent Agreements," UNCMAC, revised October 1, 1976.

—— Headquarters, United Nations Command, *Annual Historical Summary, 1 January 1991–31 December 1991*, compiled by the Command Historical Branch, United Nations Command, Unit 15259, APO AP 96205-0032.

—— *Command Historical Summary, 1 January 1992–31 December 1992*, compiled by the Command Historical Branch, United Nations Command, Unit #15259, APO AP 96205-0032.

—— *Command Historical Summary, 1 January 1994–31 December 1994*, compiled by the Command Historical Branch, United Nations Command, Unit #15237, APO AP 96205-0010.

—— *Command Historical Summary, 1 January 1995–31 December 1995*, compiled by the Command Historical Branch, United Nations Command, Unit #15237, APO AP 96205-0010.

—— "Report of the Activities of the United Nations Command for 1995," Annex.

—— *Command Historical Summary, 1 January 1996–31 December 1996*, compiled by the Command History Office, United Nations Command, Unit #15237, APO AP 96205-0010.

—— "Report of the Activities of the United Nations Command for 1996," Annex.

—— *Command Historical Summary, 1 January 1997–31 December 1997*, compiled by the Command History Office, United Nations Command, Unit #15237, APO AP 96205-0010.

—— "Report of the Activities of the United Nations Command for 1997," Annex.

—— "Conflict & Tension on the Korean Peninsula! A Chronology (28 Jul 53–Aug 98)."

—— "Report of the Activities of the United Nations Command for 1998," Annex.

—— Proceedings of the Seventh General Officers Talks, June 22, 1999.

—— Proceedings of the Eighth General Officers Talks, July 2, 1999.

—— Proceedings of the Ninth General Officers Talks, July 21, 1999.

—— Proceedings of the Eleventh General Officers Talks, September 1, 1999.

—— "Report of the Activities of the United Nations Command for 1999," Annex.

—— Military Armistice Commission (UNCMAC), "We own the Zone," a briefing material.

United Nations Command/United States Forces Korea/Eighth United States Army, *The 1976 Annual Historical Report*, p. 15, in file 350.018-3, "Axe Murder, 1976 (assorted)," United Nations Command, Combined Forces Command and United States Forces Korea, Command History Office.

United Nations Command/United States Forces Korea/Combined Forces Command/ Eighth United States Army, Public Affairs Office, "Serious Incidents in the DMZ," USFK Backgrounder, no. 16, current as of June 1993.

Commission to Assess the Ballistic Missile Threat to the United States, "Executive Summary of the Report of the Commission to Assess the Ballistic Missile Threat to the United States," July 15, 1998.

Congress, House, Hearings before the Special Subcommittee on the U.S.S. *Pueblo* of the Committee on Armed Services, *Inquiry into the U.S.S. Pueblo and EC-121 Plane Incidents*, 91st Congress, First Session, March 4, 5, 6, 10, 14, 17, 19, 20, April 25, and 28, 1969, H.A.S.C. no. 91–101 (Washington, DC: U.S. Government Printing Office, 1969).

—— Hearing before the Subcommittees on International Political and Military Affairs and on International Organization of the Committee on International Relations, *Deaths of American Military Personnel in the Korean Demilitarized Zone*, 94th Congress, Second Session, September 1, 1976 (Washington, DC: U.S. Government Printing Office, 1976).

General Accounting Office (GAO), *Nuclear Nonproliferation: Difficulties in Accomplishing IAEA's Activities in North Korea*, Report to the Chairman, Committee on Energy and Natural Resources, U.S. Senate (Washington, DC: GAO, July 1998).

Japan

Defense Agency, *Defense of Japan 1999* (Tokyo: Urban Connections, year not indicated).

Ministry of Defense, *Defense of Japan 2007* (Tokyo: Inter Group, 2007).

International organizations

International Atomic Energy Agency, "In Focus: IAEA and DPRK."

Korean Peninsula Energy Development Organization, *2005 Annual Report.*

English-language publications

Albright, David, and Kevin O'Neill, eds., *Solving the North Korean Nuclear Puzzle* (Washington, DC: The Institute for Science and International Security, 2000).

Albright, David, and Paul Brannan, "The North Korean Plutonium Stock, February 2007," Institute for Science and International Security, February 20, 2007.

Albright, Madeleine with Bill Woodward, *Madame Secretary*, New York: Miramax Books, 2003.

Armbrister, Trevor, *A Matter of Accountability* (New York: Coward-McCann, 1970).

Arms Control Association, "Background Information on North Korea's Nuclear Program," May 5, 1994.

—— "Chronology of U.S.–North Korean Nuclear and Missile Diplomacy," June 2003.

Auster, Bruce B., Kevin Whitelaw, and Thomas Omestad, "Upping the Ante for Kim Jong Il: Pentagon Plan 5030, a new blueprint for facing down North Korea," *U.S. News & World Report*, July 21, 2003.

Bamford, James, *Body of Secrets: Anatomy of the Ultra-Secret National Security Agency* (New York: Anchor Books, 2002).

Bechtol, Jr, Bruce E., *Red Rogue: The Persistent Challenge of North Korea* (Virginia: Potomac Books, 2007).

Bermudez, Jr, Joseph S., *Terrorism: The North Korean Connection* (New York: Crane Russak, 1990).

—— "New Developments in North Korean Missile Programme," *Jane's Soviet Intelligence Review*, vol. 2, no. 8 (August 1990).

—— "Ballistic Missiles in the Third World: Iran's Medium-Range Missiles," *Jane's Intelligence Review*, vol. 4, no. 4 (April 1992).

—— "North Korea's Nuclear Infrastructure," *Jane's Intelligence Review*, vol. 6, no. 2 (February 1994).

—— *North Korean Special Forces*, 2nd edn (Annapolis, MD: Naval Institute Press, 1998).

—— "Taepo-Dong Launch Brings DPRK Missiles Back into the Spotlight," *Jane's Intelligence Review*, vol. 10, no. 10 (October 1998).

—— "North Korea's Musudan-ri Launch Facility," Missile News: Special Report, CDISS.

—— "Estimated Flight Paths of Known DPRK Ballistic Missile Tests: 1984–1999," http://www.cdiss.org/DPRK_Missile_Tests.pdf (accessed on August 5, 2002). No longer available at this URL.

—— *A History of Ballistic Missile Development in the DPRK*, Occasional Paper no. 2, Monitoring Proliferation Threats Project (Monterey, California: Center for Nonproliferation Studies, Monterey Institute of International Studies, 1999).

—— *The Armed Forces of North Korea*, The Armed Forces of Asia Series (London: I.B. Tauris, 2001).

—— "Proliferation in Pyongyang," *Jane's Defence Weekly*, May 25, 2005.

—— "Moving Missiles," *Jane's Defence Weekly*, August 3, 2005.

Bermudez, Jr, Joseph S., and W. Seth Carus, "The North Korean 'Scud B' Programme," *Jane's Intelligence Review*, vol. 1, no. 4 (April 1989).

Bolger, Daniel P., *Scenes from an Unfinished War: Low-Intensity Conflict in Korea, 1966–1969* (Washington, DC: U.S. Government Printing Office, 1991).

Caminos, Hugo, *The Legal Régime of Straits in the 1982 United Nations Convention on the Law of the Sea* (The Hague: Kluwer International, 1987).

Carter, Ashton B., and William J. Perry, *Preventive Defense: A New Security Strategy for America* (Washington, DC: Brookings Institution Press, 1999).

Center for Nonproliferation Studies, Monterey Institute of International Studies, "Chronology of North Korea's Missile Trade and Developments."

Center for Strategic and International Studies (CSIS), "Nuclear Confrontation with North Korea: Lessons of the 1994 Crisis for Today," March 20, 2003, Seoul, Korea.

Chinoy, Mike, *Meltdown: The Inside Story of the North Korean Nuclear Crisis* (New York: St. Martin's Press, 2008).

Cordesman, Anthony H., and Abraham R. Wagner, *The Lessons of Modern War*, Volume IV: *The Gulf War* (Boulder, CO: Westview Press, 1996).

Creekmore, Jr., Marion V., *A Moment of Crisis: Jimmy Carter, the Power of a Peacemaker, and North Korea's Nuclear Ambitions* (New York: PublicAffairs, 2006).

Chung, Chin O., *Pyongyang between Peking and Moscow: North Korea's Involvement in the Sino-Soviet Dispute, 1958–1974* (Alabama: University of Alabama Press, 1976).

Diamond, Howard, "U.S., North Korea Meet on Missiles; Japan, S. Korea Press on Defense," *Arms Control Today*, vol. 28, no. 7 (October 1998).

Downs, Chuck, *Over the Line: North Korea's Negotiating Strategy* (Washington, DC: The AEI Press, 1999).

Federation of American Scientists, "Nuclear Weapons Program," updated on November 16, 2006.

—— "Nuclear Forces Guide-Missiles," updated on March 17, 2008.

Freedman, Lawrence, ed., "Introduction," and "Strategic Coercion," in Lawrence Freedman, ed., *Strategic Coercion: Concepts and Cases* (Oxford: Oxford University Press, 1998).

—— *Deterrence* (Polity Press, 2004).

Funabashi, Yoichi, *The Peninsula Question: A Chronicle of the Second Nuclear Crisis* (Washington, DC: Brookings Institution Press, 2007).

Gerardi, Greg, and Joseph Bermudez, Jr., "An Analysis of North Korean Ballistic Missile Testing," *Jane's Intelligence Review*, vol. 7, no. 4 (April 1995).

Gills, B. K., *Korea Versus Korea: A Case of Contested Legitimacy* (London: Routledge, 1996).

Gleysteen, Jr., William H., *Massive Entanglement, Marginal Influence: Carter and Korea in Crisis* (Washington, DC: Brookings Institution Press, 1999).

Hamm, Taik-young, *Arming the Two Koreas: State, Capital and Military Power* (London: Routledge, 1999).

Hayes, Peter, *Pacific Powderkeg: American Nuclear Dilemmas in Korea* (Lexington, KY: Lexington Books, 1991).

Head, Richard G., Frisco W. Short, and Robert C. McFarlane, *Crisis Resolution: Presidential Decision Making in the Mayaguez and Korean Confrontations* (Boulder, CO: Westview Press, 1978).

Hecker, Siegfried S., Senate Committee on Foreign Relations Hearing on "Visit to the Yongbyon Nuclear Scientific Research Center in North Korea," University of California, January 21, 2004.

—— "Technical summary of DPRK nuclear program," Center for International Security and Cooperation, Stanford University, 2005 Carnegie International Non-Proliferation Conference, Washington, DC, November 8, 2005.

—— "Report on North Korean Nuclear Program," Center for International Security and Cooperation, Stanford University, November 15, 2006.

Iredale, Harry, "*Pueblo* Incident: Attacked by North Korean Military Forces."

International Institute for Strategic Studies, *The Military Balance, 1973–1974* (London: International Institute for Strategic Studies, 1973).

—— *Nuclear Black Markets: Pakistan, A.Q. Khan and the Rise of Proliferation Networks — A Net Assessment*, IISS strategic dossier (London: The International Institute for Strategic Studies, 2007).

Jacobs, Gordon, "The Korean People's Navy: Further Perspectives," *Jane's Intelligence Review*, July 1993.

Jane's Fighting Ships, 1986–87 (London: Jane's Publishing Company, no publication year indicated).

Jane's Fighting Ships, 1987–88 (London: Jane's Publishing Company, no publication year indicated).

Katzman, Kenneth, and Rinn-Sup Shinn, *North Korea: Military Relations with the Middle East*, CRS Report for Congress, 94-754F, September 27, 1994.

Keaney, Thomas A., and Eliot A. Cohen, *Gulf War Air Power Survey*, Summary Report (Washington, DC: U.S. Government Printing Office, 1993).

Kessler, Glenn, *The Confidante: Condoleezza Rice and the Creation of the Bush Legacy* (New York: St. Martin's Press, 2007).

Kim, Se-Jin, ed., *Korean Unification: Source Materials with an Introduction* (Seoul: Research Center for Peace and Unification, 1976).

Kim, Seung-Hwan, *The Soviet Union and North Korea: Soviet Asian Strategy and Its Implications for the Korean Peninsula, 1964–1968* (Seoul: Research Center for Peace and Unification of Korea, 1988).

Kirkbride, Wayne A., *DMZ: A Story of the Panmunjom Axe Murder*, 2nd edn (Seoul: Hollym, 1984).

Kissinger, Henry A., *White House Years* (Boston, MA: Little, Brown and Company, 1979).

Lee, Chung Min, *The Emerging Strategic Balance in Northeast Asia: Implications for Korea's Defense Strategy and Planning for the 1990s* (Seoul: Research Center for Peace and Unification of Korea, 1989)

Lee, James M., "History of Korea's MDL & Reduction of Tension along the DMZ and Western Sea through Confidence Building Measures between North and South Korea," in Chae-Han Kim, ed., *The Korean DMZ: Reverting beyond Division* (Seoul: Sowha, 2001).

Mazarr, Michael J., *North Korea and the Bomb: A Case Study in Nonproliferation* (New York: St. Martin's Press, 1995).

McClintock, Ralph, "*Pueblo* Incident: AGER Program Background," http://www.uss*Pueblo*.org/v2f/background/agerback.html.

Medeiros, Evan S., "U.S., North Korea May Hold Talks On North's Missile Sales, MTCR Status," *Arms Control Today*, vol. 26, no. 1 (February 1996).

Nanto, Dick K., and Emma Chanlett-Avery, *The North Korean Economy: Overview and Policy Analysis*, CRS Report for Congress, April 18, 2007.

Niksch, Larry A., *North Korea's Nuclear Weapons Program*, CRS Issue Brief for Congress, updated October 5, 2006, http://fpc.state.gov/documents/organization/74904.pdf.

Nixon, Richard, *The Memoirs of Richard Nixon*, vol. 1 (New York: Warner Books, 1979).

Oberdorfer, Don, *The Two Koreas: A Contemporary History* (Reading, MA: Addison-Wesley, 1997).

Park, Chi Young, "Korea and the United Nations," in Youngnok Koo and Sung-joo Han, eds., *The Foreign Policy of the Republic of Korea* (New York: Columbia University Press, 1985).

Pritchard, Charles L., *Failed Diplomacy: The Tragic Story of How North Korea Got the Bomb* (Washington, DC: Brookings Institution Press, 2007).

Radchenko, Sergey S., "The Soviet Union and the North Korean Seizure of the USS Pueblo: Evidence from Russian Archives," Cold War International History Project, Woodrow Wilson International Center for Scholars, Working Papers Series #47.

Reiss, Mitchell, *Bridled Ambition: Why Countries Constrain Their Nuclear Capabilities* (Washington, DC: Woodrow Wilson Center Press, 1995).

Reiss, Mitchell B., Robert Gallucci et al., "Red-Handed," *Foreign Affairs*, March/April 2005.

Roy, Denny, "North Korea and the 'Madman' Theory," *Security Dialogue*, vol. 25, no. 3 (1994).

Samore, Gary, "U.S.–DPRK Missile Negotiations," *The Nonproliferation Review*, vol. 9, no. 2 (Summer 2002).

Schaefer, Bernd, "North Korean 'Adventurism' and China's Long Shadow, 1966–1972," Working Papers Series #44, Cold War International History Project, Woodrow Wilson International Center for Scholars (October 2004).

Schaub, Jr., Gary, "Compellence: Resuscitating the Concept," in Lawrence Freedman, ed., *Strategic Coercion: Concepts and Cases* (Oxford: Oxford University Press, 1998).

Sigal, Leon V., *Disarming Strangers: Nuclear Diplomacy with North Korea* (Princeton, NJ: Princeton University Press, 1998).

Simmons, Robert R., *The Pueblo, EC-121, and Mayaguez Incidents: Some Continuities and Changes*, Occasional Papers/Reprints Series in Contemporary Asian Studies, no. 8 (School of Law, University of Maryland, 1978).

Snyder, Scott, *Negotiating on the Edge: North Korean Negotiating Behavior* (Washington, DC: United States Institute of Peace Press, 1999).

Wit, Joel S., Daniel B. Poneman, and Robert L. Gallucci, *Going Critical: The First North Korean Nuclear Crisis* (Washington, DC: Brookings Institution Press, 2004).

Wright, David C., "An Analysis of the North Korean Missile Program," in Report of the Commission to Assess the Ballistic Missile Threat to the United States, Appendix III: *Unclassified Working Papers*, Pursuant to Public Law 201, 104th Congress, July 15, 1998.

—— "Cut North Korea Some Slack," *Bulletin of the Atomic Scientists*, vol. 55, no. 2 (March/April 1999).

Yoon, Tae-Young, "Crisis Management on the Korean Peninsula: South Korea's Crisis Management towards North Korea within the Context of the South Korea–U.S. Alliance, 1968–1983," Ph.D. Dissertation, Department of Politics and Philosophy, Faculty of Humanities and Social Science, The Manchester Metropolitan University, October 1997.

Zagoria, Donald S., and Janet D. Zagoria, "Crisis on the Korean Peninsula," in Barry M. Blechman, Stephen S. Kaplan et al., *Diplomacy of Power: Soviet Armed Forces as a Political Instrument* (Washington, DC: The Brookings Institution, 1981).

Zelikow, Philip, "The Plan That Moved Pyongyang," *Washington Post*, February 20, 2007.

Zoellick, Robert B., "Long Division," *Wall Street Journal*, February 26, 2007.

Korean-language publications

An, Seung Beom, ed., *2000 Hanguggun Jangbi Yeongam* (ROK Armed Forces Equipment Annual 2000) (Seoul: Gunsa Jeongbo, 1999).

Choi, Sun-Jo, *Seohae Haejeon* (Naval Battle in the West Sea) (Seoul: Jiseong-ui-saem, 2007).

Choi, Zoo Hwal, "Gim Jeong Il 30-nyeon Noryeog Kkeut-e Gunbu Wanjeonjangag (Kim Jong Il Perfectly Consolidated his Position in the Military after 30 Years of Efforts)," *Win*, June 1996.

Chun, Yong Taek, interview by Nam Mun Hui, "Bughan, No Dong misail gaebal pogi yagsoghaessda (North Korea promised to abandon No Dong missile Development)," *Sisa Jeonal*, no. 597, April 5, 2001.

Gang, In Seon, "Inteobyu: Yuengun Saryeongbu Daebyeonin Jim Kolseu (Interview: UNC Spokesman Jim Coles)," *Wolgan Joseon*, June 1996.

Gwon, Yeong Gi, "Seohae 5-do-neun 'Hwayaggo' Hanbando-ui Noegwan (The West Sea Five Islands are "Powder Keg" and a Detonator)," *Wolgan Joseon*, July 1999.

Habdong Yeongam 1977 (Seoul: Habdong Yeongamsa, 1977).

Hahm, Sung Deuk, ed., *Gim Yeong Sam Jeongbu-ui Seonggong-gwa Silpae* (The Kim Young Sam Government: Its Successes and Failures) (Seoul: Nanam, 2001).

Heo, Man Ho, "Hyujeon Cheje-ui Deungjang-gwa Byeonhwa (Emergence and Transformation of the Armistice Regime)," in Hangug Jeongchi Waegyo Haghoe, ed., *Hangug Jeonjaeng-gwa Hyujeon Cheje* (The Korean War and the Armistice Regime) (Seoul: Jibmundang, 1998).

Hwang, Il-do, "Bug Jangsajeongpo: Alryeojiji anhneun Daseos gaji Jinsil (North Korea's Long-Range Artillery: Five Unknown Facts)," *Sindong-a*, December 2004.

Hyun, Seong Il, *Bughan-ui Guggajeonryag-gwa Pawo-elriteu: Ganbu Jeongchaeg-eul Jungsim-euro* (North Korea's National Strategy and its Power Elite: Focusing on the Leader Personnel Policies) (Seoul: Seon-in Doseochulpan, 2007).

Je, Seong Ho, *Hanbando Pyeonghwa Cheje-ui Mosaeg: Beobgyubeobjeog Jeobgeun-eul Jungsim-euro* (Search for a Peace Regime on the Korean Peninsula: Focusing on a Legal-Normative Approach) (Seoul: Jipyeong Seowon, 2000).

Jeong, Hyeong-Gon, "Bug-Jung Gyeongje Hyeobryeog Ganghwa-ui Pageub Yeonghyang (Consequences of the Upgraded North Korea-China Economic Cooperation)," *KIEP Segye Gyeongje*, February 2006.

Jo, Seong Gwan, "1976-nyeon 8-wol 21-il Gaeseong Jingyeog Jagjeon Gyehyoeg (Operation Plan to Advance into Kaesong, August 21, 1976)," *Wolgan Joseon*, October 1992.

Jo, Seong Sig, "Haegun Janggyo Chulsin Jo Seong Sig Gija-ui NLL Daehaebu (Detailed Anatomy of the NLL by Reporter Jo Seong Sig, a Former Naval Officer)," *Sindong-a*, January 2008.

Jung, Chang-Hyun, *Gyeot-eseo Bon Gim Jeong Il*, rev. and enl. edn (Kim Jong Il Seen from the Side) (Seoul: Gimyeongsa, 2000).

Kang, In-duk (Institute for East Asian Studies), ed., *Bughan Jeonseo, 1945–1980* (North Korean Handbook) (Seoul: Geugdong Munje Yeonguso, 1980).

Kim, Byeong Seog, "Eonron-i Milgo Gun-i Abjangseon NLL Sasujagjeon (An Operation to Defend the NLL without any Conditions: The Media Backed It and the Military Led It)," *Wolgan Joseon*, July 1999.

Kim, Chang Hui, "Bughan, 80-nyeondae jungban Seodog-eseo Haegmuljil Guib (North Korea Purchased Nuclear Material from West Germany in the mid-1980s)," *Sindong-a*, no. 434 (November 1995).

Kim, Chang Sun et al., ed., *Bughan Chongram* (A General Survey of North Korea) (Seoul: Bughan Yeonguso, 1983).

Kim, Chung Yum, *Hangug Gyeongje Jeongchaeg 30-nyeonsa: Gim Jeong Ryeom Hoegorog* (Thirty Years' History of South Korean Economic Policy) (Seoul: JungAng Ilbosa, 1995).

Kim, Tae Seo, "Bughan-ui Seohae Dobal-gwa Geu Chimryagjeog Jeoui (North Korea's Provocations in the West Sea and its Aggressive Intensions)," *Bughan*, vol. 3, no. 1, serial no. 25 (January 1974).

Kim, Yeong Gu, *Hangug-gwa Bada-ui Gugjebeob* (The Republic of Korea and the International Law of the Sea) (Seoul: Hangug Haeyang Jeonryag Yeonguso, 1999).

Kim, Yong Sam, "Hangug Haegun-ui Jeolchibusim: 56-ham Chimmol hu 32-nyeon man-e Bughan-e Bogsuhanda (Struggle of the ROK Navy: Revenge against North Korea 32 Years After the Sinking of the ROK Navy Ship No. 56)," *Wolgan Joseon*, July 1999.

Kim, Young Sam, *Gim Yeong Sam Daetongryeong Hoegorog* (President Kim Young Sam's Memoir), vol. 1 (Seoul: Joseon Ilbosa, 2001).

—— *Gim Yeong Sam Daetongryeong Hoegorog* (President Kim Young Sam's Memoir), vol. 2 (Seoul: Joseon Ilbosa, 2001).

Ko, Yeong Hwan, "Bughan Woegyo Jeongchaeg Gyeoljeonggigu mich Gwajeong-e Gwanhan Yeongu: Bughan-ui Dae-Jungdong/Apeurika Woegyo-reul Jungsim-euro (A Study on North Korea's Foreign Policy Decision-Making Organizations and Processes: Focusing on North Korea's Foreign Policy towards Middle East and Africa)," Master's Thesis, Kyunghee University, August 2000.

Lee, James, "'Panmunjeom San Jeungin' Jeimseu Ri Yugseong Jeung-eon (1) ("A Living Witness of Panmunjom," Oral Testimony of James Lee)," *Sindong-a*, December 1997.

—— "'Panmunjeom San Jeungin' Jeimseu Ri Yugseong Jeung-eon (2) ("A Living Witness of Panmunjom," Oral Testimony of James Lee)," *Sindong-a*, January 1998.

Lee, Jang-Hie, "Bugbang Hangyeseon-ui Gugjebeobjeog Bunseog-gwa Jaehaeseog (Analysis and Reinterpretation of the NLL from the Perspective of International Law)," *Tongil Gyeongje*, no. 56 (August 1999).

Lee, Jong-Seok, "Hanbando Pyeonghwacheje Guchug Noneui, Jaengjeom-gwa Daean Mosaeg (Debate on Establishing the Peace Regime on the Korean Peninsula: Issues and the Search for Alternatives)," *Sejong Jeongchaeg Yeongu* (Sejong Policy Research), vol. 4, no. 1 (2008).

Lee, Jung Hoon, "Haegun 2-hamdae Yeonpyeong Haejeon-ui Juyeog Pilseunghaegun-ui Seonbong (Navy Second Fleet: The Main Actor of the Battle of Yeonpyeong and the Vanguard of the Navy of Certain Victory)," *Sindong-a*, February 2002.

Lee, Ki-Tak, "Hanbando-ui Saeroun Gunsa Hwangyeong-gwa Haeyang-eseoui Anbo (New Military Environment on the Korean Peninsula and Security of the Seas)," *Strategy 21*, no. 1 (1998).

—— "Seohae-ui Jeonryagjeog-in Jungyoseong-gwa Munjaejeom-deul: Gugbang Jeonryag Damdangja-deul-ege Alrinda (Strategic Importance and Problems of the Yellow Sea: Informing the Defense Policy-Makers)," *Gunsa Segye*, no. 75 (August 1999).

—— "Gugje Jeongchi-neun Seon-ida. NLL-eun Sasuhaeya Handa (The International Politics is about the Line. The NLL must be Defended Unconditionally)," a speech by Professor Lee Ki-Tak, *Wolgan Joseon*, July 2001.

Lee, Mun Hang (James M. Lee), *JSA-Panmunjeom, 1953–1994* (Seoul: Sohwa, 2001).

Lee, Sang Myeon, "Seohae Gyojeon-i Namgin Beobjeogmunje (Legal Issues that the West Sea Battle Left)," *Joseon Ilbo*, June 21, 1999.

Lee, Seon Ho, *Hanbeon Haebyeongdae-neun Yeongwonhan Haebyeongdae* (Once You are a Marine, You Will Always be) (Seoul: Doseo Chulpan Jeongudang, 1997).

Lee, Young Hun, "Bug-Jung Muyeog-ui Hyeonhwang-gwa Bughan Gyeongje-e Michi-neun Yeonghyang (Current Status of North Korea-China Trade and its Impact on North Korean Economy)," Institute for Monetary and Economic Research, February 13, 2006.

Park, Hee-do, *Doraoji Anhneun Dari-e Seoda* (Standing in the Bridge of No Return) (Seoul: Saemteo, 1988).

Park, Ung Seo and et al., *Bughan Gunsa Jeongchaegron* (On North Korean Military Policy) (Seoul: Gyeongnam Daehaggyo Geugdong Munje Yeonguso, 1983).

Sin, Gyeong Wan, "Gyeot-eseo Bon Gim Jeong Il (Kim Jong Il Seen from the Side)," *Wolgan JungAng*, June 1991.

Song, Hyo Sun, *Buggoe Dobal 30-nyeon* (Thirty Years of North Korean Provocations) (Seoul: Bughan Yeonguso, 1978).

Yu, Jae Min, "Nambughan Bulgachimseon Hyeobsang-gwa Hangye (Negotiations for the Demarcation Line for Nonaggression between South and North Korea and their Limits)," *Gugbang Daehagwon Anbo Gwajeong Usu Nonmunjib* (Collection of Excellent Articles of the National Defense University Security Course) (Seoul: Gugbang Daehagwon, 1998).

Yu, Yong-Weon, "Sudogwon-eul Sajeonggeori An-e Neohgo Issneun Bughan-ui Dayeonjang Rokes Mich Jajupo Yeongu (Study on North Korean Multiple Rocket Launchers and Self-Propelled Artillery that Put Seoul Metropolitan Area within their Range)," *Wolgan Joseon*, March 2001.

Yun, Gyeong Won, "'Yeonpyeong Haejeon' dangsi Saryeonggwan 'Chong Majeul Sigan Gidaryeossda (The Commander at the Time of the Battle of Yeonpyeong, "I was Waiting to be Shot)," An Interview with Park Jung Sung, *Deillian*, June 19, 2006.

Japanese-language publications

Akimoto, Chiaki, "Inpa Kakujikken-no Shinso (Real Facts of Nuclear Experiments of India and Pakistan)," *Chuuoukouron*, August 1998.

Asagumo Shimbunsha Henshuusoukyoku, *Bouei Handobukku 2000* (Defense Handbook 2000) (Tokyo: Asagumo Shimbunsha, 2000).

Asahi Shimbun *AERA* Henshuubu (Asahi Shimbun *AERA* Editorial Staff), *Kitachousen karano Boumeisha: 60-nin-no Shougen* (Defectors from North Korea: Testimony of Sixty of Them) (Tokyo: Asahi Shimbunsha, 1997).

Cho, Gab Je, *Kitachousen Onna Himitsu Kousakuin-no Kokuhaku: Daikankoukuuki Bakuhajiken-no Kakusareta Shinjitsu* (Confession of a North Korean Female Agent: Hidden Truth of the Bombing Incident of the Korean Airliner), trans. by Kikutoshi Ikeda (Tokyo: Tokuma Bunko, 1997).

"Dokusen! Kita-misairu Chakudan 'Zen Deta' (Scoop! The North's Missile Impacts 'Perfect Data')," *Yomiuri Weekly*, vol. 65, no. 34 (August 6, 2006).

Eya, Osamu, *Kin Shounichi Daizukan* (An Illustrated Book on Kim Jong Il) (Tokyo: Shougakkan, 2000).

Gekkan Chousen (Wolgan Chosun), ed., *Kin Shounichi: Sono Shougeki-no Jitsuzou* (Kim Jong Il: The Shocking Reality), trans. by Hwang Min Gi (Tokyo: Kodansha, 1994).

Hideya Kurata, "Chousenhantou Heiwataisei Juritsumondai-to Beikoku (The United States and the Issue of Establishing a Peace Regime on the Korean Peninsula)," in Yoshinobu Yamamoto, ed., *Ajia Taiheiyou-no Anzenhoshou-to America* (Security in the Asia-Pacific and the United States) (Tokyo: Sairyuusha, 2005).

Lee, Gwang Su, *Senkoushirei: Shougen Kitachousen Sensuikan Gerira Jiken* (Order to Go Underwater: Testimony on the North Korean Submarine Guerrilla Incident) (Tokyo: Za Masada, 1998).

Quinones, C. Kenneth, *Kitachousen: Bei-Kokumushou Tantoukan-no Koushou Hiroku* (North Korea's Nuclear Threat: "Off the Record" Memories) (Tokyo: Chuuoukouron-sha, 2000).

Suzuki, Masayuki, *Kitachousen: Shakaishugi-to Dentou-no Kyoumei* (North Korea: Resonance between Socialism and Tradition) (Tokyo: Tokyo Daigaku Shuppankai, 1992).

Newspapers, monitoring reports, and periodicals

Asahi Shimbun
Associated Press
Aviation Week and Space Technology
Daily Telegraph
Dong-A Ilbo
Executive News Service
Financial Times
Gekkan Chousen Shiryou
Gugbang Sosig
Gunji Kenkyuu
Gyeonghyang Sinmun (*Kyunghyang Sinmun*)
Hangug Ilbo (*Hankook Ilbo*)
Joseon Ilbo (*Chosun Ilbo*)
JungAng Ilbo (*JoongAng Ilbo*)
KBS-1 Radio Network
KCNA
Kitachousen Seisaku Doukou
Korea and World Affairs
Korea Herald
Korea Times

SELECT BIBLIOGRAPHY

Kulloja
Kyoudou Tsuushin
Mainichi Shimbun
Minju Joseon
New York Times
Nihon Keizai Shimbun
OhmyNews
Pacific Stars and Stripes
Pyongyang Times
Reuters
Rodong Sinmun
Sankei Shimbun
Segye Ilbo
Seoul Sinmun
Sisa Jeonal
U.S. News & World Report
Washington Post
Washington Times
Yeonhab (*Yonhap*) and *Yeonhab Nyuseu* (*Yonhap News*)

Interviews

Republic of Korea

Ahn Kwang Chan
An Pyong Tae
Bae Kwang-Bog
Cho Gab Je
Cho Myoung-Gyon
Choi Kang
Choi Zoo Hwal
Do Il Kyu
Hamm Taik-Young
Han Sung-joo
Hyun Seong Il
Jang Hae Seong
Jun Bong-Geun
Jung Chang-Hyun
Kang In-duk
Kim Gwang-u
Kim Gyu
Kim Hee Sang
Kim Kook-Hun

Kim Kyung-Won
Kim Seong Min
Kim Sun Wook
Kim Young Rim
Lee Chung Min
Lee Jang-Hie
Lee Jeong-Seok
Lee Ki-Tak
Lim Dong-won
Lim Sungnam
Moon Seong-Mook
Park Yong-Ok
Park Jin
Rhee Sang-Woo
Sim Sin Bok
Suh Choo Suk
Yeo Suk-joo
Yoo Young-Ku
Yoon Taeyoung
Yu Yong-Won

United States

Soong-bum Ahn
Guy Arrigoni
David Asher
Bruce Bechtol, Jr.
Stephen Bradner
Kurt Campbell
Robert Carlin
Victor Cha
Richard Christenson
Morgan Clippinger
Robert Collins
Toby Dalton
James Delaney
Chuck Downs
Michael Dunn
Nick Eberstadt
Robert Einhorn
Michael Finnegan
Gordon Flake
James Foster
Ryan Gage

SELECT BIBLIOGRAPHY

Robert Gallucci
Michael Green
Donald Gross
Frank Jannuzi
James Kelly
Sung Kim
Bruce Klingner
James Lee (Lee Mun Hang)
Michael McDevitt
John Merrill
Anthony Namkung
Larry Niksch
Don Oberdorfer
Kongdan Oh
Christian Ostermann
James Person
Jonathan Pollack
Charles Pritchard
Kenneth Quinones
Mitchell Reiss
Glenn Rice
Alan Romberg
Rinn-Sup Shinn
Leon Sigal
Scott Snyder
David Straub
Dae-Sook Suh
Stephen Tharp
Nathaniel Thayer
Aaron Trimble
Jon Wolfsthal
Joel Wit
David Wolff

China

Jin Jingyi
Li Chunhu
Qi Baoliang
Xia Liping
Yang Bojiang
Wang Shaopu
Zhao Huji

Japan

Yoichi Funabashi
Kinji Koyama
Hideya Kurata
Chiharu Mori

Germany

Bernd Schaefer

INDEX

124th Army Unit 8–9, 24

A-12 reconnaissance aircraft 37
"Abuses of Socialism Are Intolerable"
115
Agreed Framework 15, 93, 103–4,
111–12, 115–16, 119–20, 122–3, 135,
163–4, 183, 185, 191; agreed
conclusions 99; Agreed
Statement 104
Agreement on Reconciliation,
Nonaggression, and Exchanges and
Cooperation between South and North
Korea *see* Basic Agreement
aircraft carrier 36, 42, 44, 49, 75–6, 102,
104
Alaska 129
Albright, Madeleine 127–8, 133
Aleutian Islands 129
An-2 transport aircraft 64, 154
Anti-Ballistic Missile Treaty 137
apology: by Kim Il Sung 90; by
North Korea 90, 150; by the Soviet
Union 45; by the United States 6, 42,
88; North Korea's demand for 30, 35,
42; South Korea's demand for 79, 88,
143, 150; U.S. demand for 36, 88
Arirang Festival 160
Armistice Agreement 10, 18, 21, 30, 52,
54–5, 57–64, 67, 69, 79, 81, 83, 85, 87,
89, 133, 138–41, 145, 147–8, 150, 152,
164, 167, 183, 194; failure to define a
maritime demarcation line 63, 65
Armitage, Richard 176
Army-first policy see WPK's policy of
giving priority to army

artificial satellite: Japanese 137;
North Korean 122, 125, 128, 132, 136;
for reconnaissance 133; U.S.-sponsored
launch of 128
Asian Games 12–13
assassination attempt 6–13, 19, 187, 189

B-52 bomber 76, 79, 81
Baeggu-class missile craft 72
Baengnyeongdo 52–3, 55–8, 60–1, 64,
71, 154, 162
ballistic missile defense 3, 16, 136–7,
196, 246n157
Banco Delta Asia (BDA) 170, 173–4
Barrett, Mark 75
Basic Agreement 111, 140, 147, 152–3,
194; as a non-aggression agreement
111; Joint Military Commission
established by 148
Battle of Yeonpyeong (1999) 145–7, 154,
189, 199
Berger, Samuel 23, 40, 45
Berlin agreement (1999) 127
Berlin agreement (2007) 173
Black Shield reconnaissance mission 37
Blix, Hans 93
blockade 54, 61, 68, 166–7
blue crab 159
Bolger, Daniel 31
Bonesteel III, Charles 18, 20, 24–5, 31–2,
38
Bonifas, Arthur 75, 87
Brezhnev, Leonid 45
Bridge of No Return 43, 73–6, 80, 84
Britain 140, 144
Brown, Winthrop 28, 30

Printed in Great Britain
by Amazon.co.uk, Ltd.,
Marston Gate.